THERE GOES THE GAYBORHOOD?

PRINCETON STUDIES IN
CULTURAL SOCIOLOGY

Paul J. DiMaggio, Michèle Lamont,
Robert J. Wuthnow, and Viviana A. Zelizer,
Series Editors

A list of titles in this series appears at the back of the book.

THERE GOES THE GAYBORHOOD?

_____

AMIN GHAZIANI

PRINCETON UNIVERSITY PRESS | PRINCETON AND OXFORD

Library of Congress Cataloging-in-Publication Data
Ghaziani, Amin.
There goes the gayborhood? / Amin Ghaziani.
Includes bibliographical references and index.
ISBN 978-0-691-15879-2 (hardback)
1. Gay community—United States—History. I. Title.
HQ76.3.U5G483 2014
306.76'6—dc23   2013038242

British Library Cataloging-in-Publication Data is available
This book has been composed in Verdigris MVB Pro and League Gothic
Printed on acid-free paper.
Printed in the United States of America
1 3 5 7 9 10 8 6 4 2

For the Princeton Society of Fellows

CONTENTS

Introduction   I

PART I. GAYBORHOODS ARE CHANGING . . .

Chapter 1. Beyond the Gayborhood   35

Chapter 2. The Happiest Ending   64

Chapter 3. Triggers   102

PART II. BUT ARE THEY DISAPPEARING?

Chapter 4. Cultural Archipelagos   133

Chapter 5. Resonance   166

Chapter 6. Reinvention   210

Conclusions   244

Acknowledgments   261

The Language of Sexuality   267

Appendix: What Are Gayborhoods? How Do We Study Them?   271

Notes   287

Works Cited   315

Index   337

Introduction

"Gay Enclaves Face Prospect of Being Passé."

This was the front-page headline of the October 30, 2007, edition of the *New York Times*, and the article predicted the demise of San Francisco's iconic Castro district. The most famous gay neighborhood in the United States, like so many others across the country, was (and still is) changing rapidly. The causes are numerous: a dramatic increase in societal acceptance of homosexuality, ramped-up urban revitalization efforts, an influx of straight people, and casual disclosures by gays and lesbians that they feel safe living pretty much anywhere in the city. "These are wrenching times for San Francisco's historic gay village," the writer of the article, Patricia Leigh Brown, sighed, "with population shifts, booming development, and a waning sense of belonging that is also being felt in gay enclaves across the nation."[1]

Such laments, indeed, are not restricted to San Francisco. Kyra Kyles published a front-page story in a Chicago paper the same year entitled "There Goes the Gayborhood," in which she similarly predicted the fall of Boystown, an affectionate term that locals use to talk about their gay neighborhood: "With more [straight] families moving in and longtime [gay and lesbian] residents moving out, some say Boystown is losing its gay flavor."[2] The people that Kyles interviewed were deeply conflicted about this "culture clash," as she calls it. "Some residents and activists welcome the gay migration, saying it's a sign of greater equality, while others say Boystown is losing its identity." A photograph of one of the rainbow-colored pylons that adorn North Halsted Street and mark it as the city's main gay artery accompanied her article—but the colors in this haunting image were fading, or perhaps even bleeding away.

Are gay neighborhoods really disappearing? There is quite a buzz about this question. Demographers who analyze the US Census confirm that zip codes associated with traditional gay neighborhoods are "deconcentrating" and becoming less "segregated," to use their words, across the entire country.[3] Fewer same-sex households lived in these zip codes in 2010 than they did in 2000 or in 1990—and the number of straight residents is increasing. Whatever the answer to the question may be, it is clear that these urban areas are in flux.[4]

We can identify a gay neighborhood—or gayborhood, as many people playfully call it—by several qualities. It is a place that has a distinct geographic focal point: locals can point it out on a map, usually by singling out one or two specific streets. It has a unique culture: gays and lesbians set the tone of the neighborhood, which is why symbols like the rainbow flag are visible as you walk along the streets, and ritual events like the pride parade take place in the area. It has a concentration of residences: everyone who lives in a gayborhood does not self-identify as gay or lesbian, of course, but many people certainly do. Finally, it has a cluster of commercial spaces: gay-owned and gay-friendly businesses, nonprofit organizations, and community centers that appeal to residents and non-residents alike are based there. Midtown in Atlanta, Boston's South End, Oak Lawn in Dallas, Houston's Montrose, Miami's South Beach, the Gay Village in Montreal along Saint Catherine Street, New York's Greenwich Village, Chelsea, and, most recently, Hell's Kitchen, Philadelphia's officially dubbed Gayborhood in Washington Square West, San Diego's Hillcrest, Seattle's Capitol Hill, Toronto's Church-Wellesley Gay Village, Vancouver's Davie Village, Dupont Circle in DC, and the entire city of West Hollywood: each is an example of a gayborhood—and depending on who you ask, each might appear on a list of endangered urban species.[5]

And yet there are numerous benefits that gayborhoods, and perhaps only gayborhoods, provide. They allow gays and lesbians—who, unlike racial minorities, are often not physically identifiable—to find one another for friendship and fellowship, sex, dating, and love. Such individuals can create unique cultures, political perspectives, organizations and businesses, families, rituals, and styles of socialization in and around their neighborhoods. These urban areas thus stand on guard against an entrenched problem of history and ancestry—they help to answer the question, who are my people?—and they offer a renewed sense of roots. At the end of a long day, gayborhoods promise an incomparable sense of safety, a place where gays and lesbians can seek refuge from ongoing heterosexual hostilities, hate crimes, discrimination, bigotry, and bias.

Gayborhoods are more than just a protective shield. They also provide a platform from which gays and lesbians can organize themselves as a voting bloc, if they seek to work within the system, or as a social movement, if they wish instead to rally against it. The personal is political, as we know, and in this regard, gayborhoods represent a space of freedom in which gays and lesbians can discover the authenticity of who they are and celebrate it without being burdened by the tyranny of the closet or the culturally crushing weight of heteronormativity. The more we look, the more we see that gayborhoods have a hand in nearly every aspect of modern life: from the municipal promotion of urban spaces to city planning and the shaping of real estate values; from the institutional development of gay and lesbian communities to their civic engagement; and from pride parades to protests to electoral influence. They promote policy discussions around sexuality, a topic that many politicians would rather ignore; they enable social service and public health organizations to distribute life-saving resources; and they assist corporations with their efforts to reach a potentially lucrative niche market. The presence of a gayborhood signals a city's commitment to diversity, tolerance, inclusion, and openness, and research shows that officials can boost their local economy when they invest in them. These are just some of the many stakes involved in the deceivingly simple question about if indeed the gayborhood is going somewhere.[6]

If you ask the people who live in these areas if they think their home is changing and what we should do about it, you will hear no shortage of opinions—and several explosive ones, at that. Consider a standing-room only roundtable session that the GLBT Historical Society of Northern California hosted on November 28, 2006. Under the urgent title "Are Gay Neighborhoods Worth Saving?," panelists debated what it means to save a gay village (rescue it from what real or perceived threat?) and whether these urban areas are worth fighting for (why are they still meaningful today in an era of gay cultural visibility and acceptance?). According to a press release for the event, the session reflected "an upsurge of dialogue about the potentially imperiled future of the Castro district as a GLBT neighborhood." Board member Don Romesburg disarmed the dubious assumptions of some audience members about the stability of queer spaces: "We tend to assume that once created, queer neighborhoods will be self-sustaining. That's not true. Our neighborhoods get built within particular economic, political, and cultural circumstances. When those change, so do our neighborhoods."[7]

Now take a quick excursion with me to Toronto. In 2007, the *Globe and Mail* published a story with a title that had a familiar refrain: "There Goes the Gaybourhood: A New, Straight Crowd Is Discovering Church and Wellesley." The writer, Micah Toub, observed, "These days, the area's character is changing as straight couples and families move in and Toronto's gay community disperses across the city." Six years later in 2013, urban planners, activists, residents, and businesses initiated a community-wide study that asked the same kinds of questions that we heard in San Francisco: "What is the role of an LGBTQ village in a modern, progressive city?" and "What must be done to support the Church-Wellesley Village to solidify its role as a major cultural and community hub?" This is a restlessness that appears in cities across North America. To wonder where gayborhoods are going, debate whether they are worth saving, or question their cultural resonance—all of this announces to us that they are in danger.[8]

I myself lived in Chicago's Boystown district for nearly a decade, starting in 1999. I remember feeling uneasy in those years as I read one headline after another about the alleged demise of my home and other gayborhoods across the country. The sight of more straight bodies on the streets became a daily topic of conversation among my friends—an obsession, to be honest. We writhed over stroller congestion on the sidewalks (though gays and lesbians also have kids, the stroller was, and still is, a politically charged symbol of heterosexual invasion into queer spaces). We denounced bachelorette parties at gay bars (we could not legally marry at the time, so why were they insensitively flaunting their nuptials in our face?). And we cheered the decision by a local gay bar to admit gays and lesbians for free yet charge a steep cover for straights ("You have ladies' nights," we would retort). We accosted straight couples who locked lips in our bars ("We risk physical violence if we do that in your bars; you should be more respectful in our spaces"). We sighed when a sex shop would close and, say, a nail salon would open in its place (much like the strollers, these salons were also symbols of change). We fumed when straight residents complained that the Center on Halsted, our queer community center, excluded them in their programming ("Are you really accusing us of reverse discrimination?"). And we deployed a stealth micropolitics of street-level resistance by staring at straight men with all the carnal lust we could muster ("How does it feel to be sexually objectified?" we tried to say with our probing eyes).

As the years went by, my friends and I bemoaned, perhaps most of all, feeling a little less safe holding hands with our partners, dates, or hookups—even as we walked down what were supposed to be our sheltered streets. I had been called a "fag" on more instances than I still care to remember, and I was shocked at the disapproving looks that I would receive when walking hand in hand with another man. I knew I could not escape this menacing straight gaze altogether, but I was so angry that I had to deal with it in Boystown. This was supposed to be a safe space.

Stroll down the streets of any gayborhood, eavesdrop on passersby, and I bet that you will hear a vast range of views about what is happening on those streets. You will quickly notice that not everyone defends the sanctity of gayborhoods like my friends and I did. Veteran activist Urvashi Vaid, for example, blasted them back in 1995, calling them "a more spacious closet." Sexual orientation is losing primacy for how we define ourselves, other people will tell you, and it is no longer the wedge that it once was, dividing gays and straights. Sophia, a Cuban-born transsexual immigrant who moved to New York in 2005, berated them for their ghetto-like qualities: "Chelsea is still a gay ghetto. I'm against ghettos, whether they're youth ghettos or black ghettos or minority ghettos or gay ghettos. I don't think there's any need to separate yourself from the rest of society." Frank, a West Hollywood resident, brought this attack to a climax in a 2013 interview with *LA Weekly*. "The gay ghetto is dead," he boldly declared. A "new gay paradigm" has ascended in its place, and it is rendering the gayborhood "obsolete." The idea (or hope, maybe) is that sexual orientation can be one aspect of our identity without being the defining aspect: we are your neighbors, not your gay neighbors.[9]

Everyday life in gay neighborhoods moves in multiple directions; the perspectives of one person will contradict what someone else says. We will never be able to learn anything from this social noise if we simply ask *whether* gay neighborhoods are changing. Of course they are. Every neighborhood will change at some point. Though cities are built of bricks and concrete, they nonetheless are living, breathing, organic entities that are perpetually shifting, even if those changes are not always evident to us. Gayborhoods certainly are not an exception to this most basic of urban insights. We therefore need to ask more penetrating questions. Who wants to live in a gayborhood? And who rejects them? What can their diverging preferences teach us about sexuality, especially its unique relationship with an otherwise common process of urban change? If gayborhoods first formed through a politics of liberation, how will they morph in our modern era—one that some people call "post-gay"—a time that is defined by unprecedented societal acceptance of homosexuality? If these areas once promised safe spaces for sexual minorities, what will happen to them as the world itself becomes safer and as being gay or lesbian becomes more normal? Will gayborhoods die, a victim of their own success, or can they still survive as vibrant cultural enclaves? Does this rise-and-fall narrative even apply to gay neighborhoods? Or can we unearth a more subtle and nuanced reality to explain what is happening today and to predict what might become of them in the future?

These are tailored versions of a general set of questions about residential choice (how do we decide where to live?) and urban forms (why do neighborhoods look and feel the way they do?). Such inquiries have inspired the imagination of anthropologists, architects, city planners, economists, demographers, geographers, migration scholars, policy experts, and sociologists since the earliest days of each respective discipline. We know much about these matters of urban choice and change—and from an interdisciplinary perspective—but we know so little about gay neighborhoods, specifically. This is a heterosexist oversight. It paints a biased picture of cities, one that erases, both intentionally and accidentally, the lives of gay people.[10]

Sociology is my intellectual home, and it struggles with its own problems related to this topic. Under the rare occasion that my colleagues pay attention to gayborhoods on their own terms, rather than merely as comparative foils or footnotes against racial and ethnic enclaves, they overplay gentrification as an explanation both for why they first formed and why they now are changing. Or, like Richard Florida, they exploit gay neighborhoods as urban amenities that local officials can use as markers of "tolerance" to lure a creative class of workers who allegedly will shape the future of our cities.[11] Sociologists like to think about gayborhoods through the lens of economic rationalities—what we can afford to rent or buy; what natural amenities, like the weather, or built conveniences, such as public transportation, are available; the quality and value of the housing stock; the investment potential of real estate; market forces, like interest rates and private lending options; and future prospects for development.

These and other kinds of economic factors are invaluable, no doubt, but I think that we rely on them too much when we talk about gay neighborhoods. They do not account for all the reasons behind gay flight out from the gayborhood. Nor does money by itself answer why straights are systematically moving into them. Gays and straights must pay the same price for their housing, after all, and rising costs are uniformly prohibitive.[12] And besides, why now, at this particular moment in time, are we witnessing all these urban changes?

A common conclusion that many members of the media, activists, some scholars, and everyday people alike make today is that gayborhoods are "potentially imperiled" and "passé" for gays, as we just heard, yet suddenly desirable for straights. To me, this implies that the resonance of their streets is changing, and that they now mean different things for different groups of people. Therefore, the heart of the matter—what these places mean, for whom, and why so many of us are troubled, or not, by all these crisscrossing developments—transcends dollars and cents. Economic arguments ignore what I think is a crucial fact about the relationship between sexuality and the city: gayborhoods, to echo the elegant words of geographers Mickey Lauria and Lawrence Knopp, are "a spatial response to a historically specific form of oppression." They are transforming in unique ways as the long arc of the moral universe bends toward justice.[13]

In this book, we will journey together to understand why gay neighborhoods are changing in the so-called post-gay era. Our goal is to better understand how shifting conceptions of sexuality—especially allegations that it is declining in its significance for how we define ourselves and how we structure our everyday lives—affect where we choose to live. We will identify the conditions under which gayborhoods can retain their resonance for certain people, despite ongoing gay flight and a steady stream of straight newcomers into them. We will also consider the possibility that new gay and lesbian settlements are emerging, if we just know how and where to look for them. In the course of our travels, we will explore the multiple, seemingly contradictory meanings that gayborhoods have for gays and straights alike, think deeply about why those meanings matter, and consider how they inform the many material stakes that are involved for those who live in and visit these places.

This is an ambitious task, I know. To make heads or tails of it, we first need to know what happened in the past. Gay and lesbian spaces in American cities have fluctuated across three periods of sexual history—what I call the closet, coming out, and post-gay eras. The heyday of the closet, which began prior to World War II, was characterized by concealment (you cloaked who you were from your family and friends), isolation (you felt disconnected from networks of other gays and lesbians), feelings of shame, guilt, and fear (which you endured because you internalized negative societal views about homosexuality), and duplicity (you lived a double life). Gayborhoods, as we think of them today, did not exist at this time. People who desired others of their own sex found each other in places that were scattered across the city: a bar here or there, a cabaret, a public park, a restroom. The coming out era, in contrast, was a radical reversal of the closet: you were now open and out about your sexual orientation, you had almost exclusively gay and lesbian friends, and you believed that "gay is good," to quote the popular phrase coined by the late activist Franklin Kameny.[14] Gay neighborhoods formed and flourished during this sexual era, which dates from World War II to about 1997.

But gay life in the Western world today is remarkably different. It is now so open that it is moving "beyond the closet," to borrow a visual image from sociologist Steve Seidman, despite a persistent privileging of heterosexuality by the state, societal institutions, and popular culture. Our new post-gay era, as we will see in more detail later, began around 1998 when the term arrived in the United States. The "new gay paradigm," as Frank from West Hollywood called it, is characterized by a dramatic acceptance of homosexuality and a corresponding assimilation of gays and lesbians into the mainstream. Assimilation then affects how we all think about sexual orientation. Take Nate Silver as an example. Silver rose to fame for predicting the outcome of the 2008 presidential election with stunning precision. In 2009, *Time* magazine named him as among "The World's 100 Most Influential People," while *Out* magazine selected him as their Person of the Year in 2012. During his interview with the editor of *Out*, Silver said something that stuck: "I'm kind of sexually gay, but ethnically straight."[15]

Sexuality has always been an important part of human life—and our ideas about it are constantly evolving, of course—but the recent post-gay shift has been nothing short of startling. Those who consider themselves post-gay profess that their sexual orientation does not form the core of how they define themselves, and they prefer to hang out with their straight friends as much as with those who are gay. Actually, they generally do not even distinguish their friends by their sexual orientation. This is not to say that people no longer claim a gay, lesbian, or bisexual identity for themselves—they do—because sexual orientation is still a part of who we are after all, because heterosexuality is still culturally compulsory, and because sexual inequalities persist. Post-gays do not pretend that the world is a perfect place. But with public acceptance of homosexuality and same-sex relationships at an all-time high, it is much easier for some sexual minorities to move into the mainstream, to participate in its most foundational institutions, like marriage or the military, and to blend into the prized, multicultural mosaic in a way that renders them no different from heterosexuals. "No one gives a good god-damn if you are gay or straight," we will hear them say in this book.

I have been thinking about gay neighborhoods, and living in them, for more than a decade, first when I lived in Chicago's Boys-town district as a graduate student at Northwestern, then in Lam-bertville, New Jersey, during my postdoctoral years at the Princeton Society of Fellows, and now through my assistant and associate professor years at the University of British Columbia in the Olym-pic city of Vancouver. To help us figure out how and why they are changing, I have collected an immense amount of information, including census data, numerous opinion polls, hundreds of news-paper articles, and more than one hundred interviews with actual gayborhood residents.

Let me say a little more about this data set. I gathered 617 news-paper articles from seventeen presses that represent all regions of the United States. This public conversation reports on twenty-seven different urban, suburban, and rural areas (since, as we will see, we have to broaden our view beyond just cities), it spans forty years of coverage (from 1970 to 2010), and it enables us to hear from gays and straights across the country. The media is an important source of information because it directs and delimits, reflects and arbi-trates our public conversations, even if journalists sometimes select quotes that are evocative rather than representative. There is no superior source that can produce a national and qualitative portrait of the perceptions that residents assign to the places they live. While we will always remain aware of potential biases, I am less interested in analyzing the coverage itself than I am in using these articles to help us explain why gayborhoods are changing across the country. To do this, we will read all these articles first to clarify the persistent claims of demise. But just as every coin has two sides, so too will we reread these articles against their own grain, so to speak, push-ing past the dramatic headlines in search of more subtle, challeng-ing themes. We will stare contradictions and inconsistencies in the eye, not turn our backs to them. This will allow us to appreciate the complexity of what is happening on the ground. Such a dual reading will also afford us some distance from potentially sensational and simplistic cries of doom.

As a means of both broadening and deepening our perspective, we will also look at demographic trends from the 2000 and 2010 US Censuses. We will use this statistical evidence to determine whether "same-sex partner households"—the only category of sexual orientation that the census includes on its form—follow patterns in where they locate and migrate. Unfortunately, the census underestimates the size of the nonheterosexual population by only counting coupled households. Excluded are those who are single (about a quarter of gay men and two-fifths of lesbians are in relationships at any given time), those who may not live with their partner, those who are not willing to self-identify as gay or lesbian, those who self-identify as bisexual or queer, and those who self-identify as transgender or two-spirited. Like the newspaper accounts, however, we will use the census not because it is perfect but because it is an optimal way to zoom out and see a bigger picture of what is happening across the country.

Finally, to dig deeper into the marrow of what it is like to live in a gayborhood—to see, hear, feel, and breathe what life is like from up close—we will meet 125 gay and straight residents of Chicago, including business owners, government officials, representatives of nonprofit community organizations, realtors, developers, and other public figures. The Windy City is the third most populous in the United States, and it has captivated the curiosity of sociologists like me since the earliest days of our discipline. Chicago is a vibrant sexual laboratory, and among the most studied cities in the world, but its gay and lesbian history pales in comparison to what we know about places like New York, San Francisco, and Los Angeles. I returned to Chicago during the summer of 2010 (from Lambertville, where I was living at the time) and chatted with newcomers and old-timers from two different neighborhoods: Boystown, which we know is the informal moniker of the city's official gay district, nestled in the East Lakeview neighborhood, and Andersonville, a historically Swedish section of the Edgewater neighborhood to the north of Boystown. Some residents playfully refer to Andersonville as Girlstown, to contrast it from the gender composition of Boystown, or Mandersonville, to emphasize its older demographic (think "boy" versus "man"). Both areas are "so strongly gay and lesbian identified that even the straight denizens of these 'hoods admit that they live in a gay neighborhood," notes one tourism guide.[16] I hung out with people at their homes, in my summer sublet, at their places of work, in coffee shops, grocery stores, restaurants, and in the local community center. These residents came from all walks of life: they were students and waiters, attorneys and physicians, copy editors and professional grant writers, massage therapists, interior designers, hairstylists, social workers, flight attendants, models, stay-at-home moms and dads, part-time bartenders and professional mixologists, graphic and web designers, cat sitters and dog walkers.

Gays and lesbians may no longer need gayborhoods to come out or to celebrate their pride. They may not look there to find friends and lovers or to network for jobs. They may not seek them out as countercultural havens or to feel sheltered, secure, and safe. But this does not mean that existing districts are culturally insignificant; nor can we conclude that gayborhoods will eventually go extinct and that new ones will never again form. Reality, as we know from our own personal experiences, is never quite so black or white. Simple binaries like persist-or-perish and durability-or-dissolution make for catchy headlines and stoke the fires of some people, but a life that is lived is far richer than any such contrasts can possibly capture. In the pages to come, we will discover a breathtaking variety of present-day gayborhoods, and we will consider surprising possibilities for the future of urban America. But first, let us take a crash course in gayborhood history so that we can more fully appreciate the streets on which we walk today.

"SCATTERED GAY PLACES"

Sex between men and sex between women is timeless. It has no history. But "the homosexual as a species" most certainly does. Men and women of this distinct social sort were not born, if you will, until 1870, notes French philosopher Michel Foucault with poetry and precision. This happened when medical professionals transposed sodomy from a mere sex act—forbidden, perhaps, but disconnected from a deeper self-concept and any cultural meaning—onto the very "soul" of the person who committed it. Prior to then, people with gay or lesbian identities simply did not exist. They, unlike sex, are "a product of history," John D'Emilio argues. A free wage labor system also developed around this same time, and it released our ideas about sex away from a Victorian "imperative to procreate." This allowed the social world to become erotically charged for the very first time. Some men and women celebrated the "experience of a heterolust," to borrow a titillating phrase from Jonathan Ned Katz, while others found the freedom to structure a life around their same-sex desires. Many of these men and women would eventually call themselves gay over the next several decades, and they saw themselves as members of a community with a collective life as rich and varied as any other, even if society condemned their sexual behavior as perverse, pathological, sinful, and illegal.[17]

A remarkably complex gay male world, in particular, emerged in New York and other major urban areas during "the closet era," a period of time that lasted from the late nineteenth century through the start of the Second World War. The city at this time consisted of what historian George Chauncey describes as a "topography of gay meeting places"—or "scattered gay places," to borrow a tactile image from urban planner Ann Forsyth. These bars, cabarets, speakeasies, theaters, public parks, restrooms, and other cruising areas were generally located in bohemian parts of the city, like Greenwich Village for white gay men or Harlem for blacks. Such areas had "a reputation for flouting bourgeois convention," Chauncey tells us. Men exploited the anonymity of urban life as they navigated these places and explored their same-sex desires. But they did not "set the tone" of the neighborhood; hence, it would be a mistake to say that the scattered gay places of the closet era were based in a gayborhood. Nevertheless, a vibrant urban gay world existed at this time, even if straights were not always aware of it, and even if that world did not cohere into a formal gay district. For example, a restaurant that two men, Paul and Joe, owned in the Village in 1924 was known by one account as "the 'headquarters for every well-known Lesbian and Queen in town,' who felt no need to hide their homosexuality there." African American gay men were denied access to many of these places, and so they crafted dynamic communities of their own several miles north.[18]

Urban histories of romantic "female friendships," as they were often called, are harder to find. Literacy rates for women, especially those who were working class, lagged behind men's, and so there are fewer written records for us to study. There is evidence, however, that lesbians formed their own spaces. Historians Elizabeth Lapovsky Kennedy and Madeline Davis document a working-class and racially diverse lesbian community that thrived in Buffalo, New York, during the early twentieth century. Women with same-sex desires cultivated social networks with others who were like them, often in the bars (or in speakeasies during Prohibition) and especially in private house parties. These places were hotbeds of lesbian identity and community in Buffalo. Many women used them to craft "cultures of resistance" and to find some relief from the well of loneliness that burdened so many of their lives at the time. And they were transformed by hanging out together. "I wasn't concentrating on my school work, 'cause I was so enthused and so happy," one woman reflected. Another added, "We wound up at this bar. Now previous to this I had never been to a gay bar. I didn't even know they existed. It was a Friday night and that was the big night . . . And we walked in and I thought, my God, this is really something. I couldn't believe it . . . [I] don't think there were any straight people in that bar that night."[19]

The visual metaphor of the closet can mistakenly suggest sweeping isolation and vulnerability for gays and lesbians. We, like Chauncey, will use the designation of the closet era in a different way: to think about a particular moment in time between 1870 and World War II when sexual minorities surreptitiously appropriated public spaces to "construct a gay city in the midst of (and often invisible to) the normative city." They socialized with each other under the radar of a punitive "straight state," to borrow an appealing alliterative phrase from Margot Canaday, and they fabricated their own urban cultures, despite the odds stacked against them. A more public (read: straight) awareness of these clusters emerged toward the end of the period. New York politicians, in one example, denounced the Village in the 1920s as "the nation's Sodom and Gomorrah." There is nothing subtle or placeless about this characterization. In 1934, the movie *Call Her Savage* featured Greenwich's gay scene and, by doing so, it circulated among national audiences the same idea: gays often hang out in distinct parts of the city. A medical journal published the "Degenerates of Greenwich Village" two years later and announced to the authorities that the Village had become "the Mecca for perverts." Amid these and other sensational exposés, a world-altering event began that, in its wake, would stamp an indelible queer imprint across urban America.[20]

GAYBORHOODS FORM AND FLOURISH

World War II was "a nationwide 'coming out' experience," John D'Emilio and Estelle Freedman tell us, and it thus hastened a new "coming out era." Military officials discharged thousands of gays and lesbians from the armed forces on the grounds of their real or presumed homosexuality. Although these young men and women hailed from across the country, the war deposited them into certain military bases. Places like Chicago, Seattle, San Francisco, San Diego, Philadelphia, New York, Miami, and New Orleans swelled with dishonorably discharged service members who created "refugee camps," in the stirring words of activist Carl Wittman, or "ghetto[s], out of self-protection." The population of San Francisco, for example, had declined during the 1930s, but it grew by more than 125,000 between 1940 and 1950. In addition, census data from 1950 to 1960 show that the number of single-person households in the city doubled following the war and accounted for 38 percent of the total residential units. The perceptible presence of gays and lesbians in these urban centers encouraged more bars to open that catered specifically to them. These bars, in turn, cemented dense social networks and inspired gays and lesbians to assert a right to gather in public places.[21]

Before the war, laws in several states prohibited gays from congregating in public places, even in the bars. But a landmark California Supreme Court decision in 1951 ruled that it was illegal to shut down a venue just because homosexuals were the primary customers. The ruling inspired a national movement to safeguard gay spaces, and it politicized the bars. Activists founded the Tavern Guild in 1962 to protect themselves from arbitrary law enforcement, and they soon realized that gay bars were ideal venues to organize voter registration drives. The Guild, which mostly attracted men, stabilized gay districts as distinct urban forms. Thus, the origins of early American gayborhoods, in the words of sociologist Manuel Castells, were "inseparable from the development of the gay community as a social movement."[22]

Winning the legal right to gather in public places and forming the Tavern Guild did not make gays immune from police harassment. The straight state flexed its muscles again on June 28, 1969, when New York City police raided the Stonewall Inn, a gay bar located at 53 Christopher Street in Greenwich Village. Compliance during these raids was often as routine as the raids themselves, but this time the bar goers and a growing crowd outside fought back. The result was five days of violent rioting that forever changed gay life in America. Bar owners and patrons had defended themselves at other raids in New York and elsewhere, but activists and academics, like Barry Adam, remember Stonewall as "a symbol of a new era of gay politics."[23]

Stonewall motivated gays and lesbians to come out of the closet en masse and to move to big cities where they knew they could find others like themselves.[24] And so began the "great gay migration" of the 1970s and 1980s, to borrow a wonderful phrase from anthropologist Kath Weston.[25] Large port cities, especially San Francisco, were the strongest magnets in this demographic movement of gay people to major urban centers, but their visibility also surfaced in unexpected areas like Cherry Grove, a small resort town on Fire Island; Worcester, Massachusetts; Columbia, South Carolina; and Des Moines, Iowa, among others. The migration and gayborhoods were mutually reinforcing: gays and lesbians fled to specific areas of the city, and their emerging concentrations reaffirmed a "gay imaginary," again from Weston—or a perception that they comprised a people who were culturally distinct from heterosexuals. In one sense, we can think about the war and Stonewall as "historical accidents," as British economist Alan Collins argues, that triggered the formation and flourishing of gay neighborhoods, respectively.[26]

This discussion should prompt us to ask some follow-up questions: Why did so many gays and lesbians move to a relatively small number of cities during the great gay migration? And once they arrived in each of these cities, why did many choose to live in the same neighborhood? To figure this out, let us momentarily pause our historical account and try to identify different factors for why people move to a gayborhood. By exploring these, we will deepen our understanding not just of the building blocks of gayborhoods in the coming out era but also why they are still around in our present day.

There are high concentrations of same-sex households in coastal cities with mild climates, places like Fort Lauderdale, Los Angeles, Oakland, San Diego, San Francisco, and Seattle. Certain noncoastal cities also have sizable populations of gays and lesbians, including Atlanta, Austin, New York, and Washington, DC. And then there are the declining industrial, midwestern, and eastern cities like Buffalo, Cleveland, Detroit, and St. Louis, which have lower concentrations. If we assume that some of these cities emerged as gay magnets during the great migration (which we must in order to approximate the past; there is no comparable data from the 1970s to the 1990s), then one lesson that we can draw is that amenities matter in gay and lesbian location decisions. Consider the counterfactual: cities with the lowest concentrations of gays today are Birmingham, Charlotte, Greensboro, and Louisville. For these Southern cities, economists like Dan Black and his colleagues "wonder" if other factors, like an area's "general political and social acceptance of gay individuals," make them less appealing. We will revisit this important point a bit later.[27]

Within a given city, there are correlations between the number of same-sex residences in a neighborhood and an older and higher-value housing stock. And there is a lot of anecdotal evidence that gays settle in places with more cultural offerings. Why? According to Dan Black, Gary Gates, Seth Sanders, and Lowell Taylor, this happens because gay households have fewer kids, which frees up resources that individual gay people can use to move to an area with a beautiful natural environment, better housing stock, an array of restaurants, and a vibrant local arts and entertainment scene.[28]

Let us look more closely at this assertion about families so that we can verify this economic argument about how amenities affect where gay people choose to live. Nationally, according to the 2010

US Census, 17 percent of male same-sex partner households and 28 percent of female same-sex partner households had their own children under the age of eighteen (children by birth, adopted children, or stepchildren). We have no reason to believe that these numbers were higher during the great gay migration of the 1970s and 1980s. If anything, they were probably lower, given greater societal animosities toward same-sex couples. Now compare the numbers with those for married heterosexual couples: 42 percent of husband-wife and 39 percent of male-female unmarried partners had children under the age of eighteen present in their household.[29] There are clear differences between same-sex and opposite-sex couples in their likelihood of having kids. The greater access to financial resources that gay people have as a result enables them to move to cities with more desirable amenities.

Gentrification is another and perhaps more common economic explanation for why gayborhoods formed. In the United States, federal interventions fueled a first wave of urban renewal efforts, which were a response to the inner-city decline that white flight caused in the 1960s. This wave involved isolated investments in what geographers Elvin Wyly and Daniel Hammel call "islands of renewal in seas of decay." Participants, many of whom were gay, imagined themselves as pioneers who were "taming the urban wilderness," adds anthropologist Neil Smith, as they searched for affordable places to live. These arguments have much popular appeal. For example, writing for the *Advocate*, Justin Ocean defined "gays and gentrification" as a "marriage" with a long history that spans the coming out and post-gay eras: "From San Francisco's SoMa in the '60s to Manhattan's West Village in the '70s to Los Angeles's Echo Park in the [20]00s, the cycle of queer pioneers turning the dilapidated into destinations seems to be an intrinsic fact of urban life." Realtors have also caught on to the insight that gays revitalize the neighborhoods in which they settle. "There's an old saying among realtors that if you want to improve a neighborhood, rent to a gay man," said Michael Lamm, president of the Greater San Diego Business Association. "Before gays started moving in [to Boystown], this place was a dump," Mary Morten, Mayor Daley's advisor on LGBT matters, conceded about Chicago as well.[30]

Economics and gayborhoods are familiar bedfellows. If we think exclusively along these lines, however, then we will see gays and lesbians merely as rational, economic actors—and thus overlook that they also respond to political and social forces, like discrimination and legislative inequalities, and cultural concerns like building a community and promoting their own visibility. The research that we just reviewed is still valuable, of course, and we can benefit from it even if we do not limit ourselves to it. Economics matter, in other words, but in concert with other factors. Where gays and lesbians choose to live is also driven by an area's "reputation for tolerating non-conformity," Chauncey asserts.[31] Historically, they have invested in areas "at a financial and social cost that only 'moral refugees' are ready to pay," Castells adds. In the coming out era, gays and lesbians perceived gayborhoods as a beacon of tolerance, a liberated zone that promised reprieve from antigay violence, a place from which they could resist all things heteronormative, and a self-controlled territory in which they could incubate an oppositional consciousness. Gayborhoods flourished following the Stonewall riots in the 1970s and 1980s precisely because sexual minorities from across the United States romanticized the endless possibilities for freedom that they dreamed about in these areas. They migrated to them as an "exodus out of bondage into the promised land," to echo sociologist Laud Humphrey's aspirational words from 1979.[32]

A promised land promises freedom and safety. This is why I prefer to think about gayborhoods as a type of "free space" or "safe space." Such areas allow minority groups to independently examine their lives. For example, telling stories about shared experiences and struggles inspired the famous slogan "the personal is political," a notion that affirmed women's collective reality in a safe space that was not occupied by men. Gayborhoods do something similar. A basic, intimate act like holding your partner's hand or sharing a sweet kiss on the street without fear is profoundly political, if for no other reason than because doing so is not always possible beyond the sacred streets of the gayborhood. Consider the language that John Gallagher used in a 1997 article for the *Advocate*. In his survey of American cities, he "uncover[ed] 20 safe and supportive havens for gay men and lesbians" that are "oases to which they have fled." But "not all cities are equally friendly," Gallagher cautioned. He then offered some important advice: "Where you live makes a difference in how you live." A 2007 *New York Times* story provided a more close-up perspective. The journalist interviewed a gay man named Brian, who reminisced about his life during the years of the coming out era: "I remember growing up in the city being gay in the '70s and '80s, and it was scary. So I'm not going to go and move into a neighborhood where I am scared. I want to be near Chelsea and the West Village, where there are safe, gay people."[33]

As gays and lesbians fled to gayborhoods across the country, they discovered a treasure trove of other possibilities. Sex and love were perhaps the most immediate. Gayborhoods cultivated sexual subcultures, encouraged the pursuit of libidinal pleasures, and fostered a sense of sexual freedom. Consider a walk down memory lane that Denny Lee took in a *New York Times* story after he interviewed gay people who had lived in Greenwich Village for many years: "Older residents recall another era when the street was paved not with gold, but with gays. That was what put Christopher Street on the cultural map, the old-timers say wistfully." The residents with whom Lee spoke painted an arousing picture of their earlier years: "'It was one big cruising street,' said Bob Kohler, a retired talent agent with a full head of platinum hair who has lived on nearby Charles Street since the '60s and is something of a father figure to the pier kids. 'There was just a bohemian quality to it.'" Later in the article, Lee shared in his own words what he learned: "Gay men (the area never attracted a large lesbian population) carried the sidewalks as late as 1990, turning the street into a genuine carnival day and night. The waterfront, once a desolate truck yard, was a 24-hour playground of sexual trysts and flamboyant acts. By day, nude sunbathers staked out an urban beach on disfigured docks." Gay men have often depended on gayborhoods for such carnal pleasures—absent moralizing straight surveillance. "Straight people avoided Christopher Street," Kohler mused with a knowing grin on his face.[34]

Gayborhoods also promised love. In an *Advocate* editorial, John Morgan Wilson reflected on this idea when he celebrated West Hollywood's twentieth anniversary as "America's first gay city" (it was officially incorporated on November 29, 1984):

I'm not arguing that West Hollywood is a perfect city, or even a gay mecca. But it is a special place . . . A passage in my latest mystery novel . . . sums up why I still live here. It refers to two young men who've just met during gay pride weekend and might be falling in love: "They deserved a chance to find each other, to test the connection, to have the same shot at intimacy and happiness as anyone else. In West Hollywood, for all its silliness and superficiality, all its self-conscious glitz and glamour, all its attention to image and gratification, they were given that chance. Whatever its flaws, it was a city that let people be themselves and make their own choices about whom they loved and how, without judgment or condemnation or shame."

Across the country, Michael Lavers, writing for the *Village Voice*, interviewed a professor in New York in 2009 who invoked similar promises of sex and love to explain the appeal of the gayborhood: "Like any identity group, gay men and lesbians want to be with their own kind. It's also easier to hook up—for a night or a lifetime."[35]

The density of gays and lesbians in specific parts of the city helps them find each other as they pursue matters of the heart and libido, but it also satisfies their social needs for friendship. In one study of fifty gay white men between the ages of twenty-three and forty-eight who lived in Dupont Circle in Washington, DC, more than 80 percent expressed "a desire to be among other gay men" as their major reason for neighborhood selection. "This is the only place to be ourselves, to be with people who are like ourselves and not be looked down on," explained one resident. Like other minorities, gays and lesbians want to be with their own kind, which is why British geographer Paul Hindle sees gayborhoods as "the physical manifestation of a gay community."[36]

The presence of particular institutions is the most prominent aspect of a community. In fact, sociologist Stephen Murray suggests that "the existence of distinctive institutions is more salient to the identification of a community—for both insiders and outsiders—than residential segregation or concentration." Gayborhoods are home to gay-owned and gay-friendly bookstores, hair salons, churches, travel agencies, realtors, medical facilities, retail stores, periodicals, and political groups. Imagine that you are an urban planner, and that you are interested in building a gay district as a way to boost your city's local economy and tourism base. Will you encourage landlords to rent to gay men and lesbians as a way to increase the area's residential density? Or will you open a gay bar? Murray would advise you to see gayborhoods as the "institutional elaboration of a quasi-ethnic community" and thus opt for the latter.[37]

Communities are not just a collection of institutions; they also have cultures. Gayborhoods highlight the symbolic and expressive aspects of a distinctively gay and lesbian way of life. Regina Quattrochi, the former director of the New York City AIDS Resource Center, said, "Even as recently as the early and mid-1980s, I think the Village was symbolic of a sort of celebration of gay culture." Tim Nolan, former president of the San Mateo County Board of Supervisors and candidate for Congress in 1992, merged culture and community with a sense of freedom: "[I]n the 1960s and '70s . . . gay men and lesbians from across America rushed to the coastal cities seeking fellowship and freedom." Consider finally Elizabeth Kastor's invocation of imagery from the *Wizard of Oz*: "For decades, the gay neighborhoods of San Francisco, New York, and Washington embodied the promise of change, freedom, friendship, and acceptance. Greeting cards and T-shirts were emblazoned with the slogan 'I have a feeling we're not in Kansas anymore.' To come out of the closet, to move to those gay utopias, was to be swept up by a tornado and dropped into Oz. The black-and-white landscape dissolved into color."[38]

Many gays and lesbians in the coming out era used the language of "mecca" when they expressed their feelings about gay neighborhoods. This is a religious reference to the capital city of Saudi Arabia, the holiest site of the Islamic faith. In a *San Francisco Chronicle* article, Dan Levy borrowed this religious emblem to write, "The Castro . . . drew thousands of gays from all over the country because they believed it was their own mecca-in-the-making." In commemorating the twenty-fifth anniversary of the Stonewall riots, Paula Span, writing for the *Washington Post*, blended the Islamic motif of mecca with the American symbol of Ellis Island: "There will be a constant stream of pilgrims coming to gaze at the brick-and-stucco facade of the Stonewall over the next few days . . . The neighborhood surrounding the old saloon, a hangout-turned-landmark, will become an international mecca, a symbol of gay liberation. But that's what Greenwich Village has always been. A kind of Ellis Island for generations of gay men and lesbians, a crucible of gay history since before the Jazz Age, it is America's most celebrated gay enclave."[39]

Invoking religious imagery is ironic, given entrenched taboos against homosexuality, especially in the closet and coming out eras, but it is not entirely surprising. At the heart of such spiritual iconography and religious experience is a communal affirmation. Joseph Coates said sublimely in a 1991 Chicago editorial, "Our eroticism is the closest thing we have to what in the past was called a spiritual life, and no one wants to be excommunicated from that church altogether. This is probably why people who are seen or see themselves as primarily homosexual have acceded to their own subculturalization in gay ghettos." That gays and lesbians "acceded" to the "ghetto"— but that the ghetto grants them certain possibilities in return—is an interesting idea that suggests the less desirable parts are worth it precisely because of the many better ones. Perhaps gayborhoods in the coming out era were like the totems erected by the primitive tribes that French sociologist Emile Durkheim studied. In these very different social worlds, there is a common motivation to seek the sacred. And in both cases, there is an apotheosis of the community.[40]

These different perspectives make it clear that we need to bring existing economic wisdom into dialogue with a more complex understanding of how our sexuality affects where we choose to live, especially the ways in which it arouses our search for sex and love, and why it does (or does not) compel us to seek safety, community, friendship, freedom, spirituality, and a political voice. If we pay attention to the overlaps and intersections of these many factors, we will be able to offer a multicausal explanation not just for why gay neighborhoods formed and flourished in the coming out era, but also why they are changing as we embark into a new post-gay world.

WHITHER THE GAYBORHOOD?

British journalist Paul Burston coined the phrase "post-gay" in 1994. It found an American audience four years later in 1998, a year that heuristically marks the beginning of our current era, when

Out magazine editor James Collard used it in the *New York Times* to argue, "We should no longer define ourselves solely in terms of our sexuality—even if our opponents do. Post-gay isn't 'un-gay.' It's about taking a critical look at gay life and no longer thinking solely in terms of struggle. It's going to a gay bar and wishing there were girls there to talk to." He clarified the urban implications of this still-murky term two months later in a separate *Newsweek* feature: "First for protection and later with understandable pride, gays have come to colonize whole neighborhoods, like West Hollywood in L.A. and Chelsea in New York City. It seems to me that the new Jerusalem gay people have been striving for all these years won't be found in a gay-only ghetto, but in a world where we are free, equal and safe to live our lives."[41]

Gayborhoods long provided sexual minorities with a safe space in an often unsafe world. But now the world itself is becoming much safer. This is an important part of the story about why gayborhoods are de-gaying (and straightening) across the United States, and in many other parts of the world, during a post-gay era. This is not to say that we today are totally post-gay—on the contrary, the idea is riddled with vexing problems, as we will see throughout this book. Yet it is still a useful pivot point for us, a way to think critically about the dramatic changes we are witnessing in the relationship between sexuality and the city.

In 2010, the census revealed that 93 percent of all counties in the United States contain same-sex partner households. Gays, in other words, really are everywhere. Over the years, their presence has been "increasing in some of the most conservative parts of the country," in areas far beyond urban gay districts. Why do so many gays and lesbians now think outside the gayborhood box? And why are straights so much more comfortable within it? As with the question of origins, economic wisdom can again help us with this related yet distinct concern with contemporary change. We know that federal intervention fueled a first wave of urban revitalization efforts in the 1970s and 1980s. Gentrification resurged in the late 1990s in a second wave that corresponded with rising home prices. Adjustments in the financing system, increased privatization, and the demolition of public housing incited this second surge. Ironically, while gays and lesbians used the first wave to build their neighborhoods, the "super-gentrifiers" of the second wave are mostly straight people who are transforming gay districts into "visible niche markets for retail commerce and realty speculation," observes American studies scholar Christina Hanhardt.[42]

Second-wave financers and straight newcomers often prefer chain stores, which threaten the cultural icons of gayborhoods—the bars, bookstores, bathhouses, and boutiques targeted to nonhetero-sexual consumers. Many gays and lesbians perceive the resulting changes as the pillaging of their cultures and communities. This makes sense, though sadly so, especially when a prominent scholar like Richard Florida appears on *The Colbert Report* and declares, "If you live in a city or neighborhood that has a large concentration of gay and lesbian people, . . . then you're going to get a premium for your house." After he heard this, Colbert asked, "Should I be follow-ing gay people around to see where they're living?" Florida replied with force, "Absolutely. Absolutely, if you want to get more return on that 12-bedroom Tudor. Absolutely"—and he indicated that he himself does so. Given that 3.5 percent of adults in the United States identify as lesbian, gay, or bisexual—and that straights will always outnumber them—the incentivizing of gayborhoods risks inevita-ble and potentially irreversible change.[43]

Another clue for the questions that concern us comes from municipal promotion and tourism campaigns, which position gay-borhoods in what Dereka Rushbrook calls a "geography of cool." In the late 1990s, a group of demographers created a "Gay Index" that ranks regions based on their concentration of same-sex households. Florida has publicly championed this index, including the time in 2007 when he went on *The Colbert Report*, and city officials often use it because it can predict economic competitiveness in a global-izing world. In fact, to compete with a small number of powerful global cities, especially as manufacturing has declined, secondary cities like Chicago, Miami, Manchester, Philadelphia, Seattle, Syd-ney, and Vancouver have reimagined and rebranded themselves as "places of culture and consumption," to borrow again from Rush-brook, by showing off their stock of ethnic spaces. City officials now use gayborhoods in the same way that they have used ethnic enclaves: as "a marker of cosmopolitanism, tolerance, and diversity for the urban tourist." The resulting Disneyfication of gayborhoods as moneymaking entertainment districts signals an underlying shift in how the state perceives these areas: from a regulatory problem that required repression and containment in the coming out era to a marketing asset more recently. To include them alongside ethnic enclaves at a cosmopolitan buffet for hungry tourists is a profound but problematic shift. The marketing ploy ignores their history, and it opens up their boundaries indiscriminately to straight newcomers. According to Collins, they have become "the chic social and cultural centres of the city—the place to be seen, . . . regardless of one's sexual preferences."[44]

Neighborhoods form and change for reasons beyond gentrification. Consider the advice of Australian geographer Brad Ruting, whose concern I share: "Gentrification and changing preferences can only provide partial explanations; in addition, reduced discrimination against homosexuals is likely to have eroded the premium that many gay men and lesbians were once willing to pay" to live in a gayborhood. From the point of view of straights, "the consumption of queer space and spectacles cannot be assumed to denote acceptance, or even tolerance," Rushbrook adds. Economic perspectives, while helpful, say nothing about how political gains, cultural motivations, and societal attitudes also affect the choices we make about where to live. Even the idea that gayborhoods have changed in the minds of government officials, from a problem of regulation to an opportunity for marketing, implies a more fundamental shift in how Americans think about the diversity of human sexuality.[45]

Social support for gay and lesbian issues and the perceived moral acceptability of their relationships have dramatically increased in recent years, and this is hastening their assimilation into the mainstream. We see this in several ways. A straight allies movement of "politically gay" heterosexuals, as sociologist Daniel Meyers calls them, has emerged in recent years. This testifies to increased interactions between gay and straight people, and we can use that to make inferences about assimilation.[46]

Changes in public opinion provide additional evidence. Several independent surveys of Americans show a shift in their attitudes toward sexual minorities. According to a 2010 Gallup Poll, "Americans' support for the moral acceptability of gay and lesbian relations crossed the symbolic 50% threshold in 2010. At the same time, the percentage calling these relations 'morally wrong' dropped to 43%, the lowest in Gallup's decade-long trend," which, incidentally, has continued to the present day. A 2012 poll from the Pew Research Center found evidence for acceptance in all regions of the country, urban and rural. Finally, a 2013 *Washington Post*-ABC News poll found that "public support for gay marriage has hit a new high." Fifty-eight percent of Americans believe that it should be legal for lesbians and gay men to marry, while only 36 percent say it should be illegal. In a striking reversal, "public attitudes toward gay marriage are a mirror image of what they were a decade ago: in 2003, 37 percent favored gay nuptials, and 55 percent opposed them." [47]

Legislation is finally catching up with public opinion as well. On June 26, 2013, the US Supreme Court, in the landmark case *United States v. Windsor*, ruled that Section 3 of the Defense of Marriage Act (DOMA) was unconstitutional under the Due Process Clause of the Fifth Amendment. This portion of DOMA defined "marriage" for all purposes under federal law as "only a legal union between one man and one woman as husband and wife." Writing for the 5–4 majority, Justice Anthony Kennedy declared, "DOMA writes inequality into the entire United States code." Its "principal effect," he continued, "is to identify a subset of state-sanctioned marriages and make them unequal." Therefore, "the federal statute is invalid, for no legitimate purpose overcomes the purpose and effect to disparage and injure those whom the State, by its marriage laws, sought to protect in personhood and dignity." Although the court did not issue a sweeping ruling, it found that the federal government cannot discriminate against gays and lesbians who are legally married in their home state. [48]

These recent and radical shifts are the latest development in the United States' long history of absorbing successive waves of immigrants into its mainstream melting pot. Sexual minorities are finally experiencing this as well—and at an accelerating rate. "Assimilation" is the word that we generally use to talk about this process of cultural absorption, and it is the primary feature of the post-gay era. For a group like sexual minorities to assimilate means that its members are adopting the perspectives and attitudes of heterosexuals, the dominant group, who, in turn, are incorporating gay people into their existing social structures, like marriage laws. This is by no means the first time in history that the question of whether to assimilate has taken center stage in gay politics, but the post-gay iteration "*is* very different," Seidman emphasizes, because gay people have many more options for how to structure their lives, and because those lives now "look more like those of conventional heterosexuals than those of the closeted homosexuals of the recent past." In prior historical periods, "individuals confronted stark choices: stay in or step out of the closet." Identity choices were also oppositional: "to deny or champion being gay as a core identity." But things are much less stark today. "As individuals live outside the closet, they have more latitude in defining themselves and the place of homosexuality in their lives."[49] Gays and lesbians in the coming out era were generally open and out about their sexuality—"We're here! We're queer! Get used to it!" went a popular refrain that defined a generation. Post-gay life, however, allows a greater range of ways to express yourself in an increasingly multicultural society. Being gay or lesbian is just one among many other identities— and one that is receding in its centrality. The new motto might be: "We're here and there and everywhere. We happen to be queer. But who really cares?"

We can use the term "post-gay" to think about many different aspects of our lives. It can be a mode of self-identification, a way to describe the vibe of a particular place or an entire neighborhood, and it can capture the zeitgeist of a historical moment. Individuals who identify as post-gay, for example, define themselves by more than their sexuality, and they disentangle it from a sense of militancy and struggle. Post-gays feel free from persecution, even while they acknowledge that inequalities persist, and they prefer sexually mixed company—hence Collard's lament for more girls in gay bars. Many post-gays are urban twenty-somethings that are part of "a new generation of young gay people," notes Paul Aguirre-Livingston in a 2011 article for a lifestyle magazine in Toronto. They are skeptical about whether their New Jerusalem can exist in gay-only ghettos, and they reject them as a result. Younger gays and lesbians feel that their sexual orientation is merely secondary to their place in life—a life that "in most ways, is not about being gay at all," Aguirre-Livingston adds. But if life is not at all about being gay, then it is only a matter of time before gayborhoods begin to disintegrate as they lose their cultural currency from one generation to the next.[50]

We can also use the term post-gay to think about specific spaces like a bar, where "the need to clearly define and delineate our sexualities is largely deemed unnecessary," says British geographer Gavin Brown, or entire neighborhoods where there is no pressure to assert "one identity or another. Most times they contain a majority of heterosexuals." This is possible in ways that it was not before because "'gay' identities have outlived their usefulness," he concludes.[51] During the coming out era, gayborhoods were "akin to what Rome is for Catholics," D'Emilio argues in his provocative analogy. "A lot of us live there and many more make the pilgrimage." But in the post-gay era, they are "more akin to what Jerusalem is for Jews," counters geographer Wayne Myslik. "Most of us live somewhere else, fewer of us make the pilgrimage than in the past, [and] our political power has moved elsewhere."[52]

As gay identity recedes, so too will distinctly gay institutions. Consider that there were sixteen gay bars in Boston and Cambridge between 1993 and 1994, but by 2007 less than half remained. This has a domino effect. "As gay bars vanish, so go bookstores, diners, and all kinds of [other] spaces," notes Robert David Sullivan in a report for the *Boston Globe*. When gay businesses leave the gayborhood, or if new ones open in other parts of the city, they sever the ties that bind residents and visitors to a once symbolically important place. This happened in New York when a beloved coffee shop called Big Cup closed in 2005. Writing for the *New York Times*, Steven Kurutz recounts the effects on the gayborhood:

> Patrons learned this week that the coffeehouse, which employees nicknamed Gay Grand Central, a place where many men found a welcome introduction to gay life, was closing . . . [Big Cup] offered a casual place for gay men to socialize. Women and straight men were welcome too, but as a review once put it, "They just seem sort of irrelevant." . . . "I'm

disappointed for the neighborhood," said Scott Silver, an owner of the business since it opened in 1994 . . . The written memorials of the customers testify to the legacy of the coffeehouse. One note read: "Every community needs its focus place—this has been that for [us]."[53]

Amid these decades-long shifts in economic, cultural, and social factors, we must also recognize the very recent, and very dramatic, entry of a new factor: technology. Some say that the Internet is displacing the neighborhood's traditional role as a broker of sex, dating, love, and romance. Sullivan, who we met earlier from Boston, explained, "When Internet access became widespread in the mid-1990s, . . . [they] usurped gay bars' most important function: a place for men to meet each other . . . As a result of these changes, there are stories of gay bars closing all over the country." The Internet enables gay people to find electronically mediated friendships, sex partners, and dates, either "for virtual pleasure" or "for real-world fun." One study of seventeen cities across the globe found that in every single one of them, "the virtual gay community was larger than the offline physical community." Sandy, a West Hollywood gay nightclub owner, told Lisa Leff of the *Washington Post* that she "has started promoting special dance nights for straight[s] . . . because her gay clientele has fallen off. [She] said that many gay men and lesbians now prefer to meet potential partners on the Internet." If gay bars are straightening as a result of hosting such "straight nights," is it any wonder that gayborhoods are becoming residentially integrated as well? William, an employee at a Boston gay bar, echoed Sandy when he said to a reporter from the *Boston Herald*: "Gay people don't come out as much as they used to because the Internet has made it easier to meet people."[54]

Gayborhoods today are an elective, not exclusive, place where some gays and lesbians come to socialize and maybe even to live. While fewer of them need gayborhoods as safe spaces, they increasingly provide such sanctuary for straight women who, according to British sociologist Mark Casey, retreat to them to "escape the heterosexual male gaze that sexualizes their bodies" everywhere else in the city. Even straight men have gotten more comfortable with gay people, especially gay men. Charles Blow captured this post-gay nonchalance perfectly in the title of his 2010 essay in the *New York Times*: "Gay? Whatever, Dude." Although straight men and women have always lived in gay neighborhoods, they have become "a common sight on the street" in recent years, as Dan Levy notes in a story for the *San Francisco Chronicle*:

> Straights have always lived and shopped in the midst of the homosexual colony, of course, but their numbers are increasing . . . Two decades of struggle for equal rights have translated into real economic and emotional progress for homosexuals—and many heterosexuals . . . If the need to carve out a gay oasis made heterosexuals feel unwelcome 10 or 15 years ago, today straight couples are a common sight on the street . . . If lesbians and gays no longer feel confined to a homosexual safe zone, straights are increasingly less likely to be threatened by same-sex attention. Relaxed attitudes about sexual identity have led to a greater permeability.[55]

The meanings of sexuality are changing in complicated, subtle, and striking ways in a post-gay era; it is our task to figure out how all of this will affect the future of gay neighborhoods.

THE ROAD LESS TRAVELED

All neighborhoods change. This is a simple fact of city life. And while gayborhoods are no exception, such changes do not indicate that they are doomed to disappear. The evolution of a place does not signal its demise and death. This is why the shuffling demographic and institutional composition of gayborhoods is the point from which we will begin our investigation, not where we will end it. We will discover numerous expressions of urban change throughout this book: the ways in which gays and lesbians are assimilating into the mainstream—and how the straight mainstream is also assimilating into gay culture—and the greater array of possibilities that result for both groups.

To take the road less traveled, we need to ask harder questions: Why do some gays and lesbians imagine a life beyond gayborhoods while others continue to flock to them? And why are more straight people these days moving into them and socializing there? How can current residents, community activists, business owners, nonprofit organizations, realtors, city planners, and politicians preserve the cultural and institutional relevance of gayborhoods without denying either the inevitability of urban change or the realities of sexual integration? In what ways, and for whom, can gayborhoods remain resonant and meaningful in a post-gay era, a time that is defined by the declining significance of sexual orientation? Is it possible for new gayborhoods to emerge? Will they remind us of gayborhoods that formed in the coming out era, or will they look and feel different? Where should we look for them? And who is pioneering their development? Armed with these more piercing questions, let us turn the page, acquaint ourselves with those people who walk the streets of gayborhoods across the United States, and begin to find some answers.

PART I

GAYBORHOODS ARE CHANGING . . .

1

Beyond the Gayborhood

"As the country opens its arms to openly gay and lesbian people, the places we call home have grown beyond urban gay ghettos. The *Advocate* welcomes you to this new American landscape." The March 2007 essay from this national gay newsmagazine concluded with a poll to its readership: "Do you prefer to live in an integrated neighborhood rather than a distinct gay ghetto?" The following issue reported the results from a self-selected group who had signed on to a website to vote: 69 percent said yes, and 31 percent said no. One year later, in a more methodologically rigorous story entitled "Where the Gays Are," a writer for the same source interviewed demographer Gary Gates, who had analyzed the 2000 and 2010 US Censuses. "Same-sex couples live virtually everywhere in the country," said Gates. In 2000, they reported living in 99.3 percent of all counties in the United States, and in 2010 they were present in 93 percent.[1] As we have seen, gays and lesbians once considered the gayborhood a mecca, a safe space to live. Why has their residential repertoire changed in recent years?

This chapter presents the beginning of an answer, which is based on a comprehensive archive of more than six hundred media reports. We will examine these articles for the perspectives they contain of those lesbian and gay residents who live in gayborhoods, those who once did but have since moved out, and those who reject them outright. Like all news reporting, and judging from some dramatic headlines, journalists who write about gayborhoods contend with their own preconceptions and drama. Selection bias, for example, is a perpetual possibility with media coverage; reporters are human, just like the rest of us, and they like a good story. Therefore, it is possible that they consciously or unconsciously interview residents whose proclamations of gayborhood demise make for a captivating pitch. Although these articles are the main source for our thinking in this chapter, we will use them to focus on how the assimilation of sexual minorities is affecting where they choose to live, and how those decisions can change the significance of gayborhoods across the country. We will harness the insights that the media promises by reading past the headlines and capitalizing on the hundreds of interviews that journalists have tirelessly conducted over forty years. This treasure trove of perspectives will allow us to appreciate the lived realities of urban change in America.

WHERE THE GAYS ARE

Assimilation reveals a great deal about the groups that are inter-mixing—in this case, the gays and straights that cross paths on the streets and in the stores of gay neighborhoods. Demographers express the extent of this mixing through what they call an "index of dissimilarity." This statistic represents the proportion of minor-ity group members who would have to exchange places, usually census tracts, with majority group members in order to achieve a relatively even residential distribution, defined as one where every neighborhood replicates the sexual composition of the city over-all. According to sociologist Doug Massey and his colleagues, the index measures residential segregation and spatial isolation, both of which tell us about the "separation of socially defined groups in space, such that members of one group are disproportionately con-centrated" in a particular area. Index values range from 0 to 100, where 0 represents total integration and 100 signifies conditions of extreme segregation.[2]

Table 1.1 shows us that male and female same-sex partner house-holds have become less segregated and less spatially isolated across the United States from 2000 to 2010. Male same-sex partner house-holds remain in the moderate range of segregation (between 30 and 60), while female same-sex partner households have scores in the low range (below 30). Using 2010 Census data, demographer Amy Spring compared these scores with those for economic and racial

TABLE 1.1 Sexual Segregation in the 2000 and 2010 U.S. Censuses

	Mean index of dissimilarity		% change
	2000	2010	2000–2010
Male same-sex partner households (from all different-sex households)	47.2	43.4	−8.1
Female same-sex partner households (from all different-sex households)	29.6	25.5	−13.6

Source: Spring (2013:699).

groups. She found that the mean index of dissimilarity of the poor from the nonpoor was 33.13, and the index of all nonwhite racial and ethnic groups from the white population was 52.26. Spring concludes, "Segregation of same-sex partners rivals that of other types of segregation and should be considered alongside economic status and race as an important factor in urban spatial patterns."[3]

Statistical segregation is not the same thing as how residents perceive one another as they decide whether to share an urban space. The dissimilarity index, however, is silent on this question of motivation. "What a neighborhood truly is," argues sociologist Meghan Ashlin Rich, "exists in the minds of social actors, its residents, and neighborhood outsiders." Perceptions about sexuality and its significance in residential decision making must also be an important part of our explorations. We need to develop a qualitative counterpart, a dissimilarity meanings measure, if you will, that can help us to better understand why lesbians, gay men, and even straights choose to live and socialize in one part of the city rather than another.[4]

Local laws exert considerable influence on such decisions. Writing for the *New York Times* in 2004, reporter Josh Benson interviewed a lesbian couple who had recently relocated to a New Jersey suburb. Neither woman considered herself "any sort of activist," Benson noted, and both wanted "to have a suburban family life that is almost boringly normal." But why Jersey? "We moved to New Jersey because the laws have just improved and continue to change in good ways for the gay and lesbian community," said Jeanne, one of the two women that Benson interviewed. "And we're specifically not moving into gay neighborhoods here. Within the state of New Jersey, we feel comfortable living anywhere." Jeanne's partner Diane added, "Here, we're just part of a neighborhood. We weren't the gay girls next door; we were just neighbors. We were able to blend in, which is what you want to do, rather than have the scarlet letter on our heads."

I suspect that Jeanne and Diane felt like they could blend in partly because of the safety that their legal environment provides them. New Jersey passed the Domestic Partnership Act in 2003, the year before Benson interviewed them. This law extended many legal rights, protections, and benefits to same-sex couples, and it made the state more progressive at the time than its neighbors: "By contrast, gay rights advocates in New York state celebrated the passage of an anti-discrimination law just two weeks ago"—on September 5, 2004—but "a similar law has been on the books in New Jersey for 12 years," Benson explained. Such legislative differences explain where gays and lesbians choose to live, especially when they are considering neighboring states: "Unlike politically influential gay constituencies in nearby urban areas, which have their centers of gravity in dynamic neighborhoods like Chelsea in Manhattan or Washington Square West in Philadelphia, New Jersey's [residential pattern] is a more diffuse phenomenon." Variation in state laws is related to whether the gay and lesbian population is concentrated (where laws permit inequality) or diffuse (where laws promote equality). In a 2007 *Washington Post* story, Lisa Leff arrived at a similar conclusion about the entire country: "Gayborhoods are losing their relevance as gays win legal rights and greater social acceptance."[5]

Favorable legislation creates a perception among some gay people that they have greater options for where to live. Strides toward legal equality, therefore, may attenuate the backbone of gay life in urban America by encouraging individuals to diffuse across a respective state. Gayborhoods will become less relevant and less resonant for these sexual minorities who, in prior historical moments of legislative injustices, may have opted to cluster for protection. In a 2004 *Boston Globe* article, reporter James McCown asked, "With the dawn of same-sex marriage in Massachusetts and the acceptance of gays across wide swaths of American society, whither the gay ghetto?" Assimilation generates feelings of acceptance, comfort, and safety. It enables gays and lesbians to feel like they are a part of the mainstream, which remained elusive for so many of them in prior generations. It also reduces their sense of otherness, or a feeling that they are different from straights. This emerging social mindset is reversing an earlier propensity of sexual minorities to residentially concentrate in distinct gayborhoods. The most revealing example comes from a directive that former National Gay and Lesbian Task Force (NGLTF) executive director Urvashi Vaid gave for gays "to leave the ghetto," which she condemned as "a more spacious closet," as we learned earlier.[6]

If gayborhoods formed during the coming out era when sexual minorities sought sanctuary from discrimination and violence, then we would expect them to gradually disappear as they feel safer and more incorporated into the mainstream. David Smith, also from the NGLTF, anticipated this possibility early in 1993 when the Cincinnati City Council banned discrimination against gay people in housing and employment: "The movement is breaking out beyond the gay ghettos," Smith observed. "It's moving out to small cities and counties nationwide." He, too, suggests that legal equality can compel residential dispersion. More than a decade later, in a 2007 story for the *Boston Globe*, Robert David Sullivan expressed the same argument: "The gay population is becoming more dispersed. As gay men [and lesbians] feel more comfortable coming out to family, neighbors, and co-workers, they may also feel more comfortable living in small cities or towns rather than in the 'gay ghettos' of large cities." Assimilation allows gay people to feel comfortable and secure. And these feelings enable them to feel safer living in areas beyond the gayborhood.[7]

Boston is another city where gays and lesbians are leaving the gayborhood. Assimilation here has expanded the local residential repertoire beyond the South End, which was formerly the nucleus of queer life. Gays and lesbians have been relocating several blocks east to South Boston. But "Southie," as locals call it, is an odd choice since it is "a neighborhood made famous for raising barricades against change," notes Phillip Bennett in his article for the *Boston Globe*. Gay people "are quietly adding a dimension to a place where, to outsiders, intolerance has seemed at times part of civic duty." How can we explain this? Based on his interviews, Bennett concluded that the dispersion of gays and lesbians into unexpected urban areas like Southie was related to feeling accepted across the city: "Several activists said that the movement of gays and lesbians into South Boston is part of the widespread dispersion of the gay community as individuals and couples seek to settle down in more established or quiet neighborhoods. 'In recent years, we've moved further out into many different kinds of communities,' said John Meunier, Mayor Flynn's liaison to the LGBTQ community. 'It reflects a general acceptance outside of our own little downtown enclaves.'"[8] As gay people feel more accepted and safer in today's post-gay era, they will make some unexpected decisions, such as opting to live in a neighborhood that they once perceived as intolerant. Very few places in the city will feel out of bounds to them if they do not perceive themselves as all that different from their straight neighbors.

Consider next the legendary Castro district of San Francisco. The city's Convention and Visitors Bureau chief Joe D'Alessandro lives there with his partner and their six children. D'Alessandro said that "he thinks gay enclaves marginalize the people who live there. He said the gay community in his previous home of Portland, Ore., a city without a historically gay neighborhood, is a model because gay and lesbian residents comfortably live in the mainstream. 'They do not live in a ghetto,' D'Alessandro said, 'and I think they're stronger because of it.'"[9] On the one hand, his comment supports the contention that gayborhoods are declining in significance. But if Portland is a model city because it lacks such a district, then why, after moving to San Francisco, did he choose to live in the most famous gayborhood in the country? Why valorize those gays who "do not live in a ghetto" but then elect to live in one yourself?

For many residents, the City by the Bay is "one of the great immigrant stories" of the United States, but "these immigrants weren't coming from Italy, Ireland or Germany, but from within their own country," notes award-winning film producer, director, and writer Peter Stein. In this case, the immigrant is the gay person—and a domestic one, at that, if not also a moral refugee. Stein suggests that gayborhoods such as the Castro are "like other immigrant neighborhoods" because "the residents staked a claim to their turf. They made it a place where they could own businesses, buy property, elect their own officials, and where they could be themselves 24 hours a day." But the Castro today is not like it used to be. It has become "a sort of gay Disneyland," he continues, "and as gay men and women realize they can live in lots of different places without fear, the need for a gay neighborhood may in fact be obsolete." Because San Francisco often provides a litmus test for the rest of the country, changes in its gayborhood either signal the loss of community or they are a powerful indicator of equality.[10]

If we spend a little more time in San Francisco, we will discover the first of two change mechanisms, or the actual, on-the-ground process through which assimilation diminishes a desire among some gays and lesbians to live in a gayborhood. "There is a decentralization occurring. Gay people are assimilating and moving to other neighborhoods," said a Castro bar owner in 1996. Eleven years later, an unauthored *Philadelphia Daily News* brief added, "Growing confidence among gays that they can live pretty much wherever they want nowadays and do not need the security of being in a 'gay ghetto' is contributing to cries around California that 'there goes the neighborhood.'" Don Romesburg, cochairman of the GLBT Historical Society of Northern California, said that same year, "What I've heard from some people is, 'We don't need the Castro anymore because essentially San Francisco is our Castro.'"[11] That phrase of his—"San Francisco is our Castro"—captures how individual decisions that people make can add up to collectively undermine gayborhoods. In a post-gay era, many gays and lesbians feel like their residential imagination is expanding. When they decide where they want to live, for example, they consider the gayborhood if they want to, but they also think about the rest of the city as well—all of it is becoming a gayborhood of sorts. If everything is the Castro, however, then nothing is uniquely or distinctively so. Hence, a post-gay paradox: assimilation expands the queer horizon of residential possibilities, yet it also erases the material and sensory location of sexuality in specific, identifiable urban spaces.

This first effect of assimilation is not exclusive to big cities like Boston and San Francisco, or to medium-sized cities like Cincinnati. A geographic reordering is happening in smaller cities, small towns, and the suburbs as well. Travel with me to Northampton, Massachusetts. "There are other gay enclaves, but there's no place I know where the gay population is so integrated into the community," said Julie Pokela, a lesbian business owner and former head of the chamber of commerce. Although some people have dubbed her entire town "Lesbianville, USA," Pokela thinks that locals discourage segregation. "The town is too small and the lesbian population is too big to have ghettos." Tracy Kidder, who is the author of a nonfiction book about the area (entitled *Home Town*), agreed: "Northampton is on the way to being a place where [being gay or lesbian] doesn't matter anymore." But if it truly does not matter anymore, then why bother calling Northampton "Lesbianville, USA?" Such a rhetorical device sends a cultural charge to the very category of sexual orientation that post-gays seek to suppress.[12]

The small town of Gulfport, Florida, is another example. Diane Daniel, a correspondent for the *Boston Globe*, reflected on how the town has changed from 1996 to 2006: "What Gulfport really has become is a place for everyone, a place where 'diverse' is not a buzzword. During a stroll along the mostly commercial Beach Boulevard on a Saturday afternoon in early February, there were children playing in front of a worn duplex, 20-somethings shopping, traditional families with children, bikers, grandparents, great-grandparents, and gay couples." Greg Stemm, an openly gay man who is the executive director of the Gulfport Chamber of Commerce, agreed with Daniel: "We at the chamber call the community 'bohemian' . . . There's a real desire not to make this a gay ghetto. We very much value an eclectic mix. For a small town, we have a remarkable blend of people."[13] For him to position "bohemian" as the opposite of "gay ghetto" carries with it a sense of historical irony. The places where gay people would gather in the closet and coming out eras were both bohemian *and* ghettoized. The rhetorical strategy in a post-gay era is to untangle what was once a fusion between bohemia and clustering.

Finally, consider what reporters who write for the *Advocate* refer to as "once-sleepy blue-collar suburbs," which lately are "attracting large numbers of gay people." These areas are appealing to those gays and lesbians who "don't feel ostracized by society" and who "feel perfectly comfortable in the burbs." The newcomers call themselves "regular Joes" and "suburban," and they perceive their expanding residential repertoire as "a positive, like a sign that they were true mainstream Americans," said sociologist Wayne Brekus in his interview with the magazine. The journalist who interviewed him also spoke with Gary Gates, who added, "It's not that [post-gays] won't need a gay community, they just won't have to move to find it." At first, it may seem odd that so many gay people have become "entrenched in conservative suburbs," but it is evidently not an issue for those who live in them. Andy, one of Coldwell Banker's top realtors in Fort Lauderdale, said as much about his local market: "The area is the most boringly accepting place. No one gives a good goddamn if you are gay or straight."[14]

Do changing attitudes about sexuality *cause* some gays and lesbians to reject big-city gayborhoods and instead move to smaller towns and the suburbs? Daniel Stewart, the openly gay mayor of Plattsburgh, New York (a small town snuggled between Lake Champlain and the High Peaks of the Adirondacks), said in a 1999 interview with the *New York Times*, "The acceptance of gays is being won in small towns and villages. It's small-town America where people know you, you can impact their lives, and they are less apt to use it against you." He confirms, though only descriptively, that small towns are a hotbed of changing sexual meanings. A counterfactual might help us to answer the causal question. What would happen in the *absence* of a gayborhood, if one did not exist? Wayne, a soft-spoken gay man who lives in Roanoke, Virginia, compared being gay in his smaller community with what he thinks it is like in a larger urban area. In Roanoke, "There is no large gay enclave to retreat into," he said in a 2001 interview with the *Washington Post*. This forces gay people like himself "to relentlessly interact with people who are not gay." As a result, "here, you mesh yourself into a larger community and forge friendships with people who haven't had exposure to gay people before." In numerous small towns like Roanoke, "we don't live our whole lives as gay." Wayne says that "it is one thing to be gay and another thing to live every part of your life as a gay person." Small-town gays "may be gay sexually, but they are not gay culturally." Their sexuality does not define them.[15]

The distinction that Wayne made in 2001 between being "gay sexually" and being "gay culturally" resembles what Nate Silver said in his 2012 interview with *Out* magazine: "I'm kind of sexually gay, but ethnically straight."[16] Both of these gay men resist a reductive understanding of their sexual orientation. In a post-gay era, it does not extend to a worldview in the same way it did before for many people. Each man asserts that who he has sex with is not necessarily related to his self-identity or to the cultural communities in which he participates. In this way, sexual identity today is much like white ethnic identity: optional, episodic, and situational.[17] Such sentiments are gaining traction today, but they are not entirely new. Wayne, for instance, overlooks the fact that few gay men and lesbians before Stonewall were able to live their "whole lives as gay" in the way that he imagines gay people do in big cities today. The crucial difference between the present day and prior sexual eras is that the ability to *not* live "our whole lives as gay" is something that gay people can do much more easily—and by choice. But they retain the option to move to the Castro, like Joe D'Alessandro did, or any other gayborhood at any time, if they want, and flaunt their sexuality all day long.

Assimilation frees lesbians and gay men from feeling like they have to self-segregate for reasons of safety, community building, or pride, while urban economic renewal, municipal promotion campaigns, and the easing of stigma against homosexuality invite straights into gayborhoods and gay bars. In other words, push and pull factors both incite this particular brand of urban change. "As gay culture becomes more mainstream, the ghettos open up. People live wherever," said Kafka-Gibbons, a former Washington, DC, Dupont Circle resident who now lives in suburban Massachusetts, in his 2002 interview with the *Washington Post*. Homophobia is not the primary culprit for gay out-migration, as we might expect. The journalist also interviewed Barrett, a longtime Dupont resident, who explained, "What's happening is not so much a transfer of gay life out of Dupont as an expansion into other areas . . . If the forces were homophobic, I'd worry and want to do something about it, but

I don't think they are." Indeed, if homophobia was the principal reason why gays are moving out of gayborhoods, we probably would not hear them say that "people live wherever."[18]

Economic factors may compel some straights to move into a gayborhood, but the primary motivation for why gays move out is almost always cultural and political. In Houston, for example, "sexual minorities . . . have not only grown in number and visibility, but have spread out from Montrose, the community's historic center," remarked Carol Christian, a journalist with the *Houston Chronicle*. To find out why, she interviewed a gay male couple, Harry Livesay and Michael Venator, about their decision against living in Montrose. Livesay said that some gays and lesbians have moved out of the Montrose area because it has become "too expensive," confirming a common economic perception about the effects of gentrification, but she also found that it had to do with increased acceptance. Livesay is the former chairman of Houston's Gay and Lesbian Political Caucus. He and Venator purchased a home in Westbury, rather than the Montrose gayborhood. Livesay remarked that ten years ago, Westbury homeowners would likely have said that they didn't want gay neighbors. "Now they say, 'We're so glad you're here . . . It's a big turnaround. We're not 'those people in Montrose.' We're the people next door." For him, this represented a fundamental shift in the meaning of sexuality. His sentiment in conservative Texas resembles what we heard earlier in Southie, and it also echoes Jeanne and Diane from New Jersey who, recall, said that they "weren't the gay girls next door; we were just neighbors. We were able to blend in, which is what you want to do, rather than have the scarlet letter on our heads." The tone of all these transcripts, however, is laced with some shame. What is wrong with being the gay girls next door? And why is the opposite of "blending in" having a "scarlet letter on our heads" or being "those people," a category whose vagueness speaks volumes? Gayborhoods are changing in a post-gay era, but if we ask questions about the implications of what people say, then we will remain alert to the subtleties and seeming contradictions that are associated with these modern urban upheavals.[19]

An expansion of the residential imagination is not the only way that assimilation works on the ground. There is one more mechanism that accounts for why so many gays and lesbians are leaving the gayborhood while straights move in: an emerging mindset among gay and straight people alike that allows them to feel that they are each not so different from the other. We have heard hints of this already. Recall Andy, the Fort Lauderdale realtor, who told us, "No one gives a good goddamn if you are gay or straight," and Nate Silver's memorable self-identification as "ethnically straight." Now consider a third example from New York, where Dick Dadey, executive director of the Empire State Pride Agenda, explained why many lesbians and gay men are rejecting gayborhoods: "There is a portion of our community that wants to be separatist, to have a queer culture, but most of us want to be treated like everyone is," he said. "We want to be the neighbors next door, not the lesbian or gay couple next door."[20] Dadey, himself a public figure, equates queer cultures and communities with separatism, which post-gays consider anathema to "being treated like everyone else." This impulse toward cultural sameness is a powerful pathway that also contributes to the dilution of gayborhoods, even if Dadey incorrectly assumes that minority cultures are incompatible with mainstream values. Although straights and gays share this mindset, they express it quite differently. For instance, have you ever heard straight people say that they are "ethnically gay"? We will explore these and other fascinating nuances later in the book.

Post-gays promote themselves as "virtually normal," to borrow a phrase from Andrew Sullivan, and thus culturally similar to their straight neighbors. In his interview for a *New York Times* story entitled, "A Milestone in the Fight for Gay Rights: A Quiet Suburban Life," Tim Nolan, who we met earlier, declared, "There are still people who clearly want to live in the gay ghetto . . . But a whole lot more, I'd guess, want to lead their lives like other people live their lives." From this statement, the reporter concluded, "Mr. Nolan and his partner are among a new cadre of homosexuals who are living openly and happily in the sort of suburban neighborhoods that they quit in the 1960s and '70s, when gay men and lesbians from across America rushed to the coastal cities seeking fellowship and freedom." To contrast the "gay ghetto" of the past with "a new cadre of homosexuals" who are "like other people" is an example of this burning desire to be culturally similar to straights, a passion that, while it certainly also existed in prior sexual periods, has decidedly deepened in today's post-gay era.[21]

The theme of cultural sameness appears repeatedly in the coverage of gay neighborhoods, although the style of this particular conversation can be a bit sensational. In the late 1990s, a reporter with the *San Francisco Chronicle* interviewed lauded gay English writer Quentin Crisp. The journalist asked, "What do you think of gays living in their own self-contained neighborhoods—in 'gay ghettos' such as the Castro District?" Crisp quipped, "When I asked somebody, 'Why do you want to cut yourself off from nine-tenths of the human race?' he said, 'I have nothing in common with them.' But he has everything in common with them except his funny way of spending the evening." Surely, the distinctiveness of queer cultures is greater than the alleged comedy of the night. Consider next the impressions of Bill, a gay resident of Sarasota, who told a reporter for *USA Today*, "Why should we be in a gay ghetto? No way. Why shouldn't we be in a mainstream community where it's beautiful?" Yet to define the mainstream as beautiful is to imply that gay districts are somehow distasteful or ugly. Shame and stigma, however subtle, disguise themselves in Bill's logic of assimilation. Next, let us meet New York playwright Craig Lucas. Speaking about his sexuality, Lucas explained, "I balk at being called a gay playwright. It marginalizes you." His self-definition affected his view of gayborhoods: "I live in the real world, not in a gay village." Lucas's opinion, much like Bill's, is also troubling for what it implies about the spatial clustering of queer cultures. To make this vivid, simply ask yourself whether the feelings of safety, pride, community, and political power that gayborhoods promise amount to mere fantasy. Finally, consider an interview in the *Chicago Tribune* with Tracy Baim, a prominent reporter who covers issues of relevance to the local GLBT community. In speaking about Halsted Street, the main queer artery in the Boystown district, Baim predicted, "Maybe, in 20 or 30 years, gays will be so thoroughly assimilated into the culture that they won't want or need their own community. Maybe then the rainbow lights will make for just another pretty street." Baim imagines a future when sexual minorities have achieved full legislative equality, and she encourages us to anticipate how cultural preservation will (or will not) be possible in such a time. We will revisit this important theme throughout our travels.[22]

Arguments about cultural sameness sometimes take a defensive tone. *Village Voice* editor Richard Goldstein, for example, published the following comment in 1998 about the relationship between assimilation and gay culture: "There is apprehension about the banalizing impact of mainstreaming—fear that it means the end of gay culture." His statement provoked vitriolic letters to the editor. One reader wrote with fury, "May I ask Mr. Goldstein what exactly is so wrong with being 'mainstream'?" Said another more explosively, "What the hell is 'gay culture' anyway? 'Fruity masculinity and feminine gravitas' in mainstream images of gays? Those stereotypes are insulting enough. Sparky the Gay Dog in South Park?!! Give us a break!" This particular writer proceeded to dismiss gayborhoods altogether: "If Goldstein spent much time outside of his gay ghetto (or New York), he would discover that all gay Americans (i.e., non-urban, rural, redneck, 'mainstream' gays) want is for others to acknowledge that sexual orientation doesn't make a dammed difference about anything . . . Goldstein doesn't realize it, but he's doing incredible harm in encouraging the notion that gay people are fundamentally different and exist outside the mainstream."

Gayborhoods historically have been crucibles for the cultivation of queer cultures and communities. Erased in these fiery letters with their defensive tones, therefore, are the legions of writers, artists, musicians, dancers, intellectuals, and other creative people who have found inspiration in them, like Armistead Maupin or Tony Kushner. Goldstein, without hesitation, responded to all these letters in one fell swoop: "I suspect that if this writer were to assert her identity—say, by holding her lover's hand while shopping at Wal-Mart—she would soon be wrenched from her illusions, and reminded that, to dispel stigma, one must first be aware of it."[23]

As we have seen several times now, and will continue to see throughout our travels in this book, "gay ghetto" is a popular—but loaded—phrase that many people like to use. On the surface, it is a fairly common, if catty, way to talk about the changes that we are seeing in gayborhoods across the country. Underneath, however, it carries significant implications about the discrimination that straight people have used against gays for decades by assuming that deviance, disease, and other pathologies are associated with segregated ghettos. The use of this term by gays to talk about other gays may, in turn, signal a certain kind of progress. Assimilation into the mainstream is always accompanied by infighting within a minority group, especially between those who are eager to blend in and those who are determined to hold on to what makes them different (e.g., compare Malcolm X's black power program with Martin Luther King Jr.'s promotion of civil rights and electoral representation). The term "gay ghetto" differentiates post-gays who strive toward cultural sameness and maintain that they have an expanding residential imagination from those gayborhood gays who stand out like a sore thumb. It is a rhetorical tool that demarcates post-gays from those who they think are among the most disreputable elements of their group, yet with whom they must share an uneasy affinity.

But the question still remains for us to answer: Is the word "ghetto" appropriate to use in the context of a gayborhood? The term originated in sixteenth-century Venice, where it described an area of the city in which authorities forced Jews to reside. American sociologists of the Chicago School appropriated the word in the 1920s "to designate urban districts inhabited predominately by racial, ethnic or social minorities, whether by compulsion or by choice," notes historian Michael Sibalis. Within fifty years, scholars, like residents, were "applying the term 'gay ghetto' to neighborhoods characterized by the presence of gay institutions in number, a conspicuous and locally dominant subculture that is socially isolated from the larger community, and a residential population that is substantially gay." Ghettos, in other words, have four defining features: institutional concentration, a locally dominant subculture, social isolation from the surrounding city, and residential segregation typically created by compulsion rather than by choice. Therefore, an urban area is a "gay ghetto" or "lavender ghetto" if it has large numbers of gay institutions, a visible and dominant gay subculture that is socially isolated from the rest of the city, and a concentrated residential population. Based on these four features, the term "gay ghetto" is an apt synonym for a gayborhood—but only in the coming out era.

The definition applies unevenly to gayborhoods in a post-gay era. The "institutional encasement" of the coming out era, to borrow a term from sociologist Loïc Wacquant, is weakening as gay bars and bookstores close across the country. New organizations and bars continue to open, of course, but many of them are setting up shop beyond the borders of existing districts. And remember from the opening pages of this chapter that even those areas are residentially deconcentrating and becoming less sexually segregated. Many gays and lesbians today describe an expanded residential imagination and praise arguments about the cultural similarities between them and their straight neighbors. As a result, significant numbers of gay people are dispersing across the city, while straights now feel more comfortable living and socializing in the center of the gayborhood. All of this is to say that gayborhoods in a post-gay era are not ghettos—if anything they are "anti-ghettos," again from Wacquant—due to their "heterogeneity, porous boundaries, decreasing institutional density and incapacity to create a shared cultural identity."[24]

All of the people who we met in this section raise another hotly debated question: Are gays really any different from straights? And how will that affect urban life? "People are different," Eve Sedgwick answered without equivocation in her book *The Epistemology of the Closet*. Furthermore, if we acknowledge that diversity is "life's one irreducible fact," as sexologist Alfred Kinsey claimed back in the 1940s, then surely there must be some valid distinctions that we can make between gays and straights. And if these differences compel certain patterns in behavior—which is perhaps the most basic insight of the discipline of sociology—then there is but a small step for us to take before we can conclude that gays and straights are indeed different from one another, and for reasons other than the funny way in which they each spend their evenings.[25]

SHOULD I STAY OR SHOULD I GO?

There are certain moments in our lives that compel us to reflect on where we want to live, and if we should stay or go. Gays and straights pass through some of these same stages, like growing older, while others, like coming out of the closet, are unique to non-heterosexuals. And then there are those junctures in life, like the decision to start a family, that both groups experience, yet raise distinct concerns for same-sex households. Each occasion—aging, the coming of age of a new generation, and starting a family—operates like a trigger that forces us to rethink our relationship with the city. Of course, gays have always aged, young people have always come out, and same-sex couples have always had children. These are not new groups of people that have suddenly emerged in a post-gay era. Instead, the growing social acceptance and assimilation that we have been seeing in recent years creates more possibilities for how these groups can structure their lives, and thus we are witnessing more variety in where they live. After we see the world through their eyes, we will wrap up this chapter by considering the astounding effects of the Internet on urban life, especially the ways in which it, too, is influencing how and where people choose to live by endowing them with an enhanced freedom of residential choice.

Gayborhoods become less appealing for some gays and lesbians as they get older. Jane Gross, a journalist with the *New York Times*, spoke with several of them who were living in New York in their late forties. This is what she learned: "With the approach of middle-age, they say the city loses its sparkle, and they grow tired of looking for parking spaces and dodging muggers. The rustle of leaves, they discover, is sweet music compared with a whining car alarm. And a little house and a yard matters more than a 24-hour nightlife." The same trend is evident across the country in the Bay Area: "San Francisco has grown up and matured, and that includes the gay and lesbian community," said supervisor Susan Leal. She acknowledged the interactions between an expanded residential repertoire and feelings of cultural sameness: "We feel more secure, so there isn't the need for such close-knit support. All over the city, people are seeing two people showing affection for each other not as a gay and lesbian thing or a straight thing, but as people just living their lives." Finally, consider evidence from aging gays and lesbians in the nation's capital, a politically charged space where we might expect sexuality to remain more salient. Writing for the *Washington Post*, D'Vera Cohn summarizes the results of a 2003 study that analyzed the American Community Survey: "Many of the Washington area's gay male and lesbian couples are middle-aged suburban home-owners, according to a new study of census data that offers the first detailed portrait of one of the nation's largest gay communities . . . The region's gay population has grown . . . [and] is increasingly liv-ing outside the best-known gay neighborhoods."[26] From New York to San Francisco to Washington, DC—in each city the story is the same. As gays and lesbians grow older, their preferences for where to live change, and many of them move out from the gayborhood.

Gay people grew older in previous generations, just as they do now, yet the gayborhood remained more salient in the lives of those from prior generations. We should ask now, before diving any deeper, why the post-gay era is different. Aging will modify what we want in ways that are not always compatible with life in a gaybor-hood, of course, but societal acceptance today has made it easier for gays and lesbians to live openly across the city. Prior generations may have perceived fewer options for where they could live safely and publicly beyond the gayborhood. To put it differently, gays in the coming out era wanted more space and less noise as they aged, just as aging post-gays do today. The difference is that previous gen-erations did not perceive the same collectively patterned freedom and flexibility to move and live in places like Westbury, Southie, or suburban New Jersey.

The maturing of certain segments of the gay population pro-ceeds alongside the coming of age of younger generations, but today's "new gay teenager," to borrow a phrase from psychologist Ritch Savin-Williams, is unique. In a provocative 2005 *New Repub-lic* essay entitled "The End of Gay Culture and the Future of Gay Life," Andrew Sullivan explains how: "While the older generation struggled with plague and post-plague adjustment, the next gen-eration was growing up. For the first time, a cohort of gay children and teens grew up in a world where homosexuality was no longer a taboo subject." Some evidence for the tumbling of this taboo comes from television and films. "If the image of gay men for my generation was one gleaned from the movie *Cruising* or, subse-quently, *Torch Song Trilogy*, the image for the next one was MTV's *Real World*, Bravo's *Queer Eye*, and Richard Hatch winning the first

Survivor." There are now more gay and lesbian characters on television and in the movies, yet their sexuality is often secondary, and their lives resemble those of conventional heterosexuals. Sure, "there is no single gay identity anymore, let alone a single look or style or culture," Sullivan says, but "gay and straight become a blur" in these post-gay images. The emphasis today is on "the interaction between gays and straights and on the diversity of gay life and lives." The only way to accomplish such cross-sexual interactions and celebrate the diversity of gay lives at the same time is to carefully and strategically select which lives we will depict in public. Which? you rightfully ask. Those lives with which straights can more easily relate. "Slowly but unmistakably, gay culture is ending," since "being gay is a nonissue." As a result, "the gay ghetto is no longer an option," Sullivan concludes.[27] His final statement is a little extreme, in my opinion, since it suggests that gays do not have a choice, that they cannot live in a gayborhood even if they wanted to, but it unveils the distinction that I think Sullivan is trying to make between "gay culture" and "gay life." The former is a product that gay people themselves create as they live and socialize in gayborhoods (and elsewhere), whereas the latter is a generic and perhaps unspecified entity in which both gays and straights can participate, at least in theory.

The new gay teenagers are rejecting gayborhoods. In a story for the *Advocate*, John Caldwell remarked, "During a time when gay people are coming out at younger ages, many cities outside of the traditional urban gay centers have become important examples of positive change. As society becomes more accepting, the need for intense gay enclaves begins to dissipate." Kyra Kyles, who we met earlier, said something similar in the *Chicago Tribune*: "Increasing social equality means gays and lesbians don't need to be confined to any one area of the city." She interviewed a resident who explained how generational changes and social acceptance jointly undermine the viability of gay neighborhoods: "Young people no longer see the need for a specific 'gayborhood,'" said Bill Pritchard, the self-described "unofficial mayor of Boystown" and senior vice president of community affairs for a local entertainment company. "This generation of gay, lesbian, bisexual, and transgender community is different . . . We don't necessarily have to live in a gay social circle to feel protected."[28]

When gayborhoods formed in the coming out era, they provided a sanctuary for sexual minorities. But the new generation is coming of age in a time of acceptance, and their experiences are quite different from those of prior generations. They assume safety, rather than seek it out, as Benoit Denizet-Lewis expressed in a 2008 *New York Times* magazine essay: "Young gay men [and lesbians] today are coming of age in a different time from the baby-boom generation of gays and lesbians who fashioned modern gay culture in this country . . . While being a gay teenager today can still be difficult and potentially dangerous, . . . gay teenagers are coming out earlier and are increasingly able to experience their gay adolescence. That, in turn, has made them more likely to feel normal." This sense of normalcy enables the new gay teenager to see him or herself as no different from their straight friends. "Many young gay men [and lesbians] don't see themselves as all that different from their heterosexual peers, and many profess to want what they've long seen espoused by mainstream American culture: a long-term relationship and the chance to start a family." The us-gays versus them-straights mentality of the closet and coming out generations, on which gayborhoods were built, is yielding to an us-and-them mindset that younger generations are pioneering and that contributes to the metamorphosis of gayborhoods.[29]

Aging and youth sometimes interact to render gayborhoods "passé," as Patricia Leigh Brown argued in her 2007 story on the front page of the *New York Times*:

> The social forces that gave rise to the Castro and other gay neighborhoods like the West Village and West Hollywood may be becoming passé. In West Hollywood, another traditional gay haven, the graying of the population . . . [has] resulted in once-gay watering holes like the Spike and the I Candy Lounge going hetero . . . [while] young gay waiters and schoolteachers move instead to Hollywood and other surrounding neighborhoods.

Perceptions of older and younger generations can work in the same direction, and when they do, they exacerbate the unraveling of gayborhoods. Brown concluded, "There has been a notable shift in gravity . . . with young gay men and lesbians fanning out" all across the city.[30]

Same-sex households with children are the final group whose circumstances in life trigger them to reassess whether they want to live in a gayborhood. Writing for the *Washington Post* in 2009, Lonnae O'Neal Parker remarked, "Gay and lesbian families are showing up in greater numbers in the nation's suburbs and rural areas" in what is a new "pattern emerging across the United States." From 2000 to 2007, "there was a 25 percent increase in the number of same-sex couples in urban areas, including inner suburbs, and a 51 percent increase in rural areas." Same-sex households with children are more visible now than they have ever been before. This new visibility represents "the arrival of gay men and lesbians at a less marginalized point, where being gay is just one identity among many," and often not the primary or "master identity," as some sociologists call it, or one that takes precedence over others and orients our action without regard for context. For many same-sex households with children, this is hardly news; they are just "quietly going about their lives." In the post-gay era, "there is both increased visibility of gay and lesbian families in areas outside the cities," and there is also "a migration [out of the city] as gay families become more likely to have children or as couples get married and have families," O'Neal Parker explains, based on her interviews and census data.[31] The notion of suburban flight, familiar to so many straight families, now also applies to same-sex households who are positioning themselves in their suburban homes by focusing on what makes them similar to their straight neighbors.

Having children affects our lives in deep ways, and it can change where we want to live. In a 2011 interview for a *New York Times* story, Mayor John Heilman of West Hollywood remarked that his city, like others, has undergone "an inevitable evolution as gay residents gained greater acceptance in society. The city's gay population has aged and," he argued, "its interests have changed. Gay residents are more likely to, say, have children and focus on family activities than stay out late at one of the gay clubs that dot Santa Monica Boulevard." This reduces their incentives to stay in a gayborhood. As gays and lesbians are more accepted in society and as more of them begin to form their own families, they become part of "a shift in cultural values in the gay community," city councilman John Duran added. The institution of marriage is responsible for some of this shift. "Marriage by nature is a conservative institution," he continued, "which often brings children and monogamous relationships." The mayor and councilman themselves make a conservative argument that has been circulating for years within certain circles of gay activists and public intellectuals. Andrew Sullivan, for instance, argues that marriage provides a "conservative reform" that can "promote stability and monogamy among homosexuals and responsibility in the society as a whole." This line of thinking begs questions about culture, sexuality, and stigma—not to mention marital heteronormativity as the gold standard of all relationships—and fierce debates about these matters are ongoing.[32]

Gays and lesbians consider new residential options as the legal landscape changes. Donovan Slack, writing for the *Boston Globe* in 2003, remarked on the role of adoption laws in particular: "A Supreme Judicial Court decision that paved the way for same-sex couples to adopt children has spurred a shift toward family values in the gay community." He interviewed a male couple who "hope to adopt children soon," in their words, about how a legal case (*Goodridge v. Department of Public Health*, 2003) might affect their preferences: "We want to raise them in a neighborhood that is both gay-friendly and child-friendly. We don't want to be in a gay ghetto." They seem to imply that a gayborhood is not child-friendly; it is another example of the criticism we heard before about "those gayborhood gays." Consider as well a 2006 article in which a reporter interviewed a Boston resident named Chris who went a step further to argue that same-sex marriage is responsible for the demise of the gayborhood: "Gay marriage seems to have exacerbated the decline of the 'gay ghetto,' created a 'profusion of conservative gays,' and it has become a 'one-dimensional definer of the community and its political platform,'" Chris emoted. He believes that the legalization of domestic partnerships, civil unions, and marriages have sanctioned certain types of relationships, and compared to singles, partnered households are less likely to live in gayborhoods.[33]

Families with children are often concerned about an area's schools. This is another issue, besides suburban flight, that is also familiar for heterosexual families. Let us travel to Plano, Texas, a place where many local same-sex families are relocating. "The school system is a big draw for families," said Bob, an openly gay realtor who moved to the area with his partner and their two kids. The reporter provided some context for Bob's assessment: "Plano's 68 public schools and at least a dozen private schools consistently score in the top percentile of the nation, producing such notables as Lance Armstrong and Chace Crawford (*Gossip Girl*). That's good news for the 20.2% of Texas's same-sex households who have children under 18." Bob agreed: "It's one of the biggest reasons families relocate to the area. I was even the secretary of my daughter's theater group at the Colony High School, and nobody batted an eyelash about a gay dad."[34] Here again we see how an expanding mindset (the decision to move to Plano rather than a gayborhood) interacts with cultural sameness ("nobody batted an eyelash about a gay dad").

Before we conclude this chapter, let us think for a moment about the dramatic ways in which the Internet is also affecting the choices we make about where to live. In a 2013 nationally representative survey, the Pew Research Center found that "LGBT adults are heavy users of social networking sites, with 80% of survey respondents saying they have used a site such as Facebook or Twitter. This compares with 58% of the general public (and 68% of all Internet users)." Among all LGBT adults, 55 percent report meeting a new friend online, and just less than half the respondents (43%) say that they have come out on a social network.[35]

The Internet is changing our relationship with the city. Some people blame it for causing a gay dispersion, though they acknowledge that gay businesses and other institutions offset some of these effects. A Boston bartender, for example, insists that "it's much harder for a neighborhood gay bar to attract a steady clientele," and he and other locals attribute this decline in businesses to the Internet. Robert David Sullivan, the journalist we met before, and who interviewed this bartender for his story in the *Boston Globe*, offered a historical perspective: "When Internet access became widespread in the mid-1990s, gay chat rooms on America Online and other sub-scription services quickly attracted a crowd. More elaborate sites such as Gay.com quickly followed, usurping gay bars' most impor-tant function: a place for men to meet each other . . . As a result of these changes, there are stories of gay bars closing all over the coun-try." Just as institutional presence and a sexual marketplace can anchor a neighborhood's gay identity, the closing of bars and other businesses can destabilize it. One reporter said as much on the front page of the *New York Times*: "There are signs that the dispersing of gay people beyond the Castro vortex and the rise of the Internet are contributing to a declining sense of community. An annual survey by the San Francisco Gay Men's Community Initiative indicated that in 2007 only 36 percent of men under 29 said there was a gay community in the city with which they could identify." In this way, gayborhood change goes hand in hand with the Internet. Doug, a medical sociologist who works at the San Francisco Department of Public Health, mused in the story, "I've had therapists who have told me they are asking their clients to go back to bars as a way of social interaction."[36]

The effects of the Internet extend across the border to Canada. One day during the summer of 2012 in Vancouver, when I was out for a lunch break, I noticed that a guerilla gay activist group had plastered fliers on lampposts in Davie Village, the city's gaybor-hood. The message they left for those of us who walked by was hardly cryptic in its all-capital font: "MORE GRINDR = FEWER GAY BARS." First launched in 2009, Grindr is a free social networking mobile application for gay men that offers, as its website states, a "quick, convenient, and discreet" way for them to meet others. At the time when I wrote these words, 3.5 million men in 192 countries had downloaded it. But is Grindr the *cause* of gay bars closing and the waning sense of community? That is a hard question to answer since we do not know if people decide not to go out to the bars spe-cifically because they are on Grindr. It is possible that the app is creatively recreating community in unexpected places, as we will consider shortly. For now, however, some social commentators fear that the app is "an intrusion of digital artifice into what was once an analog gay Utopia."[37]

The electronically mediated interaction that Grindr provides is not new. It is an enhanced version of technologies that date back to online chat rooms (e.g., AOL or Gay.com) and, even before then, to telephone lines, which enabled gays and lesbians to talk to each other from the privacy of their own homes. The new capabilities that Grindr brings to the mix are mobility and GPS-enabled proximity. Users can see what a person looks like and read his constructed persona or profile, and they can also learn where he is in space at any given moment. In this sense, Grindr is not a mode of using technology as a substitute for in-person interactions, as the flier and the San Francisco therapist both accuse. It can facilitate those very interactions by situating them in specific spaces. With respect to community formation, Grindr may function today as gay bars did in the coming out era. The density of nearby contacts creates a proxy queer space, albeit an electronic one, whether in a gayborhood or beyond it, since users are visibly mapped. In theory, a gayborhood can manifest anywhere within a reasonable proximity where there is a critical mass of other men who are logged on at the same time as you. The app can also supplement, rather than supplant, bar attendance, and I personally know many men who use it while they are inside a gay bar or at a house party. Still, the flier is a meaningful form of cultural discourse that expresses anxiety in a very public way about the effects of technology on queer spaces.

Besides the bars, the Internet is also "challenging the position of gay papers as the main sources of news in their communities and the diaspora of gays from traditional urban enclaves is making readers harder to reach," noted Keith Darc in his *San Diego Union Tribune* story. "Gay papers face other challenges that are unique, such as contending with what some people call gay sprawl. With the increasing acceptance of gays and lesbians into mainstream American culture, a growing number of gay newspaper readers are moving out of compact urban gay ghettos and into the suburbs. 'That shift is making it harder for papers to reach their target audience,'" said Sue O'Connell, publisher of *Bay Windows* in Boston, in her interview with Darc. "They aren't frequenting the same places where gay publications traditionally have been available, like bars, clubs, and gay bookstores."[38]

Notice Darc's metaphor of a "diaspora." This idea refers to the dispersion of a group away from its homeland. The Internet decreases incentives to live in a gayborhood since gays and lesbians can easily meet others online for anything ranging from sex, through apps like Grindr, or parenting advice. It therefore subverts the sexuality and community functions that gayborhoods provided in the coming out era. The Internet also indirectly affects the economic viability of gay organizations, since bar and bookstore closings and newspaper deaths all undermine the character and composition of gayborhoods, and this feedback loop further lowers the incentives for living in these spaces. The closing of Oscar Wilde Bookshop in New York is one particularly sad example. Located at the intersection of Christopher and Gay Streets in Greenwich Village, this was the world's first gay bookstore, which opened in 1967. Its closing in 2003 sent ripples across the city: "'There's simply no community support,' said Larry Lingle, who bought the store from founder Craig Rodwell in 1996. 'Many gays and lesbians now feel comfortable outside of 'gay ghettos' such as Christopher Street.'"[39]

SEXUALITY AND THE CITY IN A POST-GAY ERA

Gayborhoods are changing. The index of dissimilarity offers statistical evidence that they are "deconcentrating" and becoming less "segregated," as demographers like to say. In this chapter, we pursued a qualitative counterpart, a dissimilarity meanings measure as we called it, that allowed residents to breathe life into these numbers. Why do some American gays and lesbians say that they want to leave the gayborhood? And why do others reject them outright? We focused on how societal acceptance of homosexuality in a post-gay era, and the assimilation that results from it, alters the way that people think about the relationship between sexuality and the city. Of course, all nonheterosexuals do not live in gayborhoods, nor are existing ones exclusively queer. Nondistrict dwellers are also more visible today. Gayborhoods are in flux, to be sure, but our wider cultural discussions about sexuality are themselves more varied, inclusive, and attentive to those gays and lesbians that live in predominately heterosexual communities—and to those straights who live in gayborhoods, as we will see more directly in later chapters.

We heard two major reasons (or mechanisms, as we called them) that residents offer for why gayborhoods are changing. First, assimilation is broadening the queer residential imagination beyond singular streets. Post-gays perceive an entire city as the functional equivalent of a gayborhood. The phrase "San Francisco is our Castro" is the quintessence of this expansion mechanism. Calling the entire city of Northampton "Lesbianville, USA" is another vivid example, one that illustrates that the pattern applies to gay men and lesbians alike, and it is not limited to large urban areas. The problem, however, is that no particular space may remain uniquely queer. Hence, a peculiar post-gay paradox: assimilation expands the horizon of residential possibilities beyond the boundaries of just one neighborhood, yet it also erases the location of sexuality in specific urban spaces. San Francisco-as-our-Castro looks and feels very different on the ground from the Castro as a place of gay community, culture, politics, and pride.

Post-gays also express that they feel culturally similar to their heterosexual neighbors, which is the second mechanism through which assimilation exerts gayborhood change. The statement "No one gives a good goddamn if you are gay or straight" is an apt, if aggressive, illustration of this emerging mindset. Post-gays promote themselves as virtually normal, and they desire to be the unmarked and thus unremarkable neighbors next door, not the gay or lesbian couple next door. They wish to erase the scarlet letter of their homosexuality. These mechanisms often work together in real life, and they illustrate how sexuality creates a type of urban change that is unlike the effects of race, ethnicity, and class.

After we discussed these two mechanisms, we turned our attention to certain stages in life that trigger us to reassess where we want to live, if we want to move, and why. These moments also have the potential to change the composition of gay neighborhoods. We heard stories from older generations of gays and lesbians, we learned about the perspectives of the new gay teenager, and we met several same-sex couples with children. Each group represents a particular juncture in life where the ideas of expansion and cultural sameness resonate a bit more deeply. Their actual experiences are far more complex than the mere preview that we saw in this first chapter, of course. As we grow older, for example, sometimes we want a quieter life with less traffic, maybe in the suburbs, and post-gays generally feel comfortable leaving the gayborhood to find such a life. But other gays and lesbians find that aging reinforces their desire to be with their own kind. Why else would some observers describe gay retirees as "the next big untapped market"? Consider what CBC News reported in 2013 in its headline: "Gay Seniors Struggling to Find 'Safe' Retirement Housing."[40] Gay seniors may not live in a gay neighborhood, but the desire to be around others who are like them is alive and well for many of them. Same-sex families with children confront a similar conundrum. Some households want to blend in with their straight neighbors and live side by side with them in communities that have a reputable public school system. For them, a parent identity ascends while their sexual identity recedes. Others, however, want to ensure that their kids go to a school where some of their peers will also have two moms or two dads.

The same goes for gay youth. Some of them are coming out early in their lives, hanging out easily with their gay and straight friends, and joining gay-straight alliances. They do not experience any significant stigma about being a sexual minority. A great example of this comes from a high school in Putnam, a small town of about six hundred people that is sixty-five miles north of New York City. In 2013, Dylan and Brad, a gay male couple at Carmel High, won the "cutest couple" title in their school. It was the first time that a same-sex couple received the honor. Kevin Carroll, the principal, remarked that it "hasn't really been a big deal in the school." The father of one of the boys agreed, "I think of it as any other normal day. He won. OK. Lots of people win 'Cutest Couple.'"[41] This story is remarkable for so many reasons. It supports the claim that society, especially younger generations, is becoming more post-gay as the years go by. But now compare Dylan and Brad's experience with the epidemic of homelessness and suicides among queer youth. On the one hand, you have the Cutest Couple, who happen to be gay, but on the other hand you have the It Gets Better Project, a brilliant campaign that Dan Savage created to communicate to young queer people that their lives will get better. Clearly, there is much more for us to explore.

Finally, we considered how the Internet affects gay urban districts. Institutional presence and a vibrant sexual marketplace contributed to the initial formation of these areas in the coming out era. The Internet developed as we transitioned to the post-gay era, and many people blame it for creating a queer diaspora by allegedly decreasing incentives for living in a gayborhood. How can independent gay bookstores like Oscar Wilde survive in an age of Amazon, after all? And why bother going to a bar to find someone for the night or for a lifetime when the search is so much simpler online, especially with a mobile app like Grindr that locates users on a map in real time? Some observers worry that as traditional brokers of sex, love, and romance, neighborhoods are being displaced by communication technologies that provide the same function with greater efficiency and more control.

We encountered a handful of intriguing questions in this chapter that still linger. Does gayborhood change signal the loss of community? Or is it an indicator of equality? And are gayborhoods necessary for the creation and preservation of queer cultures? We have only just begun our journey, of course, and these puzzles require more time, attention, and careful analysis. For now, let us move our focus away from the printed page of newspapers to the streets of everyday life. We now will travel to Chicago, a paradigmatic American city, and explore how the cacophony of this national debate over gayborhoods looks, feels, and sounds to people on the ground. Thus, it is time to shift our view away from the somewhat distant proclamations of journalists to a close-up of daily encounters and opinions of those lesbians, gay men, and straights who call this great city their home.

2

The Happiest Ending

Chicago has captivated scholars for more than a hundred years. It even inspired its own brand of sociology, known as the Chicago School of Urban Sociology. The professors who developed this intellectual tradition in the early twentieth century focused on the importance of place in everyday life. Today, the city remains "as much a sexual laboratory as a social one," notes Chad Heap, a historian who studies the legacies of the Chicago School, and this makes it a logical site for a case study. As of the 2010 Census, Chicago (population 2,695,598) was the third most populated city in the United States, after New York (8,175,133) and Los Angeles (3,792,621).[1]

There are many ways to think about the Windy City. Some observers remark that it is a global city: a command point in the world economy, a key location for international finance and specialized services, a crucible for innovation, and an exciting hub for the circulation of people and products. Others disagree and view Chicago instead as a secondary city: one that is decidedly not global and thus incapable of competing at that level. Globalization promoted the development of world-class cities like Frankfurt, London, New York, and Tokyo. As these grew in importance, and as manufacturing declined, secondary cities engaged in clever strategies to attract capital. One way they did this was by rebranding themselves as places of culture, cosmopolitanism, and consumption, and they showcased their stock of ethnic enclaves like Chinatown, Greektown, and Little Italy. In recent years, city officials have added gayborhoods to the menu. Competing under the cosmopolitan canopy of a globalizing world motivated Chicago to go a step further and formally mark its gayborhood.[2]

The disagreement among scholars and urban planners about whether Chicago is a global or secondary city tells us that it is at once a quintessential American city, yet it is also unusual or atypical in some notable ways. Of course, no one city can ever represent the entire nation, but zooming onto the streets of one place can still teach us something about another. Although there is no shortage of studies about Chicago, especially its rife racial and class dynamics, its queer narrative is vastly underwritten compared to New York, San Francisco, or Los Angeles. These are all reasons why it makes sense for us to spend some time in Chicago, in addition to the many other places to which we are traveling with our journalist guides.[3] In their news reports, however, they sketch a picture of urban America in fairly broad strokes. We cannot fully appreciate how gayborhoods are changing unless we talk to people ourselves, and take the time to understand the sensory details of their everyday lives from up close. We will see this texture in this chapter and in chapter 3 through the eyes of 125 self-identified gay men, lesbians, and straight residents, business owners, government officials, representatives of nonprofit community organizations, realtors, developers, and various public figures. In this next part of our journey, we will explore the hopes and fears of ordinary residents—their banal concerns and their greatest ideals about the gayborhoods that they more simply call home.

WELCOME TO THE GAYBORHOOD

Chicago has two active gayborhoods: Boystown, the nickname of the city's thriving commercial and nightlife district that is tucked into the Lakeview neighborhood, and Andersonville, another area, although quieter, with a large concentration of same-sex households that is located farther north in the Edgewater neighborhood (figure 2.1). In 1997, the city installed tax-funded rainbow-colored art deco pylons along North Halsted Street in Boystown and, in doing so, made it the first officially designated gayborhood in the United States. But residents also recognize Andersonville as another queer space. We will meet locals who live in each northside hub.[4]

A triangle-shaped area defines the boundaries of Boystown (figure 2.2). Belmont Avenue is at the southern end, Grace Street at

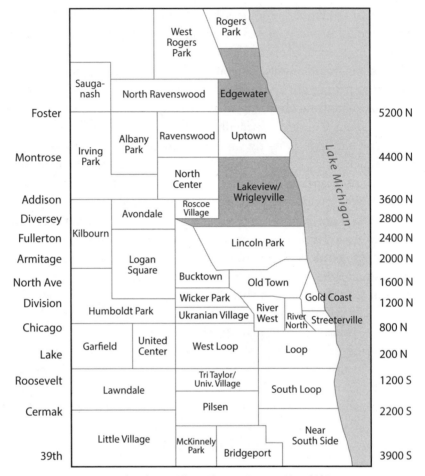

FIGURE 2.1 Boystown and Andersonville in Chicago. Source: City of Chicago.

the northern end, and the angular Broadway Avenue serves as the hypotenuse. Boystown is Chicago's gayest neighborhood, but its composition is changing fast. "It's now very mixed, culturally," remarked Ed Gargano, a longtime manager of Gaymart, a novelty shop located on Halsted Street. But Boystown still has the largest concentration of gay bars, and it is home to the Center on Halsted, the Midwest's largest LGBT community center.[5]

A second gayborhood in Andersonville emerged over the last twenty or thirty years. It is a rectangle-shaped subsection of the Edgewater neighborhood (figure 2.3). Andersonville is a Swedish

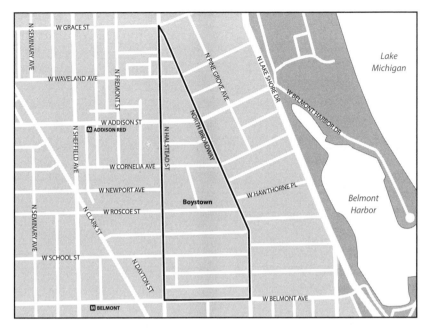

FIGURE 2.2 Boystown.

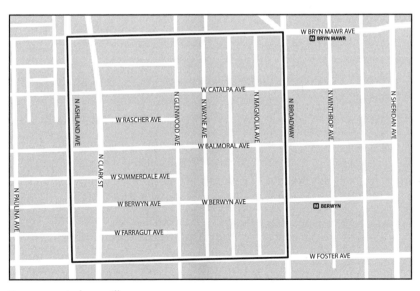

FIGURE 2.3 Andersonville.

American landmark neighborhood. It is home to the Swedish American Museum; an iconic water tower painted in the colors of the Swedish flag; numerous Swedish delis, bakeries, and restaurants; and a popular Midsommar Festival that annually celebrates the area's ethnic heritage. A lesbian population arrived in the 1970s, drawn by the presence of a feminist bookstore, Women and Children First, which opened in the neighborhood. Gay men soon followed, many of whom moved directly from Boystown. These days, some residents feel like Andersonville is gayer than it is Swedish.[6]

At the time of the 2010 American Community Survey collection, half of Illinois's estimated 25,710 unmarried partner households lived in Cook County, which includes Chicago and several suburbs to the north, south, and west. Forty percent of these households resided in the four northernmost neighborhoods along Lake Michigan (see figure 2.1). Lakeview, which contains Boystown, has the largest concentration. It is home to 1,106 same-sex households, or 12 percent of the city's total, followed by Edgewater (home to Andersonville: 951 households, or 10.3 percent), Rogers Park (736, 8 percent), and Uptown (635, 6.9 percent). Lakeview's rate of self-reported same-sex households (2.1 percent) is above the city's average (0.9 percent), but these days its ranking is falling behind Edgewater (3.2 percent).[7]

The two neighborhoods differ in their gender composition and in their proportion of same-sex partner households. Joseph Erbentraut, a journalist who writes for the *Windy City Times*, a free gay newspaper, reported 2010 Census results to highlight the distinctions: "Comparing the community areas' ratios of queer male households to queer female households, Edgewater (1.60 male households for every one female household), Uptown (3.04:1) and Rogers Park (3.91:1) are much more in line with the city average (1.89 male households for every one female household) than Lakeview. Lakeview is estimated to be home to 10.77 queer male households for every one female household." We can better appreciate these ratios when we narrow the comparison to the specific census tracts that comprise Boystown and Andersonville. Erbentraut continued, "Andersonville's male-to-female ratio is estimated to be 1.33:1, while Boystown's is 12.15:1." More men than women live in Boystown, whereas Andersonville has a more balanced gender profile. In addition, "Andersonville's rate of queer couple-led households as a percentage of all households (5.3 percent) is also markedly higher than Boystown (2.4 percent)," meaning that, compared to Boystown, more same-sex couples live in Andersonville.[8]

How do Chicago residents make sense of living in a city with multiple gayborhoods? Do they consider Boystown and Andersonville culturally equivalent, or do they think about them as different from each other? Why do straight people live in these two areas, especially a place like Boystown, which is municipally marked as queer? What meaning do straights assign to the sexual iconography that lines their streets and the queer bodies that move along them every day? All neighborhoods change, of course, and they are shaped and reshaped by a constellation of factors. Here, we will listen to self-identified gay, lesbian, and straight residents reflect on the effects of assimilation in general, and we will ask them to talk about the significance of older generations, younger generations, same-sex families with children, and the Internet in chapter 3. Our goal is to take the bird's-eye view we gleaned from the media and color it in with texture, voices, and views from the streets of one great American city.

AN EXPANDING RESIDENTIAL IMAGINATION

Assimilation, as we have seen, is broadening the spatial location of homosexuality away from the specific streets of a gayborhood to the entire city itself. This is a significant shift in demography and cultural consciousness, as gays and straights are actively reimagining their relationship with the city. To better appreciate how they talk about this, reflect for a moment on the cultivation of our own perceptions. According to sociologist Eviatar Zerubavel, "What we perceive through our senses is normally 'filtered' through various interpretive frameworks." People carve out from an essentially continuous reality distinct "islands of meaning," he says. We group together acts, events, and objects that we think are similar. In this way, each neighborhood of a city is an island of meaning that residents use to "outline rather elusive social differences."[9] Ethnic enclaves, gayborhoods, theater and nightlife districts, well-known shopping areas—all of these are examples of categories that we create to navigate the city. We then seek confirmation of a neighborhood's character through various symbols that we identify as meaningful. With gayborhoods, this might include two men or two women holding hands as they walk down the street, rainbow flags that hang in storefronts, or particular ads that are visible on billboards and bus stops.

If our perceptions are social, then they are also subject to the tides of human history. Recall how the relationship between sexuality and the city has changed over time. The scattered gay places of the closet era paved the way for the formation of distinct gayborhoods in the coming out era. Gay and lesbian moral refugees carved out these islands of meaning, along with gay-friendly areas and straight areas, because they were seeking safe spaces. Post-gays, however, imagine an expanding set of options about where they can comfortably live, and they suppress the perceptual act of classification that defines them as different from straights. What interpretive frameworks do Chicagoans use to explain this change? And what do those teach us about gayborhoods as islands of meaning?

Let us begin with a series of responses from public officials, business owners, realtors, and community leaders, all of whom agree that Chicago gays and lesbians are reimagining their relationship with the city. Openly gay alderman Tom Tunney of the Forty-Fourth Ward, which includes Boystown, sees queer islands of meaning merging with the rest of the city: "It's not just one neighborhood. Gay is okay in major cities. Period. It's just not as ghettoized. It's not this pocket and this pocket. It's everywhere." A realtor added, "The overall urban mentality is more accepting of the gay community. I'm selling homes to the gay community all over the city." Meanwhile, more straights are moving into gayborhoods, as another realtor remarked: "In the last few years, I've only had straight people that wanted to be in Andersonville or Boystown." Such urban changes reflect cultural shifts in queer life, says bar owner Stu Zirin: "From a cultural standpoint, there's an acceptance. It's not 'Oh, you're gay? You have to live over there.' We don't need our own ghetto anymore." Art Johnson, who owns one of Chicago's most popular gay bars, called Sidetrack, agreed: "I think gay people are dispersing throughout the city. I think it's a really significant social change." Dyke March organizer Edith Bucio concluded that gayborhoods have lost their meaning: "What's a queer neighborhood? There are queers all over the city." Jason Cox, the associate director of the Andersonville Chamber of Commerce, spoke with me about how societal change affects the waning need to self-segregate: "As society has become a little more open, there's less that need to ghettoize yourself. There's much more willingness to spread much wider." Tico Valle, the director of the Center on Halsted, thinks that the gay community is "taking the whole lakefront" these days, while Bernard Cherkasov, who directs Equality Illinois, offered a sweeping vision: "The LGBT community is everywhere in the state."

Some urban sociologists argue that the city is a "growth machine," and that the perspectives of public officials, realtors, and business owners may not always align with the lived experiences of everyday residents.[10] In this case, however, residents agree. A Boystown gay man explained, "It used to be that everybody was here. But now, we're all over the place. Everybody's really spread out." Another man declared, "There has to be a gay aspect to every neighborhood." A lesbian who lives in Boystown added, "Our friends in the city live all over," while a male couple in Andersonville observed, "Gays and lesbians are more spread out." One man in Boystown linked a conventional economic perspective with cultural change: "Gays will move wherever they want to as long as they can afford it. It doesn't have to be the gayborhood." Finally, a man in Boystown and another in Andersonville echoed the expansion mechanism that we heard in chapter 1: "The argument can be made that the entire North Side is homosexual," said the former, while the latter added, "The gay neighborhood? It's pretty much all of Chicagoland." Their intuition is worth stating in more general terms: many residents today equate the gayborhood with the entire city.

Chicago residents like to compare their home with other places, especially New York. Many of the people who I met felt that a similar perceptual expansion was happening in the Big Apple. "Our friend who lives in New York said the entire island of Manhattan's gay," recalled a Boystown gay man. Notice the similarity between the phrase "the entire island of Manhattan" and the earlier remark about "all of Chicagoland." In both cases, the gayborhood becomes interchangeable with much of the city. Another Boystown gay man similarly said, "New York is really spread out. All the gays are really spread out. You go in different areas, and you're going to see a lot of straight people, and you'll see gay people, too. It's really mixed."

San Francisco is another city that often came up in my conversations, especially among straight residents. One woman in Boystown characterized the City by the Bay as "the king of the gay community," while her husband elaborated, "San Francisco doesn't care if you're gay; just go live wherever you want. You don't need your own spot where you feel safe." Another married couple in Boystown referenced both New York and San Francisco: "I think you get to a certain point where, like a New York City or a San Francisco, or maybe we're now seeing that in this Lakeview part of Chicago, where people are just kind of okay with it . . . Maybe Halsted Street is losing its rainbow colors, but I think it's partially because it's spreading out. And I think with the Castro district, it was the Castro district, and now it's San Francisco."

San Francisco looms large in the queer imagination as well. A gay man who recently moved to Chicago from San Francisco explained, "My perception of San Francisco is that it's almost like a much larger version of the gayborhood." Similarly, a gay man who lived in Andersonville, who moved to San Francisco for law school but then returned to Chicago after graduating, said, "Yeah, the Castro might have a higher concentration of gays, but everybody was gay in San Francisco. There are gay people everywhere."

Queer and straight minds both equate gayborhoods with an entire city. It was Boystown (or the Village in New York or the Castro in San Francisco) in the closet era, but now, in a post-gay era, it is the entire city, which we can think about as a much larger version of the gayborhood. While city dwellers once carved out queer islands of meaning from an essentially continuous urban reality, now they are reversing the view and merging gay people and gayborhoods back into the continuous reality.

Gayborhoods will attenuate as fewer gays and lesbians consider themselves moral refugees, and as they no longer perceive an urgent and inescapable need for a safe space. One gay man in Andersonville predicted that gayborhoods will "shrink" as the country becomes more accepting of same-sex relationships: "I think we're probably in for an extended period of shrinkage in gay neighborhoods because as other places become more comfortable, people are going to go where they really want to be. They're going to vote less with their sexual orientation and more with their desire for space or their desire for access to work, or whatever, all the reasons people choose neighborhoods." An expanded residential imagination emerges when feelings of safety and comfort prompt people to downplay the primacy of sexual orientation in their everyday lives. As a result, gays and lesbians make decisions about where to live based on a broader array of conventional factors, like affordability and access to nature, work, or public transportation. A lesbian in Boystown explained, "You might live in any neighborhood in town and feel equally comfortable among straight and gay people." A gay man in Andersonville identified greater tolerance as the cause: "I think our society is becoming more tolerant of gay people, so you can be gay in more places than just your neighborhood." The entire city then opens up with possibilities. A Boystown lesbian found freedom in this new post-gay world: "Gay and lesbian people can move in other areas of the city, out of the gay-identified places. I think that there is freedom to go out and explore." Citing an expanded repertoire, a male couple in Boystown argued that gay people today "choose to live where they want to live and not, like, 'I'm a gay man. I must live in Boystown.' It's interesting. I do not hear Lakeview always or even predominately referred to any longer as 'Boystown.'" This incisive observation suggests that some residents perceive the name Boystown itself as limiting. A lesbian in the neighborhood found the name outright "offensive," not because of its gendered overtones, as we might expect, but instead because "it feels very narrow." A gay man also objected to the ghettoization that it implies: "I don't want a gay ghetto. I don't think every gay man in the city should live in one neighborhood." All these arguments define a queer concentration as narrow and limiting, rather than as a source of pride or community, as many residents felt when gayborhoods first formed.

We must also consider the role of power and politics as we try to understand why gayborhoods are changing. A gay man in Andersonville drew a savvy comparison with race: "Some say, 'If your mayor is gay, the whole city is gay.' It's sort of like what people feel about black mayors. If the mayor is black, that means the whole city is black." His argument echoes what we heard following the election of President Obama in 2008. Some years later, in a 2013 commencement address at Morehouse College, the alma mater of Dr. Martin Luther King Jr., Obama told the graduates, "Laws, hearts and minds have changed to the point where someone who looks just like you can somehow come to serve as president of these United States." With sexuality, as with race, the assimilation of a minority group expands their horizon of possibilities. As a result, "there's no need to have these safe spaces anymore," the same gay man in Andersonville concluded. "This space [Boystown] was really important when there was this invisibility of the population, this marginalization. But if they've been assimilated into the local area, then the area no longer serves any purpose. If the whole city has been imagined as gay, then you could do that anywhere. The city is redefining itself." Gayborhoods provided much-needed safe spaces to sexual minorities when they suffered from cultural invisibility, stigma, and powerlessness. But assimilation and strides toward social equality have redrawn the landscape, and residents now imagine the entire city as gay in some ways. A lesbian attorney in Boystown linked dispersion with politics and the law: "Our community has really dispersed. It is not residentially concentrated anymore or rentally concentrated anymore. I think over time, as we have made political gains, it has really forced neighborhoods to open up and rent to us. And that really happened with the passage of the city human rights ordinance. Rather than having protection municipality by municipality, all of Cook County is protected by the county human rights ordinance, and it really has allowed us freedom to move and live wherever we want."[11] By banishing housing discrimination, the Cook County Human Rights Ordinance helped to transform the entire city into a place of possibilities.

Straights are aware that the queer residential repertoire is expanding. A straight man in Andersonville observed, "Boystown's becoming less gay as gay people don't have to live in Boystown. It used to be that if you wanted to be gay or open about your sexuality, that's where you went because that's where you could live and be open. But as society gets more open, you can live in Lakeview or Wicker Park." Did his argument also apply to Andersonville? "Even Andersonville will become less gay over time as it starts dispersing as well," he replied. A single straight man in the same neighborhood agreed: "What's the point of it now? You don't really need it [a gayborhood] anymore." He then explained how the world itself has changed: "I can see why in the beginning you wanted it, to feel safe. But if you're feeling safe everywhere, then I think you're able to spread out instead of being almost forced to live in a gay area [like you were] thirty years ago." Finally, a straight married man in Boystown remarked on the relationship between normalization and where gays and lesbians live: "If you're a gay couple, you don't have to live in Boystown. You can live in a lot of areas. You can even live comfortably in most suburbs now. I think part of it [the change over time] is the gay community being normalized and not something to shove aside in an area and just say, 'Okay, let's close off these five blocks and let gay people do whatever they want.'"

Residential possibilities for gay people are expanding—but they still have some very real limits. When I asked a straight woman in Boystown if gay people can comfortably live *anywhere* in the city, she replied, "Not anywhere, no. I think in the gay neighborhoods, you could definitely be openly affectionate and that's accepted. But I don't think that's the case in every neighborhood." So yes, the residential imagination is expanding beyond the gayborhood, but those areas still offer the strongest sense of social acceptance, personal safety, community support, and freedom. Expansion, therefore, is an incomplete yet ongoing and complex perceptual process that plays out on a day-by-day basis as legislative victories compete with lingering homophobia.

CULTURAL SAMENESS

Queer Points of View

Working as part of the Chicago School, sociologist Louis Wirth characterized American cities in 1938 by their size, density, and heterogeneity. He predicted that these three aspects of urban life would create, in his words, "the spatial segregation of individuals according to their color, ethnic heritage, economic and social status, tastes, and preferences."[12] Wirth was right about race and class—islands of meaning existed for both in his home city of Chicago—but he would be shocked to see what the city looks like in today's post-gay era. Chicago residents now talk about a social blending that occurs as a result of the same variables that Wirth used to argue for segregation. Gays and straights perceive one another as culturally similar, and this is the second of two mechanisms that accounts for why gayborhoods are changing. Consider, for example, the reflections of a lesbian in Andersonville: "This urban life that we choose would suggest that you're okay with blending. We are at the seams. We just kind of blend." Blending minimizes the need to carve out islands of meaning, as another woman explained: "It's less important to say this is a gay neighborhood versus this is a straight neighborhood. It's blending, right? We don't have to put a stake in the ground anymore because 'yeah, we're gay.' It's more acceptable now than it was twenty years ago, and there are a lot more people in the public eye that are outwardly gay, and that's also helped people wherever they are in the world to understand it." How can we account for the reversal of Wirth's long-standing insight about American cities?

Contact reduces sexual prejudice, and visibility facilitates familiarity.[13] Perhaps this is why so many gays and lesbians who I met perceived themselves as similar to straights—no longer culturally foreign—and as a result, they asserted that "it's no big deal" to be gay. "There is more of a mix now, like people just don't care," commented a lesbian who lived in Andersonville. Another added, "If you're gay, nobody really cares. If you're not, nobody really cares." Yet a third projected this sensibility onto the entire neighborhood: "If you ask me to describe Andersonville, it's a place where sexuality doesn't matter."

Public officials offered a perspective that again aligned with those of residents. Alderman Tunney said quite simply, "We have more in common than we have apart." Bernard Cherkasov agreed. When I asked for his thoughts on straights who move into Boystown, he replied, "I love it, because it indicates that the idea of gayness used to be controversial or unusual in a negative way, that people thought, 'Oh my goodness, I am never going to move within close proximity of gay people because that just means immoral behavior or lifestyle.' What it means now is that they recognize that there is nothing particularly unusual about gay people." Consider last the familial feeling that Clarissa Gonzalez offered: "You don't need to be queer for me to feel like you're family." The political philosophies of the alderman, the CEO of a mainstream lobbying organization, and a Dyke March organizer, respectively, range from centrist to far left, yet they all perceive themselves to be just like their straight neighbors.

Many gays and lesbians today feel integrated into the American mainstream. "Our society has become more gay," said a gay man in Boystown. "Gay has been mainstreamed." A male couple in Andersonville agreed: "It's mainstream to be gay." For these and other residents, gayborhood integration "is a sign that we're being more accepted," a Boystown gay man told me, and that "we're more welcomed" across the city—and indeed the country. Another added that sexual integration "reflects the way society is moving, which is that gay people in general are more accepted." An Andersonville lesbian said the same: "Straight people do need to see gay couples, and that we're normal. We're just like them. We love the same way, we want to have the same sorts of fulfillment in our lives." These individual perceptions of sameness add up to a collective embrace of sexual integration. Another Andersonville lesbian explained how this works: "The more we are accepted and the more it's not considered to be the least bit unusual to see two women or two men walking down the street arm in arm, the more you're going to see more diffuse populations." A third woman summarized this mindset with some rhetorical questions: "Isn't our point that we're not different? Isn't that what we want, how we want people to look at us?" She then linked both mechanisms, cultural sameness and expansion, and offered a beautiful image for the future of urban America: "We can live anywhere. You could live with us. And at the end of the day, that's the happiest ending."

As gays feel more accepted by straights, many feel that they should also welcome straights into the gayborhood. A lesbian in Boystown defended this notion: "These are neighborhoods that were established when we had nowhere to go, so I could see how it would be very hard for everybody to let some of it go. But if we all want to be accepted, then we've got to let them in, too. We just can't keep ourselves isolated, or it's going to be harder for acceptance." If we take this line of thinking to its logical conclusion, then we can appreciate why so many Chicagoans believe that gayborhood demise is inevitable. Another lesbian added, "Isn't this what we should have been aspiring to? Does it have to be a straight neighborhood versus a gay neighborhood? Can't we all be in a very nice neighborhood?" As sexual orientation recedes into the background, gayborhoods begin to lose some cultural significance, yet we cannot help but wonder if the aesthetics of a "very nice neighborhood" are now more important than queer culture or community.

Several gays and lesbians supported the idea of being straight-friendly. Consider first the barrier-busting sentiment of Tico Valle. Living in an integrated neighborhood, he told me, is "how we break down the barriers of hatred and bigotry in our society. The day will come that we can go into a bar, and it doesn't matter if you are gay or straight. And you can kiss your partner, and people will be like, 'Who cares?' That's the society I'm looking for. So if this neighborhood becomes a diverse neighborhood of baby strollers and straight and gay and black and white and transgender and all, the true rainbow colors, that's fine with me. I love that, because that's what my world is about." Consider next the soothsaying skills of Stu Zirin, who tells us that the days of "strictly gay" are gone: "The way of the future is that we're combined. I don't think that there will be an establishment open that would just be strictly gay. I just don't see that. I think the days of 'strictly gay' are gone." His business partner John Dalton calls this "the new gay," much like Frank from West Hollywood, who we met earlier. Stu and John operate their businesses according to this post-gay principle. During the summer of 2010, for example, one of their two bars displayed a flag for the Chicago Cubs baseball team in its front window. What makes this worthy of remark is that a gay bar located in one of the most commercially dense entertainment districts in the United States did not display any symbols of the queer community, such as a rainbow flag, or any explicitly sexual iconography. It is one thing to suggest that the days of "strictly gay" are gone and quite another to promote a business model that erases all community symbols.

A heightened sense of sameness with straights prompts many gays and lesbians in Chicago to de-emphasize their sexual differences. This is precisely what it means to be post-gay. Consider Alderman Tunney's thoughts on the role of sexuality in electing a public figure to city office:

> We bring more to the table than our sexuality. I think what's happening now, especially in a city like Chicago . . . , people say, "I get it. It's okay. It's cool. What else do you bring to the table?" And I think that's where we as a community need to move on. I think a lot of us have set the trailblazing for, you know, you can represent everybody as their elected official by being openly gay or an open lesbian . . . People want to know about three or four things that—why would they vote for you? Because boom, boom, boom. And I don't think it has anything to do with being gay, at least in most parts of Chicago.

Several residents echoed Tunney. A Boystown lesbian in her mid-fifties added, "I do think how gays once identified themselves is changing," while a forty-year-old Boystown gay man elaborated, "I've never defined myself, number one, as a gay person. There are any number of factors that I will list first . . . So, I'm fine with neighborhoods not being so gay-gay-gay focused."

These abstract changes in how we think about our sexuality concretely affect the choices that we make about where to live. A thirty-one-year-old lesbian in Andersonville defined post-gay as "a trend away from needing to identify [as lesbian or gay]," which, for her, translates as a diminishing need to "gather in a gay space or a gay bar or in a gay neighborhood." Linda Bubon, co-owner of Women and Children First, the feminist bookstore that is credited with spurring Andersonville's queer identity, added, "I think it's so much healthier that people don't feel the need to segregate themselves, that they feel that they can go anywhere with their friends, that they don't necessarily have to be in an all-women or all-lesbian space." A lesbian in Boystown agreed on all counts, although she preferred the language of "fluidity," "blending," and "blurring," which tends to be more common among women:[14] "Everything is very fluid and very blended and much more blurred than it was previously, where you felt, 'Oh, I don't want to live there because that's not Boystown.'" In the coming out era, gayborhoods operated as a safe space. However, a gay man in Andersonville predicted that they will "lose their salience" in a post-gay era of greater overall safety: "These places are indicators about where the population is, both socially and politically. And I think if the idea is that America's become more okay about gayness or about being a lesbian or transgender, then it seems like by virtue of that, these spaces will lose their salience. Part of the draw to it was because you didn't want to feel like when you walked out of your door you were going to be persecuted by your neighbors. Places are just reflections of that population."

I also heard some confusing claims in my conversations about the declining significance of sexual orientation. Before we visit with straight residents in the next section, let us first consider three of these vexing puzzles, each of which reminds us that the relationship between the post-gay era and gayborhoods is quite complex. The first pertains to cause and effect: Does neighborhood integration come first, which later compels gays and lesbians to rethink the importance they place on their sexuality? Or did a critical mass of gays and lesbians first change the way they thought about their sexuality—as a result of other factors—which later caused them to move out from the gayborhood, or if they chose to stay, to celebrate the arrival of straights? Equally unknowable is whether gays and lesbians first felt a sense of affinity with straights, which later caused them to subordinate the significance of their own sexual orientation, or if instead gays and lesbians first muted the importance of sexual orientation in their own biographical profiles, which later caused them to feel more similar to straights.

I also heard a lot of circular reasoning. For instance, Judy, a pseudonym for a thirty-nine-year-old lesbian in Andersonville, took me for a walk down her personal memory lane: "When I was in Darien [a suburb of Chicago], in order for me to kiss my girlfriend, I didn't want to sit on the balcony [of my own home] and hold her." It was only after she moved to Andersonville that Judy felt her sexuality no longer mattered. This is where we need to think carefully about circularity. For Judy and many other lesbians and gay men, spatial clustering comes first; it is necessary to develop a post-gay sensibility that later rejects a need for that very same concentration. In other words, those who say that being gay or lesbian does not matter anymore also happen to live in an area, or they once did, with a sizable presence of other gays and lesbians. Thus, an experience of living around other sexual minorities is a necessary antecedent for a belief, which comes later, that lesbians and gay men no longer need to define themselves centrally by their sexual orientation. Consider what Sarah, a pseudonym for another Andersonville lesbian, said, "I have no consciousness of even being gay when I'm here. It's just so easy and normal that I never really have to worry about it." When I asked her why it was so "easy and normal" in Andersonville but not in other parts of the city, Sarah replied with a similar circular logic: "Because everybody's gay. When I'm in that neighborhood, I don't even think about that. If I'm annoyed [when I leave the neighborhood and have to navigate a straighter world], then I'm conscious of being a gay woman. If I'm just going through my day [in Andersonville], then I'm not conscious of it." Ironically, living in a gayborhood is what enables gays and lesbians like Judy and Sarah to believe that their sexual orientation is secondary—or even irrelevant.

A similar circular logic applies to the idea of gay rights. Later in our conversation, Sarah added, "You fight for all these rights, and you want equality—and then you're like, but no, I'm not different, and I don't stand out." This argument for social equality is subject to the same troubled reasoning as arguments against spatial concentration. The fight for equality in a pluralist political system requires the recognition of personhood, of belonging to a group, and of social distinction. Yet at the same time as they fight for equal rights, many lesbians and gay men also insist that their sexual orientation does not matter and that they are culturally similar to straights. In doing so, they undermine themselves as an electoral bloc, which is a necessary political logic in the United States. It is one that requires specificity and distinction.[15]

The final puzzle pertains to the relationship between gayborhood change and cultural preservation. Many American subcultures and ethnic groups were once or still are spatially rooted in urban enclaves.

"Through this linkage, areas acquire symbolic qualities that include their place-names [such as Boystown] and social histories [such as the Stonewall riots]," notes sociologist Mark Abrahamson. "Each place, both as a geographic entity and as a space with social meaning, also tends to be an object of residents' attachments and an important component of their identity."[16] The stories of many ethnic groups include their gradual dispersion out from their respective enclaves and into the rest of the city. Americans cite this out-migration as evidence that an immigrant group has successfully assimilated into society. But we need to ask whether the preservation of a minority group's way of life—its culture, essentially—requires a spatial component. Can queer cultures, communities, and identities persist in the *absence* of gayborhoods? A gay man in Boystown mused along these lines: "I think the challenge for the gay community is, 'How do we continue to be a community? How do we maintain a sense of community regardless of whether we have a physical community, centralized, or a more virtual community?'" Later in our conversation, he struggled to determine how his own sexual identity affected his decisions about where to live: "Do I identify being gay by where I live? And is how I live who I am?" He conceded that "where I live is who I am," and he added that he knew "a lot of people [who] identify themselves that way," but this realization prompted more questions. "What does it mean if there is no gay neighborhood? Does that mean I'm not gay? Or not necessarily not gay, but am I not a part of the gay community? If I'm not in these small enclaves of gay communities, if they don't exist, what does that mean?" As we move farther into this book, we will revisit these three puzzles of causality, circularity, and cultural preservation. For now, however, let us speak with straight people who live in gayborhoods and ask them to talk as well about the effects of assimilation.

Straight Points of View

Straights also remark on a social blending, rather than segregation, that occurs as a result of the population size, density, and heterogeneity of Chicago. A married man in Boystown told me, "I think it's such an interesting paradox, you've got Boystown and

Wrigleyville, hand in hand." Wrigleyville is the informal name of the streets that surround Wrigley Field, home of the Chicago Cubs baseball team. Many residents consider Wrigleyville its own island of meaning—not to mention a bastion of heteronormativity. "You've got this thriving gay community, and you've got frat boy sports guys all in the same cluster of blocks," he added. The close proximity between these two social worlds was precisely why he moved to Boystown, and it is also why he refuses to define the area as a gayborhood:

> That's one of the reasons why I was more comfortable living here, because it's not so much that I was living in the middle of a gay neighborhood. I was living in the middle of a neighborhood where there are all these different groups of people together. When you stand at Halsted and Addison [two major intersecting streets where Boystown and Wrigleyville overlap] on a Friday night, you see every kind of person imaginable. It's not that you are living in a gay neighborhood. You're living in a neighborhood that's really diverse. Everybody exists peacefully together.

Separated in some places by one mere city block, Boystown and Wrigleyville are the colloquial names that designate two subsections of the same Lakeview neighborhood. Figure 2.4 shows Wrigley Field on the left and the Center on Halsted, the LGBT community center, on the right. It is this close collision between the "gay community" and "frat boy sports guys" that is a "paradox" for this resident, but such disparate types of people nonetheless "exist peacefully together" in a neighborhood that is "not so much" a gayborhood as it is "a neighborhood that's really diverse." Diversity, in other words, ascends in place of sexual specificity.

Straight expressions of cultural sameness have three parts. First, many of them are benignly indifferent to their gay neighbors; they do not think about them or notice them very much at all. Second, when I pressed straights to comment specifically on the gay part of the phrase "gay neighborhood," some of them defensively retorted that integration is the desired outcome that everyone seeks. This is how they minimized the area's sexual tone and also how they drew a bridge between themselves and their gay neighbors. Finally, a

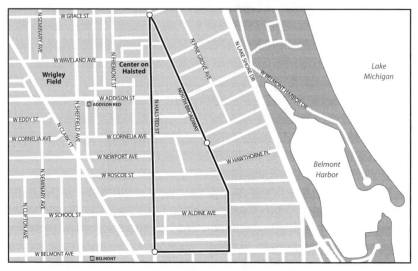

FIGURE 2.4 Boystown and Wrigleyville.

minority of straights responded to anxieties about their presence in Boystown with accusations of reverse discrimination. Let us look at each one in turn.

The most common sentiment that straights expressed was a feeling of benign indifference toward gays and lesbians who lived in the same neighborhood, despite nervously acknowledging that they might actually live in a gay neighborhood (this hesitation is revealing, as we will see). A fifty-year-old single straight woman in Boystown told me, "Am I aware [that this is a gayborhood]? Do I see men walking down the street holding hands? Do I care or look twice? No. I just don't give it that much thought. I'm of the mind-set, 'Who cares what your sexual orientation is?'" When I asked a thirty-eight-year-old married man in the same neighborhood how his awareness of the area's queer character factored into his fam-ily's decision to purchase a home, he replied, "It wasn't a big deal. Frankly, the fact that there are gays, it's like no difference. I don't feel anything." Another married man agreed: "Never really thought too much about it," he confessed. "I'm not looking for the differ-ence. I just don't feel like that's the first thing that comes to my mind." Yet another married straight man added, "For me, it didn't jump out as anything remarkable. I was just like, 'That's cool.' It wasn't anything surprising."

These responses were so repetitive, almost rehearsed, that sometimes I found it hard to tell if the residents were being honest with me or if instead they felt a need to be politically correct. In fact, one of the biggest surprises for me was just how insouciant so many straights—men and women, single and married—were about gays and gayborhoods. A thirty-one-year-old single straight woman in Boystown waved her hand dismissively, "We're over that as your personality. That's no longer interesting enough for you to be the gay foil of the friend group. It's just that's who you happen to be. It's not interesting. It's so not relevant to people anymore. I think a lot of people see it as an odd reason to single out anyone. It's becoming irrelevant." A thirty-six-year-old single straight man in Andersonville was equally unmoved: "It shouldn't even be a thing. It should be what it is. It's just your sexuality. That's it." Homosexuality is less interesting for these straights because they see it as pretty normal. "To me, it's almost normal," said a twenty-eight-year-old single straight man in Boystown. "I've always been immersed and at least had some degree or some local proximity to a very prominent gay, liberal culture. It's always been somewhat a part of my life. It doesn't impact me one way or another." A married man in Boystown hardly even noticed it anymore when men flirted with him: "If I go out in Boystown, I get hit on a little bit. It doesn't bother me. I'm okay with that. It doesn't make a difference to me." Even anal sex was sometimes insufficient to distinguish gays and straights, as this fifty-nine-year-old married woman in Boystown argued: "My father is a good example, god rest his soul. He's dead now, but I remember going home. He was a strong Episcopalian, and he loved the church. A lesbian pastor came out, and he was beside himself. He couldn't handle it. I sat down with him one day and said, 'Dad, tell me what you have against gay people.' It was like their way of life would rub off on somebody, and he didn't agree with that. I said, 'What particularly do you dislike about their lifestyle? They live together. They have families. They connect.'" And then she delivered the punch line in the form of a question—and her father was just not prepared for it. "And then I said, 'Is it anal sex?' And his eyes just—and I said,

'Well, Dad, did you know that heterosexual people do it, too?' And I thought he was going to have a heart attack! In his mind, he must've thought, 'Oh, I've missed all that with my dear departed wife.' I just thought, 'What's the big deal? I don't get it.'"

I was equally taken aback by some straights' explicit passion for sexual integration and implicitly, their rejection of separate urban spaces. A twenty-eight-year-old single straight man in Boystown emoted, "I personally think it's fantastic that straights are moving in because it's a sign of acceptance rather than a sign of loss. It's a sign of 'nobody cares that your neighbor may be gay. Nobody cares that there may be a gay bar around the corner as opposed to a straight bar.' To me, it's a beautiful sign of a melding together"—or social blending, as we called it earlier. I followed up and asked if acceptance of homosexuality was the same thing as not caring about having a gay neighbor. He answered, "I think from a social perspective, the stigma becomes less relevant, which I happen to think is progress. It's like no big deal, whatever. If everybody's gay or everybody's not gay, it's yesterday's news." He thought that straight people moving into Boystown was "a sign" that sexuality is becoming "irrelevant," that "if you're gay or if you're straight, sexual orientation is not a big deal." This young man thought the same thing about his own heterosexuality: "I'm attracted to women. It is what it is. It's what I practice. Somebody else may see the same sex, and that's okay. That's what's intrinsic, that's important to them. That's fantastic." Be who you are; this was the dominant theme of our conversation. Who you are, furthermore, does not warrant a separate neighborhood: "I don't necessarily think that you need a neighborhood to have everybody be the same as you in terms of sexual orientation." For him and a number of other straights that I met, there was no relationship between gay identity and gay neighborhoods, probably because they restricted their responses to individual identification rather than concerns of culture, community, and politics.

When they endorsed neighborhood integration, some straights sounded quite utopian. The same man added, "I think it's one of the beauties of America, the fact that gay people and straight people can coexist." This was a two-way street: "I think that a lot of minorities have a responsibility to try to remove barriers, along with asking the rest of society to accept them. It's important for society to really open up, gay people living beside straight people and being able to say that it doesn't make a difference to anybody." A straight woman in the same neighborhood objected to the very topic of this book and protested, "Can't we all just live in peace, in harmony?" Finally, another woman resisted classifying her world into gay or straight islands of meaning: "I don't like the distinction." When I pressed her to explain why, she responded, "Why can't everybody just be equals? I like it when everybody gets along and can just hang out together." Rodney King made the question of why we cannot all get along famous following his brutal beating by Los Angeles police officers in 1991. Several straight residents, like this woman, expressed a version of it. It is a nice thought, of course, but it says little about the nature of heteronormativity, the structure of our laws, and whether such matters actually facilitate coexistence.

Just as interactions with straight people enable some gays and lesbians to perceive themselves as similar to straights, so too do they fuel straight indifference toward gays. A married couple in Andersonville noted that their friendships have reduced a sense of gays as the "other": "It's already part of our lifestyle to participate in their lifestyle. I'll go to a gay bar with a friend. It's just part of our daily lives, so it's not necessarily an 'other' to us." Here again we witness a rejection of an us-versus-them mindset. A thirty-seven-year-old single straight woman who recently moved from the suburbs to Boystown added how immersion in the gayborhood creates this outcome: "Living in the suburbs makes me sick to my stomach because it's so bland. The city provides such a flavor for me, and if I didn't live where I live, I wouldn't see the many flavors of Boystown. It's just one big happy rainbow of thirty-two flavors. I feel like [living in Boystown has] really opened my mind to humans as humans first, rather than a group." Living alongside gays and lesbians and interacting with them on a daily basis creates a perception of "humans as humans." Boystown is "one big happy rainbow"—until gay people try to get married, of course, or up until the moment that your gay neighbor is fired from work because of his or her sexual orientation. Rainbows are conveniently unhinged from institutional systems of inequality.

Many straights struggled to understand why gay people still want to have their own neighborhoods. For example, a fifty-year-old single woman in Boystown said, "Isn't that what gays have always wanted? People are moving into a space that you originally carved out, and now it's just okay. You're accepted. We're all in this together. You don't need to have a segregated space anymore." This sounds supportive on the surface, but she conflates the idea of a "segregated space," which has specific meanings in the historical context of racial oppression, with some gay people's desire to live among those who are like them in order to feel safer, to shield themselves from discrimination, and to celebrate their community. Consider as well the remarks of a forty-two-year-old single woman in Andersonville: "Do we really need this anymore? Can't we just accept that gay people live everywhere, and they don't need their own separate neighborhoods?" But it is not that simple. One study from 2011 found that same-sex couples are 25 percent more likely to be rejected by landlords seeking renters. Housing discrimination is real, and it, along with the lack of employment protections or relationship recognition, are precisely the types of institutional structures that straight people often ignore in their otherwise accepting, if sometimes idealistic, remarks. The same study found that rates of discrimination plummet when same-sex households apply for housing in gay neighborhoods. This should give us pause about the material significance of these queer islands of meaning.[17]

One reason why straight people forget about institutional inequality, and thus a reason why they think gayborhoods are outmoded, is that homosexuality is less stigmatized in their minds. A straight man in Andersonville said, "It doesn't have the stigma that is used to, even in areas that are very far away from Boystown." As the stigma wanes, so too does the perceived need for safe spaces. "Maybe it's not necessary to have a separate area, safety in numbers, strength in numbers now," he concluded. A man in Boystown situated this perceptual change in broader political and cultural currents in American society: "You're exposed to gay celebrities. We have a black president. We have women in politics. We didn't used to have these back when we were young. It's just become quite normal." As a sense of normalcy increases, the need for gayborhoods decreases. "Little by little, it's going to become quite the norm where people will be entwined in society to the point where you may not even consider it a gay neighborhood. It'll become a neighborhood that was at one point a gay neighborhood. Maybe it just so happens that gay people live here, but what does that mean anymore?" For him and other straights, the stigma against homosexuality is falling by the wayside in a post-gay era.

Many straights hotly rejected the premise that Boystown, with its rainbow pylons, is a gay neighborhood. One man shrugged his shoulders and said, "It's hard for me to see this neighborhood as a gay neighborhood because it has become so natural for at least the [gay people] that I know of to be open about their sexual orientation. Whether it's at work, whether it's friends who are going out, it has become such a part of life." For him, a gayborhood depends on sexual secrecy; the increased visibility of gay people today makes it hard to imagine any neighborhood as distinctly gay. A single woman in Boystown who self-identifies as "mostly heterosexual" agreed: "I don't think it's a particularly gay neighborhood. I think it's way more integrated. There's a huge proportion of people who want to live in the neighborhood who have nothing to do with being GLBT." A straight man took this argument one step further and dismantled the gay community itself: "You don't need to have your own community. You don't need the neighborhood. You just kind of live." Here, too, are queer lives that are somehow unencumbered by discriminatory laws and heteronormativity.

Straight residents cited two specific organizational symbols to support their contention that Boystown is no longer a gayborhood. They first pointed, perhaps stereotypically, to the presence of a new sports bar. The same man continued, "Before, it was like, 'You don't want a sports bar on Halsted. That's not gay.' But now you see a sports bar that has a gay flavor, and it fits with the neighborhood very well. It's a gay place, but it's a sports bar. You can have both." The gay sports bar in Boystown is called Halsted's. Its "gay flavor" is based on its clientele, rather than any explicitly queer iconography, which is absent on the exterior of the building, in its windows, or on its logo. In fact, if you were a tourist in Chicago and you walked by Halsted's, you would not have any reason to suspect that it was a gay bar.

Straights also referenced organizational names and name changes, especially, to argue that Boystown is no longer a gayborhood. "You used to have the Manhole," recalled a married man, referencing a lasciviously named after-hours nightclub on Halsted Street. "Every gay neighborhood used to have a Manhole. Alright, great, Manhole, you know it's a gay bar." In 2002, Manhole, a gay leather bar, closed and rebranded itself as "Hydrate," a new martini bar that was sexually nondescript. There is "nothing particularly gay" about the redesigned neighborhood club. It's just a "place to hang out," and "you don't have to call it Manhole to prove the point," he added.

Organizational names and name changes are a useful lens through which to study the meanings of sexuality since they embody a group's history. Thus, the transition from Manhole to Hydrate provides an archaeological record of how the neighborhood has changed. There is a "diminishing in the bathhouses and the leather bars and an increasing in wine bars and straight-friendly martini bars and fine olive oil stores," remarked a thirty-one-year-old straight man in Andersonville. Even if mostly gay people hang out in these "straight-friendly" places, they still are not explicitly gay. Notice the different bar signs in figure 2.5. The Manhole had an awning with black and blue stripes and a red heart—the official flag for the gay leather subculture. "The businesses that would have catered to the overtly sexual gay people are diminishing in number," the same man added. His observation speaks to the new Hydrate awning that leaves out all gay community symbols in its solid blue color scheme. Gays and straights have reimagined sexuality as implicit and inclusive—and maybe even asexual, evidenced by the disappearance of the bulging, half-naked muscle men donning leather gear as they drink, socialize, and dance inside the Manhole.[18]

In a second expression of cultural sameness with gays and lesbians, some straights assert that urban sexual integration is the desired outcome of the gay rights movement. This opinion cut across marital status, gender, and neighborhoods. A married man in Boystown asked me a rhetorical question that illustrated this view, "Isn't it a good sign that straight people are moving more and more into Boystown? Isn't that a sign that it's not a big deal?" A

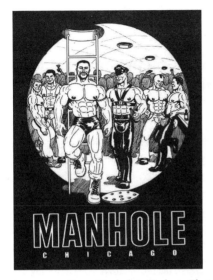

FIGURE 2.5 From Manhole to Hydrate. Photos courtesy of Mark Liberson.

single man in Andersonville said more directly, "If they [gays] really wanted to have equality, then we should all live in the same neighborhood." According to his logic, full legislative equality will be the death knell, once and for all, of gay neighborhoods.

Some straights became visibly defensive at this point in our conversation. The same man from Andersonville aggressively waved his index finger in my face and said, "This is what *you* wanted. *You* wanted equality. *You* wanted your rights. This is it!" In another encounter, after some back-and-forth, a single straight man in Boystown confessed, "I guess I am two-faced about this, if I'm being frank with you. On one side, I would like to see the signs [the rainbow pylons] taken down and things along those lines [like all visible rainbow flags]." When I asked him why, he accused gay people who lived in gayborhoods of causing political harm:

It [an explicitly signified gayborhood] may hurt the progress of the gay movement. To me, it's putting a stake in the ground and claiming a particular piece of dirt where you're supposed to hang out and almost segregate yourself, as opposed to, it's a part of town, it's Lakeview, and there's a high gay population here, but what's the big deal? We don't feel the need to stick a stake in the ground and say, "This is our neighbor-hood. This is where we all congregate," and almost segregate yourself.

His opinion serves his best interests since it permits him to live in the neighborhood guilt-free. The other side of this twenty-eight-year-old man's "two faces" revealed the benefits that gayborhoods offer: "The other feeling that I also have is recognizing that it is probably a minority of the population of the world by far, and there is a movement behind it. It's a good spot for gay people to go and identify and find others who are similar to them in terms of sexual orientation and a place where they can feel much more comfort-able." His inconsistency should remind us that urban change moves in multiple, often conflicting directions.

To support their arguments, some straights compared sexual minorities with people of color. A married man in Boystown, for example, invoked the initial presidential victory of Barack Obama in 2008:

> It's the interesting struggle of when minority groups are fighting for equality and start to get to the point where they're getting closer to that equality, what effect does that have? You've seen it in the past couple years with Barack Obama becoming president. All of a sudden, for all this talk for so long that a black person's not going to be president any-time soon, all of a sudden you have someone who does it. And then all the questions start to change in the media and as people talk. "Well, what does this mean now, and does this mean that black people aren't as disadvantaged as we thought, and are the opportunities different now?" It's a whole shift in the conversation.

I wish he would have compared what it means to be post-gay with being post-black or post-racial, since I think he was on to some-thing quite profound in his remarks about the president. Both ideas are a part of the same seismic cultural shifts that are forcing us to reexamine the categories of race and sexuality that we use all too often in our society. As another example, consider how a straight, single, Jewish man in Boystown drew on his religion:

> I was brought up Jewish. And to me, I never wanted to be in the Jewish part of town. I knew what my religion was, I knew what my beliefs were

or are, and that's what's important to me. It wasn't necessarily being in the all-Jewish part of town. I never liked that feeling. I felt like Jews were segregating themselves by doing that, as opposed to immersing themselves into the everyday world of what has made America so great, being a melting pot that it is. If you want to be gay, be gay. If you want to be straight, be straight. I want you to be happy and enjoy your life. To me, that's a good neighbor.

Here, we see how the post-gay era is shifting our conversation away from gayborhoods to sexual integration and, as we will see later, from identity politics to a privatized pride.

Andersonville residents speak of their neighborhood in similar terms. One man characterized the area as "one big neighborhood, whether you're black, Puerto Rican, gay, lesbian, or straight. That's the way it should be." But this conjures the same conundrum that we encountered earlier when we heard the queer points of view: Does the cultural preservation of a group of people require spatial concentration? Many straights say no, and they reach this conclusion, again, by comparing sexuality with race. Consider what the following white man, who is married to a Latina woman, said as he argued that the goal is for gayborhoods to become "passé":

> Every race is working on this constantly, right? Like the blacks are working on it, the Mexicans are working on it, gays are working on it. You want to be passé. You don't want to have your own neighborhood. You want to be so ingrained in society where it doesn't matter. You don't need a gay neighborhood. We hang out with heterosexual people, and it doesn't matter that they're heterosexual. It doesn't matter if they're homosexual. We just do stuff together. We walk by each other. We say hi on the street. We go out to dinner. We go to Cubs games together.

He dreams of a world where "you don't need to have your own community."

Some straight residents of Boystown defended sexual integration by redefining the meaning of the annual gay pride parade. A single woman did just that: "I heard an interesting comment on the train yesterday. There was a woman talking to somebody and she said, 'I looked around, and there were more straight people than gay people at the parade.' I didn't know what to think because it's like, well, geez, I'm your neighbor. I live on the parade route. I come out. I have a good time. I never took it as just for gays. It's for people who want to show their support, and people who just want to not discriminate against you just because of your sexual orientation." According to this liberal view, heterosexual attendance at gay urban festivals is an indicator of integration, but she neglects to consider how the population size of the majority group can mask power disparities between it and minority groups. Straights will always outnumber gays. This is why more straight presence in queer spaces does not signify acceptance by default. For generations, straights have slummed in them for reasons other than expressing their political support. In fact, some straight people move into gayborhoods *despite* their sexual identity, not *because* of it, as the following straight woman in Boystown told me: "I think most people who are not gay who live in this neighborhood don't think of it as a gay neighborhood." This struck me as odd, since Boystown is municipally marked. She agreed, "It totally strikes me as odd." Some straights do not even perceive Boystown as a gayborhood. This conveniently eases any political pressure they may feel to support gay rights.

During the summer of 2010, the Chicago Cubs and the Chicago Blackhawks both had floats in the annual gay pride parade. The Blackhawks won the Stanley Cup that year, and they proudly displayed it in the parade. Participation by both teams was unprecedented. A local journalist interviewed Brent Sopel, the player who carried the cup in the parade: "We teach our kids about accepting everybody, tolerate everybody, to understand where everyone is coming from." His words resonated with a single woman in Boystown, who remembered reading the article: "The *Sun-Times* had an article about the Stanley Cup coming [to the parade], and they were interviewing the Hawk who is coming. And he's like, 'Of course I'm coming. I have a wife and three kids, but that's awesome [participating in the parade].'" That the Cubs were also in the pride parade is further evidence of gayborhood change, as another woman argued: "Just showing how the neighborhood's changed, this was the first year that the Cubs participated in the pride parade, and their reasoning is they're showing we recognize this community, and we recognize that there are Cubs fans in Boystown, and we want to give back to that community. They had a float with Ernie Banks on it [a former Cubs shortstop and first baseman who was elected to the Baseball Hall of Fame in 1977] because he's 'Mr. Cub' [as he has been nicknamed]. It's nice to see how predominant sports were involved in this year's pride parade." ESPN also remarked on the presence of both teams in the parade: "Parade coordinator Richard Pfeiffer believes the prominent representation of two of Chicago's major sports teams reflects a major step forward in breaking down stereotypes and fostering positive attitudes . . . 'I think it says something about the changing of our culture,'" Pfeiffer commented. If being post-gay means to not define yourself primarily by your sexuality and to prefer sexually mixed company, and if sports are a stereotypically heterosexual domain, then the presence of a hockey team and a baseball team in a gay pride parade provides compelling evidence to support the claim that gayborhoods are integrating—not just demographically but also culturally.[19]

In the final expression of arguments about similarities between gays and straights, a minority of straight residents charged some gays who live in gayborhoods with reverse discrimination, of making straight people feel excluded and unwelcomed. A thirty-seven-year-old single white woman in Boystown, let us call her Ann, angrily addressed this theme in one of my most heated and memorable conversations:

> *Ann*: If you're gay, what does it matter if there's a neighborhood or not? And if you're black, what does it matter if you all have your own little section? It just feels very segregated to me . . . I don't know why me being a single white female is different than being gay. I don't feel like I need to go live where there are a bunch of single white females to feel safe. And I don't necessarily need a neighborhood for all of us together, you know? Because I feel like it's just them calling us out or making us appear that we want this attention. So, in the same way, I feel like if you're gay living in a straight neighborhood—why does there have to be a neighborhood to create a safe place?

Me: That's an interesting analogy: Do we need a neighborhood for single white females? Can you tell me more about what you're thinking?

Ann: Being a woman, and then on top of that being single, I feel like I'm part of a group or a minority maybe myself. And yet, I don't want to live in an area where we're all just single white females because that is very bland, and there are more interesting people and areas that I would want to be a part of, rather than blending into a single white female area where everybody's the same. It doesn't allow for any sort of differentiation or independence or comfortability in who I am compared to my neighbor.

As I have asserted several times in this section, homophobia and heterosexism are institutional systems that are held in place by visible and invisible webs of laws, media images, socialization, school curricula, employment policies, housing ordinances, and so on. Each individual strand in the system sustains tension around the others, and the web stays taut even if a few strands break (e.g., heterosexism is systemically unchallenged even when a pro-gay law is passed or if a gay-affirmative character appears on television). Ann's argument that gay people can discriminate against straights is unconvincing because there is no comparable cultural web that supports anti-heterosexuality. When, for example, have you heard someone say homosexism or heterophobia? Gays and lesbians cannot institutionalize anything against straights in a way that is similar to the intricate system that straights have designed to discriminate against them. Defensive protests, like "I don't know why me being a single white female is different than being gay," are thus misguided for several reasons. First, reverse discrimination is systemically illogical, even if it is still possible on an individual level, given that heterosexism and homophobia comprise an institutional system that straights design and control. Second, gays and lesbians are responding to this system when they react against straights who are moving into their gayborhoods. The reverse is not possible because the discriminatory system is unidirectional (e.g., straights are not systematically targeted in housing discrimination in a way that resembles what gays experience). Third, heterosexual cries of reverse discrimination are plausible and palatable only because we as a society have not articulated a compelling logic in which acts of queer cultural preservation and resistance make sense as life-saving, identity-affirming, and community-building. Finally, history instructs us that minority cultures thrive in concentrated safe spaces that are protected from infiltration by the majority. The Harlem Renaissance is a terrific example. This was a black cultural movement of racial pride during the 1920s and 1930s that was centered in the Harlem neighborhood of New York. The concentrated urban setting served as a crucible in which black culture, identity, and consciousness flourished. It also enabled black residents to appreciate the tremendous diversity of their own lives. Now compare this with the question we heard earlier: "If you're gay, what does it matter if there's a neighborhood or not? And if you're black, what does it matter if you all have your own little section?" Clearly, it does matter.[20]

I have referenced Louis Wirth, who is a well-respected urban theorist, in several sections of this chapter. Why did he paint a picture of city life in Chicago as segregated, while the people we met, who live in the same city, see the opposite? Wirth, like other scholars of his time and even those from today, focused on race. But there is an "epistemological distinctiveness of gay identity and gay situation in our culture," the late Eve Sedgwick argued. The experiences of sexual minorities are not the same as those of racial and ethnic groups, and doing research about the latter does not mean that we have nothing left to say about the former. The contrasting ways in which we acquire knowledge about race and sexuality, along with the trajectories through which these respective discourses and silences flow, account for why an urban landscape constructed by considerations of race cannot adequately account for gay neighborhoods. Furthermore, Wirth's Chicago in 1938 existed in the closet era, whereas the city today is increasingly post-gay and characterized by a cognitive shift away from an us-*versus*-them view of the world toward an us-*and*-them paradigm. This shift from opposition ("versus") to inclusion ("and") implies that gays and straights wish to build bridges, not turn their backs, toward one another.[21]

FROM ISLANDS OF MEANING TO THE MEANINGFUL CITY

The world today is a much safer place for sexual minorities, and their ongoing assimilation and integration into the mainstream is changing gayborhoods in two ways: it is expanding the queer residential imagination, and it is creating shared feelings among gays and straights alike that they are culturally similar. We encountered both in the first chapter as well, but here we have enriched our understanding of how these mechanisms look, feel, and sound on the ground in Chicago.

The first mechanism, an expanding perceptual set of possible places where gays and lesbians think that they can now safely live, encodes a long-standing historical relationship between sexuality and the city. The scattered gay places of the closet era came together into full-on gayborhoods in the coming out era. And where are these gayborhoods going in the post-gay era? "It's pretty much all of Chicagoland," said an Andersonville gay man in an apt summary of the contemporary period. Gayborhoods have stretched beyond specific streets to the entire city itself. When they first formed, gayborhoods functioned as safe spaces for the many queer moral refugees who undertook the great gay migration in search of them. Gayborhoods were islands of meaning in a city that was flooded with heterosexual hostilities. But things are changing rapidly in today's post-gay era. No longer limited to isolated islands of meaning, the perceptions of gay and lesbian city dwellers are expanding to include the entire city as a meaningful and livable place. Meanwhile, many straight residents do not even define the municipally marked Boystown as a gayborhood. If it is true that "most people who are not gay who live in this neighborhood don't think of it as a gay neighborhood," as one straight man told us, then the "islands of meaning" metaphor is losing its utility for how we think about sexuality and the city. The entire city is now a place where gays and straights blend together. Ironically, however, we risk wiping queer sexualities, cultures, and communities off the map. But then, where does the young gay person who has just moved to Chicago from a small midwestern town go if he or she seeks sanctuary, friendship, and fellowship? How does someone who comes out later in life meet other gay people? Or find them for sex, love, and romance? Simply asking these questions suggests that there are limits to post-gay arguments with which we will have to contend.

Cultural sameness is the second mechanism that explains why gayborhoods are changing. The way residents articulated these arguments, however, varied by their sexual orientation. Lesbians and gay men offered two versions. First, they perceive themselves as similar to their straight neighbors. Assertions like "we have more in common than we have apart" and "we are just like you" erase the scarlet letter of sexuality. Post-gays do not feel culturally foreign, or like domestic moral refugees, both of which characterized the mentality of many gay people in the closet and coming out eras. Second, the centrality of sexual orientation is receding in the post-gay mind. "We bring more to the table than our sexuality" is how one resident described it. Sexuality does not define the core of a gay person's self-identity. This is an important lens through which post-gays see the world, but the underlying logic is burdened by contradictions of causality (did neighborhood integration come first, or did changes in sexual self-identification come first?), circularity (is spatial concentration a necessary antecedent for a post-gay sensibility, which later rejects a need for that very same concentration?), and cultural preservation (does a distinct way of life require a spatial component?).

Straights talk about cultural sameness in three unique ways. First, many of them feel a benign indifference toward their gay and lesbian neighbors; homosexuality does not have much of a charge for them anymore. We commonly heard straight residents declare, "Who cares if you're gay?" and also "Who cares if you're straight?" Some said that they were "over" sexuality as a primary feature of identity. Even anal sex was insufficient to distinguish gays from straights. Others were quite passionate about sexual integration. "I personally think it's fantastic that straights are moving in because it's a sign of acceptance rather than a sign of loss," one resident emoted. These endorsements sounded utopian, but also a bit naive, as when one resident opined, "I think it's one of the beauties of America, the fact that gay people and straight people can coexist." This type of thinking suggests that contact creates feelings of familiarity and acceptance, even if some straight people are blissfully unaware of how discrimination, power, and inequality operate.

Second, some straights defensively retorted that integration is the desired outcome for which gays have been fighting all these years. We heard this opinion from men and women, from singles and married couples, and from residents in Boystown and Andersonville. The rhetorical question, "Isn't this what you wanted all along?" captures it well. I felt the brute force of this perspective when some residents pointed their index finger in my face and said, "*You* wanted equality. *You* wanted your rights. This is it!" Equality somehow became my fault. To support their argument, some straights compared sexuality with race (e.g., being black does not matter anymore now that we have a black president) and religion (e.g., as a Jewish person, I know what my religious beliefs are, and they do not require that I live in the all-Jewish part of town), while others redefined the meaning of the annual gay pride parade (e.g., it is not just for gay people anymore).

Finally, a minority of straight residents accused those gay people who desired their own neighborhood with reverse discrimination. As one restless resident asserted, "Being a woman, and then on top of that being single, I feel like I'm part of a group or a minority maybe myself. And yet, I don't want to live in an area where we're all just single white females." This straight woman saw her plight on the same political grounds as sexual minorities, and in the process she demonstrated a startling lack of understanding that heterosexism and homophobia are institutional systems that work in one direction. Another extraordinary example of this sentiment comes from efforts that began in 2012 on Facebook—and quickly spread beyond it by popular demand—to designate July as "Heterosexual Awareness Month." The mission of the group, according to its website, is "to promote, celebrate, and protect heterosexuality." Participants are trying to organize a "straight pride day" to show their support and solidarity for heterosexuality. Ironically, however, this event shows how the straight mainstream is also assimilating into queer culture.[22]

Several facets of the post-gay era ring truer for us as we travel through particular junctures in our lives: as we grow older, as young people come out of the closet, and as households decide whether to have children. The Internet is also a part of this urban upheaval, and it, too, makes the abstract ideas of expansion and cultural sameness resonate more concretely for us. We gleaned a somewhat distant view of these diverse life stages and technological capabilities in the first chapter, but there is still more to learn. So, let us walk the streets of Chicago again and ask people to talk about how these "triggers," as we called them once before, are remapping the relationship between their sexuality and the Windy City.

3

Triggers

Diversity is "natural to big cities" since "so many people are so close together," notes Jane Jacobs, a pioneer of urban studies. To manage a city life that is filled with differences, birds of a feather tend to flock together. Sociologists call this "homophily," and a vast amount of evidence supports it—from free blacks in nineteenth-century Philadelphia, Pakistani immigrants in 1960s Queens, Sri Lankans on Staten Island, and Arabs in Brooklyn in the 2010s. We generally expect minority groups to settle in close proximity to one another, patronize the same businesses, rely on the same community organizations, and build their own support systems. This tendency certainly applied to lesbians and gay men in the postwar years as they were building their first gayborhoods. But does it still hold true in a post-gay era?[1]

Chicago residents these days talk about a social blending that occurs on their streets, as we saw in chapter 2—not segregation—despite the diversity of city life. One gay man in Boystown dismissed the assumption that all sexual minorities would ever live in the same area: "I don't think it's productive to have this idea of all gays living in one space." When I asked him why not, he explained, "Because the gay, the queer community—whatever label you want to use—is not one community." He is right, of course. "To label it as such is to try to imagine something that it is not." Similarly, a gay man in Andersonville connected the heterogeneity of homosexuality with the dispersion of gays and lesbians across Chicago: "I have no idea what the gay community is anymore. Twenty years ago, it was a more politically focused, socially focused kind of idea. But now I feel that there are gay people everywhere. They don't have to have this core [in one neighborhood]." From this preview, we can already surmise that the post-gay era is potentially thwarting predictions that are based on homophily.

Sexuality does not have a singular spatial expression. This is becoming truer over time, and it is a strong indicator of assimilation.[2] Post-gays insist that they are culturally similar to straights, and they perceive many different neighborhoods in the city as possible places to live. In this chapter, we will see with greater granularity how these two familiar mechanisms work as gays and lesbians pass through certain momentous junctures in their lives. These triggers include growing older, the coming of age of a new generation, and the decision to have children. Each forces us to reevaluate where we want to live and socialize. The Internet is also a crucial part of this story, and it enhances the varieties of experiences that are possible in the city—and beyond it. Thus, the "idea of all gays living in one space," if it was ever true, is now moribund in a post-gay era.

THE PARTY'S OVER WHEN YOU HIT A CERTAIN AGE

Changes that we experience in the life cycle affect the choices we make about where to live and socialize. A forty-year-old gay man in Boystown remarked, "As you get older, you don't necessarily need to live in that [a gayborhood]. I think gay guys who make it out of college or are in college, they want to be in the thick of it. They want to be in the heart of it. And they don't mind bar noise until four in the morning. As you get older or settle down, you don't want that as much." Aging creates a desire for more living space and less noise, especially the throbbing bass of nightclubs or the drunken shouts that spill out from the bars. Younger people, he says, tolerate all this better. His thirty-two-year-old partner added, "A lot of them [recent university graduates] move to Boystown, get little studio apartments, and then once they settle down a little bit and realize they can be anywhere in the city, they do move out, because they know they can get a bigger place in a better area, and they don't need the gay bars anymore." A lesbian who lived in the same neighborhood commented on how aging and partnering overlap to alter the role of the gayborhood as a matchmaker: "I think that twenty-year-olds for sure like to be by the bars, and maybe thirty-year-olds. But I think a lot of people kind of age out of that. They get partnered, and there's not such a need or desire to be in that meat-market space." Boystown is especially meaningful for younger gays and lesbians who move to Chicago from small towns and smaller cities, as the following fifty-nine-year-old gay man told me: "I meet a lot of young guys who just moved here from Kentucky or out of town. They come here for a year or two and say, 'Okay, I've done my gay thing. I'm going to move somewhere else.'" Needless to say, the relationship between maturation and neighborhood preferences is not unique to gay people. In one playful conversation, a thirty-four-year-old married straight man summed things up: "The party's over when you hit a certain age."

These ideas emerged regularly. A thirty-five-year-old gay man in Boystown suggested that aging encourages gays to depart from the gayborhood: "I have some friends who are around my age or a few years older that have now moved out of the neighborhood. They've just kind of done their own thing. For me, it's age. I wouldn't follow a gay community now. When I first moved here? Oh, absolutely. I had to be in the heart of it! Now? Not so much." To "follow" is an interesting choice for a verb. It echoes arguments that developmental psychologists make about aging. The older we get, they say, the less susceptible we are to social influences and conformity pressures, and we are less likely to use what other people do to orient our own preferences.[3] Another gay man, a forty-three-year-old, hinted at this in our chat about friendship, bars, and gayborhoods: "When I was twenty-four, I thought I had to live in a place where a lot of my friends who are gay would live or people that I might become friends with, or where the bars are. But when I was forty, I was less likely to do that." A thirty-year-old gay man added, "A lot of us get tired of drinking and get tired of partying all the time and feel like the gayborhoods are really kind of centered around that. When you get to a certain age, I don't want to be out until three in the morning every weekend drinking and getting cruised. Let me go somewhere else where I don't have to deal with that." When I asked him what else gayborhoods offer besides parties, he offered a surprisingly limited portfolio:

My gut reaction is that gay neighborhoods are gay bars, a few restaurants that are gay-friendly, and a bunch of cheesy novelty shops, like, we have Gaymart, which sells dildos, T-shirts, and shiny things and dolls. And then there's Tulip, which is sex toys. And there are more sex-toy places. And more bars. And I think that there are community organizations that are trying to develop a presence and trying to provide services and safe places to the community, like the Center on Halsted and Howard Brown [a medical services facility for the LGBT population] and other smaller and equally important ones. But aside from those, I'd really be hard-pressed to think of what the community does provide other than what I just talked about. It provides people, and it provides social opportunities, and novelties.

His impressions may reflect what is visible on the streets. After all, novelty shops and sex stores have more memorable window displays than nonprofit community or political organizations.

Any major decision we make in life is the result of multiple factors, and even those interact in crisscrossing ways. This was the case for Bill, a pseudonym for the following thirty-year-old gay man who was about to leave Boystown:

When I first moved to Chicago and lived in Boystown, I relished the community. I was still settling into my sexuality, though saying it that way perhaps minimizes my difficulty in doing so. I felt the need to be surrounded by the LGBT community for a myriad of reasons. Among them, I wanted to feel accepted, have the opportunity to go out in bars catering to my community, and find friends and lovers right outside my doorstep. A lot has changed since then.

When I asked him to tell me about those changes, he identified textbook signatures of post-gay life:

My sexuality is no longer the lynchpin of my identity. I've grown into a more multifaceted person. I enjoy many aspects of myself, rather than merely focusing on my life as a gay man. Today, my friends aren't limited mostly to gay men. Rather, I have friends from all backgrounds and sexual orientations. That really adds to my life. I've integrated my sexual orientation into my life, which has alleviated my need to focus on it.

Aging and romantic partnership were also contributing factors for Bill: "I don't miss going to the bars, as I don't drink much anymore and am in a committed, long-term relationship. My need for external acceptance has significantly diminished as I fully accept myself. I don't need the comfort of living in a gay community, and I know it's still there for me to enjoy visiting. It's exciting to move past the stage where surrounding myself with LGBT people was essential to my emotional security." All of these developmental factors enabled Bill to perceive himself as culturally similar to straights and to see the city as filled with residential and social options. He could elect loft living in the South Loop or be with hipsters in Wicker Park. He saw so many possibilities beyond the gayborhood that he eventually moved out. Leaving symbolized an achievement of sorts, a marker of Bill's personal growth, and a moment in life when his sexuality was no longer the primary way in which he defined himself.

Once you believe that "sexuality is no longer the lynchpin" of your identity, then a cascade of changes soon follow. Bill moved past a focus on his "life as a gay man" and decided that his friends did not have to be "limited mostly to gay men." Instead he "integrated [his] sexual orientation into [his] life" and no longer needed gay people as "essential to [his] emotional security." For Bill, like so many other post-gays that I met in Chicago, personal growth meant not feeling as reliant on the larger gay community, although he and others were comforted by knowing that they could visit anytime they wanted. "I know it's still there for me to enjoy visiting." But this is true only if other gay people do not make similar decisions en masse. Post-gays like Bill leave behind a trace of contradiction as they move out from the gayborhood: If everyone leaves, then what gay community will they go back to visit and enjoy?

Andersonville lesbians also suggest that safe spaces are no longer needed. A thirty-two-year-old woman told me, "Boystown used to be somewhere where you would go to feel like you could totally be gay and totally not worry about anything and be whoever you want. That's what it was when I was growing up, and that's where I would go when I cared more. Now, I don't think about my sexuality as much as I used to. No one really cares." She shows us how individual maturation ("I don't think about my sexuality as much") can merge with a collective, post-gay sensibility ("No one really cares") to influence how people think about gayborhoods. She, too, left Boystown:

> It is not as big of a deal to be gay as it used to be, in terms of the need for a strict gay ghetto. I don't really feel like you need it the way that we used to, the way that I used to. I've grown up a little bit and changed, and my focus has shifted. I don't really need to just be around lesbians. I don't need that experience. It just doesn't seem as important to me as it used to.

She assumes that the gayborhood as a whole is not as important as it once was—"no one really cares"—just because she herself no longer needs it. But her dismissal ignores many other realities, such as what life is like for queer youth, people of color, or transgender individuals, many of whom still need exactly what she needed when she first moved to Boystown. Such groups may perceive the presence of straights in the gayborhood as still threatening or dangerous. This is an example of confirmation bias: we sometimes interpret the wider world falsely based on our own personal experiences and on what we want to see rather than competing realities that are different from ours yet true for others.

Like their lesbian neighbors, gay men also discussed how aging, partnering, and starting a family can interact in the hard choices they make about where to live. "Now that I'm thirty-six and I've been out for a really long time and married to my partner, and we have two kids, and we live a pretty out gay life, I don't really care as much, and it doesn't really bother me [to not live in Boystown]," a gay man in Andersonville told me, as his partner tended to their crying babies. "But when I was twenty-four, twenty-five, and coming out, I wanted to be around people who were gay . . . I think as you age, living in the gay ghetto is less important." But then he interrupted himself and redefined maturation as "not even necessarily as you age." When I asked for clarification, he mentioned general changes that occur over a lifetime: "It's life stages. I think it becomes more important when you're single, or if you've had a big change in your life, and you suddenly are without a lot of friends, that's more important to have that community." A forty-nine-year-old single gay man in the same neighborhood agreed: "I was very gay-identified [in my younger days]. I was of a generation, I think, where that [living in a gayborhood] was very important. And I was living in San Francisco at the time. I was living in the Castro. It was important for me to move someplace where I felt like I was in a neighborhood with other gay people." A male couple, also in Andersonville, who were thirty-nine and forty-six years old, respectively, offered a fun analogy of university life: "As you get older, maybe you don't want to live on campus. You want to graduate and move to another neighborhood and be an adult settler." They used to live in Boystown and later moved to Andersonville. "Once we left the neighborhood, we said, 'Okay, let's move into something that isn't as gay. We can leave campus and still feel like we're connected to it,' because it's really just a spiritual thing, not really a physical thing."

Growing older is unavoidable, and it is linked to urban development. Everyone we have met in this section told us that aging makes the gayborhood less appealing and less essential for them. "The party's over when you hit a certain age." The line is lighthearted, but its insights are not trivial. Living in a post-gay world makes it easier for some gays and lesbians to disperse across the city, beyond the gayborhood, and the fact that they feel culturally similar to straights helps to remove the roadblocks. Prior generations may have perceived fewer options because they lived in a world that was fundamentally different than ours, and the gayborhood probably remained more salient in their life as a result. Some Chicagoans were quite "excited to move past the stage" where they felt the need to be surrounded by other gay people. They saw it as a sign of personal growth and as evidence for the cultural shifts that are occurring in our post-gay era. Two simple sentences capture this complex melding: "Now I don't think about my sexuality as much. No one cares." This mindset makes it easier to leave the gayborhood. But even if they detach from it physically, a "spiritual" connection lingers. This word offers us a clue that we will pursue in later chapters: maybe there are ways in which existing gayborhoods can still remain resonant and impactful after all.

THE NEW GAY TEENAGER

The Policy Institute of the National Gay and Lesbian Task Force finds that 3 to 6 percent of adolescents are attracted to members of the same sex, or they identify openly as lesbian, gay, or bisexual.

Today, the average age at which teenagers first identify in one of these ways is sixteen. In 1980, by comparison, the average age was twenty for gay men and twenty-two for lesbians. The "new gay teenager," to borrow a phrase from psychologist Ritch Savin-Williams, is coming out earlier and, more important, self-identifying in unprecedented ways. "They have same-sex desires and attractions," Savin-Williams explains, "but, unlike earlier generations, new gay teens have much less interest in naming these feelings or behaviors as gay . . . The notion of 'gay' as a noteworthy or identifying characteristic is being abandoned; it has lost definition."[4]

The coming of age of a new generation is a perpetual part of the life cycle, but growing up in a post-gay era is creating a cohort of youth that is the first of its kind. They are more likely to self-identify as "post-gay," "gayish," "queer," "questioning," "open," or even to opt for no label at all—"anything but gay," quips Adam Vary in his cover story for the *Advocate*. As part of his essay, which he provocatively titled "Is Gay Over?," Vary spoke with Arnold Zwicky, a Stanford linguist who came out of the closet one short year after the Stonewall riots. "Gay as an identity, as we used to know it, may be pretty much at an end," Zwicky declared, because "people are thinking of their sexuality in a much more diffuse way" than they were in the 1970s. This is true for both gays and straights, but the cultural changes in how we think about sexuality today are especially visible in this next generation of queer youth. If the young will inherit the future, then the fate of gayborhoods lies in part in their hands as they decide in later years whether to live and socialize in them. But how meaningful are gayborhoods for these young people who are coming out earlier and embracing an altogether different sense of what "gay" means?[5]

A thirty-year-old gay man in Boystown described the tidal shift: "I know that people are coming out earlier and seem to be much more comfortable with it." When I asked him to speculate on how this will impact gayborhoods in the future, he replied, "As this generation has had less conflict coming out and growing up, I think that people aren't going to feel as much of a need to amass with their people." Gays and lesbians in the coming out era were moral refugees who built their gayborhoods as safe spaces, but youth today are coming of age in a post-gay era of greater acceptance and safety, and they feel culturally similar to straight people. Many residents that I met suspected that this change in context will affect the relationship that queer youth will eventually have with gayborhoods. A forty-four-year-old gay man in Boystown offered a forceful prediction: "I think they will disappear." Assimilation is the culprit. "When you look at them [queer youth], they really don't identify with other gay people," he continued. "They identify with their straight friends. And so, I don't imagine that that generation will have any interest in living in a gay neighborhood."

The post-gay era is not unfolding in isolation of other currents in our society; it is part of a broader shift, one that is characterized by the rejection of identity politics in the United States. A forty-two-year-old single straight woman in Andersonville painted this bigger picture by comparing the new gay teenager with third-wave feminists:

> I think the feminist movement is the same thing. They talk about third-wave feminism, and how these young women can take for granted that they can do whatever they want. For certainly first wave, but also second wave, of which I consider myself a part, there was still a sense that you had to define that identity in that space. For young gays, it's like, "What's the big deal? We can live wherever we want." Maybe people don't need to flock to enclaves because you're not flocking to go where you won't be excluded.

As identities like gender and sexuality recede in centrality, minority spaces will follow suit. Lisa Bubon offered a similar comparison between the experiences of women and sexual minorities:

> That whole concept of women-only space, younger women related less and less to it. The whole notion of separatism, which was so big in the early '80s, is really a distant memory . . . It just seems like the fact that this was Girlstown is less significant than the fact that this is a community that is open and accepting to all kinds of folks, gay, straight, transgendered, gay families, straight families. We figured out how to coexist. And I think that's a much greater achievement than having some shrine to lesbian presence in this neighborhood.

What reason do we have to believe that gayborhoods are separatist spaces? Straights have always lived, shopped, and dined alongside their queer brethren. Gayborhoods are residentially concentrated with same-sex households and sexually integrated at the same time, and they can be culturally and commercially queer without alienating straight neighbors. Reflect on what a thirty-two-year-old gay man in Boystown observed about straight people in the neighborhood: "A younger generation, especially straight guys, can move into a gay neighborhood and not think anything of it and be like, 'So? What's the big deal? I don't care if my friends think I'm gay. I'm moving into a gay neighborhood because I like the apartment.'" This line of thinking—"What's the big deal?"—is one that we have heard several times now from gays and straights alike. A forty-six-year-old gay man in Boystown added, "If you look at the straights who are living here, they're younger . . . It's a fact of life that there are gay people in every aspect of their lives: work, play, friends, brothers, sisters, fathers in some cases, mothers in some cases. It's just there." They "don't feel nervous about it," a thirty-four-year-old Boystown lesbian shrugged, because gay people are now familiar, family members, and friends—a part of everyday life.

Now push this logic a step further: if we continue to define gayborhoods as minority-only or segregated spaces, many queer youth will reject them since their friendship circles are sexually mixed. A forty-three-year-old Boystown gay man commented, "There are some gay people, especially the younger ones, who are less identified with having some sort of gay exclusivity in their life. They may go to gay bars, but they also go to straight bars, do different things, and have a broader range of friends. They are not heavily focused on having gay friends." Another gay man from Boystown, who is forty-four, was dating a man in his early twenties who does not live in the same neighborhood. He shared how his partner viewed Boystown: "I'm dating someone who's young, and he never even considered moving to Boystown." When I asked him why not, he also remarked on the influence of a heterogeneous social network: "Because most of his friends are straight. And so why would you move into a gay neighborhood?" He does not see himself as any different from his straight friends, and this, he predicted, will affect the future of city life: "The neighborhoods will disappear . . . The young gays are not flocking to a gay neighborhood. When you look at and talk to young gay people, they're all over the place. And they're where their straight friends are at." The younger gays "couldn't care less" about Boystown. "It's a fun place to go visit," he continued, "but you would never want to live there because you socialize with your straight friends, and you live with your straight friends," who are spread out across the city. Post-gays do not define themselves solely in terms of their sexuality, nor do they feel that their sexuality makes them all that different from heterosexuals. "You'd only live in a gay neighborhood if your whole identity was being gay, and all your friends were gay, and everything you did was gay. But that's not how they are anymore." Several residents remarked on the straight friends of queer youth. Perhaps this means that gayborhoods will fail to resonate with queer youth as long as we define them as gay-only spaces. It also implies that older gays have fewer friends who are heterosexual, a supposition that is controversial (and difficult for me to test unfortunately) yet consistent with the defining features of the coming out era.

As sexual orientation declines in its significance for how queer youth self-identify, fewer of them feel compelled to be around other gay people all the time or to structure their lives with their sexuality at the center of it. A gay man in Boystown remarked, "The younger generation said, 'If it's easier for me to live downtown because I work downtown, fine, I can take a train or cab to Boystown to the bars. But why do I really need to be there?'" This is the same expansion mechanism, but it is projected here as a hypothetical statement. Another gay man in the same neighborhood, who was a professor at a nearby university, spoke about his students, who distinguish where they live from where they play: "I see that a lot with my students. They like to go to Halsted for the bars, but they don't have any need to live near the bars." And then he sighed, "I'm envious of the new generation because they don't have this whole gay identity thing." Why exactly was he envious? He replied:

> They're gay, but it's not like they have to wear it on their sleeves or live in a gay neighborhood or have gay friends. Their gayness is a small part of their life. They did normal things: they went to their prom, they came out to their parents really young, and nobody made an issue of it. Most

of their friends are straight, and their straight friends are cool with it. They didn't need to go to gay people for acceptance because they got acceptance from straight people. They just don't have this gay identity thing like we do.

In this statement, he gives us some hallmarks of post-gay life. Younger queers enjoy sexually mixed company. A gay, lesbian, or bisexual identity is not as meaningful for many of them since they see themselves as normal and just like their straight friends. They come out earlier and do not need gayborhoods as safe harbors. And why would they, since times themselves have become so much safer?

To drive home the point that queer youth are different, some of the residents that I met offered cross-generational comparisons. Consider first the remarks of those, both straight and gay, who live in Andersonville. A forty-two-year-old straight woman used San Francisco as an example of how the gayborhood is losing its grip on gay life:

> When the Castro was created, people moved there deliberately. It was a safe space where people could enjoy their lifestyle . . . Younger generations of gays are taking it for granted, and they don't feel like they have to live there. They can hang out there because there are good bars or whatever. But they don't feel like they have to live there. They take for granted that they are welcome in other places in the city as well.

A forty-three-year-old straight man added dimensions of power and inequality, yet with a familiar element of spirituality: "There's a collective consciousness. Each generation gets wiser and wiser at a younger age when it comes to social stratification or the views of the world. Things are more accepted with each generation . . . It's just an education-slash-spiritual thing." A thirty-four-year-old lesbian remarked about the new generation's casual outlook, even in the face of rejection by parents and persistent bullying by classmates: "The younger generations are more, 'It's not a big deal. So what?' I'm sure they still get teased and kicked out of their houses by their parents. There are still a lot of issues, but it's not like it was when I was growing up." A thirty-three-year-old gay male high school teacher thought about his own students to predict the future:

You have to look at the kids in high school today to know where we're going to be in ten, fifteen years as far as gay neighborhoods are concerned . . . When I went through school, I had all straight friends, and then because of that, after coming out, I had predominately gay friends. That was a big thing for me, versus one of my students who's coming out as a freshman, who's already come out to some of his straight male friends, and they've been accepting of it. He may have far less of a need to live in a gay community because he may have felt through his life far less excluded. And so his desire to live in a gay neighborhood may be greatly diminished.

Each generation will have a different relationship with the gayborhood, he concluded, and they will react differently to the possibility of their demise: "For my generation [those who came of age in the coming out era], it might be ambivalence. For an older generation [those who came of age in the closet era], it might be sadness. For a younger generation [those who are coming of age in the post-gay era], it might be joy to not feel ghettoized in some enclave."

Boystown gay men offered similar assessments. A thirty-year-old said, "If you look generationally, there are a lot of people who are ten, twenty, thirty years older than me that will never want to leave a gay neighborhood. They feel very comfortable there. That's where they've lived their lives. I think generationally, the older generations are probably more likely to stay. I just think the younger generations are not going to feel as drawn [to live in a gayborhood]." The university professor we met earlier added that "being gay is just a small part of their lives. People who struggled with coming out, it was a huge part of our identity." Those in the younger, post-gay generation, however, "don't struggle with issues of dealing with their sexuality. It's not an issue. And so, they don't need to live in gay neighborhoods." This is an overstatement, I think, since it flies in the face of policy initiatives like Dan Savage's It Gets Better Project. The program's website defines its mission as follows: "to communicate to lesbian, gay, bisexual, and transgender youth around the world that it gets better, and to create and inspire the changes needed to make it better for them."[26] The professor implies that gays "need" the gayborhood in order to deal with their "issues." But the gayborhood is not a panacea for all psychological problems, even if it can ease feelings of isolation. Similar to the view that gayborhoods are minority-only spaces, this is another misconception that, if it circulates widely enough, will likely repel young people.

Queer youth are coming of age in a post-gay era, as we saw in this section, and this will affect their relationship with the gayborhood. Unfortunately, I was not able to speak with any queer teenagers. University-based Institutional Review Boards, which are ethics panels that oversee research proposals involving human subjects, have special requirements to protect minors, such as parental permission for an interview. Requiring such a signature from a parent presents an obvious challenge for those young people who are not yet out at home. There are, of course, limits and biases when we ask older people for their impressions of the young, like feeling "envious of the new generation" or declaring that "it's not like when I was growing up," but the procedure is ethically sound. Furthermore, gays and straights from Boystown and Andersonville offered consistent views, and their impressions were in line with theoretical understandings of what it means to be post-gay, along with empirical research studies. All of this should give us confidence in what they shared with us. Still, a curious discrepancy requires our attention. On the one hand, we heard in this section that queer youth do not need the gayborhood, yet some older lesbians and gay men from the prior section said the opposite. Perhaps members of older generations were reflecting on their own youth and personal development. They came of age in the coming out era, not the post-gay era, and so their teenage years were different than what we are seeing for the most recent cohort of queer youth. This again is an issue of context, and one that we should always keep in mind as we appraise who says what and when about the gayborhood.

The new gay teenager is coming out earlier, many of them identify equally with their gay and straight friends, and sexuality is just one part of their self-identity—and sometimes a small one. All of this makes gayborhoods potentially less meaningful for them. Of course, there is a lag between when kids come out, which happens today around the average age of sixteen, and when they decide to move out of their parent's home. This means that the changes transpiring in gay neighborhoods right now, at this very moment, are not immediately shaped by teenagers. But they will inherit the future, and coming of age in a post-gay era will influence whether and how gayborhoods will resonate with them down the road. But the precise nature of how queer youth will relate with gayborhoods is not predetermined. Although we have reason to believe that these urban areas are losing cultural significance for them, we also encountered clues for how they might remain meaningful. The more we insist on defining gayborhoods as minority-only or separatist spaces, for example, the less they will appeal to queer youth who, compared to prior generations, have more sexually mixed friendship circles. Similarly, the more we define gayborhoods as something that queer people "need" in order to deal with their "issues," the less they will appeal to queer youth who are not burdened by their sexuality in quite the same way.

THE GAYBY BOOM

The 2010 American Community Survey shows that approximately 594,000 households of same-sex couples live in the United States, or 1 percent of all households with couples in the country. Of these, 115,000, or nearly 20 percent, report having children. Seventy-three percent of these households have only biological children, and 21 percent have stepchildren only or adopted children only. The Williams Institute, a national think tank dedicated to researching sexual orientation and gender identity, found that these families live throughout the country: 26 percent are in the South, 24 percent in New England, and 21 percent in the Pacific states. Some commentators call this newly visible trend of same-sex couples having children a "gayby boom," and it has the potential to transform the metaphorical adult playground of the gayborhood into literal playgrounds with monkey bars and sandboxes. And so we must ask: Are same-sex households with kids more likely to stay in the gayborhood, to leave the gayborhood, or to categorically reject it?[7]

A thirty-two-year-old lesbian in Boystown, who recently had a baby with her partner, explained why same-sex households with children think differently about gayborhoods: "I think to some extent neighborhoods are going to be identified by gay bars. And then when you do have children, there are all these other considerations that come into play, like what kind of house can you buy? What's the school system like?" All these things affect the texture of gay neighborhoods:

> Those move to the top of your consideration list, rather than gay bars. So, I feel like when you have a child, there's a constellation of considerations that might drive your actions, whereas if you're a young gay person, it could be all about—your number one consideration would be, "Put me in a neighborhood where I can quickly and easily meet other gay people."

A thirty-six-year-old lesbian left Boystown for Andersonville because she was "getting older and wanting to start a family." This inspired her "to identify a little more with straight people" and a little less with Boystown. A similar shift affected her friends, all of whom have "come to the age where we're all starting to think about having kids of our own." A twenty-nine-year-old partnered gay man in Andersonville anticipated the same adjustments in his lifestyle, even though he did not yet have any children: "I see neighborhoods as a reflection of the population that lives in it. So, as marriage becomes a gay issue, I wonder if part of that population is participating in a change of the neighborhood." I asked him to tell me more about this "change of the neighborhood":

> You have a population that's grown older, survived HIV and AIDS, and is in a place where it's no longer about being single but having a family. I wonder if the aspirations of gay people, contemporarily speaking, have in many ways produced some of these changes, because gay people in some ways have become more family-oriented than once upon a time. That in many ways has this adverse effect on this space.

By "adverse effect," he meant the dilution of gayborhoods and the specific queer spaces within them. But that did not matter so much for him and the other parents that I met. The developmental process for them was the same: parent identity ascends, gay identity recedes. Their calculations about what will work for the family trump their sexuality as they decide whether to stay or go.

Straights also recognize that same-sex parenting affects gay-borhoods, as the following fifty-nine-year-old married woman in Boystown told me: "As gay families develop, Boystown will be more blended; it won't be so separate." Her notion of blending reminds us again of what we learned before about assimilation. In fact, one married couple saw Andersonville as "the culmination of assimilation" because it houses families "in all different forms." They described their local clothing store, Green Genes, as an example: "Typically, when people think of a children's store, it's run by a heterosexual couple," the man explained. "Or a woman, a straight woman," his wife added. While the idea of a gay couple owning a children's store is plausible, the man guessed that such a store would have "some gay theme, like a 'Mommy and Mommy' shirt or something." Green Genes, however, is a lesbian-owned store that defies both of their expectations. "It's just a store that happens to be owned by a gay couple, and it's for everybody," the man noted. If Andersonville typifies assimilation, then this store is its most potent symbol: "I think that's a symbol for how our neighborhood is," he said. "And hopefully the future," his wife added. On the webpage, there is no mention of the store as "lesbian-owned" or "gay-identified." While the site acknowledges that the store is "founded by best friends and partners, Heather Muenstermann and Christina Isperduli," the "About" section focuses on the store's "eco-friendly" mission "to help leave the planet just a bit better, if not a whole lot better, than its current state." The owners make no mention of whether their products are produced by queer companies, if they intend them for queer families, or if they donate any of their profits to queer causes.

Same-sex parents shape a gayborhood as they go through the arduous process of choosing a school. A lesbian couple in Boystown explained, "As younger gay men and women, as couples, have started having and adopting children, perhaps being in the city itself is not an option because of education. Many of them have decided to live life in the suburbs. Part of it is because of the schools in the city: if you're not going to get into a magnet school, you're going to hope that you're going to get into a private school." But what if private education is not financially possible? They recognized that "it isn't for most people," in which case "you have to go to an area where there is good public education if it doesn't exist in your own neighborhood in the city." For straight couples, this idea is well established; families move to a neighborhood because it has a strong public school system. But the experience is fairly new for same-sex families with children. And it will affect the future of gay neighborhoods as more gays partner up, if more of them have kids, and if gayborhoods do not have strong public schools.

Boystown is a subsection of Chicago's Lakeview neighborhood, which is home to the Nettelhorst School, one of the best public elementary schools (prekindergarten through eighth grade) in the city today. In fact, the school's recent improvements have been dubbed the "Nettelhorst revolution," and some residents see them as a "blueprint" for a national success story. There are other schools in Boystown and Andersonville, but the prominence of Nettelhorst among locals makes it worth considering at length. Susan Kurland, the school's principal, and Jacqueline Edelberg, a neighborhood mom, cowrote and published *How to Walk to School: Blueprint for a Neighborhood Renaissance*. The book, published in 2009, tells "the story of an entrepreneurial principal and visionary neighborhood parents who took a leap of faith together and transformed an underutilized, struggling urban elementary school into a successful, vibrant institution." Conflict exists between gay and straight neighbors, the authors freely admit, but both groups have learned how "to live and let live. Tolerance cuts both ways: Stroller moms needed to share the sidewalk with a diverse segment of society—goth-punks, openly gay couples, panhandlers, buskers, Cubs fans, Krishnas, Orthodox Jews, and Lake Shore Drive socialites." Kurland and Edelberg acknowledge the gay identity of the neighborhood: "The school's proximity to Boystown, Chicago's vibrant gay community, delivered a seemingly endless supply of creative talent to Nettelhorst's front door."[8]

Neighborhood residents echoed themes from the book. The school is "a tremendous draw, not just for straight people, but also for gay parents. The school is what's tying a lot of the community together, and it doesn't have to be straight people with kids," one Boystown straight man, whose child attends the school, told me. Nettelhorst does "a great job of integrating, of celebrating the differences" in the neighborhood, commented a gay male couple in the same neighborhood. Consider the following vivid example of the school's commitment to diversity and integration. Every year in June, to celebrate gay pride, Nettelhorst faculty and students adorn the fence that surrounds their school with rainbow colors. In 2009, school officials posted the following sign next to the brightly arranged pieces of fabric:

> Each Nettelhorst student has tied a piece of fabric to the fence as a tangible sign of his or her personal intention to create a better world. At Nettelhorst, we've also made a collective intention: that each of us becomes kinder, gentler, and more tolerant. Here, the rainbow colors of gay pride are a visible sign of our respect for the neighborhood of which we are a part, and the diversity of families that we serve. In June, Nettelhorst will be the first public school to walk in Chicago's Gay Pride Parade. We believe family means everybody. Enjoy the summer: SPF 50, baby![9]

A gay male couple reacted to this groundbreaking effort: "If every institution or every business was able to celebrate that commingling of straight and gay in the same way that the school seems to have done, I think that would be a really great template for how things could be in the future."

I spent time with parents who occupied leadership positions at the school. Rachel Gross, the 2010 Nettelhorst parent group president and a married straight woman, told me: "[The school provides an] environment for everyone. There are a ton of same-sex couples at our school. And we were the only school last year to march in the Pride parade, and we were at the very front of the parade." I asked if her own children attended the school, and what she thought about the neighborhood's gay identity. Rachel replied, "My children, because I'm their parent and because they go to a school like Nettelhorst, and they are exposed to all different types of people, and if it's a gay neighborhood or whatever neighborhood it is, they're just learning that there are people who are different than they are, and maybe they're not so different. I just love the exposure that my children get, and the acceptance." David Neubecker, who is a school council member and chair of the diversity committee, added, "We wanted our kids to see that the school was part of the larger LGBT community, which our families were a part of, but we also wanted the LGBT community to realize that their neighborhood school was also supportive."

Nettelhorst became the first public school in Chicago to walk in the city's annual gay pride parade in 2009. Monique Bond, a spokesperson for Chicago Public Schools, noted, "Parents, both gay and straight, organized the school's entry, viewing it as an important step to make in a community with a large GLBT population." Richard Pfeiffer has coordinated the parade since 1974, and he also commented on this extraordinary event: "We've never had a grammar school, or a school for that matter. The remarkable thing about the gay pride parade is that it's the one day that you get that full cross-section of the GLBT community. We're young, we're old, and a growing portion of our community now has children. And I think that has often gone unnoticed."[10] Recognizing the growing presence of gaybies compels gays and straights to conclude that sexuality is not a meaningful marker of difference between them. Ironically, the visibility of lesbian moms and gay dads makes them seem *less* diverse since the decisions they make about where to live closely resemble the considerations that straight parents have to make as well. Lesbians and gay men are becoming more integrated, more like the dominant group, and the diversity of queer lives now oddly merges into the mainstream. Parents champion the school because their enrolled children will be "exposed to all different types of people." While some admit that "it's a gay neighborhood," they, like Rachel, quickly add "or whatever neighborhood," perhaps as a way to understate its gay identity. On the other hand, the fact that an annual pride parade still occurs, that it proceeds through the streets of Boystown, and that Nettelhorst participates in it all suggest that the gayborhood remains culturally vibrant and resonant.

Consider another example that also highlights the jousting between assimilation and diversity in a post-gay era. As chair of the diversity committee, David, who we met earlier, uses a "Welcoming Schools Guide" produced by the Human Rights Campaign (HRC), the largest LGBT political lobbying organization in the United States. The guide describes "ways to make schools more welcoming and inclusive in the areas of gender stereotyping, family diversity, and anti-bullying." The HRC published this material for wide use, he said, "because LGBT issues were not brought up in other guides that dealt with diversity issues in schools. Our community was always left out because it was a little too difficult to talk about in some communities. Schools seem a little more scared to talk about gay and lesbian issues at the elementary school level." This does not seem very post-gay at all. In an ironic twist, however, David modified the LGBT guide for use at Nettelhorst: "For our school, they wanted all the issues treated the same. So I had to bring this guide back down to a level where everyone was on an equal plane instead of it always focusing on the LGBT community." This made the idea of diversity relevant for all the parents, although it suppressed the distinctiveness of gay and lesbian sexuality. His decision also raises questions about the authenticity of acceptance: Is it the outcome of living in a sexually integrated neighborhood? Or is acceptance strategically manufactured, at least for the parents of schoolchildren who attend this particular elementary school in Boystown?

The relationship between gayborhoods and parenting is not all about schools, of course. Parents must also decide if they want to raise their kids in the culture of a gayborhood. Some worry about exposing their kids to what they consider the seedier parts of the gayborhood, things like bars, bathhouses, and sex shops. Others fear that their kids will feel ghettoized. Yet others, however, desire the support system of lesbian moms and gay dads specifically. They are troubled by the thought that their kids will be the only ones in school with gay parents. The story is multifaceted, and we will have to revisit it again in later chapters to get at more angles of it. In this section, however, we focused on one important part of the puzzle: the ascendance of a parent identity while sexual identity recedes in comparison. This can compel some same-sex families to leave a gayborhood and move somewhere else, especially if the gayborhood does not have a strong public school system. Boystown, home to Nettelhorst, is not necessarily a representative gayborhood in this respect. The residents we met asserted that geography is still an important part of raising their kids. What remains unclear, however, is whether their observations are indicative of gayborhood demise. We can imagine the existence of a hypothetical gaybor-hood, filled with queer parents with kids, that looks nothing like a straight neighborhood. Maybe the children who live in such a place are encouraged to explore and express fluid sexual and gender iden-tities. Perhaps parenting is more communal here, and single queer adults can interact with local kids without suspicion or malicious stereotypes, such as those that create false associations between homosexuality and pedophilia.[11] This brief thought experiment allows us to resist the specious claim that same-sex families will invariably undermine the vitality of existing gay districts.

COMMUNITY AND GEOGRAPHY, UNHINGED

Sociologist Edward Laumann and his colleagues published *The Sexual Organization of the City* in 2004. The *New York Times* reviewed their book, which was about Chicago, as "the most important study of American sexual behavior since the Kinsey reports of 1948 and 1953." Individual chapters cover a wealth of topics, includ-ing race, life course, family formation, commitment and jealousy, intimate-partner violence, forced sexual activity, sexually trans-mitted diseases, and religion. Notably missing in this otherwise comprehensive list is a discussion of how the Internet affects urban sexuality. The editors offer one easy-to-overlook footnote in which they acknowledge that "geography plays a diminished role" in an electronically mediated world. As a point of comparison, a differ-ent group of researchers surveyed 810 men who had sex with men (MSM) about their first sexual encounter between the years 1993 and 2003. Their results show "a significant increase in the percent-age of MSM who met their first male sexual partner through the Internet" and a "corresponding decrease in the percentage who met their first sexual partner at a gay venue" like a gayborhood bar or bathhouse. The tendency to meet others online, whether for sex, love, or friendship, has increased over the years. To understand the sexual organization of the city, therefore, we must contend with how the Internet is redefining the meaning of urban spaces. Unlike the other triggers that we have considered in this chapter, however, the Internet is obviously not a stage of life through which we pass.

Yet the ease with which it enables us to participate in virtual communities also forces us to reexamine how we relate with the material city. Has the Internet unhinged our sense of community from geography?[12]

The impact of the Internet on our culture, commerce, and global communication has been intense and irrevocable. Digital technologies were responsible for 1 percent of the information flowing through two-way telecommunication networks by 1993. The rate jumped to 51 percent by 2000, a whopping 97 percent by 2007, and it continues to grow today.[13] Since its introduction, the forms and functionalities of the Internet have rapidly evolved from e-mails and instant messages, to chat rooms of online communities like those that AOL pioneered, to dating sites like Match.com, sex sites like Manhunt.net, social networking sites like Facebook and Twitter, and finally to mobile apps like Grindr. Many gay men that I met in Boystown suspected that all of this is "damaging to the neighborhood" because it makes the gayborhood "obsolete," in the words of a thirty-two-year-old who voiced a common refrain. "I've got Manhunt, and I've got Match.com, and I've got all kinds of websites where I can meet guys," added a thirty-two-year-old gay man. "I don't need Boystown anymore." A thirty-year-old gay man explained how these online options affect the way we relate with one another:

> I think people socialize differently now with the advent of, at first, chat rooms, and then dating sites, and then mobile apps like Grindr, where you can see who's gay around you and ostensibly sleep with them. People are interacting differently and are coming together differently. That wasn't an option ten years ago. You had to go to a gay neighborhood and go to a gay bar to meet people and to socialize, and that's just not true anymore.

While lesbians are less likely than gay men to rely on such websites and apps for sex, they, too, believe that the Internet contributes to the decline of gay neighborhoods: "You really can't underestimate the communities that are available online," a thirty-four-year-old self-identified "open" Boystown woman told me. "That is something to think about when you think about neighborhoods and identities and networks. People, to a large extent every day, rely on online virtual networks," rather than a friend or lover who lives down the street.

Andersonville gays agree that online options are unhinging our perceptions of community from geography. "[The Internet] has made it so you can have community in ways that don't have to be geographic," said a thirty-nine-year-old gay man. "We can do some of that on Facebook. We can do some of that through e-mail. In some ways, it gives you flexibility in where you're living in order to still hold that community." A thirty-five-year-old gay man added, "The need for the neighborhood has expanded into more of a virtual community. Maybe there isn't the need for the physical [place] because we have opportunities to connect with gay people in so many other forms." Another gay man, aged thirty, added that the Internet is "making physical place obsolete in a lot of ways. It's not really as important that your friend lives within a mile or two miles of you. Technology is definitely related to issues of space." If you can experience community in ways that are not dependent on geography, then the places where you think you can live also increase in number. The gayborhood goes virtual and spreads across the city.

Themes of technology, community, and geography emerged repeatedly in my conversations. "It's too easy to find gay people," a thirty-three-year-old gay man in Andersonville commented. "I don't need to walk out my door. I just turn on my computer, and it doesn't matter where I am. I can imagine ten or fifteen years ago, if you were going to hook up, you needed to be in Boystown. Now you can get on one of these websites and meet a guy who lives in the next suburb, and you don't have a need for Boystown." Even a straight man who lives in Boystown recognized this: "You have these applications for your iPhone where you can find someone to hook up with. You don't necessarily have to go to your gay community, your gay bars to find someone these days. Technology may eventually do away with some neighborhoods."

Not everyone painted such a grim picture. A forty-three-year-old gay man in Boystown, for example, was not convinced that the Internet would unravel gayborhoods: "I think you can meet people by going online," he acknowledged, "but I think that there are still quite a few people who don't find that very rewarding and don't find people that way." There is something irreplaceable about face-to-face contact and interactions in person. For Andy, a gay man in Andersonville, the world was "very different online." His partner Jim explained what he meant, "There are people like [Andy]. He would never do that [try to meet someone online]." Andy then spoke for himself: "I don't feel safe to go online because I don't know the people I'm talking with. I just don't think I'm getting a realistic profile of the person I'm talking to because sometimes they have created a fake profile and things like that." Jim added, "I don't know that virtual communities will ever fully replace real communities for one-on-one interaction. I don't think that's going to happen." The Internet adds to, and builds on, other forms of communication and community; it does not supplant them. This is why the impact on gayborhoods is uneven, as it is for Andy and Jim, and thus difficult to predict precisely. It is changing the needs and meanings of urban spaces, to be sure, but there will always be different strokes for different folks.[14]

We talked about sex a lot in this section. Unfortunately, I did not design my interviews to talk about the Internet in any great depth, and so the residents that we met were not primed to think about it in more subtle ways. Gayborhoods certainly facilitate sexual opportunities, but they do much more than that as well. They enable social networking for a group of people who face unique challenges in not being physically identifiable to one another, and they are crucibles of culture. They are also—and still—safe spaces where gay people can seek refuge from heterosexual hostilities, discrimination, bigotry, and violence. And they are sites of resistance, a place where gays can organize themselves politically as a voting bloc or as a grassroots social movement. Gay neighborhoods provide a space of personal freedom, an atmosphere where it is easier to come out and celebrate your sexuality. They house gay-owned and gay-friendly businesses like churches, travel agencies, realtors, medical facilities, retail stores, newspaper and magazine offices, and political lobbying groups. Basically, they provide a path to membership in the gay community, and they link its diverse members together in ways that can be episodic or enduring. The

Internet has the potential to affect these other nonsexual aspects of the gayborhood as well.[15]

DIVERSE AND DYNAMIC CULTURES

Our ideas about "the gayborhood" often rely on a static understanding of queer lives and cultures. In fact, "one of society's favorite myths about gay people is that we are all alike," asserted Jim Owles of the New York Gay Activist Alliance in an important movement document that he published in April 1971.[16] The myth is tenacious, and it rears its ugly head in the form of damaging stereotypes or media images that flatten the texture of urban queer lives. Examples include the 1971 film *Cruising* (gayborhoods will lure in and sexually confuse straight men, even Al Pacino), the 1989 film *Longtime Companion* (gayborhoods are bastions of HIV/AIDS and other diseases), the 1996 film *The Birdcage* (did you know that Miami's gayborhood in South Beach is filled with drag queens and drag clubs?), and *Brokeback Mountain* from 2005 (it is an open secret among men like that to travel to the gay village in Mexico for sex). Even gay-themed independent films like *Circuit* (2001) and *When Boys Fly* (2002) fall into this trap by depicting gayborhoods as promoters of drug-fueled dance parties. Or consider the HBO series *Queer as Folk* (2000–2005), which showed us images of urban gay men as sex-crazed or Bravo's *Queer Eye for the Straight Guy* (2003–7), which circulated stereotypes of them as having a superior sense of fashion, design, and taste. By the end of the decade, however, the images had changed. *Modern Family* (first aired in 2009) and *The New Normal* (2012–13) presented gay households as culturally similar to those of heterosexuals. Both groups now are partnered—and suburban (a theme we will explore in later chapters), monogamous, and raising children inside what anthropologist Gayle Rubin would call "the charmed circle" of normative sexuality.[17]

No way of life of a group or subgroup of people is ever uniform or singular. On the contrary, cultures are always diverse and dynamic. One reason why the culture of a group like sexual minorities is always changing is because people themselves are always changing. We know that there is an "intense bond between urban life and diversity," to quote sociologist Claude Fischer, but the problem is that we know so little about how the diversity of queer lives is related to the de-gaying of the gayborhood. To better grasp this reality, we attended to some major life transitions: aging, coming out, and starting a family. Each occasion, along with the incredible opportunities that the Internet provides for creating connections that are not dependent on geography, triggers a reassessment of our relationship with space and place. As people talked about how these triggers changed their lives in large and small ways, we saw how the physical encasement of the community—the gayborhood—also changes. Yet our discovery goes against what scholars like Fischer conclude about racial and ethnic groups and immigrants. "City people, more than others," he argues, "*resist* assimilation, cling most tightly to foreign ways, and even *personify* cultural diversity" (emphasis added). This is not necessarily true with sexuality and the city. Many urban lesbians and gay men, unlike racial and ethnic minorities, *embrace* assimilation. They say that they are culturally similar to straights and imagine that they can live pretty much anywhere in the city that they want. If anything, they *downplay* their diversity as a marker of difference. The tenacity of homophily as a residential principle wanes as a result. What we are left with is quite ironic: the shifts that come with aging, coming out, and parenting make the gay community look, feel, and sound less diverse, since its members now make the same types of decisions that straights make. From this vantage point, not only are post-gays mainstreaming—and moving out from the gayborhood—but they are also *straightening.*[18]

We encountered numerous problems and puzzles in our travels in this chapter, and these should make us pause before we arrive at any conclusions. Why, for instance, does a spiritual connection with the gayborhood linger for so many gays and lesbians, even after they move out from it and despite an increasing presence of straight people within it? And why are there mixed feelings about whether gayborhoods will remain meaningful for queer youth later in their lives? Or even for certain same-sex parents today? And what about queer people of color and transgender people? We have not yet delved into their unique perspectives. Nor have we carefully compared whether lesbians and gay men make similar or distinct residential decisions. There are even broader questions that beg to be asked. Gayborhoods are changing, to be sure, but does this change indicate that we finally have arrived on the doorstep of equality? Or does it signal the loss of community? Are gayborhoods necessary for the creation and preservation of urban sexual cultures, especially in a digital world? How do we reconcile the need that some queer people express for gayborhoods against the mindset of cultural sameness that others advocate? And what do we make of the fact that lesbians and gay men are living in so many more neighborhoods all across the city—and even in the suburbs and in rural areas?

Black-or-white answers to these questions will never satisfy. Context matters. It helps us to understand who says what to whom, where, when, and why. We already know this, and we need to keep it in mind for the rest of our journey. It is now time for us to travel down a different trail. In part 2 of this book, we will confront the many problems and puzzles that surround post-gay perspectives. The voices and views from the streets that we will hear and see next will caution us against overstating that all the world is post-gay and that gayborhoods have no place or purpose within it.

PART II

BUT ARE THEY DISAPPEARING?

4

—

Cultural Archipelagos

It is quixotic to think that gayborhoods have always been around, that they will remain stable in their character and composition, or that they will never change. All neighborhoods, along with the cities that surround them, are organic, continually evolving places. But it is equally naive to declare the death of the gayborhood. Any persist-or-perish binary about the fate of these areas is simply untenable. In the first part of this book, we tried to understand why gayborhoods are changing. Along the way, we encountered puzzles and problems that forced us to suspend making any definitive conclusions. Going forward, we will see how an impulse of assimilation and distinction, of sameness and difference, can coexist. What can we forecast for the future of gay neighborhoods—and indeed for urban America more generally?

The post-gay era is undoubtedly reconfiguring the decisions that individual gay and straight people make about where they wish to live. The range of possible outcomes, however, is far more diverse than either sexual separatism or the integration and inevitable demise of the gayborhood. What we find instead is a shifting balance of beliefs: gays swing between disfavoring gay districts, articulating the variety of arguments that we have already heard, yet still seeking some semblance of a community that is based in a specific, identifiable part of the city. In this way, gayborhoods reflect the complexities of the post-gay era itself, and they contain seemingly contradictory features that we need to untangle. Our objective in part 2 of this book is to discover how gayborhoods can persist in the present and how they will live on into the future. We will begin our journey by examining clues from the 2000 and 2010 US Censuses.

But remember that this book is about gay neighborhoods, not the gay population. After we look at these demographic trends, we will return to our vast archive of media reports, with its hundreds if not thousands of voices and views from streets across the country, to think about the surprising and sometimes subtle ways that our sexuality continues to direct the decisions we make about where to put down our roots.

CENSUS CLUES

The census first asked about same-sex households in 1990, offering hope for a revolution in how we might study the national gay and lesbian population. Unfortunately, however, the data proved unusable because government officials recoded it in a biased way. "When same-sex households identified themselves as being legally married," explain David Smith and Gary Gates, "the Census Bureau in most instances changed the gender of the spouse. Such households were therefore counted as a heterosexual married couple." It was not until the year 2000 that the Census Bureau collected the first set of unaltered data, but even that survey, along with the next one in 2010, did not ask about individual sexual orientation, sexual behavior, or sexual attraction, which are the three most common ways that researchers identify lesbians and gay men. Census forms only ask about "unmarried partners," a category that demographers use to approximate the population of nonheterosexuals. Gary Gates, in a separate article with Jason Ost, elaborates, "If the householder designates another adult of the same sex as his or her unmarried partner, the household counts as a same-sex unmarried-partner household." The 2010 collection enabled those couples to define themselves as "spouses" or "unmarried partners." This was not an option in 2000 since same-sex marriage was not yet legal in any state. But by 2010, the District of Columbia and five states—Connecticut, Iowa, Massachusetts, New Hampshire, and Vermont—had legalized it. The total number of self-reporting same-sex households in 2000 was 594,391, or 0.564 percent of all households in the United States. In 2010, 901,997 households self-identified as such, or 0.773 percent of all households. This is a 52 percent increase in ten years (307,606), and it indicates that same-sex households feel more comfortable revealing themselves.[1]

Same-sex couples live in virtually every county in the country, as we know from earlier chapters. If our society is truly and totally post-gay, then in theory these households would be randomly dispersed. But such is not the case. "The distribution of gay and lesbian families is far from uniform across the nation," Gates and Ost discovered in their analysis. Census 2000 shows "high concentration levels of gay and lesbian couples along nearly the entire California coast, in southern Florida, and throughout New England." Ten years later, the pattern persisted. In their analysis of the 2010 collection, Martin O'Connell and Sarah Feliz similarly find that "states with above average percentages are found along the east and west coasts of the United States and in the southwestern part of the nation" (see figure 4.1).[2]

In the late 1990s, a group of demographers and economists created a "Gay Index" that ranks regions based on the presence of same-sex households. The index measures "the concentration of gay

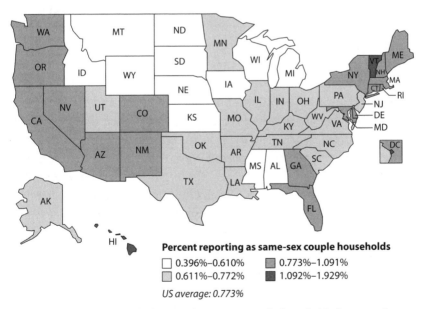

FIGURE 4.1 Geographic distribution of same-sex couple households in 2010. Source: O'Connell and Feliz (2011:7).

and lesbian couples among households in a particular geographic region," Gates and Ost explain. It is, they add,

> a ratio of the proportion of same-sex couples living in a region. This ratio, then, measures the over- or under-representation of same-sex couples in a geographic area relative to the population. A Gay Index value of 1.0 indicates that a same-sex couple is just as likely as a randomly picked household to locate in a particular region. A value of 2.0 indicates that gay- and lesbian-couple households are twice as likely as the "average" U.S. household to locate in that region, while values less than 1.0 indicate that gay and lesbian couples are less likely than the average household to locate there.

We can use this index to rank the cities in which same-sex households are disproportionately concentrated (table 4.1), to rank smaller towns (table 4.2), and even neighborhoods (defined as zip codes, table 4.3).[3]

All quantitative measures that researchers create using census data are based on same-sex "unmarried-partner households," for the 2000 collection, and/or spouses, for the 2010 count. The census does not track the presence of single gays and lesbians. Table 4.4 shows why this matters. Lush with data, this table shows the most recent distribution of same-sex households across the country. It also ranks cities based on their population size. As a result, we can compare large cities (population greater than 250,000 people) with midsize cities (population between 100,000 and 250,000) and small cities (population less than 100,000). Notice that New York is not listed among the top twenty-five large cities. This means that there are fewer same-sex *couples* in New York than, say, Austin. But that does not mean that there are fewer gay and lesbian *individuals* overall. We know that gayborhoods have unique appeal for singles since they offer opportunities to meet a mate. These spaces may be more appealing for this unhitched demographic, yet the census focuses only on partners.

All this data should make us scratch our head in curiosity. Are gayborhoods really disappearing? The census offers clues to the contrary. The emergence of a queer concentration in places like Twin Peaks, Oakland Park, and Haight-Ashbury in table 4.3,

TABLE 4.1 Top 25 U.S. Cities with the Largest Gay Index, 2000

	Gay index
San Francisco	3.11
Oakland	1.76
Seattle	1.68
Miami–Ft. Lauderdale	1.47
Austin	1.47
New York City	1.47
Los Angeles	1.43
Albuquerque	1.40
Atlanta	1.40
Portland	1.38
San Diego	1.36
Boston	1.36
Washington	1.33
Dallas	1.29
Denver	1.29
Orlando	1.28
Louisiana	1.23
Phoenix	1.19
Houston	1.19
Columbus	1.16
Minneapolis–St. Paul	1.08
Chicago	1.03
Nashville	.99
Philadelphia	.99
Kansas City	.88

Source: Gates and Ost (2004b:21).

Albuquerque and Louisiana in table 4.1, or any of the small cities in table 4.4, introduces a new narrative thread for us to follow. What looks on the surface like disappearance in some places may in fact be a reshuffling and redevelopment somewhere else. Instead of a single, clearly defined gayborhood in a big city, which is our popular perception, we now see cultural archipelagos: multiple clusters of gay and lesbian populations are emerging in cities of different sizes and, as we will see, in the suburbs and in rural areas as well.

TABLE 4.2 Top 10 Towns with Greater than 50 Lesbian and Gay Couples, 2000

	Gay index
Provincetown, MA	22.72
Guerneville, CA	13.91
Wilton Manors, FL	9.63
West Hollywood, CA	7.38
Palm Springs, CA	7.20
Miami Shores, FL	5.82
Decatur, GA	5.64
Key West, FL	5.53
North Druid Hills, GA	5.50
Northampton, MA	5.35

Source: Gates and Ost (2004b:19).

TABLE 4.3 Top 10 Neighborhoods with Greater than 50 Lesbian and Gay Couples, 2000

	Zip code	Gay index
Provincetown, MA	02657	23.39
Castro, San Francisco	94114	20.07
Guerneville, CA	95446	12.93
Twin Peaks, San Francisco	94131	12.12
West Hollywood	90069	10.06
Oakland Park, Ft. Lauderdale	33305	8.93
Haight Ashbury, San Francisco	94117	8.10
Chelsea, New York	10011	8.06
South End, Boston	02118	8.01
Montrose, Houston	77006	7.93

Source: Gates and Ost (2004b:19).

Recall that post-gays perceive an expanding set of options about where they can settle without compromising their sense of safety. This is affecting existing gayborhoods, as we know, but now consider the flip side. The post-gay era is characterized by unprecedented societal acceptance of homosexuality. Gays and lesbians

TABLE 4.4 Top 25 Large, Midsize, and Small Cities Ranked by Same-Sex Couples, 2010

Rank	Large cities Population above 250,000	Same-sex couples (adjusted)	Same-sex couples per 1000 households (adjusted)	Mid-size cities Population between 100,000 and 250,000	Same-sex couples (adjusted)	Same-sex couples per 1000 households (adjusted)	Small cities Population below 100,000	Same-sex couples (adjusted)	Same-sex couples per 1000 households (adjusted)
1	San Francisco, CA	10,461	30.25	Fort Lauderdale, FL	2,324	31.08	Provincetown, MA	237	148.08
2	Seattle, WA	6,537	23.06	Berkeley, CA	949	20.61	Wilton Manors, FL	781	125.33
3	Oakland, CA	3,359	21.84	Salt Lake City, UT	1,145	15.36	Palm Springs, CA	2,440	107.28
4	Minneapolis, MN	3,555	21.74	Cambridge, MA	633	14.39	Rehoboth Beach, DE	76	99.97
5	Atlanta, GA	3,656	19.75	Orlando, FL	1,414	13.80	Guerneville, CA	185	80.36
6	Portland, OR	4,784	19.25	St. Petersburg, FL	1,500	13.78	West Hollywood, CA	1,397	62.05
7	Long Beach, CA	3,128	19.13	Madison, WI	1,358	13.24	Pleasant Ridge, MI	61	54.77
8	Washington, DC	4,822	18.08	Alexandria, VA	776	11.39	Rancho Mirage, CA	462	52.29
9	Denver, CO	4,117	15.65	Pasadena, CA	627	11.35	New Hope, PA	63	49.99
10	Boston, MA	3,715	14.70	Jersey City, NJ	1,080	11.15	Oakland Park, FL	865	49.41
11	St. Louis, MO	1,998	14.06	Arlington, VA	1,087	11.08	Cathefral City, CA	790	46.33
12	Sacramento, CA	2,271	13.00	Providence, RI	693	11.05	Miami Shores, FL	155	42.87
13	Dallas, TX	5,610	12.25	Richmond, VA	908	10.42	Avondale Estates, GA	58	42.78
14	San Diego, CA	5,910	12.23	Vallejo, CA	420	10.34	Northwest Harbor, NY	56	42.74
15	Austin, TX	3,820	11.76	Lansing, MI	501	10.34	Northampton, MA	484	40.31
16	Columbus, OH	3,786	11.42	Rochester, NY	894	10.28	Ocean Grove, NJ	78	40.16
17	Baltimore, MD	2,689	10.76	Santa Rosa, CA	650	10.22	Eldorado at Santa Fe, NM	115	40.00

(Continued)

TABLE 4.4 (Continued)

Rank	Large cities Population above 250,000	Same-sex couples (adjusted)	Same-sex couples per 1000 households (adjusted)	Mid-size cities Population between 100,000 and 250,000	Same-sex couples (adjusted)	Same-sex couples per 1000 households (adjusted)	Small cities Population below 100,000	Same-sex couples (adjusted)	Same-sex couples per 1000 households (adjusted)
18	New Orleans, LA	1,518	10.68	Durham, NC	951	10.17	Lambertville, NJ	77	39.28
19	St. Paul, MN	1,179	10.62	Richmond, CA	367	10.16	Asbury Park, NJ	255	37.91
20	Phoenix, AZ	5,450	10.59	Ann Arbor, MI	476	10.12	Signal Hill, CA	157	37.85
21	Chicago, IL	10,849	10.38	Eugene, OR	663	9.98	Decatur, GA	294	34.15
22	Tampa, FL	1,410	10.37	Enterprise, NV	387	9.72	Vashon, WA	152	33.03
23	Kansas City, MO	1,955	10.16	Concord, CA	426	9.62	Brisbane, CA	59	32.39
24	Los Angeles, CA	13,292	10.08	Hollywood, FL	558	9.55	North Druid Hills, GA	311	31.99
25	Albuquerque, NM	2,260	10.07	Paradise, NV	857	9.52	Ferndale, MI	303	31.72

Source: Gates and Cooke (2011:7).

are rapidly assimilating and thus integrating into the mainstream, and they are living their lives in places well beyond the gayborhood. Yet we also know that birds of a feather flock together. "Similarity breeds connection," note sociologists Miller McPherson, Lynn Smith-Lovin, and James Cook in their review of research on homophily, an idea that we have now encountered a couple of times. This is not unique to sexual minorities. Like attracts like along the lines of race, gender, and class as well, not to mention in marriage, friendships, and work. "Homophily limits people's social worlds," they say, and it is this tendency to delimit what we do, and who we do it with, that generates cultural archipelagos.[4] Although some gay people are moving out of existing gayborhoods, many of them are making similar choices about where to go next. Same-sex households, for instance, are pioneering new settlements in smaller towns. This might explain why their concentration is higher in smaller cities than it is in larger ones (30.25 in San Francisco compared to 148.08 in Provincetown; see table 4.4). Guerneville, California, and Decatur and North Druid Hills in Georgia, are not places that come to mind when we think about iconic American gayborhoods, yet as of the 2010 Census, a disproportionate number of same-sex households reside in such areas. These are the new hotbeds of queer lives, cultures, and communities, off the beaten path, and they complicate conclusions about gayborhood demise. The center of gravity is shifting as gays and lesbians congregate in a wider array of unexpected places. So, let us travel off that proverbial path so that we can learn more about these fascinating cultural archipelagos.

CHASING RAINBOWS

Gayborhoods can reform from one place to another. Gays and lesbians in Chicago, for example, have moved steadily north for more than a century now, colonizing one neighborhood after the next. This is an aspect of the city that we have not yet explored. From the late 1800s to the 1930s, they socialized primarily in two areas of the city: the vice districts on the South Side and in Towertown, which was the city's liberal enclave located near the Loop, just north and west of the famed Gold Coast. It would be a mistake to call either area a gayborhood. But still, these free-spirited slices of the Windy City were "alive with gay tea rooms and cheap lodging," and other scattered places where men and women would gather during the closet era, remarks Alex Papadopoulos, a local professor of geography. Lesbians were less visible during these years, especially those who were working-class, since some of them passed as men to seek better jobs and better wages. It was not until after the repeal of Prohibition in 1933 that "the first bars catering exclusively to lesbians and gay men opened in Chicago," Chad Heap finds. Downtown had a bohemian reputation, similar to the Village in New York, which enabled it to become a place where gay men could meet with relative safety. They patronized the area's theaters, restaurants, and bars in large numbers. The concentration of gay residences and social venues along Rush Street was so pronounced that it attracted Alfred Kinsey to the area in 1939 when he was conducting his influential research on sexual behavior.[5]

After World War II, Old Town, located about a mile north of the Loop, became "a new Chicago Bohemia, exhibiting clear marks of gay and lesbian residence and entrepreneurship," Papadopoulos notes. The white gay male community flourished there, where it "percolated in an atmosphere of activism and defiance." During the 1950s and '60s, the community collectively migrated farther north near the intersection of Clark Street and Diversey Parkway in an area that residents then called New Town. Today, we would recognize this as the boundary between the Lakeview and Lincoln Park neighborhoods.

And then came the Stonewall riots of 1969 in New York. The effects of the riots reached Chicago. According to Papadopoulos, an early pride parade in 1973 solidified a subsection of the Lakeview community area as "the place that was soon to be known as 'Boystown.' For the next thirty years, gay men, and to a lesser extent lesbians, have recognized Boystown as Chicago's premier gay 'village.'" Writing for the front page of the *Chicago Tribune*, Stephanie Banchero explained how this happened: "Gays and lesbians began moving into the North Halsted Street area when few others would." Economic factors contributed to the emergence of the Boystown gayborhood. "They poured their paychecks and their energies into rehabilitating the run-down housing, pushing out the gang members and transforming boarded-up storefronts into lively restaurants, retail stores and bars. In the end, they created a vibrant community that now ranks as one of the city's most desirable."[6]

As we transitioned into our current post-gay era, Boystown began "losing its character along with longtime residents," remarked Jeff Shand, general manager of the Ram, an adult bookstore that is located on the main commercial strip. Gay people, he said, are "moving out as new [straight] neighbors move in." But rather than disperse broadly across the city, many gays and lesbians are systematically settling north in Andersonville. The current migration, therefore, is the latest iteration of a long historical cycle: as one gayborhood dissolved, gays and lesbians revived a new one in an adjacent neighborhood (to the north, in this case).[7]

The Chicago outcome is common among big cities. Consider New York. While Greenwich Village was the site of the famous Stonewall riots, the queer nucleus has since shifted. A 2009 *Village Voice* essay, revealingly titled "The New Gay Neighborhoods" (note the plural), provides an overview. Michael Lavers noticed the same pattern: "Gay men, pushed out of Greenwich Village, went north of 14th Street to populate Chelsea, then past 34th Street to Hell's Kitchen. Now, many of them are pioneering some unlikely neighborhoods that are emerging as future gay neighborhoods." He, perhaps a bit defensively, recognizes the complex interplay of economic and political motivations for moving: "Some of us would as soon keep our gayborhoods a secret. As happened in Chelsea and Park Slope, high-rises and high prices usually follow queer sensibility, to the detriment of those who originally sought refuge in them. 'We transform neighborhoods once undesirable into desirable neighborhoods that become too expensive,' said political science professor Kenneth Sherrill. 'They stop being the kind of funky, creative places we enjoy, and become sedate and snobby—and so we move on.'"[8]

Although Christopher Street was once gay ground zero, it "is no longer quite as central to gay life in New York," said Kim Brinster, former manager of Oscar Wilde Memorial Bookshop in the Village, in 2003 when the store closed. Writing for the *Washington Post* three years later, Michelle Garcia put it more bluntly, "Forget the image of the Village as gay haven; forget the liberation movement that rose from its cobblestone streets. The scene has moved north to Chelsea, and what's left in the Village is a gay neighborhood gone older, wealthier, and stodgier." Despite her recommendation to "forget" the Village, Garcia does not suggest that all gays and lesbians have fled the area. Instead, both she and especially Lavers hint at a cultural archipelagos model of multiple gayborhoods—pluralism, in other words. Some may be older, wealthier, and stodgier, while others are at the center of the new queer scene. Despite these tectonic shifts in New York, however, the Stonewall Inn remains an institutional anchor in the Village—and not just any old anchor but one that received an important designation as a national historic landmark in 2000.[9]

In the stories that are coming out of Chicago and New York, we hear a familiar refrain about urban change. Gays move into run-down areas of the city, the conventional argument goes, where property values are cheap and where they can be with their own kind without moral judgment, fear, or discrimination. They fix up the area, and once it has a certain amount of amenities and conveniences with broader appeal, straight people are drawn to it. As more straights arrive, however, they price the gays out and, through the culturally destructive processes of gentrification, the neighborhood loses its queer sensibility. Lavers and Professor Sherrill nod to this notion, and Garcia implies it, but they all avoid answers to follow-up questions that we must ask: Who wants to keep "our" gayborhood a "secret"? A secret from whom? All people with money or just straights with money? What about gays with money? They presumably play some role in the Village's vibe as "wealthier and stodgier." Complex class dynamics are clearly at play here, and they interact with politics, a drive for territoriality, and fears about the loss of community.

There are some differences between Chicago and New York in terms of collective memory. In the Windy City, the status of each former area as a gayborhood is all but forgotten (except perhaps among certain circles of historians), whereas in New York, many locals are aware that they live in a city with multiple gayborhoods.

How can we explain this difference? To draw a map of queer cultural archipelagos, each area requires property ownership, institutional anchors, or the designation of a queer business as a national historic landmark. In Chicago, gay and lesbian business owners were not economically independent in prior gayborhoods the way they are now in Boystown, and this may account for why there is so little memory about Towertown and Old Town. Similarly, we would be hard-pressed to find a queer institutional anchor or a historic landmark if we visited these other neighborhoods. Boystown, however, is different. It has several anchors, such as Unabridged Bookstore, Sidetrack, and the Center on Halsted, and many gay and lesbian business owners control their real estate. Although no particular site has yet to receive a landmark status, local activists have recently installed the world's first outdoor museum, as we will see when we visit Chicago again in later chapters, and this commemorates the area's queer cultural heritage. All of these are reasons why Boystown has a greater probability of surviving as a gayborhood in the lives and memories of locals.

Some key historical events have impacted the gay migration, especially but not exclusively in New York. HIV/AIDS is perhaps one of the most powerful examples. "In the 1980s and '90s, with AIDS, when a lot of our neighbors died, it created a void [in the Village]. And there was a movement of businesses to Chelsea," said Brinster from Oscar Wilde. Here we bear witness to how a public health crisis, and the specter of death that it left behind, compelled gayborhood change. Consider as well a 1995 *Washington Post* piece in which Gary Lee notes, "Hit by the AIDS crisis and changing times, the heart of gay New York began to gradually shift a decade ago to Chelsea, which borders Greenwich Village to the north." In a 2002 *New York Times* article, Denny Lee agreed about the impact of AIDS, but he added a provocative twist to our understanding of what happened to "America's gay Main Street":

If Christopher Street was once America's gay Main Street, today it conjures a gay Potemkin Village. AIDS wiped out an entire cohort of gay men who had flocked there, even as Chelsea attracted a younger generation of gay, mostly white residents by offering cheaper rents.

Eventually, Eighth Avenue outpaced Christopher Street as the city's gay standard. Until the mid-1990s, when Chelsea took over, the West Village zip code, 10014, had indicated the most populous gay neighborhood in the city.[10]

Notice the imagery of a "gay Potemkin Village." Potemkin was a Russian soldier, statesman, and one of Catherine the Great's lovers. He helped her seize power in 1762 by creating hollow facades of sham villages along the Dnieper River, hoping to impress the European powers-that-be with Catherine's supposed new conquests. From this mythology was born the phrase "Potemkin village" to designate a veneer that seems impressive but that lacks any substance underneath. To call Greenwich Village a gay Potemkin Village implies a superficial relationship between it and Chelsea, which I think is unfair. A symbolic relationship is a more accurate assessment: even though businesses and residences shifted north to Chelsea, the Village has retained its status as home to Stonewall, a major emblem of gay life.[11]

After the Village came Chelsea, and now there is Hell's Kitchen. In her 2004 story for the *Village Voice*, entitled "Chasing Rainbows," Lynn Yaeger remarks, "Chelsea, a neighborhood that was until recently hailed as the new gay ghetto, replaced Christopher Street, which long held that distinction. Now, an increasing number of straight hand-holders crowd the sidewalks on sunny afternoons." Straights in New York eventually overran the gayborhood, just as they did in Chicago. In both cities, therefore, a certain threshold of heterosexual presence motivates gays and lesbians to move on and to revive the gayborhood somewhere else. In her *New York Times* story, vividly entitled "TURF: Edged Out by the Stroller Set," Motoko Rich makes a similar comment about hetero-invasion in Chelsea: "For the last decade, Chelsea, on the West Side just north of Greenwich Village, has been the epicenter of gay male life in New York. Gay bars, novelty shops and coffee shops (notably, Big Cup, on Eighth Avenue), have drawn pilgrims from all over the country . . . [But] as mostly straight families move into Chelsea, gay residents are now gravitating toward Hell's Kitchen and beyond." She places the plight of Chelsea in a historical context to help her readers appreciate how the same thing happened in the Village decades earlier:

> Twenty years ago, when gay men and women began to leave the West Village for Chelsea, straight families moved in to take their place. Now, as Chelsea's gay incumbents disperse to Hell's Kitchen and Washington Heights as well as Fort Greene and Williamsburg in Brooklyn, they are again being replaced by straights . . . For some residents, the [straight] baby boom [in the gayborhood] signaled the end of an era. "I did notice that when I started to get run over by those double-truck strollers, it was probably time to get out of Chelsea," Ted Davis, a 40-year-old magazine art director, said with a chuckle. He moved to Hell's Kitchen last year and this fall will pick up again, this time for Williamsburg.[12]

This is now the third time that a journalist writing for a major news outlet identifies straight in-migration, specifically, as a factor that pushes the gays out. If they leave the gayborhood because there are "too many straights" (and their "double-truck strollers"), then this refutes romanticized notions that we can all get along in the same sexually integrated urban space. It also requires us to reconsider the cultural resonance of gay neighborhoods. If they were outmoded and on their way to becoming obsolete, then we would expect gay people to just stay put. If straight presence signals "the end of an era," and if the gayborhood is less meaningful in a post-gay era, then why go through all the trouble of moving and reviving a new one? If the neighborhood's queer identity wanes, and if sexual orientation is receding in a post-gay era, then what incentive is there to put down a pride flag somewhere else? Who needs such a flag anyway? That gays and lesbians leave, and that they relocate in ways that are systematic, flies in the face of post-gay arguments. Some of the confusion may stem from word choice. Rich tells us that Chelsea's gay incumbents are "dispersing to" Hell's Kitchen and other neighborhoods. Her imagery of dispersion, which is common among other journalists and the many residents with whom I personally met, implies that gayborhoods are disappearing. But to suggest that they are dispersing *to* particular places connotes the reverse: there are distinct patterns in their migration. When we read an article like this and then reread it against its own grain, therefore, we discover multiple realities. The meaning of sexuality is changing in a post-gay era, but it continues to structure our everyday lives. Gays and lesbians are still "chasing rainbows," after all, and they are making similar choices about where they think they will find them.

Rather than identifying continuities between the present and the past, some reporters try to distinguish between them. David Shaftel, for example, in his 2007 *New York Times* story, argued that the "new gay presence" in Hell's Kitchen "is very different from what went before. In the West Village and Chelsea, gay culture was in many respects the prevailing culture. But in Hell's Kitchen, the gay community is just one of many subcultures that share and sometimes compete for a common turf." He interviewed a local resident who described the difference in terms of identity: "Chelsea is more of a rainbow flag-flying destination, like Christopher Street. Hell's Kitchen doesn't have any one character. It just has the cheapest rents around."[13] But is the current migration from Chelsea to Hell's Kitchen really all that different from what preceded it when the queer epicenter shifted from the Village to Chelsea? The final statement from the resident that Shaftel interviewed—Hell's Kitchen has "the cheapest rents around"—echoes economic wisdom. In its earlier days, Chelsea also supported multiple subcultures, like Hell's Kitchen does today, and rents were cheaper then as well. Perhaps Hell's Kitchen is in an earlier stage of gentrification, a time when a neighborhood can retain economic and cultural heterogeneity.

Whereas the Village is an example of a symbolic (or Potemkin) gay village, Chelsea and Hell's Kitchen are both apparently queer. Whether and for how long this is sustainable is to be seen. "Despite Hell's Kitchen's growing appeal to many of the city's young gay men, an attraction fueled by its strengthening gay identity," Shaftel finds that "many residents predict that the area may never have the gay identity that Chelsea has and that the West Village was once famous for, that it will endure simply as a gay-friendly district, less a scene than simply a neighborhood." His scene/neighborhood distinction is fascinating to me. Why did Chelsea and the Village once have a distinct gay identity, but Hell's Kitchen seems like it never will? And how would a resident feel the difference between a "gay neighborhood" and a "gay-friendly district" on the ground? If we can find answers to these questions, then we can also clarify the relationship among multiple gayborhoods. Do they coexist materially, symbolically, or does one supersede and eventually supplant the other?

Whatever the case may be, it is clear that the gay and lesbian population in New York is spread out yet still multiply clustered; these are unexpectedly compatible observations. For his story, Shaftel also interviewed Gary Gates, who "analyzed census data broken down by ZIP code and concluded that Chelsea's central ZIP code, 10011, followed by the West Village's, 10014, are the city's highest numbers of households made up of same-sex unmarried couples. By 2000 . . . the 10036 ZIP code in Hell's Kitchen already had the third-highest number of gay couples, indicating that the gay settlement of Hell's Kitchen was already well under way." From this Shaftel concludes, "The conventional wisdom is that the emergence of Hell's Kitchen as a gay-friendly neighborhood simply continued the gay migration up the West Side."

The idea of a general migration obscures generational differences. Gregory Angelo, editor for a queer lifestyle magazine called *Next*, offers the following qualification for New York:

> I wouldn't say it's just a migration; it's also a new generation of gay people. . . . I found there were enough young gay men and women who, like me, wanted to be a part of Chelsea but didn't have the funds and couldn't find an apartment there. So we all moved to Hell's Kitchen . . . It's very much a gay neighborhood now, . . . which is basically the way I hear older friends of mine describe Chelsea when they moved there in the '90s, and how other gay friends described the West Village when they moved there in the '80s.[14]

His generation/migration difference clarifies why the evolution of gayborhoods will be an ongoing part of our lives. Not all "new gay teenagers," as we called them before, are alike—or post-gay, for that matter. People like Gregory are part of the new generation, but he and his friends still want to be around other gay people. Young adults usually have less money than those of us who are in our thirties, forties, and beyond, and when they graduate from college, leave home, and want to move to the city, they need to find places with cheap rents. If enough of them make the same choice, a new gayborhood can emerge, one that, in its earlier days, is economically mixed. Over time, however, it will achieve cultural unity as "more of a rainbow flag-flying destination."

Several puzzles are rumbling underneath New York. First, is Hell's Kitchen a gay-friendly neighborhood or an actual gayborhood? If it is just the former, whatever that even means, can it develop into the latter? Second, when the center of gay gravity shifts, does an emerging district replace what came before it? In other words, is Hell's Kitchen the *new* or *next* gayborhood? And if there are multiple contenders, how are they all related? Which image is more valid, supersession or coexistence? Third, are the urban dynamics of Hell's Kitchen different from those in Chelsea and in the Village from prior decades? If so, what explains this historical discontinuity? Maybe Hell's Kitchen will house multiple subcultures for the time being, but will it eventually concentrate with gays and lesbians? And then will straights soon follow, as they have before?

I suspect that urban areas will develop in a sequence from gay-friendly places initially to full-on gayborhoods later. The former are those where gays and lesbians feel safe and comfortable to be themselves, but they do not "set the tone," to borrow a critical phrase from the historian George Chauncey. Once they do, a gay-friendly area becomes a gayborhood. The notion of a sequence supports an image of cultural archipelagos, and it is also consistent with stage models of gentrification.[15] Whether it is the next or new gayborhood, on the other hand, depends on the same three factors that I proposed earlier: property ownership among queer business owners, institutional anchors of immediate relevance to queer communities, and historic preservation of sites that are meaningful for queer people. The more of these factors that a place has, the more likely we are to have a new gayborhood—and possibly another gayborhood— somewhere else. The words "new" and "another" imply multiplicity. The fewer of these factors that are in place, however, the more likely we are to see the "next" gayborhood, a term that suggests singularity, supersession, and replacement. Whether new or next, the gayborhoods of today and tomorrow are and will be different than those of yesterday because the indelible imprints of the post-gay era on urban America. These days, it does not make much sense to ask whether straights will follow the gays. Straight people have always been in and around queer spaces. Gayborhoods are no longer out of bounds for them as the stigma of homosexuality continues to ease. Their proportional presence, however, will shift: more straights will move in later, as economists correctly predict.

Chicago and New York are parts of a much bigger pattern. DC residents, like the journalist Marc Fisher, also wonder, "What if Dupont Circle isn't a gay neighborhood anymore?" In his 2002 *Washington Post* piece, he talks about "the de-homosexualization of Dupont":

> Census data indicate that nearly three of every four same-sex couples in the city live outside the Dupont area. Apartment buildings that were once almost entirely gay are now largely occupied by straight people. New gay businesses are popping up not along Connecticut Avenue or long-since gentrified side streets, but a neighborhood or two away, east of 14th Street in rapidly changing sections . . . The de-homosexualization of Dupont is neither total nor speedy. In fact, plenty of people believe . . . that gay life is alive and well in Dupont Circle.[16]

Fisher's story reflects the complexity of the gayborhood and indeed the complexity of human life more generally. The post-gay era is neither "total nor speedy"; it is uneven and incomplete. Dupont today may not look or feel like it once did, but "gay life is alive and well," even as "new gay businesses" open "a neighborhood or two away," adjacent to Dupont, which is the same geographic and urban planning pattern we saw in Chicago and New York. In this short excerpt from his article, we hear what sounds like post-gay thinking (e.g., from "once almost entirely gay" to "now largely occupied by straight people") and an expanded residential mindset (e.g., "three of every four same-sex couples in the city live outside the Dupont area"). On the other hand, Fisher also hints at the persistence of the Dupont gayborhood, even while he describes the revival of a new one.

There are many other examples. Consider South Boston, or "Southie." "We're seeing the glimmering of a trend [of gays moving into Southie from the South End]," said Don Gorton, chairman of the Greater Boston Lesbian and Gay Political Alliance. "It's not a tidal wave. But it's certainly a trend." Although the traditional gayborhood of the South End is changing, a new district is emerging in Southie, as we heard earlier. Something similar is happening in Oakland, California, which has "quietly become home to more lesbian couples per capita than any other big city in the nation, and ranks third for gay and lesbian households combined, behind San Francisco and Seattle," reported Jim Herron Zamora in his 2004 *San Francisco Chronicle* story. He then offered a curious observation: "Oakland is also the largest major American city without a pink ghetto—no Castro Street or Greenwich Village—even as it was second behind San Francisco as the hometown for same-sex couples married there this year." Castro Street and Christopher Street are commercially dense areas that have great symbolic value for queer communities. Oakland does not have such a street, nor does it have the same symbolic status. This suggests that an emerging residential concentration of same-sex couples in an area is not enough to designate it, or perceive it, as a gayborhood.[17]

Yet there is a known relationship between gay households and a local economy. Perhaps this is why Danny Wan, an Oakland city councilman, is "pushing to create a new gay and lesbian business district southeast of Lake Merritt, near a heavily gay swath of the city." Zamora spoke with the city councilman to learn more about the plan:

> Wan said he hopes that creating a gay district for Oakland will have economic benefits for a once-rundown area and enhance community pride by having a cultural center . . . "A city of our size usually has some kind of district, a place where you can go and find these types of businesses, catering to gays and lesbians," said Wan . . . "Oakland needs something like this."[18]

This example instructs us to separate residential and commercial compositions and to inquire whether claims of gayborhood demise are based on one, the other, or both. Oakland's current lack of a main commercial street may lead us to conclude that the city is post-gay. Residentially, however, Oakland has "more lesbian couples per capita than any other big city in the nation, and ranks third for gay and lesbian households combined, behind San Francisco and Seattle." This distinction makes sense because homosexuality is not visible on the body in the same way as race or gender. Queer institutions, however, provide an unmistakable proxy that locals use to confirm that they do, in fact, have a "pink ghetto."

We have just visited Chicago, New York, Washington, DC, South Boston, and Oakland, all of which provide evidence for the declining significance of sexual orientation and gayborhoods. But they also exhibit a new national pattern. In her 2007 front-page story for the *New York Times*, Patricia Leigh Brown explains, "Cities not widely considered gay meccas have seen a sharp increase in same-sex couples. Among them: Fort Worth; El Paso; Albuquerque; Louisville, Ky.; and Virginia Beach." Like so many other journalists we have met, Brown also interviewed Gary Gates, who added, "Twenty years ago, if you were gay and lived in rural Kansas, you went to San Francisco or New York. Now you can just go to Kansas City."[19] Big-city gayborhoods are sexually integrating, but new queer pockets—or cultural archipelagos, as we are calling them—are also forming in those same cities through a systematic pattern of adjacent resettlement: gays and lesbians move from one neighborhood to another that is near it. Sometimes, a residential concentration emerges without a corresponding area of commercial density. If we define gayborhoods exclusively by their institutional composition, we may fail to acknowledge that a gayborhood exists (assuming gays and lesbians set its tone).

Cities are an obvious place to find gayborhoods, to find evidence for their potential disappearance, and even countervailing trends for their surprising revival. It is no surprise, therefore, that journalists, scholars, and everyday people alike all tend to look there first. But there is more to this story than what is happening in American cities. Additional evidence that gayborhoods are creatively reconstituting comes from the suburbs that satellite those cities. Jen Christensen and John Caldwell, writing for the *Advocate* in 2006, tell us, "[The] suburbs are attracting large numbers of gay people . . . And the gays are bringing a strong sense of community . . . [by] turning what once was a straight, conservative suburban neighborhood into what some affectionately call a 'gayborhood.'" To call a suburban area a gayborhood is a radical act of cultural redefinition that severs the concept from its urban roots. Christensen and Caldwell recognize the plasticity of the idea and its portability beyond city boundaries. Later in the story, they offer several arguments for why gayborhoods are forming in the suburbs: "As growing numbers of gay and lesbian Americans seek affordable roomy houses with a yard, along with safe streets and a good school for their children, they are changing the American suburbs . . . It's a widespread movement, but it remains a quiet one." Its quietness—not to mention the "widespread movement" that is happening outside the borders of a city, where we tend to look first for queer lives—may lead us to overlook this new phenomenon. "Mainstream America doesn't see this population on shows like *Will & Grace*," said sociologist Wayne Brekhus in his interview with Christensen and Caldwell. "Suburban gay people aren't reflected in popular culture."[20]

Consider a specific example from a New Jersey suburb where a gay male couple confessed, "Living in a neighborhood, among everyone else, is what we wanted." Their straight neighbors agreed, "They're living here to live here, not to be confrontational or group together for parades . . . Not making an issue of it or wearing a badge is the best way to break down potential hostility." This resembles the "scarlet letter" remark that we heard from a lesbian couple in an earlier chapter. In her article for the *New York Times* in 2000, Jane Gross notes that the vestiges of gay identity also appear in the suburbs, even if straights do not always see them:

> In this suburb, rainbow flags, the symbol of gay pride, flap outside grand Tudors and gracious Colonials, sometimes several per block. At the Maple Leaf Diner, children blowing bubbles in their chocolate milk often have two fathers or two mothers. And at day care centers and Sunday school, there is rarely a class without several children who have same-sex parents. This Essex County community, and neighboring South Orange, which shares its school system, are considered by scores of real estate brokers and gay homeowners to be the most welcoming suburb in the region for gay men and lesbians . . . Nobody knows how many gay families live in Maplewood and South Orange, but a stroll in either village suggest that many do, and they go about their daily routines as openly as they might in Chelsea or West Hollywood. The difference is that this is not a gay ghetto, but rather a place where sexual orientation is not the defining fact of life.[21]

It is difficult to reconcile statements like "not making an issue of it or wearing a badge," "this is not a gay ghetto," and "a place where sexual orientation is not the defining fact of life" with Gross's observation that "many gay families live in [the area]," children at diners and day care centers with two moms or two dads, her mention of flying rainbow flags, and several per block, and her comparison of this suburb with Chelsea and West Hollywood, two very obvious gayborhoods. Gross's story nicely captures the contradictions of post-gay life.

Similar developments are happening in rural areas. A 2001 *Seattle Post-Intelligencer* story by Ruth Schubert identified one particular manifestation of this pattern: "Randy Marinez didn't move here because he thought it was 'gay-friendly.' It was the sense of community, the rural cadence of the land, the breezy ferry ride to downtown Seattle that drew him and his partner to the island [Vashon Island] 12 years ago . . . While a lot of same-sex couples say they didn't choose where they live based on the presence or absence of other gays and lesbians, there is comfort in numbers." Here again we stumble over the same tension between that which sounds post-gay (gay couples choose where they live without regard for the presence of other gays) and other things that do not (there is still comfort in numbers). Schubert also interviewed a lesbian couple who further complicated Marinez's experiences: "I have noticed that the island is full of lesbians. We joke about that." Like New Jersey, some gays and lesbians on Vashon Island declare that they do not want to live in a gayborhood, but the decisions they make seem predicated on the presence of other gay people in the area.[22]

Consider as well Chestnut Hill, Massachusetts. In his 2001, front-page *Philadelphia Inquirer* article, Thomas Ginsberg interviewed a male couple who explained how the residential psychology of many gay people has changed over time: "The whole 'gay ghetto' thing, which was so crucial to your peace of mind in the past, doesn't seem to be there anymore." But this couple was "astonished," in their words, by "how many [gay] friends have [also] moved" near them. If the "whole gay ghetto thing" has passed, then why are so many gay people making similar decisions about where to live? We might miss this development in Chestnut Hill, and elsewhere, if we focus

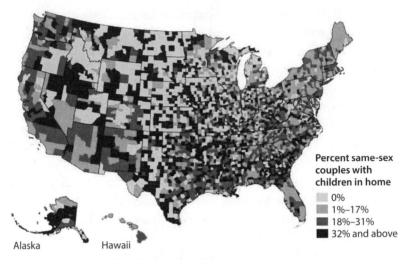

Percent same-sex
couples with
children in home

0%
1%–17%
18%–31%
32% and above

Alaska   Hawaii

FIGURE 4.2 Distribution of same-sex families with biological, adopted, or foster children under the age of 18 in the home in 2010. Source: Gates (2013), http://williamsinstitute.law.ucla.edu/wp-content/uploads/LGBT-Parenting.pdf.

exclusively on the presence of institutions, our usual indicator for a gayborhood, at the neglect of residential density, which is apparently not enough to earn such a designation.[23]

Additional evidence about the creative constitution of other types of queer settlements comes from the experiences of same-sex families with children. Census data from 2010 shows that same-sex couples are raising children across the country, although their presence is unevenly distributed (figure 4.2). About 37 percent of LGBT-identified adults have had a child at some point in their life. Currently, more than 110,000 same-sex couples are raising an estimated 170,000 biological, adopted, or stepchildren. Those couples who consider themselves "spouses" are more than twice as likely to be raising children, compared to couples who define themselves as "unmarried partners." Among those individuals who are younger than fifty and who are living alone or with a partner, nearly half of LGBT women (48%) and a fifth of LGBT men (20%) are raising a child under the age of eighteen. Among couple households, specifically, 2011 American Community Survey data shows that 27 percent of female couples and 11 percent of male couples are raising children.[24]

In a closer analysis of this trend, Gary Gates finds a surprising pattern in the places that same-sex couples choose to raise their children. Child rearing, he notes, is "most common in Southern, Mountain West, and Midwest regions of the country." States that have the highest proportion of same-sex couples with children include Mississippi (26%), Wyoming (25%), Alaska (23%), Idaho (22%), Montana (22%), Kansas (22%), North Dakota (22%), Arkansas (21%), South Dakota (21%), and Oklahoma (21%).[25]

Many same-sex couples are raising children in states that have a legal environment that is at best not supportive and at worst openly hostile toward them and their families. Some of us might read this as proof that we are post-gay: gays and lesbians are just as likely to live and parent in conservative parts of the country, far from traditional gayborhoods. I think there is some truth here, but if we look at the national- and state-level data with an even greater level of granularity, as the Williams Institute did in 2013, we find discernible pockets of concentration—and unlikely ones yet again—within this broader distribution (table 4.5).[26] Same-sex families are moving systematically to particular places. This results in the multiplication of the total number of gayborhoods and other sexually identified settlements.

Remarking on this information, the Williams Institute notes, "the metro areas with the highest percentages of same-sex couples raising children are in states that have a constitutional ban on marriage." That these families cluster in areas that are potentially hostile to them reiterates a continuing need for safe spaces, even in a post-gay era. One implication is that these clusters themselves create the safe spaces that gays and lesbians need and that they seek, although this enables them to deny the need for a gayborhood since such clusters are located outside the boundaries of more identifiable and stereotypical places.

The final example for us to consider comes from the experiences of seniors, whose decisions about where to live also reveal striking patterns. In November 2005, Claire Wilson published an article in the *New York Times* entitled, "Gay Retirement Communities Growing in Popularity." She described "a growing number of communities aimed at the gay, lesbian, bisexual, and transgender population

TABLE 4.5 Metro Areas with the Highest Percentages of Same-Sex Couples Raising Children

Population below 1 million		Population above 1 million	
Metro area name	% same-sex couples raising children	Metro area name	% same-sex couples raising children
Grand Forks, ND-MN	65	Salt Lake City, UT	26
Bismarck, ND	61	Virginia Beach-Norfolk-Newport News, VA-NC	24
Hinesville-Fort Stewart, GA	46	Detroit-Warren-Livonia, MI	22
Laredo, TX	45	Memphis, TN-MS-AR	22
Visalia-Porterville, CA	44	San Antonio-New Braunfels, TX	22
Cheyenne, WY	43	Baltimore-Towson, MD	20
Rapid City, SD	43	Columbus, OH	19
Sioux City, IA-NE-SD	43	Hartford-West Hartford-East Hartford, CT	19
Brownsville-Harlingen, TX	42	Houston-Sugar Land-Baytown, TX	19
Longview, WA	42	Oklahoma City, OK	19

Source: Williams Institute, May 2013.

across the country," including relatively new developments in Palmetto, Florida (Palms of Manasota); Fort Myers, Florida (Resort on Carefree Boulevard, a women-only community); Santa Fe, New Mexico (RainbowVision); and Boston, Massachusetts (Stonewall Communities). By 2030, the number of GLBT people in the United States who are over sixty-five is predicted to double to about three million people, and so we can expect more retirement communities to emerge that are targeted specifically for them.[27]

Wilson interviewed two men at the Palms of Manasota to find out why they purchased a place at a GLBT retirement facility: "I want to be able to walk around holding John's hand or give him a hug," said Billy, a seventy-one-year-old retired professor, referring to his partner of fourteen years, John, seventy-five, a retired Episcopal priest.

"I can do that here without feeling the pressure of being straight." As it did for same-sex parents, the safe space theme emerges for seniors as well, even in the post-gay era of presumed safety. Wilson discussed the importance of safe spaces for this group: "Aging gays and lesbians fearing discrimination and sometimes abuse in mainstream care facilities are often forced back into the closet if they require long-term care, and rarely are same-sex couples permitted to share rooms in these facilities. Reluctance to be open about sexual preference leads to isolation that can affect the level of care elderly gays get." Billy and John challenge the claim that we are now beyond the closet. They make us sit with the unthinkable possibility that, after a long life, these men and other GLBT seniors might be forced back into the closet.[28]

GLBT retirement communities are not allowed to discriminate. As a result, some straights also live in them. Two such couples live at the Palms. The gay residents generally do not mind their presence. "I don't need it to be exclusively gay," said one of the residents. When Wilson asked about what the optimal balance of composition should be in their community, the same individual backtracked: "I just want to be in the majority for once in my life." The impulse of integration and separation can coexist in a post-gay era. But for some GLBT seniors, the right balance is one in which they, not straights, are in the majority. However much society accepts queer people, the fact is that they will always be gender and sexual minorities. Sometimes, it is nice to find a little space in the world, whether in a gayborhood or in a retirement community, where that is not the case.

QUEER GEOGRAPHIES

It is difficult to assess cultural changes that are happening today. By definition, nearly all such shifts, though they may eventually seem historically significant and thus obvious in retrospect, are in the present moment simply collections of choices that people make as they go about their everyday lives. The fate of the gayborhood is no different. There is no grand sense of destiny at work here, just the numerous decisions of many different individuals that gradually, with and without intention, cohere into something that we can describe as general trends. As we looked at what people were doing and how they were thinking in this chapter, we discovered a surprising number of these trends.

The prediction that gayborhoods are on a trajectory toward demise and disappearance is flawed. It oversimplifies a much more complex reality. Gayborhoods are changing, to be sure, but the decisions that gays, lesbians, and straights are making about where to live are not random. Many queer people stay in the gayborhood—even in a post-gay era—and even those who move out often make similar choices about where to go next.

While the post-gay era is likely to last, gays and lesbians have more diverse options for how to structure their lives. This means not the end of American gayborhoods, as some observers predict, but rather their unexpected growth. Queer geographies are plural. The image of a gayborhood as a singular island of meaning, a safe space that is surrounded by a sea of heterosexual hostilities, may lose some resonance as the city presents more livable options. The people we met in this chapter encouraged us to imagine those options as cultural archipelagos. Table 4.6 summarizes these binary-breaking possibilities for the future of urban life.[29]

Gayborhoods are changing. Some of them are de-gaying and diluting (or "deconcentrating," as demographers say) as sexual minorities disperse across the city (T_1). As we saw in the first three chapters of this book, post-gays perceive expansive possibilities for where to live, and the feelings of cultural similarity that they experience with their heterosexual neighbors reduce the unease that in the past may have prevented many of them from imagining a life beyond the gayborhood. Our goal in this chapter, however, was to consider how gayborhoods are evolving in the present and how they will live on into the future based on observations from across the country.

When the residential composition of a neighborhood changes, some activists, like those in San Francisco and Toronto who we met in the introduction, ask if they are "worth saving." This is a version of "save our neighborhood," a common chant that we hear

TABLE 4.6 Queer Geographies

Trend	Prediction	Examples
T_1: De-gaying	Existing gayborhoods will sexually integrate and lose much of their cultural and institutional character.	See Chapters 1–3
T_2: Safe harbors	Acceptance has limits; existing gayborhoods will remain as a refuge.	Gayborhoods are a safe space for queer youth of color, transgender people, and those who hail from small towns.
T_3: Survival	Existing gayborhoods will sexually integrate yet retain much of their cultural and institutional character.	Gayborhoods house anchor institutions and commemorative markers.
T_4: Revival	A new or the next gayborhood will form as gays leave an existing area and collectively resettle into another one nearby.	Chicago gays have moved northward from Towertown to Old Town to New Town to Boystown to Andersonville.
T_5: Multiplication	New gay-identified areas will form, in addition to existing gayborhoods, as specific groups systematically settle into them.	Distinct spaces are emerging for same-sex families, retired gays, people of color, and lesbians.
T_6: Small- and Medium-Sized Cities	New gayborhoods and gay-identified areas will form in small- and medium-sized cities.	See Table 4.4, column 2
T_7: Suburbs and Rural Areas	New gayborhoods and gay-identified areas will form in the suburbs and in rural areas.	See Table 4.4, column 3

across the country in those areas that experience racial and class-based transitions. If activists were confident that gayborhoods, in our case, would not change, then they would not worry about saving them. Thus, the very need to "save our gayborhood" manifests only because some people are concerned that the area will not maintain its queer character. They worry that the gayborhood needs to be saved by their conscious effort—or else it will die. But we know that all neighborhoods change; it is an unavoidable fact of city life. Therefore, a desire for the status quo, for the good old days that never really existed the way they do when we look back at them through rose-colored glasses, is untenable.

Gayborhood change does not mean that these urban areas are meaningless. On the contrary, gayborhoods are culturally relevant as refuges for queer youth of color, transgender individuals, and queers who hail from small towns (T_2), because antigay bigotry still affects their everyday life. These groups are not creating new gayborhoods or reviving old ones; instead, they are seeking solace in those that currently exist. They do not deny the realities of sexual integration, but neither do they remark on them very much. It is the search for a safe space that matters most to them. Even the acknowledgment of sexual integration does not require us to forfeit the sustainability of gayborhoods. They can retain their cultural and institutional character despite ongoing residential flux (T_3). We saw this in New York, and the same is true in Chicago.

Urban life is much more complex than what is happening to existing gayborhoods, which is the emphasis in the first three trends in the table. In cities like New York, Chicago, and Washington, DC, we discovered that gayborhoods have been slowly moving over time; locals have reformed, resurrected, and indeed revived them from one place to another over the years (T_4). They have continually "reconcentrated," a demographer might say, as gays and lesbians moved in a way that suggests a collective pattern of resettlement into a different area. Sometimes, however, specific groups, like same-sex families, older gays, people of color, and lesbians, demonstrate unique trends of their own. They reconcentrate in particular places that do not necessarily overlap with the overall collective migration. This increases the total number of queer spaces in the city, resulting in multiple gayborhoods (T_5), even if each one has become sexually integrated over time, regardless of the precise nature of their relationship with one another, and regardless of whether any of them ever develop into a formal gay district.

The emergence of gayborhoods beyond big cities presents yet another alternative for the future of urban America (T_6). We do not generally think about medium- and small-sized cities as home to gay meccas. Where, for example, is the gay mecca in Salt Lake City? Or in Decatur, Georgia? Lately, however, such cities have seen sharp increases in same-sex households.[30] We spent a fair amount of time in Oakland, but other cities include those that are listed in the second column of table 4.4. Consider as well the remarks of a Boystown lesbian, who we have not yet met, who was once a high school teacher in Nebraska. She used the memorable analogy of a toddler walking to emphasize the staggered sense of gayborhood change and redevelopment:

> We're saying, "We're post-gay." Maybe in some cities. It's like, great, the toddler's walking. But now we need to look at other places where we haven't even begun to crawl. Maybe the gay neighborhood in the Castro isn't worth saving. But maybe the one in Arizona or Nebraska or New Mexico or Iowa or Idaho are absolutely worth cultivating.

Finally, all twenty-five places that are listed in the third column of table 4.4 illustrate an equally compelling observation of suburban and rural emergence (T_7). To learn about it, we visited Essex County suburbs in New Jersey, Vashon Island in Washington, and Chestnut Hill in Massachusetts.

These seven trends add up to a landscape that is pulsating with texture, dynamism, intriguing complexity, and an abundance of life. We cannot categorize our world using simple or singular binaries. It is more compelling to think about the map using an image of cultural archipelagos. But even these are not arranged nice and neatly. New Yorkers and Chicagoans, for example, differ in the extent to which residents think of themselves as living in a city with multiple gayborhoods. In the City of Big Shoulders, locals barely remember or feel any connection with prior places like Towertown or Old Town. The situation is different in New York, where the

Village maintains an intimate connection with queer communities, even if there has been a collective out-migration from it. Three variables account for this difference: control over real estate by queer business owners, the presence of institutional anchors that are directly related to queer lives, and inclusion in the National Register of Historic Places, again in a way that is relevant to queer lives. None of this happened in places prior to Boystown, and this is why those older gayborhoods have not imprinted in the local collective memory.

Just because there is more than one gayborhood or area in a city does not mean that they are all alike—any more than the fiction that all nonheterosexuals are the same. There are gay-friendly areas where queers do not set the tone and gayborhoods where they do. There are "new" and "next" gayborhoods and "gay Potemkin villages." Sometimes, one gayborhood supersedes what came before it, while at other times they coexist. Whatever the degree of queerness, and however many different spaces there are, straights are always around them in a post-gay era. But if there are "too many" of them, then gay people leave and "chase rainbows" somewhere else. While big cities are the most obvious places for us to look for them, gays and lesbians are settling in more diverse places than just that. These days, we see concentrations of same-sex households in medium- and small-sized cities, the suburbs, and in rural areas. Sometimes, as they settle in these nontraditional areas, they build up their residential density without a corresponding commercial concentration of their own businesses and organizations. This looks post-gay at first, and it can make it hard for us to recognize that a "pink ghetto" exists. We are equally likely to overlook the gayborhood if we do not take the time to recognize the unique migration patterns of certain groups like families and seniors.

To better understand this colorful queer complexity, we must continue onward with our journey. It is time to return to Chicago and to walk the streets of this great city once again. Our consideration of the sixth and seventh trends must necessarily end in this chapter since the rest of our travels will be limited to this one big city. Of course, this does not mean that we have learned everything there is to know about medium- and small-sized cities, the suburbs, and rural areas, but alas, there is only so much we can accomplish in one book. In the first part, we carefully considered the question of why gayborhoods are changing—and from many different angles. In the second part of our journey, which we began in this chapter and will continue in the next two, we will try to understand how Boystown can retain its queer character, how an increasing presence of straights affects this possibility, and how different types of sexual minorities perceive the cultural significance of gayborhoods in Chicago. On our last stop, we will explore how entire communities and also specific groups migrate in ways that expand, evolve, and indeed reinvent the very meaning and material expressions of gay neighborhoods.

5

Resonance

Gayborhoods are indeed changing. Some of us have experienced this firsthand, and now many more can appreciate it as a result of all the people we have met in this book. These residents tell us that being gay or lesbian today is not all that different from being straight. Sexual orientation is declining in its significance, they say, and it does not always affect their everyday life. Post-gays feel "ethnically straight," and they assume that they can live almost anywhere in the city, since all of it resembles a gayborhood of sorts. They, along with particular groups like same-sex parents and teenagers, reject visible gayborhoods on the grounds that they prefer a more sexually integrated lifestyle, and because they do not let sexual orientation define their core sense of self.

Although this worldview rings true for many gays and lesbians, we have added layer after layer of complexity to it by identifying several surprising trends that suggest gayborhoods will persist in the present and live on into the future. Our task in the next two chapters is to travel across the cultural archipelagos of Chicago, these queer geographies that are thriving on its streets, to better appreciate why they continue to resonate deeply for those who live in them and for those who seek them out. Here, we will reconsider the role of existing gayborhoods as safe harbors and think about how they can retain their cultural and institutional character despite the arrival of more straight newcomers.

WE STILL NEED THE GHETTO

Social support for gay and lesbian issues and the perceived moral acceptability of their relationships among heterosexuals have increased rapidly in recent years, as we know, but what this means on the ground is less obvious. Although Americans are more tolerant of gay people in general, one study, using nationally representative survey data from a Gallup poll, found that more than a quarter of Americans still prefer to not have them as their neighbors (figure 5.1). This percentage has decreased over time, but 27 percent as late as the year 2006 is significant. The number is higher for sexual minorities than it is for Muslims, immigrants, or foreign workers.[1] A gay man in Boystown summarized the lesson for us—acceptance has limits—when he noted that societal support for homosexuality "does not mean it's accepted universally." If the prediction that sociologists Manuel Castells and Karen Murphy made back in 1982 holds true—"as long as gays are insulted, beaten, and killed because of whom they love, . . . they [will] still need the ghetto"[2]— then the persistence of social intolerance will preserve our need for gay neighborhoods. As we again walk the streets of Chicago, we will discover that post-gay does not mean that gays and lesbians are immune from bigotry and bias. Gayborhoods resonate as a refuge for them in a world that many still perceive as unsafe.

We often assume a narrative of progress when we think and talk about queer lives. But several Chicagoans questioned such an

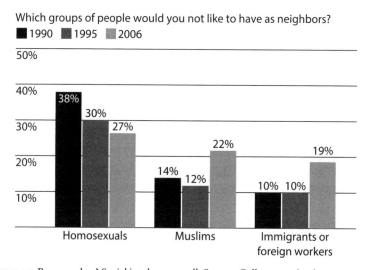

FIGURE 5.1 Be my gaybor? Social intolerance poll. Source: Gallup organization.

assumption. A gay male attorney in Andersonville, for example, wondered whether the world will ever be truly safe:

> There's always going to be bigots and homophobes in the world, and they're always going to have really loud voices. And people who are in minority groups are always going to perceive that lots of people are discriminating against them, even if they're not. Sometimes, when somebody slights us we think, "Is that because we're gay?" Probably not. It's more like the perception by gays that the world is out to get them or that there are people out there who are homophobic, which is going to cause them to want to go to places where they feel safe.

A Boystown gay man agreed that perceptions of danger may be unfounded, but this mattered less than the effects of those perceptions: "Those who've been tormented or rejected come to gay enclaves. They always have, and they always will." The notion that gayborhoods are dwindling presumes a level of acceptance, safety, and comfort that some residents reject and that others argue will never come to pass.

Where we choose to live is a personal and intimate decision. And like all of our most important deliberations in life, the perceptions that guide us are often as important as the external "facts" of the matter. The same is true for gay people. What matters to them, more than opinion polls that show increasing societal acceptance, is the intangible feeling "that lots of people are discriminating against them, even if they're not." This is what sociologists call the Thomas Theorem: "If men define situations as real, they are real in their consequences."[3] Perceptions affect our decisions about where to live, as a gay man in Andersonville told me: "As people come out, there's a tendency to want to live where there are a lot of gays, which means there are always going to be little enclaves or neighborhoods that are predominately gay. It's like their little safe harbors. Whether or not they're needed, I think the perception will be that they are needed." A gay man in Boystown agreed: "The central driving feature [for why gayborhoods exist] is that a lot of LGBT people see it as a refuge. And as long as it's perceived that way, people will still come there and live there. The perception's more important than what's probably becoming the reality." Antigay bias, both real and perceived, will sustain a need for gay neighborhoods, regardless of whether sexual minorities ever achieve full equality.

Many gays and lesbians wonder about the right balance between inclusion and straight dominance in the gayborhood. Austin and Nate, pseudonyms for a male couple in Andersonville, reflected on how this has changed in recent years. "Straights moving into gay neighborhoods isn't happening at the same rate that the world is accepting us as being a normal, natural part of the human race," Austin said. "So what if the neighborhood de-gays?" I asked them. Nate answered, "If we don't have a place to call a haven, then there's really no way that any of that's going to get any better. Someone who has been kicked out of their home because they're gay, they're sixteen years old, they need the Center on Halsted. If they don't have it or if it doesn't really exist anymore because that's no longer a gay neighborhood, then what's this kid going to do?" Austin chimed in again: "Everybody's in favor of the idea of complete inclusion, but society isn't ready for that yet." These "generalized beliefs," sociologist Neil Smelser might say, are "akin to magical beliefs" that provide catharsis and ease the social stresses associated with being a sexual minority.[4] Knowing that you have a safe space to go to, regardless of whether the world is statistically safer, allows many gays and lesbians to exhale in relief. That is its magic.

Many other residents also struggle with the ratio of gay-to-straight in the gayborhood. An Andersonville gay man explained, "People can live where they want to live. The rational side of me knows that. But there are so few areas in the world where gay people can live openly and walk down the street hand in hand. I'm a little bit of a separatist: 'Go live in your own neighborhood. Let us have our neighborhood.' We have so few areas." Said another, "I like my community of gay people. I'm not hostile to straight people. But I wish they would go live someplace else. Some famous artist [Giuseppe Verdi] said, 'You may have the universe if I may have Italy.' Let us have our little island. I just want our little tiny piece of space in the sea of hostile territory." An Andersonville lesbian shared the sentiment: "There are two neighborhoods that are truly queer-friendly, but then there are, let's say, ninety-eight communities that are straight-friendly and not queer-friendly. Why do you want to take away the two pieces from me?" Her partner added, "If ninety-eight percent of Chicago is straight, you can live in the ninety-eight percent. Don't come into the two little corners of my universe." A paradox unfolded as her partner asked, "But do you really want that? Do you only want two little communities that you feel comfortable in, or do you really want to live in the hundred percent? You're stuck between a rock and a hard place. You want to be open to people of all sorts, but you want your own space too."

Perceptions matter, but so does the legislative landscape. "It's still legal, on the federal level, to discriminate against people because they're gay," cautioned a gay male attorney in Andersonville. This discrimination will prevent full integration. "So, I wouldn't expect the city of Chicago to be completely integrated when it's still part of our society," he continued. Gayborhoods will persist "until that's gone, until people are treated equally and feel that they're being treated equally at all levels." A lesbian in Andersonville said that "in a perfect world, we shouldn't have to have Boystown, Girlstown, Hispanic, and African American communities, but we just do until things improve." The world is imperfect, and it probably always will be, regardless of changing laws and societal advances. "The social stigma is still there," a Boystown gay man noted. Another added, "These neighborhoods exist because we're still a community that suffers from discrimination."

Straights will always outnumber gays, and the world will never be rid of homophobia—any more than it will be of racism and sexism. It is not surprising, therefore, that many gay and lesbian residents feel territorial about "our little tiny piece of space." The sea change in attitudes toward sexual minorities comes in no small part from their growing visibility. The two reinforce each other: acceptance makes it easier for gay people to come out, and seeing more openly gay men and lesbians forces heterosexuals to think about the discrimination that their friends, family members, colleagues, and neighbors must endure. Sexual integration and gayborhood dilution threaten to unravel this relationship—and arguably before we as a society have reached a point beyond which additional visibility no longer promotes further acceptance. When straights move into a gayborhood, their presence changes the balance of who is in the majority, and who is in the minority. This has consequences, not just for feelings of safety, community, and acceptance, but also for how power is distributed, how groups are represented, public opinions, and the capacity of minorities to preserve their unique culture.

Even if the US government overturned all its discriminatory laws, the sheer inertia of human habits is painfully slow to change. Our individual biases, and the institutions that we mold along them, maintain social inequalities. Consider the notion of "Driving While Black (DWB)"; persistent police brutality; racial profiling; the prevalence of hate crimes based on race, ethnicity, and religion; or the epidemic of rape and how difficult it is for women to prosecute their perpetrator. In a similar vein, Chicago residents assert that homophobia, in its many vicious forms, is alive and well. Some remarked on verbal epithets, as did the following male couple in Boystown: "Remember that person who screamed 'faggot' at you on Saturday?" His partner sighed, "Yeah. They were slowly driving the car to the Cubs game, and they're like, 'You faggots!'" The memory compelled the first man to lament, "There's always the fear that if a straight guy finds out that you're gay, he's going to beat you up, which a lot of gay men have to live with growing up." Another gay man in Boystown offered a similar sentiment about the omnipresence of threat and fear: "We always live in fear of being gay-bashed, outed, stigmatized. As long as that fear's out there, we'll want to form our own place where we can feel safe. Hence, the gayborhood." Sometimes an encounter is indirect but no less menacing. One gay man was walking down the street in Boystown when he passed a woman on the sidewalk who he overheard say, "God, you see fags everywhere in this neighborhood." That the sight of gay men walking down the street in a gayborhood elicits a remark at all—let alone such an audibly homophobic one—bespeaks the mentality of some straights, even in an area that is presumably a safe space for sexual minorities.

Straight residents shared discomforting stories of their own. A woman in Boystown described the "cultural shock" that her friends from the suburbs feel when they visit her: "I have conversations with people from the suburbs who have a completely different view of the world just because they live in the suburbs. When I'm having conversations with them about where I live, that [the neighborhood's gay identity] will inevitability come up. Most of the people that I'm friends with are straight, and they don't really understand a gay lifestyle and automatically judge it. It's a cultural shock." Another woman added, "When I say I live in Boystown, I've gotten a few chuckles, almost like they were uncomfortable." The malaise that the informal name of the neighborhood elicits among some straights, and their nervous laughter, suggests a tangle of conflicting emotions. Some straight people are anxious about the very idea of living beside gay people or socializing in the same neighborhood as they do.

There are more extreme examples. A married straight couple, Wendy and Aaron, shared an unbelievable story with me: "Two guys moved next door to us," Wendy began. "They're heterosexual, and when they found out that a gay man had formerly lived in their bedroom, they asked us, 'What can we do? Can we bleach the walls?' They were such homophobes." This convinced her that gays and lesbians still need a safe space like Boystown: "Even though you wish there wasn't a need for these enclaves, there is a need because you still have someone acting like there's some kind of contamination in his space because a gay man lived there." Aaron had friends who would "go down Halsted [Street] and pick fights and go and try to beat up [gay] people." After he revealed this, Wendy opened up a little more too: "I've had people in my family who would fear bringing their child into a gay space because something's going to happen. I have an aunt, who is a conservative Christian, who told me that her church was teaching that gay couples want to adopt children because they want to molest them." The more relaxed that she became in our conversation, the more personal and unsettling became her stories: "I was raised in a Catholic family, and if I hugged a gay man, my mamma made me go home and take a shower. She literally made me. She said that I could get AIDS like that. I almost want to cry just telling you that because it's so abusive and cruel to teach a child that." Those days are long gone for Wendy, but the effects linger. She maintains that "there is a need" for Boystown today, even if she, as a heterosexual person, creates a contradiction by living there.

Conflicts in Boystown often revolve around Cubs baseball games. A straight woman said that she was "most aware" of tensions

FIGURE 5.2 World's largest gay bar. © Jeff Michel, 2014.

between gays and straights right "after Cubs games when a lot of drunk frat boys come into the neighborhood and start making fun of people. I hate that these are the straight people who come to this neighborhood." A straight man described a culture of homophobia that baseball games perpetuate in Chicago. "You see guys selling T-shirts" before a game, he began. "When you go down to the South Side [where the White Sox have their home field], they have shirts that say, 'Wrigley Field: World's Largest Gay Bar.' And the reason is because the field is right next to Boystown" (figure 5.2).[5] He confessed with regret that a friend shared this homophobic attitude: "We've got a friend who is very adamant that 'Hey, if I'm coming up to your neighborhood, we're not going to Boystown.'" He recounted one story after another about "straight couples—it's always the guys who say, 'Hey, we don't want to go into Boystown'—even when they come up with their wives and girlfriends." Admittedly, some of these tensions are with people who may not live in the neighborhood, but they are an important part of what it means for the gayborhood to integrate with straights. I thanked him for his candidness, since those are precisely the people who would reject my request for an interview. After I said this, he disclosed yet another troubling episode:

> We were out with a group, and we went to a bar that one of the guys thought was in Boystown just based on the fact that he didn't see enough women. The next day, he was like, "How dare you let me go out in Boystown? How could you do that to me?" He was pretty upset about it, and the funny part was that we weren't at a bar in Boystown. And he didn't believe me. And when I told him, "No, no, no. This is where you went," he said, "No, no, no, you're just trying to make me feel better. We went out in Boystown. How could you do that to me?"

"Post-gay" is a useful concept that can help us understand broad cultural shifts. People's lived experiences, however, are more complex than any one term like this can possibly capture. Similar to the chuckles we heard earlier, here again we find that subtle forms of bias have deep roots in the ground.

Urban cultures are crafted block by block. This is why we should not think about gay neighborhoods in isolation from the others that surround them. By default, all gayborhoods are bordered by straight areas. When we observe life at those fuzzy border zones, as we have just done with conflicts surrounding baseball games at Wrigley Field, we can appreciate why gayborhoods still matter. A straight woman told me that she often notices that two men who are holding hands as they walk through Boystown "will want to let go" once they get to the intersection of Clark Street, which is where the Cubs ballpark is located. I myself have done the same thing. The adjustment feels necessary, despite the fact that Clark Street is just one short block west of Halsted Street, the gay ground zero of Boystown. Another straight woman observed this as well when she was with her friends. She asked the men why they stopped holding hands. "It makes straight people feel uncomfortable," they said. Some gays and lesbians will not hold hands at all for this reason, and they certainly will not kiss beyond the boundaries of whatever they feel is the safe zone of the gayborhood. Self-consciousness about such basic acts of human intimacy speaks volumes about the continued need for the safe space that gay neighborhoods provide. It also illustrates how one city block can represent vastly different social worlds.

The stories that circulate about these kinds of everyday acts leave behind psychological scars. "That really affects how we choose to live our lives, where we want to live," an Andersonville gay man told me. "Going through that process, you feel like an outsider. And you never want to feel that again. The gayborhood represents that common thread. It allows us to never feel like we're the outsider . . . When you dig down deep, that kind of psychological struggle that we all went through governs a lot of what we do and where we live." A shared history of struggle bonds some gays and lesbians together, and it grounds them in a symbolically charged place in the city. Their feelings are not easily shaken, regardless of the era in which we are living, regardless of the broader cultural shifts that are happening today, and regardless of the undeniable presence of gay people in everything from schools to reality television to professional sports.

Our conversation so far animates the living, breathing benefits of the gayborhood, and it offers several compelling reasons why sexual minorities still need them as a safe haven. First, while acceptance is increasing in a post-gay era, it has some very real limits. Antigay bigotry still exists. Gay people sometimes experience that bigotry firsthand, when they are called a "faggot" or "dyke" on the streets, while at other times it is a vague yet omnipresent fear. Second, discrimination takes many forms, both de jure and de facto, which regenerates the importance of a sanctuary, despite the legal and cultural advancements that we are living through today. Third, many gays and lesbians believe that individual straights are moving into the gayborhood at a faster rate than society is accepting them. This is why the latter is an unpersuasive reason to conclude that we no longer need gay neighborhoods. And finally, the cumulative life experiences and collective memories of being a sexual minority can leave behind emotional wounds, even if life today is better than it was once before. All of these mean that the gayborhood will remain a potent and resonant symbol of the lives, communities, and cultures of sexual minorities.

In addition to these general trends, three particular groups within the lesbian, gay, bisexual, and transgender umbrella also demonstrate why existing gayborhoods will remain as a refuge. To begin our conversation, recall Steve Seidman's proclamation that gay life in the Western world today is "beyond the closet." But we must ask: Beyond the closet *for whom?* Controversies surrounding Chicago's grand LGBT community center illustrate some of the difficulties that we may encounter if we generalize societal change for all queer people. In 2007, the city opened the Center on Halsted, a 175,000-square-foot building, financed by a $20 million capital campaign, that is "not your average LGBT center," observed David Sokol in his article for the *Advocate*. What kind of center is it then? And whom does it serve? The answers are implicit yet quintessentially post-gay: the Center, like its name tells us, is *on* Halsted, the street that comprises the residential and commercial heart of Boystown. The Center is thus read as gay by its association with this street. Of course, not everyone who lives in the neighborhood or on this one street is gay or lesbian, and the publicity surrounding the opening of the Center strategically used this to advance an assimilationist agenda: "An Equal-Opportunity Hangout: The Center on Halsted to Welcome Gays and Lesbians—and Everyone Else," ran a headline in the *Chicago Sun-Times*. Journalist Mike Thomas quoted the openly gay alderman Tom Tunney: "This thing is expensive to build and expensive to operate . . . I'd be pretty upset if it wasn't made available to everybody." Thomas also quoted then executive director Robin Burr, who said, "Nearly every person I've walked through this building—gay, straight—they all want to come and be here." One message is that sexuality is either irrelevant or taken for granted; it does not need to be articulated or expressed, apparently not even in the name of an LGBT community center.[6]

During my interviews in the summer of 2010, several residents remarked on an influx of teenagers—and particularly youth of color and transyouth—who were spending more time in the neighborhood to use the Center's services. As I mentioned earlier, I was not able to speak with any of these young people. University-based ethics boards have special requirements, like written permission from a parent or guardian, to protect minors who are under the age of eighteen. This presents a challenge for many young people. To learn secondhand about their experiences, I spoke with representatives of nonprofit organizations who work with these groups. Joe Hollendoner, the twenty-nine-year-old director of the Broadway Youth Center (BYC), was one such person with whom I chatted for quite a while. "What we still see is that young people are being bullied based on perceived gender identity and expression, and perceived sexual orientation, so I don't think there is this harmonious experience that we fantasize about," he said. "Young people definitely have a different experience in high school and elementary school than even my generation did, and certainly other generations, but violence still disproportionately occurs to people because of sexual orientation and gender identity." He explained that these young people still seek safety:

> If you think about the schools that have gay-straight alliances, those are likely schools that are in higher socioeconomic status areas or that are in neighborhoods where there are lots of LGBT families. Those students who come from lower socioeconomic status schools or where there aren't a lot of out visible LGBT families are clamoring for that support, and they don't know where to go for it. And so again, they're coming here. Lots of these young people maybe don't have those gay-straight alliances in their high schools or maybe don't go to high school [and] are coming to this neighborhood because they're reporting that their home communities are less safe than here. If LGBT young people were safer in their home communities, I think they wouldn't need a go-to destination in this way.

Hollendoner seldom sees LGBT young adults who are white "because they have their social support through their GSA [gay-straight alliance], they have MySpace, their Facebook, those other means. There's a certain level of privilege that community has, whereas folks who have lower socioeconomic status are really just fighting to survive." Gayborhoods still resonate for these young people of color, many of whom are African American and some of whom are also transgender. "Boystown is where they target as being the LGBT neighborhood," he said. It is a beacon, a haven, a safe space for these kids. "That's where they go for acceptance around their sexual orientation and gender identity." For them, "to be gay means to go to this community." While many of these kids are too young to get into the bars, they still come to "bear witness to it" and "be connected to the energy and diversity and the experience of Halsted Street."

Toward the end of our conversation, Hollendoner guided me through a thought experiment about what it is like to be closeted and to fear for your life:

> Imagine being so closeted on a daily basis and having a social circle of friends who are in the same boat you are of being so closeted because they're afraid for their lives, literally, and that the only place they can go is Lakeview. That's going to get romanced in a way that I can't even comprehend. I remember being a gay youth from the south suburbs and being like, "Oh my god, here I am in Boystown" and buying the ridiculous rainbow necklace that all of us have to buy because it's just part of the coming-out process, and everything rainbow and everything gay. I wasn't nearly at risk for violence or harassment as these young people who are on the South [a predominately black area] or West Side [a predominately Hispanic area] or further North Side of Chicago [which has a large concentration of different racial groups]. I think that's something really neat that Lakeview offers, that this is one neighborhood where different types of youth interact and are able to build community. I see the beauty of that in our waiting room, where this young transwoman of color can sit next to this white girl from Loyola University, and they have dialogue. How cool is that? Where else could that happen? It's happening here at BYC, but it's happening here because we're located in Lakeview.

The presence of these young people of color on the streets of Boystown is not without problems. Hollendoner continued, "Even though they may be experiencing violence and profiling here in this neighborhood, they're willing to deal with that profiling and that violence because the experience of being closeted in their home communities is worse, or the violence that they've experienced for being out in their neighborhood is much worse." They travel to Boystown to benefit from social services that are unavailable in their home neighborhoods and for the socializing opportunities that it makes possible.

Many public officials echoed Hollendoner's observations. A professor at a nearby university remarked on the magnetism of Boystown:

> I think for queer youth across the city, this neighborhood has become more of a destination than it had been . . . Since the opening of the Center, there are a lot of people that come to the neighborhood, queer people, queer youth particularly, that come to this neighborhood to be gay, and that's very visible in a way that it wasn't before the Center opened. Queer youth of color, often transyouth, are drawn to the Center because it's there; they go to their programs. Sometimes they're too young to go into the bars, so they end up on the streets or going in and out of businesses. If a gay neighborhood's going to mean anything, if you are going to have a community center to mark it, then this means it's succeeding and actually drawing people from all over the city to come here so that they can affirm their identity.

Tico Valle, who is the director of the Center on Halsted, offered information on the populations that they serve: "We see two hundred young people per week who come to us, about fifty a day, and thirty percent are homeless. When you look at the demographics on where they come from, it's thirty-five percent from the neighborhood, and thirty-five percent from the South Side. So it's a mix of individuals that do come because of the Center, but it's also individuals who are coming because it's a safe neighborhood. It's where the gay community is." The bustling Center and its well-used services demonstrate that while sexuality may be less central for some youth as they come of age, for other teenagers, being gay or trans remains crucial to their identity—and just as fraught as it was in previous eras.

Residents, like the following gay man in Boystown, expressed something similar: "Other parts of the city are not as accepting of their gays, so those gays come up here." Experiences of violence and discrimination, along with being closeted in their home communities, loom large for many young queers of color. They travel to Boystown because they feel safer there, as another gay man said: "The

Center on Halsted has done a tremendous job of trying to provide a space for young, black, gay youth that don't have a space in their own neighborhoods." Straight residents also recognize this role of the Center and the gayborhood. One woman in Boystown commented, "It's almost like a support group, having that community there for them. It's nice to be able to come in from the West Loop or the South Side, to be able to come up here and feel comfortable in this environment." A man added, "There are some times when we notice that there's a big group of young, black ladyboys that congregate here. You don't necessarily see them during the day. Ever. So, our assumption is that they live where they live, and that this is their opportunity on weekends to go out and let loose. This is the place for them to congregate and get together." In these examples, it is not current or former residents who affirm the relevance and resonance of Boystown but young queer visitors who travel to the neighborhood for the services that are anchored there or simply to revel in their own otherwise disguised identities.

Many straight residents struggled with the influx of these queer youth of color into Boystown. Consider the following statement from one woman: "It brings people from the South Side, for example, like transgender or gay people who understandably cannot even hang out or let alone express themselves in their neighborhoods. And so they come here. And that's certainly fine by us, but if that makes me feel unsafe, then that's the downside of it. It's not because they happen to be gay or transgendered. It's just that they come from a different neighborhood; that they are more violent." For her to say that she feels "unsafe," to characterize these young people as "violent," and to define their home as "a different neighborhood" are all expressions, I think, of a subtle racism that is inflected with homophobia. A gay man in Andersonville summarized what he thought was the general response by straights to black bodies in Boystown:

I've heard anecdotally or read a few news stories about some complaints that hit me pretty hard. One in particular was about straight people complaining that a congregation of black men, "scary-looking" young black men [were hanging out] on the corners in Boystown. Well, a limited amount of research revealed that these were African

American youth coming from all over the city to go to programs at the Center on Halsted who were then hanging out afterward. So, these are gay, young black men who aren't comfortable in their own neighborhoods who congregate in Boystown because it's the safe place to hang out together. They're not going to get shot, and they can be flamboyant, but the straight people were complaining. Come on, now.

To explore this kerfuffle, we can also ask public officials for their response. Hollendoner from the BYC, who we met earlier, tried to change the causal direction: "I'd like to reframe the conversation. Young people aren't in the neighborhood because we're here [all the social service organizations]. We're in the neighborhood because young people are here. Historically, lots of service organizations developed in this neighborhood in response to the fact that there were youth in need who were coming to this neighborhood." That young people flock to Boystown despite the inflammatory ways in which they are racially profiled speaks volumes about the ineffaceable value of safe spaces for them. Hollendoner continued, "These young people are still coming to the neighborhood and still hanging out in the neighborhood because they're incredibly resilient and just beautiful and amazing in that way, that despite the fact that police are profiling, despite the fact that neighborhood groups or block clubs are getting together in meetings to talk specifically about 'How do we eliminate the youth on Halsted?,' these youth are coming and adding to the beauty of this neighborhood." Situations like this also provoke "internalized racism" for residents, Hollendoner says, when "they see large groups of young people of color congregating on the street." Some residents say that they feel "unsafe" as a result. His mention of "internal" racism indicates that it is not only straights who struggle with the presence of queer youth of color on the streets; some gays and lesbians also hold biased views. After all, gays and straights share the same street corners in this "gentrified community."

Hollendoner was not convinced that these kids were committing any crimes. "I don't think that's necessarily true," he said. "Now, that's not to say that these young people that we serve are always angels out on the street. I know they're loud. I know they're rowdy. But I don't think that these young people hanging out on the street corners is necessarily a criminal act, and I think that oftentimes people want to peg what those young people are doing as a criminal act when it's actually not." Many residents were ambivalent about their presence. They were concerned about their own personal safety, especially at night, yet they also wanted to promote the neighborhood as a diverse place. But Tico Valle, the director at the Center on Halsted, questioned what residents really mean by "diversity":

> Some people say they're very respectful and welcoming of diverse people, but when you drill down, what does that mean for them? Let's talk about the challenges of our community welcoming trans, homeless, black males to Halsted Street. I would say that every single person who would complain about that would be saying that they respect diversity, and they're not bigots. But yet, they would say they don't want those trans, homeless, black individuals on the street. And quote-unquote, they have said that "They should go back to their neighborhoods." I often say that if the individuals were white young men, it would not be an issue . . . But it isn't acceptable if a trans, homeless, black male is standing on the sidewalks minding his business.

The post-gay impulse to suppress differences between gays and straights is more difficult when we factor race and gender variance into the urban mix. This is why diversity, as an idea that we value and promote in our neighborhoods, misaligns with how we experience it on the streets.

Transgender individuals are a second group for whom existing gayborhoods remain culturally compelling. A lesbian in Boystown pointedly asked me, "And transfolk? Where are they?" She pushed me to broaden my own perspective from gayborhoods to transneighborhoods: "We never talk about transneighborhoods. And I don't think that's the gayborhood. Transfolk never really get considered anywhere." She is right. As little as we know about sexuality and the city, we know much less about transgender people and their relationship with cities. In one study, urban planning scholar Petra Doan found that "the gendered nature of these spaces," or the ways in which gayborhoods enforce traditional norms of what it means to be a man or a woman, "results in continued high levels of harassment and violence for this [transgender] population." She argues that gayborhoods erase the lives of transpeople as a result:

> Today in most overtly gay spaces there is little to no gender queerness or any indication that such variance is tolerated. Even in San Francisco's Castro District, often considered the archetype of queer space, the streets are filled with well-muscled men and even the window displays are masculinely gendered. Other spaces such as Chicago's Boys Town [*sic*] use . . . "phallic rimming" of the main street (North Halsted St.) with metallic pillars topped by rainbow-colored rings. Both through its name and in its most visible symbols this area is also clearly masculinized. Philadelphia's queer space uses a similarly masculinist play on words, to call itself the Gayborhood.[7]

Doan surveyed 149 transgender people, both male-to-female and female-to-male, to learn about their experiences in gayborhoods.[8] Thirty-three percent of her sample reported "hostile stares," 22 percent experienced "hostile comments," and 17 percent described instances of "physical harassment." She also asked respondents "how safe" they felt their city was for GLB and transpeople, respectively. Table 5.1 shows her results. Minority group members can sometimes have an exaggerated sense of how much easier their life would be if they were in the majority. It is telling, in this regard, that a third of Doan's transrespondents who lived in a city with a gayborhood felt that the area was either unsafe or tolerable, at best, for lesbian, gay male, and bisexual residents. Nearly half felt that the gayborhood was unsafe or tolerable for transgender people. Thus, while we still need gayborhoods as safe harbors, transpeople do not perceive even these areas as necessarily all that safe.

Gays and lesbians who hail from smaller communities that satellite Chicago comprise the final group for us to meet. A gay man in Boystown argued that big-city gayborhoods across the country will remain meaningful for such people: "I want to defend Boystown. I still see, to this day, the influx of gay youth from small towns around the Midwest to Chicago, just like in the South it's to Atlanta, just like in the Northeast it's to New York City. Every area has that big town that all the small-town kids move to after they graduate high school or college." A straight woman in Boystown agreed: "It's nice

TABLE 5.1 Perceptions of Safety among Transgender Residents

		City has a queer area?		
		No	Yes	Total
How safe is your city for gays, lesbians, and bisexuals?	Unsafe	14 (16%)	1 (2%)	15
	Tolerable	47 (55%)	19 (31%)	66
	Safe	25 (29%)	41 (67%)	66
How safe is your city for transgender people?	Unsafe	18 (21%)	3 (5%)	21
	Tolerable	44 (52%)	26 (42%)	70
	Safe	23 (27%)	32 (53%)	55

Source: Doan (2007:66).

for people who come from smaller towns where homosexuality isn't accepted. If you're a guy from Topeka, and you want to move to Chicago, and you're in the closet, and you don't want to tell your family, Boystown is a great place to go to be free." Her comment makes sense only if we assume that the family back in Topeka does not know where in the city he moves, or that they are unaware that Boystown is a gay district. Nevertheless, the wisdom is that those who live in smaller communities sometimes seek "to get thee to a big city," to borrow the title of an article that anthropologist Kath Weston wrote, where there is an identifiable gayborhood.[9]

A city is a beacon of tolerance for some people who live in the suburbs or smaller towns.[10] A gay man in Boystown explained, "That's what we forget: in San Francisco, New York, Boston, and wherever in these big cities, people are tolerant or accepting. The problem is that most of America is smaller communities and less progressive towns . . . And the problem is that that's where it's too dangerous [to be out], and it's still shameful or quiet or closeted. It's nice to look at the big cities and say, 'Yeah, gayborhoods are passé.' Well, maybe in San Francisco. But not in Lander, Wyoming. We just ignore all these states as flyover."

Consider next the story of a sheltered, suburban lesbian for whom the mere presence of a place called Boystown, and another area in Chicago that locals affectionately called Girlstown (which we know as Andersonville), helped her to come out of the closet. She had a "sudden awakening that I was a lesbian," after which she promptly "broke off the engagement with my fiancé, who was a man." She was afraid that she "didn't know anyone who was gay" and so she did what many in her situation would do next:

> I just went on the Internet, and I researched and researched. I was a teacher at the time, an art teacher. And I had remembered that there was a student of mine who had talked about a place called Boystown in Chicago. I had no clue about any of this; I was so secluded from all this. And so she told me about Boystown, and then she said something about a Girlstown. So I went on the Internet, and I found out where Boystown was, and I would go down to Boystown. I think I went to two bars, and finally something came up that there were a lot of lesbians in Andersonville. I was in awe, as far as like, "Wow, they're everywhere." It was just amazing to me. It was sensory overload. It was exciting. Then I eventually moved there.

We assume big cities and small towns offer very different lifestyle options. The former are tolerant places, we think, while the latter are less so. This is why some people call smaller, especially rural areas "flyover country."[11] As we saw in chapter 4, however, unexpected clusters are emerging in these areas.

To conclude this section, let us sit for a little while with a thirty-four-year-old masculinely self-presenting white lesbian who lives in Andersonville and a twenty-one-year-old white gay man from Boystown. For them, finding a way to the gayborhood was a matter of life or death. Carolyn (a pseudonym) moved to Andersonville four years ago from a small town in upstate New York. "No gay people lived where I lived. I didn't know any gay people. I was the only gay person I knew," she told me. Carolyn experienced "different scary events surrounding my sexuality where I lived," which is why she desperately wanted to move to Chicago. "Just going to the grocery store, I would be coming out with my stuff and getting in my car. And all these young guys would be like, 'Fucking faggot.' And they'd chase me in my car, and I'd be like, 'Okay, I need to find somewhere I can pull in that's safe, and then they'll leave me alone. I can't go home yet, because I don't want them to know where I live.'" Her story is an agonizing reminder of the isolation that some queer people feel. Gayborhoods in major urban centers enable them to "peel off that armor" they wear in a heterosexual and cisgender world.[12] Her thoughts are worth repeating at length:

> I think we need our own little areas where we don't have to worry. There's always a constant worry in the back of our minds [she and her partner's] when we're not in a gay neighborhood. If we're at a restaurant and not in a gay neighborhood, and I have to go to the bathroom, am I going to get told, "Sir, you're going into the wrong restroom?" In gay neighborhoods, I never worry about that. If I'm holding Katie's hand [a pseudonym], is there going to be a comment? Is there going to be a look? In gay neighborhoods, I don't even think about that. So many little things like that. When we're not in Andersonville, Katie and I don't hold hands. We're very conscious of it. I think it's so important to have these places where we can peel off that armor for a little bit and just relax and just be.
>
> So, gay neighborhoods are important, especially for people like myself and Katie that have been victims of discrimination because of our sexuality. Where I'm from, I had garbage thrown at me, I've been chased with lead pipes, I've been called so many names, things were thrown at my car. And I can't hide. I'm a lesbian, and I just can't hide it. Gay neighborhoods offer some sense of safety for somebody that has experienced those things. At least here I can relax and breathe and not be so hypervigilant.

Now let us meet Brian, a pseudonym for a young gay man who lives in Boystown. He moved to the city less than a year ago from a small town in Missouri where "there aren't any openly gay people." His story is also heartbreaking:

> People used to smash my mailbox. I came home one day, and it was on fire. And people used to write "fag" on my car, and I would have to

wash it off because I didn't want my parents to see it because I wasn't out to them . . . I lived on a farm, and I had livestock. People would talk about shooting my livestock or poisoning them. It's nice to be somewhere where you don't have to deal with that all the time.

I graduated high school with twenty-nine people, and that's made up of three different towns . . . It's a really poor community . . . Everyone was white in my school. Everyone was Southern Baptist. There were no gay people. You could call someone a "fag," and it's not a big deal. The administration thinks being gay is gross.

When I came out, I became this gossip. People were talking about it; it would be dinner conversation. And that it's gross. My best friend, she lived with her aunt who was her guardian. Her aunt told her, "Don't ever drink out of Brian's glass or share anything with him because you'll get AIDS."

One of my friends was visiting from Missouri yesterday, and he's from a really small town, too. It's a culture shock to go into a neighborhood like this, because where we live, you don't see people holding hands. Guys do not hold hands walking down the street. If you do, you might get jumped, or somebody's going to say something or throw something at you, and it's not safe to do. But here, if somebody says something to you, there are a lot of gay people around, so I feel protected. When you're suddenly surrounded by so many people that are all gay, you feel like, "Maybe this is okay." You're not just this odd one out. It makes us feel better about ourselves, I guess.

I hated living in Missouri. I never go back and visit my family. I'm just really unhappy there. Gay people should move to cities. There are a lot of other gay people there. Once you find out there's a gay neighborhood, you're like, "Wow, I can go there, and I'll be around other gay people, and I'll feel safe." And that's really the feeling that I have whenever I'm in Boystown.

The detailed profiles of Carolyn and Brian help us to "dig down deep," as we heard before, where "that kind of psychological struggle" lies, every single day, for many gay, lesbian, bisexual, and transgender individuals. If you can identify with them from your own experiences or simply through their eyes, then you can better appreciate why gayborhoods are sacred sanctuaries. To say that they are life-affirming—and indeed life-giving—is not an exaggeration.

HOW TO SURVIVE IN A WORLD FILLED WITH FLUX

So far, we have articulated the role of gayborhoods as safe harbors. The many residents who we met meditated on the limits of acceptance, and in doing so they reaffirmed the importance of existing gayborhoods. By focusing the persistence of subtle and extreme forms of homophobia, however, they bracketed explicit comments about sexual integration. But this is an undeniable reality in gayborhoods, perhaps even to the point where we can take it for granted. Societal acceptance may have limits, but it is real and responsible for an assimilation of some sexual minorities into the mainstream. This normalization of gays and lesbians removes psychological roadblocks that once prevented straights from moving into the gayborhood in the numbers that they are today. In fact, these days you can always see straight people walking the rainbow-lined streets of Boystown. This creates a new and interesting perspective on a hard question about endurance. How can gayborhoods remain resonant for gays and lesbians as more straights move into them?

If gays and lesbians rejected gayborhoods as these straights moved into them year after year, we would expect places like Boystown and Andersonville to eventually lose their cultural significance as queer hubs. But this is hardly the case. A gay man in Boystown remarked about the past and the future, "They're going to be mixed neighborhoods. To some extent, they always have been." Boystown and Andersonville have never been exclusively queer, of course, and they never will be. To think so would be to commit what sociologists call an "ecological fallacy," or the mistaken assumption that everyone who lives in a gayborhood is gay. Nevertheless, "I don't think they're going to completely lose their gay character," he continued. "Boystown is still very meaningful, and Andersonville is still very meaningful for a significant number of people who care that those are areas identified as gay-friendly."

In explaining the enduring attraction of existing gayborhoods, several residents remarked that they allow people to explore and express their sexuality. The following gay man in Boystown endorsed such a psychological and performative view:

[Gayborhoods] create a space for people to explore sexuality, to explore what sexuality means, to explore how they display their sexuality in public. I think having spaces where we feel free to explore our sexuality is really critical. And I think even insofar as sexuality is psychological or is personal or is internal, figuring out what that means for myself requires having space to express it to others. It's through the process of expressing it that I can figure out what it means for me. And it's through the process of seeing other people express their sexuality that I can figure out more about what the range of sexualities is or more about my blind spots, both in my own sexuality, which maybe I haven't explored, and also my own consciousness of what is out there in the world.

It is because gayborhoods enable such explorations, expressions, and performances of sexuality that some people, like the following lesbian from Andersonville, speak of them in almost mythical terms: "Andersonville's not like a real place. It's kind of like a dreamland place. There's no other place in the city like it." It was not unusual to hear residents describe gay districts as a homeland, mecca, or utopia, a place at once real and imaginary. Another lesbian in Andersonville who recently moved to the city echoed, "I found it very transformative to live in a gay neighborhood and feel comfortable holding [my girlfriend's] hand and seeing other people like us holding hands and having friends that are lesbian and gay, and being able to talk about gay issues that straight people don't necessarily totally get, where you could just say something and you don't even have to explain it or how you feel. The other person just knows. It's amazing." At the heart of these devotional sentiments is a communal affirmation that recasts the group in a spiritual light. Recall what journalist Joseph Coates, who we met earlier, said: "Our eroticism is the closest thing we have to what in the past was called a sacred spiritual life, and no one wants to be excommunicated from that church altogether."[13]

Gayborhoods also house anchor institutions, like certain businesses and organizations. These are the engines of community building, and they allow gayborhoods to resonate as queer spaces for residents and visitors alike.[14] Stephen Murray, recall, insists that the "existence of [such] distinctive facilities is more salient to the identification of a community—for both insiders and for others—than is residential segregation." Public figures affirmed this vision when I asked them what made Boystown a gay district. Sidetrack bar owner Art Johnson, for example, said that he could "remember the first time I saw Halsted referred to in the same sentence as Greenwich Village and Castro." It happened in the 1980s when "a few of us went out of our way to encourage other gay businesses to relocate there. And we were successful in that. We helped a number of businesses come to the street. Our sense was that we needed more gay businesses there." Today, Sidetrack anchors the Boystown gayborhood. "We began as an eight-hundred-square-foot place, and we're now over fourteen thousand. We've been there a long time, and we're a large presence on the street." Unabridged bookstore owner Ed Devereux agreed about the impact of institutions in anchoring a community: "Businesses anchor a neighborhood." Johnson's bar and Devereaux's bookstore promote a quasi-ethnic gay identity that is rooted in a specific part of the city. "They are an important part of anchoring the gay neighborhood and defining it in the same way that ethnic businesses would help define an ethnic neighborhood," Devereaux added.[15]

Control over real estate enables the permanence of institutional anchors. Devereaux offered a useful overview of migration in Chicago, which illustrates the importance of economic ownership:

> Historically, gays have pioneered. And they pioneered in this neighborhood in '78 and '79, '80. And I was part of that. We all helped the community become safer. We did a lot of renovations. And, contrary to other parts of our movement, gay business owners bought their property, so they weren't leased out, you know? I bought as early as '84. And now the real estate's worth more than the business. And Sidetrack's the same thing. If you look at the history of the migration of the gay community, they never owned that kind of real estate. I think that's why the roots here in Lakeview are still pretty deep. In Lakeview, people like myself own their properties and are committed to the community.

Property ownership is a major reason why gay businesses will continue to anchor the community in Boystown, despite residential flux, despite the arrival of nongay businesses, and despite escalating real estate values. Valle added, "One of the realities is that the community has moved from the Gold Coast to Diversey and now Lakeview and Andersonville. What happened in Lakeview [that did not happen before] was probably the laying of the foundation where a lot of LGBT individuals finally started buying homes and buying their businesses as opposed to renting. So, in Lakeview, there is a foundation and an anchor of LGBT owners."

As Valle and Devereaux distinguish the current phase of the gayborhood from its long history in Chicago, they imply a useful thought experiment. How would the current migration be different if gays and lesbians had *not* purchased their property? In the absence of ownership, the gay community of Boystown may have moved more completely, similar to what happened in prior transitions. Indeed, there are few archaeological indicators that gay and lesbian communities were once concentrated in Old Town or on the Gold Coast.[16] While another wave of residential reshuffling is actively transpiring, Boystown is economically anchored in a way that no other gayborhood was before. This will allow its cultural and institutional character to survive into the future.

Residents echoed this wisdom. A gay man in the neighborhood said, "There does need to be some sort of institutions identified with a community to really make it a gay neighborhood." Residential concentration is necessary but insufficient: "I think if there's a group of gay people that live someplace, I think you can have a gay community, but to really move to a neighborhood, I think there needs to be something more. In Boystown, you have this very strong institutional presence." He predicted that businesses would anchor the community despite a "residential drift": "Even though you have this very strong institutional presence, the residential presence is that a lot of gays have left Boystown. So, you sort of have a residential drift while there continues to be an institutional presence. So, in the institutional sense, Boystown will continue to be a gay neighborhood for a long time." This reminds us of what we heard in Oakland, which recall is "the largest major American city without a pink ghetto," even though many gays and lesbians live there. Oakland needs some queer anchors to color its urban landscape.

Some organizations, like the Center on Halsted, are especially powerful anchors. The Center provides a safe space for queer youth of color and transyouth, as we have seen, but it also anchors the community more broadly. "The gay and lesbian community center is an anchor space for that neighborhood," a Boystown lesbian told me. "It was key to keeping the neighborhood to its roots," despite the increasing presence of straight people. "The Center brought over two hundred jobs to the community," said Valle, and it also answered an anxious concern about the future of Boystown. "There was a question about whether the LGBT community was moving farther north," Valle explained, as part of a long historical pattern of northward migration and gayborhood reconstitution. "With the presence of the Center, it really became an anchor." Boystown is here to stay.

Women and Children First bookstore is a major institutional anchor in Andersonville. When I asked owner Linda Bubon when a lesbian identity first came together in Andersonville, she pointedly replied, "When we moved here." Jason Cox of the Andersonville Chamber of Commerce agreed: "When businesses like Women and Children First moved into the neighborhood, a migration followed." But Bubon admits, "It was not our intention to be a gay and lesbian bookstore." Instead, "it was our intention to serve women who were lesbians because they were women and because all women should be at home here. We were a feminist bookstore, and feminists care about all women." There is a special relationship between the bookstore and its patrons. "While I know many, many straight women who love the store and have been loyal customers over the years, there's something about the love and loyalty of women-who-love-women who love our business and know that there's this love for them there, too, that just kind of goes beyond. I think our lesbian customers know that we feel that way about them." Alex Papadopoulos confirmed the symbolic status of the bookstore: "The most important visual marking in Andersonville is Women and Children First, the bookstore, with its lavender awning," which "to us . . . would be kind of a lesbian family connotation." When I inquired about the meaning of the marking, he replied, "It's definitely a gay marking. It's a Girlstown marking."

The awning is to Andersonville, in other words, what the rainbow pylons are to Boystown.

Residential and commercial clusters both buffer urban change. Yet in the absence of the former, which is dwindling today, a strong institutional presence can still promote a vibrant queer culture. A gay man in Boystown said, "As long as those businesses are still here, that's a big thing that keeps the perception in people's head that Lakeview is still gay." That the institutions are grounded in a physical place adds a homelike quality to the area. I asked a gay man in Andersonville if it makes any difference to him whether he goes to a gay bar in Boystown or somewhere else in the city. He replied, "You want it to be an area, a land. You want to be attached to something. Take Italians, for example. It's not enough that there's an Italian restaurant that's over there . . . That doesn't feel like home. That feels different for me than saying, 'I'm in this area, an Italian area. I'm in the French area. I'm in the Greek area. I'm in the gay area.'" The culture of a group acquires materiality when it is located in an institutionally anchored, symbolically charged, and discrete physical space.

The Halsted strip in Boystown is one of the most concentrated nightlife, entertainment, and tourist districts in the country. Although gay and lesbian residents have become "much more dispersed and less concentrated," Boystown is "still a destination," remarked a local lesbian. "People come from all over the state," region, and even the country to check it out. While gays feel safer living in a wider number of neighborhoods—and they certainly are spreading out across the city—Chicago gays and those from the surrounding areas still flock to the Boystown strip as an entertainment hotspot. "It feels like it's becoming more of a destination, as opposed to a neighborhood for gay people to live," the same woman concluded. When I asked Maureen Martino, the executive director of the Lakeview East Chamber of Commerce, what makes Boystown gay, she similarly replied, "The business district. I think if you were to dig in to see what percentage of gays are still living in Lakeview East, you'd see more migration than you probably thought. When people think 'Boystown,' they're really thinking about an area where people go out. They're not really thinking that everybody is living here."

Being an entertainment and tourist destination will allow the gayborhood to survive, but it will feel very different than a residentially concentrated area. Thus, while the cultural and institutional character of Boystown will endure over the years, we probably will encounter a new tension in the future between the gayborhood as a destination, on the one hand, and the lived-in gayborhood on the other. Where you party at night is different than who you pass on the street during the day as you go about your daily routine.

Several residents made this distinction between residential and commercial concentration. During the course of our conversation, a gay man in Boystown asked me if I was interested in "where people live or where people congregate? There's a difference." "What is the difference?" I asked. He answered, "I think in the next ten years, we won't see areas where most gay people live." This sounded like a post-gay prediction to me. "I think we're going to be all spread out everywhere as people get bolder to make nongay neighborhoods more comfortable," he added, alluding to the expanding residential imagination among gays and lesbians that we explored in the first part of this book. But there was more to his story than this familiar mechanism. "Because the majority of the bars are here [in Boystown], this is the mecca of where you go to have drinks and party and all that stuff—and then you go home somewhere else," said another gay man who apparently equated the existence of a mecca with commercial anchors. "Boystown means where you go to play." A third predicted, "There will be gays and straights living together, but they'll be dispersed in more and more neighborhoods. And then there will be the strip," which will light up the cultural and institutional character of the neighborhood. A gay man in Andersonville offered an explanation for this divergence: "The cost-benefit analysis has shifted because the residential comfort is no longer an issue, but gay people still don't have many spaces to go to party and gather." It is this lasting need for a place to socialize with other gay people that will allow Boystown to survive.

This is the same pattern that major retailers follow. A gay man in Boystown explained:

> I know a lot of retailers [who] won't go to a certain place unless there's a gel of similar retailers. So, like, Banana Republic won't build a store

off in the middle of nowhere where there is no other clothing store or no other chain store. They actually want to be near other stores because it tends to bring people into those stores. That's why you have pockets throughout the city of little retail areas, not just because they're zoned for that. Over the long term, the strip of bars near Roscoe and Halsted have stayed despite the Internet, despite people moving north. My sense is that people still want to go to zones like that where they have options.

Car dealerships do the same thing. "Concentrations of businesses work better," said Devereux. "If you notice car dealerships, they're not dispersed throughout the city. You'd think that, 'Wow, why would you want to put one right next to a competitor?' Clearly, it does something, like 'This is where you go and get cars. This is the car-buying neighborhood.'" From clothing stores to car dealers to gay bars, the logic is the same. "Gay bars tend to open in proximity to one another. And that tends to anchor a gayborhood," a lesbian in Boystown remarked. "Even if people don't live there, it's a congregating space. You'll find community there, and you know it's a safe space." A straight man and mixologist in Andersonville described this clustering as a "mall effect," and he, too, indicated that it anchors the gayborhood: "You've got that mall effect, where it's better to have three or four gay bars close to each other. It becomes a destination for people. There will be an anchor because of it."

Bar owners in Chicago admitted that this logic informed their own business decisions. Stu Zirin, for example, told me that the community-enhancing effects of clustering motivated him to open a second bar on the Boystown strip: "We chose to be in Boystown. We chose to be in the environment that we're across from Minibar [the first bar that he opened], and we're next to Roscoe's [another popular gay bar], and I think we're building a destination, a zone where there are all these gay bars that are reinvesting and building." He then thought about other locations: "We could have been on Clark Street"—one block west of Halsted, where straight bars are concentrated. "We could have been on Belmont," which is the southern edge of Boystown. "We could have been somewhere else. But we chose to be in the neighborhood. We chose to add something to Boystown."

While Zirin was wistful about residential dispersion—"I want gay men to come back to Boystown and live in Boystown," he sighed—he was confident that the entertainment district would seal the area's cultural and institutional character for years to come. His business partner, John Dalton, agreed with him: "Boystown I think of as an entertainment district. However, in the past, I'm sure more gay people lived centrally around here than in other places. I think that's because it was more comfortable to hold hands down the street and be who you are in this area. But now I think you can do that in more areas of Chicago . . . Discrimination has dropped, and people feel more comfortable moving around." Their remarks offer an intriguing comparison between residential and business options. Growing acceptance of gay people has created more freedom for where they can live, even if they do not always feel comfortable holding hands outside of Boystown. But gay-identified businesses, like clothing stores and car dealerships, are still dependent on the cluster effect that a gayborhood allows.

Institutional and commercial presence begets concentration, which guards an area's character. This is why residential dispersion by itself provides inadequate evidence for the withering away of gay districts. "As long as the commercial concentration exists, that lends a certain identity to a neighborhood," said a Boystown gay man. "As time goes on, there will be more acceptance, and people won't feel the need to cluster. There will be a group of people that will feel comfortable living anywhere." This appears true in a post-gay era, but people will still want nightlife options. "Boystown is such a gay commercial stronghold that I feel like it isn't going anywhere," added a gay man in Andersonville. The first qualifier we heard—"as long as the commercial concentration exists"—is not trivial. Devereux imagined what would happen to Boystown if Unabridged or Sidetrack left the area:

> Say Unabridged wasn't here, and say Sidetrack wasn't there. If Sidetrack closed tomorrow, or say Sidetrack decided to move to Andersonville, I think it would be a huge shift in how people looked at a neighborhood. So, certainly bars anchor a neighborhood and maybe a couple major businesses anchor at least this neighborhood strip. Businesses

are an important part of anchoring the gay neighborhood and defining it in the same way that ethnic businesses would help define an ethnic neighborhood.

The survival of a gayborhood does not necessarily require that gays and lesbians actually live there. According to a gay man in Boystown, the objective instead "is to preserve the culture of the people who made that neighborhood what it was. It's not so much to say who's there [now]. It's a cultural marker to say who used to be there." But "the gay history that's embedded in it—I don't think will ever go anywhere," he added. To remember the history of an area, however, is quite different from a living, breathing gayborhood that is animated by actual queer bodies.

Scattered gathering places existed in the closet era, and gayborhoods have been around since World War II, but concentrated gay and lesbian commercial zones are among the most recent inventions. Gay and lesbian business owners are responsible for some of this, but city officials also play an important part, especially in the formal districting of gayborhoods. Cities now promote queer spaces in much the same way that they show off their stock of ethnic enclaves: both are an "indicator of cosmopolitanism," geographer Dereka Rushbrook argues. In Chicago, this made the Halsted strip "iconic," as Alderman Tunney characterizes it, especially for tourists. "It's been a great boost to tourism for the gay community," he told me. When I asked him how Boystown became such a magnet, he responded, "Boystown draws more tourists because it is a self-identified public expression of respect for our community. I think what's happened is that we've been able to solidify the tourist dollar." The explicit desire among city officials to attract tourists is a victory for gay politics and culture, even while it exploits gayborhoods for profits.[17]

So far, we have considered two major reasons why gayborhoods in Chicago will survive, despite the fact that city life is inevitably filled with flux. Boystown and Andersonville provide a psychological space that makes it easier for gay people to explore and express their sexuality. They also house anchor institutions—and many gay and lesbian business owners now have economic control over their real estate—and dense commercial zones that create an entertainment district for locals and tourists alike. Commemoration is the third and final urban life support system that we will look at in this chapter. In 1997 in a nationally unprecedented move, city officials in Chicago installed tax-funded rainbow-colored pylons—that cost $3.2 million—along Halsted Street to celebrate the area's queer identity (figure 5.3). A gay travel guide describes the gleeful scene on the street:

> You'll pass some rainbow pylons. You may think they look like rocket ships, or sex toys, or pieces of electrical equipment that got left behind an unfinished construction project, or you might even think they are simply fabulous. In any event, they are visible indicators that the city of Chicago felt fondly enough about its gay community to put several million dollars into marking the area as Gay Central—and how many cities like their gay hoods enough to do that?[18]

Over the years, the pylons have established the strip as the center of gravity for gay entertainment options and businesses. The Northalsted Business Alliance, for example, represents more than eighty businesses along Halsted Street as a single bloc. They feature the pylons on their brochures as a part of their organizational logo, and they have also added a local business listing onto several of the pylons themselves (figure 5.4).[19]

Chicago is a city of neighborhoods, and former mayor Richard Daley marked many ethnic enclaves in a similar fashion, including Chinatown, Greektown, Little Italy, and Pilsen. Political scientist Larry Bennett calls this reimagined city the "third Chicago." It is "the most self-conscious of cities" with a "shifting population mix, including a very large segment drawn from Mexico; a smaller but significant immigrant stream from south and east Asia; a substantial population of middle-class professionals working in corporations, universities, and other 'creative class' economic niches; and many thousands of 'out' gays and lesbians." The municipal government is aware of this mix, and it "routinely invokes the idea of multiculturalism through its annual sponsorship of myriad neighborhood and ethnic festivals and as it 'themes' local commercial strips as Greek, African American, Puerto Rican, or gay."[20]

FIGURE 5.3   Rainbow pylons in Boystown. Photo courtesy of Dave Frech.

FIGURE 5.4 A rainbow pylon with a business listing. Photo courtesy of Gary Baker.

Both public figures and residents in the city perceive the pylons as a commemoration of the queer community, its history, and its heritage. "Boystown is Boystown now because we have the pillars, and it's marked as a community," remarked Zirin. Bernard Cherkasov, CEO of Equality Illinois, used a territorial image of planting these stakes into the ground to emphasize why Boystown will survive. "We planted an anchor in Boystown, and with these pylons we're saying, 'This is our community space.' We planted them and anchored them deep into the ground. People move in and out of this neighborhood for different reasons, but the community isn't moving. Boystown is still here." A gay man in Boystown exuberantly added, "If one day the gayborhood is no longer on Halsted Street, they [the pylons] still designate the space that was. It's cool that, if nothing else, like, 'Oh, this is the first designated gayborhood.'" He then imagined himself as a much older man who was having a conversation with his great-grandchildren: "This is where, back in the day when we needed gayborhoods, great-grandpa had safe enclaves." A lesbian in the same neighborhood said that she liked the pylons for what they represented: "I like that, from a city planning perspective, the idea of some protection is given to the historical nature of the neighborhood. It's a social marker or a historical marker." She then offered insights about the long arc of our moral universe:

> I think societies go through periods where people that are disempowered get together, and maybe over time, they get rights, they get acceptance, and then they become more permeable. So, maybe it's a symbol of society. It's important to have a social memory that it wasn't always this way—and a sense of history, too: this is where initially people that didn't have the ability to be open and be out the way that they do now, this is where it started. It's a historical marker.

Amnesia can accompany assimilation; hence, the value of a marker that embodies the memory.

Even residents who were less certain about the future of Boystown recognized the significance of the pylons. A gay man in Boystown acknowledged that they "serve as markers," but he felt that they also "serve as monuments." "What is the difference?" I asked. He clarified with verb tense: "One [a marker] says this *is* here. One [a monument] says this *was* here. We are commemorating this." But there is a short distance from monument to mortality: "I don't mean this as macabre as it sounds, but this is almost like, 'Gays lie here.' This is like a gravestone, almost. Or it could be. It may be a gravestone someday." He was soon reading the epitaph: "Here lie gay people. Here lie gay activities." The pylons aid in memory-making. "It's a historical marker of the neighborhood," said a lesbian in Andersonville. Markers bestow a sense of permanence in a world that is filled with flux. Her partner quipped, "You don't move Plymouth Rock, right?" These comments capture the conundrum and anxieties that are invariably linked to any such markers. In their desire to affix a permanent commemoration, many gays and lesbians acknowledge that life, in the end, is itself impermanent.

But still, many residents said that it was crucial to commemorate queer history in an urban context. "What can we do to preserve our community? What can we do to preserve what we've had from a historical perspective?" a gay man in Andersonville wondered out loud. He was trying to find the words to explain the symbolic importance of the pylons: "If we don't preserve these types of things, we don't remember what we came from or where we came from or what we did or what the struggle was like along the way." Without the pylons, "we're just losing a sense of history and ourselves." In this capacity, gays and lesbians are like "any other cultural group" in that "we have our own history, and we have our own sufferings that we went through. It's important to remember that." The pylons achieve this objective. A different gay man in Andersonville added, "Lakeview is my gay history. It's part of my history. It's part of being gay. It's really important that we're not just learning about our gay history in a museum, but you can go and actually see it and that the neighborhood is preserved." In Boystown, a gay man said the same: "I want some sense of history to be preserved." Added another, "That's part of living in Chicago and especially being gay is knowing your history and knowing your neighborhoods." The pylons, I found, inspired a tremendous amount of self-reflection, at least when I asked people to slow down and think about them. Once they took that opportunity for reflection, many discovered a desire to position themselves as part of something bigger and more permanent.

Commemoration also happens in Andersonville. That neighborhood is "explicitly Swedish and implicitly gay," says Jason Cox, and this affects how public officials market it. "A lot of the marketing and language is Swedish: the water tower [which is painted in the colors of the Swedish flag], the [Swedish American] museum. But there's also a huge gay population," Cox added. Figure 5.5 shows some major Swedish markers that help to preserve the ethnic identity of Andersonville. The travel guide that we read earlier references them as well: "The history books will tell you that Andersonville is a Swedish neighborhood, and indeed, in one short stretch of Clark Street north of Foster Avenue, you can find two Swedish restaurants, a Swedish bakery, a couple of Swedish deli/food-specialty shops, and a Swedish cultural center. But for our purposes, lesbians founded Andersonville . . . Once lesbians paved the streets . . . , the Johnny-come-lately gay boys followed. Andersonville still boasts the most visible lesbian community in the city."[21] It is unclear why Boystown has markers of sexuality but Andersonville does not. It may have to do with the visibility of the community at the particular time and place when the mayor installed them. But gender matters too. Lesbian clusters are more residential; they have fewer commercial institutions that announce a queer sexuality in the same way as those that gay men create. This may also explain why there are so few commemorative markers of that history, even though "lesbians paved the streets."

Compared to ethnic markers in Andersonville, a lot more conflict surrounds the commemoration of sexuality in the Boystown pylons. Consider a critique that a gay man offered about the difference between what he called "community-building" and "revenue-building":

I'm more critical of the city's decision, for example, the way it marked North Halsted. I've begun to see it not necessarily as community-building but as business-building, as revenue-building, and in fact, as cleaning up what the gay community should be, as the city saying, "We're going to mark this as a gay space." But that means we're going to clean it up and make it the kind of gay space that we want to present to the outside world. That means that to be accepted into this gay space, some elements might need to be cleaned up more.

FIGURE 5.5 Swedish markers in Andersonville. Photos courtesy of Dave Frech.

Papadopoulos responded to this concern by emphasizing the political importance of the pylons: "Whether you like the pylons or not, it is a political victory, an urban political victory to have any metropolitan or municipal authority allow you to fix identity to space. So many struggles are really about contestations of space. So, when you are allowed to plant your flag anywhere, I think it's a victory for lesbigay identity politics." To be victorious, however, is not the same thing as being effective. "What are you trying to effectuate?" he asked. In his own struggle for an answer, he thought about the meaning of commemoration in light of residential dispersion. "In a perfect world of equality and acceptance, they [lesbians, gay men, and bisexuals] will simply weave themselves into the fabric of the metropolis. And those pylons and the designation of Boystown may live on. So, it becomes a heritage space and an origins space that is devoid of the demographic, but it's still politically very important because it says we are here or we were here: this is an important dimension of the city."

The pylons and other iconic institutional markers fossilize the collective memory of a group in space and place. An African American gay man offered a comparison with the black community: "It's like Harlem or Bronzeville: even if these spaces aren't black anymore or aren't what they once were, they still matter because they are pieces of something. They are the urban product of a lot of work that people put in, lived for, died for." Commemorative markers for racial, ethnic, gender, and sexual groups inspire its members to reflect, congregate, and celebrate their respective communities. And they enable a sense of permanence amid the realities of ongoing demographic migrations and urban change.

ANCESTRAL HISTORY

Our world is dynamic; we cannot flatten it into an urban picture of death or durability. Hence, our objective in this chapter: to render a more complex portrait of the contemporary gayborhood. In seeking a multidimensional view, we first focused on the limits of acceptance. Although we live in a time of greater public acceptance of homosexuality, Chicago residents spoke at length about the persistence of antigay bias, both real and imagined, and discrimination, both de jure and de facto. They also expressed concerns that straights were moving into the gayborhood at a rate that was faster than what opinion polls show about the overall social climate. Finally, we explored the particular plight of queer youth of color, the spatial invisibility of transgender individuals, and the struggles of those who, like Carolyn and Brian, live in smaller communities. In these voices, we heard resounding evidence for the continuing resonance—and indeed resilience—of gay neighborhoods.

The people we met in the first half of this chapter did not remark much on sexual integration. This prompted us to engage the issue more directly in the second part. Here, we asked how gayborhoods can retain their cultural and institutional character *despite* the presence of more straights on the sidewalks. We identified three factors that can promote their survival. These include the psychological and performative possibilities that gayborhoods promise (queer people can rely on them to explore and express their gender and sexuality); economic and institutional anchors (certain businesses and organizations, in tandem with property ownership, allow gayborhoods to deepen their roots); and commemorations (markers like the rainbow pylons embody the collective memories and histories of queer people, and when they are located in a place of symbolic importance, they provide physical form to a group's culture). Each factor enables us to feel a sense of perpetuity despite the unremitting passage of time.

To ensure that gayborhoods live on, we have to preserve a memory of their past. The absence of such memories induces widespread amnesia about queer lives. This is one of the most insidious forms of homophobia. During my third year of undergraduate study, for example, I remember feeling stunned when I learned that the history department was offering a course entitled "Gay and Lesbian History." I had never imagined that such a class could be possible. The narrowness of my worldview reflected the burden of queer communities then and perhaps even to this day. We lack ancestral history and a clear sense of answerability. Commemorative efforts stand on guard against the risk of forgetting. Because they have immeasurable impact on queer lives, it is worth taking the time, in the final moments of this chapter, to reflect on new developments in Chicago and elsewhere in the United States.

Until recently, no museums whose sole purpose was to preserve the lives of gay, lesbian, bisexual, and transgender people existed in the country. San Francisco made history in January 2011 when local activists opened the first GLBT museum. Writing for the *Chronicle*, Jessica Kwong reported on this momentous event:

> Long recognized as "one of the great ground zeroes of queer liberation," the Castro becomes the site of the nation's first lesbian, gay, bisexual and transgender history museum today. "Our letters were burned, our names blotted out, our books censored, our love declared unspeakable, our very existence denied," spell out words from a 1979 San Francisco Gay History Project flyer inscribed along one of the museum's walls . . . [T]he GLBT History Museum is the world's second museum dedicated solely to gay and lesbian archives and materials, museum officials said. The only other one is in Germany.

Telling stories is at once a personal and political act. It "transforms our lives and our society and takes us out of the margins," said Don Romesburg, a curator at the museum. It lets us dig down deep where our history is hidden.[22]

Chicago followed San Francisco's lead in 2012 when it unveiled the Legacy Project, a nonprofit organization dedicated to creating memorials of GLBT figures. The group constructed "the world's only outdoor museum walk celebrating the rich and diverse accomplishments of the GLBT community." Called the Legacy Walk, this fresh-air exhibit is located on the sidewalks of Boystown between Belmont Avenue and Grace Street. In the inaugural first phase, organizers installed eighteen bronze plaques onto the existing rainbow pylons. In doing so, they converted the pylons from markers to museum exhibits. Each plaque features an image cast relief portrait and a paragraph that has a brief biography of a historically important queer individual, symbol, or event that "marked a turning point in history." Notable people include Jane Addams, Alvin Ailey, James Baldwin, Barbara Gittings, Keith Haring, Alfred Kinsey, Harvey Milk, Bayard Rustin, and Oscar Wilde. Important symbols and events consist of the pink triangle that the Nazis used during the Holocaust to mark queers, the Harlem Renaissance, the American Psychiatric Association's decision to declassify homosexuality as a mental illness in 1973, and the Stonewall riots.[23]

In addition to the museum in San Francisco and the Legacy Walk in Chicago, there have been a variety of other restorative efforts around the country, including the honoring of Dr. Franklin Kameny, one of the most significant figures in the gay rights movement, by naming a street in Washington, DC, "Frank Kameny Way" in December 2010. Activists in San Diego succeeded in something similar in 2012 when they convinced city officials to rename Blaine Avenue, a two-block street in the Hillcrest gayborhood, as the nation's first "Harvey Milk Street," a dedication to the first openly gay man who was elected to public office in the United States. Additional examples include President Obama's designation in 2009 of the month of June as Lesbian, Gay, Bisexual, and Transgender Pride Month; installing George Segal's "Gay Liberation" sculpture in Christopher Park in New York; and including the Stonewall Inn on the National Register of Historic Places. All of these commemorative devices redress the absence of ancestral lineage by connecting queer people with their own rich history—and, not coincidentally, all of them are built in a particular place.[24]

For gayborhoods to resonate in the present and into the future does not require us to deny nor resist sexual integration. Bevan Dufty, a former supervisor for the Castro district, argued in May 2011 that residents, activists, business owners, and city officials should promote integration *and* preserve the sanctity of gay neighborhoods at the same time: "You can't take the Castro for granted. It's worth fighting for." While being "inclusive" is something that "we seek," he said, noting the particular role of politicians and businesses in welcoming straights into the gayborhood, "it's essential that we remain anchored in our LGBT heritage." Commemorations accomplish this objective. Sociologists who study collective memory call items like the pylons and Legacy Walk in Boystown, or the new museum in San Francisco, the "facts of representation." But the perceptions of everyday people, or the "facts of reception," such as the ones that we have discovered in this chapter, imbue those memories with meaning. The past, present, and future all blend together as a result, and they promote the longevity of gayborhoods. But here, we glimpse an additional angle that is worth mentioning, even if only briefly. Gayborhoods may remain significant not despite but *because* straights are moving into them. Their swelling numbers may actually enhance the gravity of gayborhoods in queer lives by making residents and visitors realize just how special this place is—and that it is something they should invest in and fight for.[25]

6

Reinvention

By now, we have a strong sense of why existing gayborhoods still matter. They are safe harbors for some people, and for others they are places to access anchors of queer culture, community, and commerce. However, just as we acknowledged the reality that straights are moving into gay districts, we also need to talk to those gays and lesbians who think they might leave. Where will they go next? We will find two main patterns as we follow their trail in this final chapter. First, when gays and lesbians leave an existing gayborhood, many of them collectively relocate to another area in the city. Their movement is purposeful, systematic, and it eventually contributes to the development of a new gay district. We called this trend a revival. It includes the formation of a new gayborhood in an area that is adjacent to the original or in one that is located farther on the fringes of the city. Second, specific groups like same-sex families with children, aging cohorts, people of color, and lesbians make distinct relocation decisions. When enough members make similar choices, they create a gayborhood of their own—a Latino gayborhood or Girlstown, as examples—in addition to the primary, typically better known, and more visible one that already exists. We called this multiplication. While gays and lesbians generally are more dispersed in a post-gay era than they were in the 1970s and 1980s, these two patterns suggest that they can creatively reattach some of the positive aspects of gayborhoods to the places where they move. As they make daily decisions about where to live and socialize, they invent and reinvent the very meanings and material expressions of gay districts.

QUEERLY FEATHERED BIRDS

Gays and lesbians in Chicago have moved steadily northward since the late nineteenth century, as we have seen, and revived the gayborhood along the way: from Towertown to Old Town to New Town to Boystown—and now to Andersonville. This long-standing sequence demonstrates what urban sociologists call "spatial contagion," "geographic clustering," a "cluster effect," or "gay concentration in neighboring tracts." The idea is the same: many gay people tend to stick together. As they leave an area in which they were once concentrated, they have the creative agency to reform a new settlement in a nearby place.[1]

Chicago business owners remember this history. Consider the reflections of Jim Gates. He owns a gay bar in Boystown called Little Jim's, which was the first such establishment to open in the neighborhood. "When I went to Chicago in 1967, the gay community was concentrated more in the Clark and Diversey area. There were a number of bars around there. In 1975, when I opened the bar, there were a few gay people in the [Boystown] neighborhood, but the neighborhood was primarily a very mixed neighborhood of old-timers, Cubans, Puerto Ricans. But by 1980, we had a nice gay community up there. By then we had four or five bars. Mine was the first." Gates lived through, and helped to shape, this northward movement.

Residents offered similar recollections. "Lots of gay people are moving out of the gayborhood," a lesbian in Boystown told me. This common refrain may be true, even if it is difficult to estimate exactly how many gays and lesbians have moved and how many are continuing to do so. If we stop here, however, we might mistakenly conclude that Chicagoans find less meaning in living in the gayborhood. A different picture emerges if we ask a simple follow-up question: Where are they moving? "In Chicago, the gayborhood's moving north," said the same woman succinctly. Another woman concurred with confidence, "There is a migration up to Andersonville now. There's no question there is." Sexuality, she said, and especially sexual integration, still motivates why people leave and where they go next. "It's changed so much [in Boystown]," as more straights move in, and gay people still "want more of a gay enclave."

For her to suggest that gays and lesbians want "more" of an enclave says something about the balance of demographic composition, as we have heard before. Residents and business owners say that they want to be inclusive, but sexual integration, along with rising property values, have a tipping point. Once the ratio between gay and straight changes on the one hand, and affordability becomes a problem on the other, many gays and lesbians move out in search of another place that is cheaper *and* where there are others who are like them. A Boystown gay man explained how Andersonville fit the bill: "I think Andersonville is really starting to populate and really booming because a lot of the gay community [in Boystown] just got tired: the rents started going up, [and] the straight couples moved in." A gay male realtor agreed, "I'm now finding [that] a lot of the gay community is moving to Edgewater because they say there are too many strollers in Lakeview." Gay male, lesbian, and straight parents all push strollers, of course. Were his clients explicit about their dislike for straights, specifically, in Boystown? "I keep hearing this repeatedly, and it's the general consensus: there are so many 'breeders,'" he said, invoking a pejorative term for straights. "There's an overabundance of heterosexuals with strollers." This compels many gays and lesbians to move out, but in Chicago, they follow a pattern in where they go next: Andersonville, which "has become the new Boystown," said a gay man in Boystown.

Once it began, the collective migration to Andersonville became self-sustaining: "I was motivated by the fact that other gay people, not just lesbians but gay men too, were migrating to this neighborhood," said a local lesbian as she reflected on why she moved to Andersonville. When I asked a gay male couple if they deliberately decided against Boystown, they answered "yes" right away—because the "hetero community moved in," they explained. "This [Andersonville] is where the gays were going from that point." Others agreed that Andersonville "is now gayer than Lakeview," a gay man said. "We expanded our search into this neighborhood since this was the new gay neighborhood," remarked another male couple. One especially articulate gay man explained why Andersonville, rather than some other neighborhood, was the focal point for the migration: "There's a proximal relationship that people have. You move to the place that's still close. Maybe the residents [in Boystown] are no longer gay, so it no longer has the residential significance that it once had. So you move somewhere, and Andersonville has a proximal relationship to Boystown: it's the next neighborhood over, and it happens to be gay-friendly." Boystown may be losing its "residential significance" as a queer hub (although, as we saw in chapter 5, not its commercial significance), but Andersonville is emerging as "the next gayborhood" in a classic pattern of adjacent resettlement.

The fact that gays are leaving Boystown should be a launching pad for our curiosity, not where we end the journey. Where are they moving next and why? "I don't think gay enclaves are passé," an Andersonville gay man began to tell me. "I think maybe what is currently or what was formerly the established one, that neighborhood might be passé. But where the new one is, that one is not passé." The significance of gayborhoods is not uniformly vanishing; it is simply re-forming somewhere else. Greater heterosexual presence motivates much of this movement. "Lakeview is passé because it's now [straight] families with strollers," he continued. "Andersonville is a vibrant gay and lesbian life center." The spirit of integration in existing gayborhoods thrives alongside the celebration of differences in the gayer districts that gays and lesbians reinvent somewhere else. "The gays are colonizing a new neighborhood. We're not totally integrating. That isn't happening," an Andersonville gay man concluded. The process that these residents describe is not limited to gay districts. As with many other things in life, those who are the tastemakers—the young, the educated, artists, and gay people—often cast aside what is "passé" in favor of what is "new" or "next." That goes for food, music, art, and gay neighborhoods alike. The economics of rising real estate informs this perpetual quest, but the search itself is universal.

Are gays and lesbians moving to neighborhoods other than Andersonville? "We don't see any gay men moving out of the gayborhood into nongay parts of the city," a gay male couple told me. "Where are these nongay parts?" I asked. "I don't see people moving to the South Loop or Bucktown or Wicker Park or something," he continued. "People are moving here [to Andersonville]." Did they know any lesbians or gay men that lived in neighborhoods other than Boystown or Andersonville? "Yes. There are gay guys that we know who live in other neighborhoods, but they're very often people who were moving to the city and decided that they wanted to buy a condo, and they decided to buy in the South Loop. But when they go out, they still socialize in Andersonville. Some say they feel very cut off." I spoke with another gay man in Andersonville who offered a powerful perspective that linked gayborhoods with safe spaces: "I think the gay neighborhoods of older times were almost like a wall-less gated community. You knew where the boundaries were, and you knew [that] inside those boundaries you were safe. You could hold hands. You could make out on the street corners. Not a problem. But you knew your boundaries. Nowadays, those gayborhoods have turned more straight, so those people have moved out to smaller colonies. Those colonies, those new enclaves, are a little smaller and not necessarily as gated because you don't need to be. People are more accepting. But you still have the little pockets."

There is no way to prevent or regulate straight people from moving into gay neighborhoods—and we know that these areas were never exclusively queer anyway. Yet gay migration in Chicago exhibits a distinct pattern, despite the effects of assimilation that we have been considering throughout this book. There may be "smaller colonies," "little pockets," and places that are "not as necessarily gated," but some semblance of a cluster does and will continue to exist. Sociologists call this homophily, as we know, and it explains the pattern that emerges from the decisions that individuals make about where to move. Miller McPherson, Lynn Smith-Lovin, and James Cook remark on the importance of geography in this process: "Perhaps the most basic source of homophily is space: We are more likely to have contact with those who are closer to us in geographic location than those who are distant." Even the Internet cannot completely counteract homophily. It "may have loosened the bounds of geography by lowering the effort involved in contact, but these new modes have certainly not eliminated the old pattern" of queerly feathered birds flocking together in specific parts of the city.[2] In the pithy words of a local university professor,

"I would be hesitant to pronounce the death of gay neighborhoods too soon."

The principle of homophily tempers post-gay predictions. One gay man in Boystown, parroting an idea that we have heard several times, said, "I can't imagine a day where gay people will be so fully integrated that they don't have a need within them to be around their own kind." A lesbian in the same neighborhood agreed, "Being gay is still different, and so there's always going to be an aspect of people feeling more comfortable around other people like them." It's "human nature," she said, "like attracts like." Her partner added, "You're always going to have those areas that tend to draw people in who are gay." Another Boystown lesbian echoed, "No matter what happens in society or how many rights are achieved, like-minded people are still going to want to meet." There is something basic, almost animalistic about homophily, a gay man in Boystown expressed: "We're like pack animals, living in packs or herds." Others offered tribal images: "You always want to be with your clan."

Several residents compared sexual minorities with other groups. A lesbian who lived in Boystown, for example, asserted that new gayborhoods will not be segregated like the older ones: "It's going to become less of a ghettoization thing and more just kind of a, you know, if you're Jewish you maybe still tend to head to a certain area, not because they're exclusively Jewish or that you would be uncomfortable there if you weren't Jewish. It's just that I'm going to be comfortable there." Another lesbian, this time from Andersonville, suggested that gays do what artists do: "I would suspect that anybody who is different or part of a community in any way would move to a place where there are more people like them. Artists do it. Where can I be where I can be inspired by other artists who share with me a common bond of creativity? Gay people do the same thing." Consider next the sentiments of a gay man in Boystown: "I think it's true of any group, whether you're gay, whether it's based on ethnicity or based on socioeconomic status. It's always nice to be around people like yourself." Another man offered a similarly sweeping comparison: "You can look at other groups and use them as analogies, like Harlem or some of the Jewish ghettos of the past. This is an issue that continues to recycle among disempowered groups throughout society, and it's an old question in the sense that people tend to cling together—and passionately—despite their visibility and their legal status." That these lists range from Jewish people to artists to disempowered groups of all sorts suggests that the effects of homophily will hold even as we approach a time of total legislative equality for sexual minorities.

The principle works in the midst of cross-cutting identities. An African American gay man in Andersonville explained how it influenced multiple aspects of his sense of self: "There is something very different about hanging out with my black friends. There's an understanding that I have that I don't necessarily get from friends of other ethnic groups. And sometimes it's just nice to be around my black folk. And in the same way, I think there's something about being around gay people as well." A white gay man in Andersonville who dates African Americans arrived at a similar conclusion:

> I typically date black men, and as open as I can be to race issues, I'm never looked at as a black man. I have no idea what it's like when people look at my boyfriend, what his experiences are—no idea . . . There's a need for him to have black friends and to be in a black space. People need to share their common experiences. People need to be comfortable around each other. People need to not present as something that they're not for fear of judgment. I feel that way about a gay neighborhood, too.

In terms of how homophily actually works on the ground, the most common theme I heard was about the power of social networks: "We started hearing all of our friends say, 'I just moved to Andersonville.' And you go, 'God, all our friends live north now, and there's nobody to hang out with anymore,'" explained a male couple in Boystown. This affected where they moved: "That becomes part of our decision, where our friends are moving to." Another couple in Andersonville offered a thought experiment: "Imagine this conversation. 'Hey, I just moved into this building, and we've got some units open. You should move into my building. It's really cheap, and it's really big. Why don't you move into my building, and we can both live here.' And if there are six units or ten units or three units, now you have two gay homes in let's say a three-unit structure. And now you're building small communities based on friends who know one another." According to this view, small queer clusters emerge by word of mouth within circles of friends.

Other residents, like the following gay man in Andersonville, emphasized a common culture and community: "The gay neighborhood represents our common thread." Being around similar others enables you to recognize that you belong to a common community. Art Johnson explained that a gayborhood "helps a community in becoming a community, [and] remaining a community when you have neighborhoods that are your own." The fact that "we're constantly a community in transition" makes it important for us to have "a neighborhood or neighborhoods that we could more clearly identify and look to with pride." A young gay man who recently moved to Boystown from a small midwestern area shared one of his experiences: "I went to Sidetrack last night, and it's show tunes night, and everybody's singing, and they know all the songs that are playing. That's part of the culture. They're all hugging, and they have their arms around each other, and they're all friends. In a gay neighborhood, gay people have other gay friends." Gays and lesbians share certain experiences with one another. "Being gay, you went through a lot of the same tribulations," another man added, "whether it was coming out to parents, whether it was dealing with things in school, whether it was coming to terms with your sexuality—you have those types of bonding experiences. That's what living in a gay community is all about is that you can share those experiences and meet other people who understand." This affects their decisions about where to live. "It's not like going into a new area or a straight area and feeling like you have to try to fit in. Here, you already fit in." All of these were among the reasons why another gay man in Andersonville selected the area when he left Boystown: "To acknowledge a common experience is powerful for me."

Several people invoked this tendency to stick together in their predictions for the future. A gay man in Boystown presaged, "You'll always have gay neighborhoods for the same reason that you'll always have Chinatowns and Greektowns and Little Italys." When I inquired about the effects of straights moving into Boystown or nonindigenous people into ethnic enclaves, he replied with the same logic: "If you have a Chinatown, and then all of a sudden a bunch of Europeans move in, I feel like it would just move somewhere else. People that have something in common are going to group together. You'll always have that." A gay man in Andersonville offered a similar prediction. "I don't think gay neighborhoods will ever disappear." When I asked why not, he similarly answered, "For the same reason that Puerto Rican neighborhoods are not disappearing, or other Hispanic neighborhoods and African American neighborhoods won't. People want to live where they know they're going to be comfortable." And where is that? "There's a tendency to want to live where there are lots of gays, which means there are always going to be little enclaves or neighborhoods that are predominately gay."

An African American gay man in Andersonville drew an analogy with the black church to make a poignant argument about "structural prominence" and "cultural importance":

> Gay neighborhoods remind me in some ways of the black church. The black church no longer has the same structural prominence that it once had for black people. But it still has this cultural importance. It still provides very important things for black people. But it isn't doing the same political work or providing the same political space that it used to, for a lot of different reasons. I think gay neighborhoods are the same thing: they're no longer structuring gay life anymore, but they are culturally resonant. I imagine if somebody said, "We are going to take Boystown away," I'm sure there would be resistance all over the place because it's important as a historical marker and as a site of cultural resources, even if it's not necessarily the heart of the rallying cry of gay people.

Soothsaying straights said something similar: "I don't see how gay neighborhoods could disappear," one man shrugged. "I can only see how they would move and relocate and reconcentrate in other places. A proportion of every minority has a need to live in a community where other people they identify with live. It's just a natural human tendency."

Implied in the modern cry of "there goes the gayborhood" is a sense of motion and movement. Like Chicago, New York gayborhoods have also moved—along the West Side in that particular

city—from Greenwich Village, the site of the Stonewall riots, adjacently to Chelsea, and now to Hell's Kitchen. In DC, there has been
an eastward march from Georgetown to Dupont Circle, to Logan
Circle, and most recently to Shaw. Even in San Francisco, the
gay mecca of the Castro may have been the most fabulous of gayborhoods, but it was not the first, nor will it be the last. Gays and
lesbians moved from North Beach in the 1950s, to the Tenderloin
(Polk Street/Van Ness) in the 1960s, to the Castro in the 1970s, and
now they are moving to the East Bay.[3] Revived gayborhoods may be
smaller and less concentrated, but they will always embody a special
link between sexuality and the city.

THE BIGGIE BANG

In my conversation with Scott, a pseudonym for a fifty-one-year-old
white, partnered gay man who had lived in Chicago for seventeen
years, I learned about a "biggie bang" that happened in the city, a
social explosion that produced "little planets of gays" across the city:

> There's a pattern of movement of where people live. Let's say it's this
> "biggie bang." Everybody lived in Lakeview. There was no question at
> the time that the place to move was Lakeview. All through the '80s,
> it was really, really heavily gay. And then it exploded. Lakeview's not
> as concentrated anymore, and it will never be as concentrated. Now
> people are settling in different areas. The explosion has made little
> mini-enclaves throughout the city. I still see concentrations in certain
> areas, but it has dispersed. So, the biggie bang happened, and now
> you've got all these little planets of gays.

Many gay people in Chicago are collectively moving north to Andersonville, as we just saw, but there is a concurrent possibility as well.
Sexual integration can also produce multiple mini-enclaves, rather
than dilute the one and only gayborhood in town and compel local
gays and lesbians to reinvent it somewhere else. Consider the intuition that a Boystown gay man shared: "It's not only one gay community, it's not only one gay neighborhood, and not everybody who
might be looking for a gay neighborhood would consider Boystown
the gay neighborhood they want." Andersonville is an alternate to

Boystown, but there are others as well—and each one is developing its own brand of identity. "Even as a gay community, we have a tendency to stick in subsets as opposed to being all-encompassing," observed one gay man. To see these "planets of gays," we need to discard an assumption of singularity.

Scott's playful idea of the biggie bang—"and then it exploded," in his words—includes an amalgamation of many factors, including signatures of the post-gay era, like societal acceptance of sexual minorities, their mainstreaming, legislative advancements for their rights, and increasing straight presence in existing gayborhoods; economic forces like housing stock, property values, affordability, amenities, and urban renewal efforts; and expressions of diversity within queer communities, which will be our focus in this section. Particular groups of sexual minorities, such as same-sex families with children, aging cohorts of gay people, people of color, and lesbians, make distinct choices about where to live. We have visited with members of the first two groups before, and we learned that becoming a new parent or growing older triggers a reflection on many aspects of our lives, including where we want to live. A lesbian in Boystown reminds us about this idea: "There are changing points in your life that drive the movement away from a gay neighborhood. Maybe it appeals less if you're in a later stage in your life and you're having children and families." Before, we investigated why members of these groups were leaving the gayborhood, but here we will focus on patterns in where they go next. After we finish this discussion, we will think critically about racial and gender differences in the geography of sexuality, and we will foreground the experiences of people of color and lesbians. Homophily motivates the migration of all these groups, and as we will see, it multiplies the total number of areas that can acquire a distinct association with sexuality.

Andersonville has a local reputation as a bastion for same-sex families with children. "The only reason why I moved to Andersonville was because I knew it was gay-friendly," one lesbian in the neighborhood told me. "And that's important to me, because I would like to have a family someday, and I would like to raise my kids in a very open-minded, very comfortable area." A male couple with two newborns felt the same way: "Living here is important for us with kids." A general gayborhood like Boystown was less appealing to these dads because fewer same-sex families reside there. "If we're walking around in Lakeview with kids in the stroller, we wouldn't see as many gay families. Up here, you'll see gay families walking around all the time." The men left Boystown, where they used to live, once their surrogate was pregnant. When I asked them to recount their thought process, they offered a three-tiered, concentric, circlelike reply of increasing specificity. Their first consideration, and the outermost ring, was a broad residential filter that correlated with the collective resettlement we saw earlier: Where in general are the gays moving? The second question they asked was tailored to their desire to be near other parents: Where are the queer families with kids? Finally, they inquired about a familiar practical matter: Where are the good schools?

Some residents incorporated one more layer, another ring in the concentric circles if you will, between the second and third residential filters when they asked: Where are the lesbian moms? Or where are the gay dads? The same couple described lesbian friends of theirs who had a newborn and who integrated this final filter: "More specifically than just gay families with kids, they have a daughter. And they want their daughter to be in a school where she will not have an isolated experience of having two mommies. And so, they're projecting on to where their daughter will be comfortable saying she has two mommies." The men concluded that "gay families with children seem to exhibit a pattern in where they relocate." In a similar vein, two moms in Boystown explained why they were about to move to Andersonville, and why they rejected Boystown as a possibility: "We perceive Andersonville as being more family-friendly. I think it's critical, whereas Boystown, that's really understood to be a little bit more of a singles atmosphere rather than necessarily family-friendly in the way you might think of Andersonville. We want to move to a neighborhood where our kids will be around other kids from similar families." Queer flight from Boystown in this case does not signal the declining significance of sexual orientation, at least not in absolute terms, as much as it reveals a subtle pattern among same-sex families with children. I heard the sentiment repeatedly from men and women alike. A male couple with kids observed, "We see lesbian couples all the time. We see gay male couples all the time. This is not an exaggeration. Every time we go for a walk through Andersonville, we see other gay parents with kids." This was important to them when they were deciding where to live: "We would only live in areas that have lots of gays and gay couples with kids."

There are other pockets of same-sex families besides Andersonville, even if they are not named or codified as a gayborhood in the same way. Oak Park is one such place. This is a suburb that is adjacent to the western edge of Chicago. I had a memorable conversation with a female couple who had lived in Boystown for five years. Jenn and Amy had recently relocated to Oak Park. They shared their thoughts about how assimilation is compatible with a desire to be around other minorities:

Jenn: The integrated aspect—that it's not us versus them—that you can live anywhere and be treated the same and not be given looks when you walk around in various neighborhoods, I think is a sign of progress and the kind of place I would like to be in, where it's a nonissue, the post-gay phenomenon. I like the more openness.

Me: Do you think the openness and integration that we see in Boystown today exemplifies this post-gay phenomenon?

Jenn: That to me is the idea of it, that it's a nonissue. The same experience we've had since we've moved here to this suburb where these middle-aged ladies who live nearby us have brought us baby gifts and just been very sweet, told us nice things, nothing—not treated [us] differently. I like it.

Amy: At work, when I came out and had a baby, nobody cared. I assumed there was going to be some trouble. [But] nobody cared.

Jenn: They threw you a shower! [throws her hands up in the air with exclamation]

Amy: They threw me a shower! I could have never known how to prepare the ground for something like that. I'm the only out lesbian in the entire school of engineering [at a local university]. The reception here in this small suburban community has been startling. I guess I wasn't prepared for as much post-gay as I got.

An us-versus-them mentality, which was common in the closet and coming out eras, is yielding to an us-and-them view of relationships in a post-gay world.[4] But this does not diminish a desire among gays and lesbians to be around other families that resemble their own. "We wouldn't have remained in Boystown forever," said Jenn. "But starting a family was the thing that pushed us [to move out]." In Oak Park, and certain other suburbs, "there are a number of same-sex parent playgrounds and things like that," she continued. "Yeah, a lot of gay families live here," Amy added. Both women explicitly factored this into their decision.

Oak Park is not in the city, and it is not recognized as a gayborhood like Boystown and Andersonville. But Jenn and Amy did not feel isolated there. "We were pretty dedicated about connecting with same-sex families," Amy told me, and they joined a parent network in the area. "They actually have a same-sex parents subunit and a pretty active group of women that we know that have a playgroup once a month, and they're pretty dedicated too." Some of these women live in Oak Park, while others live in the North Shore suburbs of Berwyn and Wilmette or in Rogers Park in Chicago. "We all get together and talk, and our kids play together. Jenn and I actually started going before we had our child so we could get to know these women." As a final example, consider the explanation that one lesbian, who recently moved to Chicago from Boston, offered for why she thinks queer families cluster together:

> In Boston, we joke that the women partner and have kids and move to Roslindale from J.P. [Jamaica Plains]. As it is, school's tough. It's hard to be a kid in school. And to be the gay kid or the kid with the gay moms or dads, it's even harder. Just like any minority kid, if you're the one, then you are the representation of all. And so, I think that it's almost out of kindness. People just simplify: we'll cluster together because then there is a community, and there's the mothering or fathering group.

The idea of belonging to a community has not lost its meaning for queer families—and it certainly is not an abstract notion for them. "You need to have community while you're child-rearing because you have all these other complicating factors being in a same-sex partnership and trying to raise children," the former Bostonian explained. "So I think people who have children cluster because it's easier, there's community, there's support, and there's understanding." These clusters may not develop into formal gay districts. There is no official urban or suburban gayborhood for queer families, for example. But awareness circulates—by word of mouth, in newspapers, and in online forums and discussion groups—that they are the place to be for gay dads and lesbian moms.

Much like becoming a new parent, aging is another trigger that prompts us to reflect on where we want to live. Growing older can sometimes drive a decision to leave a gayborhood, as we have already seen, but it can also produce patterns in where older gays and lesbians choose to relocate. Sociologist Sharon Zukin calls this a "lifecycle" or "cohort effect."[5] One gay man explained that he arrived at his decision to move to Andersonville gradually as he grew older. "Age plays into the Andersonville area. A lot of the younger people still stay in the Lakeview area or the Boystown area because the clubs are there, and they want the sense of being able to be in that environment." A straight man in Boystown recognized this as well: "A lot of gay people that used to live in Boystown grew up, wanted something a little calmer, moved to Andersonville, settled down, bought property, and now they're just kind of there." This is the same issue of maturation that we considered before. In our prior discussions, however, we focused on how growing older creates disincentives for living in a gayborhood. Although we again will hear from gays and lesbians who want to move out of Boystown, the people we will meet this time around still want to be around other gay people of a similar age.

Andersonville might exemplify the trend of a collective northward migration, but it is also possible that Boystown and Andersonville attract different types of people. "The older generations are more likely to move to Andersonville. The younger generations are not going to feel as drawn," said a gay man in Boystown. Two others spoke more directly: "Old gays flock to Andersonville," said one. "It's like gay Mayberry up there," added the other. While Boystown appeals to gay men more than it does to lesbians, there are generational patterns in neighborhood selection that cut across gender, as the following lesbian couple in Andersonville observed: "I know that there are a lot of younger lesbians that move to Boystown versus Andersonville. There are some here, don't get me wrong, but it is very much a trend for the younger community—that's a draw for them, for the younger lesbians, to live in Boystown." Similarly, Heather Muenstermann and her partner Tina Isperduli, who we met before as the co-owners of the eco-friendly Green Genes in Andersonville, indicated, "As far as the gay people, men and women, who live up here, I feel like it's a little older demographic, a little more settled, gays and straights having families." If younger people patronize bars more than those who are older, and if nightlife is concentrated in Boystown, then it is not surprising that younger gays and lesbians will want to live there. "Boystown is nightlife and singles," a gay man in Andersonville summed up. As they age, however, many move out—and systematically choose Andersonville as the place to go next.

My interviewees regularly addressed this pattern. Tim Weber, who owns a hair salon in Andersonville, made the point by referencing colloquial neighborhood names: "It's *Man*dersonville, man versus boy. *Boys*town is the young gays who want to party. They move to Mandersonville when they become men who want houses and careers and maybe kids and want to calm down a little bit." Several residents expressed differences between the two gayborhoods through such tongue-and-cheek terms. "It's Boystown and Mandersonville," a thirty-nine-year-old Andersonville gay man echoed. "And I felt like I was ready for Mandersonville. That's where you go to be an adult, not just to play." A lesbian in the same neighborhood added, "Someone had at one time described Andersonville as Shady Hills for gay men. Once they were ready to grow up, they would move to Andersonville. I see more gay male couples and older people. Once they tire of the party scene and they still want that gay neighborhood but want to settle down a little bit more, they move here." Her phrase—"and they still want that gay neighborhood"—is important. It is unclear if Andersonville will ever be as concentrated as Boystown, replace it altogether, or morph into something distinct. Regardless, many older gays and lesbians still want to connect with a community of similar others, and this produces a pattern in the choices they make about where to live.

Straights are aware that this is happening on the streets of their home, and they also mention age to explain the differences between the two gayborhoods. A man in Boystown said, "This is more of the party town, and Andersonville's a lot more grown up." A woman in the same neighborhood agreed that "[Boystown] is where you would live if you were young and you were gay. Andersonville is for older gay people. That's just the maturation of what a gay neighborhood is." In comparing the two areas, a straight man in Andersonville asserted that his home was unlike Boystown: "Andersonville's different than Boystown." "How so?" I asked. "It's older," he replied. "It's tamer. It's more integrated." A straight woman in Andersonville identified a tipping point in the life course: "The fellows that have moved up to this neighborhood are older. They're usually past their thirties and maybe lived in Boystown. Now they want a more quiet life. Andersonville is where the boys from Boystown come to settle down."

Chicagoans, like the New Yorkers who we met in an earlier chapter, disagree whether Andersonville is a *new* gayborhood, the *next* gayborhood, or something totally different. Each word or phrase—new, next, something else—hints at multiplicity. Gays and lesbians must set the tone for Andersonville to become the new or next gayborhood, but even if they do not, there is an association between the area and gay people, regardless of whether that association is limited to gays and lesbians of a particular age.

We have now reconsidered two triggers, becoming a new parent and growing older, both of which stimulate the formation of cultural archipelagos. But we have not yet isolated the role of race and gender, two elemental social categories that shape our experiences in life. Rhetoric professor Charles Nero is puzzled by the "paradox," as he calls it, "that gayness is multicultural yet gay neighborhoods are overwhelmingly white." This prompted him to ask, "Why are the gay ghettos white?" Nero suggests that black gay men and women do not participate in the social networks of the middle-class white gays who are often instrumental in building gay districts. His argument may explain why existing gayborhoods are white, but we need to follow up and ask whether people of color make unique relocation decisions in response—and form their own districts.[6]

Chicago residents echo Nero when they say that Boystown feels white. "Unfortunately, what we consider our queer neighborhood or gay neighborhood also comes along with a lot of other things, like there are mostly going to be white people around there," said Dyke March organizer Edith Bucio. "Boystown is a very white-specific place that caters to black audiences on particular nights," added an African American gay man who lives in Andersonville. He noticed that some Boystown nightclub owners promote a "salsa night" or a "hip-hop night," which reads to him and other people of color as a code for Hispanic and black crowds, along with the white men who sexually desire them.

Lesbian spaces contend with the same paradox. A man from Andersonville described his neighborhood as "lesbian and white. And my experience with white lesbians, both in the neighborhood and in general in life, it's been [that] they're very territorial." Clarissa Gonzalez, another Dyke March organizer, sensed something similar: "Lots of my really Latina-looking friends or lots of my African American friends don't ever want to go up there [to Andersonville] because they don't see similar faces. They were like, 'I don't like white people.' And I was like, 'Why? Why don't you like white people? How are you going to be racist if you're complaining about other people [not liking you]?' And they were like, 'It's not about being racist. I just don't feel safe.'"

Some people of color respond to the racial homogeneity of the gayborhood by building their own separate communities. "Boystown is overwhelmingly white," a Latina lesbian in Andersonville declared. But "there are pockets on the South Side that have developed into mini gay areas." These "mini gay areas" are not formal gayborhoods per se. They are "essentially, like a club here or there or something, or more closed, secretive places." Nevertheless, some Chicagoans realize that the South Side, an area of the city with a large African American population, offers a safe space for queer people of color. On the other, far north side of the city, Rogers Park is also emerging as an enclave for people of color. A white gay man in Boystown reflected, "For some people, instead of trying to make Boystown the kind of neighborhood they want, they would rather look for a community someplace like Rogers Park, where maybe they can build another gay community that might be more receptive to queers of color." To call Rogers Park "another gay community" is different from the "mini gay areas" on the South Side. Both developments are important, of course, and they can occur simultaneously, but they are not identical. The "club here or there" on the South Side reminds us of the scattered places of the closet era. A nonreceptive context of homophobia played a large part in creating this topography during that particular historical period—and compared to the North Side today, it evidently still does, although in a way that also intersects with experiences of racial isolation. Recall, for instance, what a gay man from Boystown once told us: "The argument can be made that the entire North Side is homosexual." Not one person said something similar about the South Side.

Several public figures also mentioned the difficult role of race in queer geographies. A straight female realtor remarked, "I do think there has been some frustration in the African American community with the white-centered gay lifestyle in Chicago that leaves out a huge group of people who are not white. It's all been on the North Side." While she admitted not knowing "if there is a gay neighborhood on the South Side," resident reflections from earlier suggest that socializing opportunities are certainly available. Bucio confirmed that this was true for queer Mexicans: "For me, my greatest passion is for my Mexican community, and just being around family in that aspect, and then within that, finding a queer-safe space." The social and residential choices that people of color make resemble those of same-sex families. The outer ring, or the most general residential (and social) filter, is the ethnic community—"my Mexican community," as Bucio called it. Within this, many people of color seek a "queer-safe space." This may not culminate in an alternate gayborhood, but it does not diminish the value of knowing that there are places where you can go to find others who are like you. "There are a lot of queer people in different neighborhoods of color that build their own spaces," Bucio concluded.

The strategy of queer people of color creating their own safe spaces is deliberate and political. Places like Boystown and Andersonville are "predominately white, and there's obvious racism within the LGBT community," Gonzalez noted. To shield themselves from this racism, queer people of color craft underground scenes:

There's a distinct African American, queer, female-identified community. There's a distinct Latina queer community. There's a little bit of an Asian community. These spaces are separate from the white spaces, which is Andersonville and Boystown. On the West Side, there's this whole underground scene of African American male parties, and they have their own scene that's not connected to Boystown at all, because they don't feel comfortable going to Boystown. And I knew this because a really close friend of mine was always throwing these parties where they would all go out. And there were these guys who look like thugs on the street, and they were gay, and they were all partying and dancing. I would have never guessed if I saw them on the street—like this whole, huge underground scene.

Gonzalez then described how "it's the exact same thing within the female world": "There's a whole scene in South Shore that's all African American. They have their own culture. They have their own history. They have the places that they go that I've heard about here and there. It's a distinct lesbian culture. In the Latina community, unfortunately, we are not that organized. But slowly, there are definitely, like Latina nights at these bars where it's lots of women who are looking for other women. And it's not yet as much of a solid set culture, but there are definitely trends within it which I feel shows that it is its own community."

The patterns we see in Chicago also exist in other cities. Michael Lavers published a story in the *Village Voice* in 2009 about "New Gayborhoods" in New York that were "Breaking the Outer Limits," to borrow phrases from his title. He discovered that people of color were forming unique settlements across the city—in places well beyond Manhattan:

Jackson Heights . . . has become Hell's Cocina in recent years—the city's main Latino gayborhood. It's one of a handful of such outposts that have sprung up in the so-called outer boroughs. Immigrants from Latin America and South Asia have transformed Jackson Heights into a neighborhood teeming with ethnic restaurants, street vendors, and legions of flamboyant drag queens and macho Latinos, who populate Friend's, Atlantis, Bar Los Recuerdos, Lucho's Place, and the many other gay bars and clubs along Roosevelt Avenue between 65th and 82nd streets. These bars provide a refuge for non-English-speaking immigrants still uncomfortable in Anglo-American culture. "The bars offer a space where they can mingle, socialize, speak Spanish, and meet people from their own culture," said one resident.[7]

Jackson Heights in Queens, Lavers says, has become "an enclave for Latino gays (and 'salsa queens,' the Anglos who love them)." In a similar way, Fort Greene in Brooklyn has become "a bastion of gay black professionals," so much that "it is called the Chocolate Chelsea." Charles Nero was right to wonder, "Why are the gay ghettos white?" Fortunately, however, his paradox does not mean that the lives of queer people of color are casualties of racism. On the contrary, what we are witnessing in Chicago and New York illustrates the powerful agency that they have in creating their own spaces and shaping their own destinies. This does not mean that there are no people of color who live in existing gayborhoods like Boystown, Hell's Kitchen, or Chelsea, any more than it implies that queer people of color who live in other areas never socialize in the gay bars that are based there. The world of gayborhoods is vibrant and multilayered, and we live in a time of expanding, not diminishing, options.

In addition to race, some of the cultural archipelagos of Chicago are also defined by gender. Many residents refer to Andersonville as "Girlstown," for example, and some also call it "the lesbian ghetto," "Lesbiantown," "Land-O'-Les," and "Dykeville." This language underscores the gendered nature of queer migrations. A gay man in Boystown explained that the biggest difference between Andersonville and his home is that "Andersonville has a bigger lesbian population." Another man recognized this as well: "It's called 'Boystown' for a reason. Lesbians don't seem particularly visible." Gonzalez agreed with these men: "Boystown is a gay neighborhood. It's *boys'* town—it's all guys. Boystown is super, super male. Andersonville is definitely more lesbian than gay, especially with establishments like Women and Children First bookstore. It's very female-oriented. It's lesbian." Straights also differentiate the two gayborhoods by gender. "Andersonville is mostly lesbians, and Boystown is men," said one woman. A man added, "Boystown is boys, and Girlstown is girls. But there are exceptions. I know gay men who live in Andersonville and gay women who live in Boystown."

Those women who are the exceptions—the lesbians who live in Boystown—say that they feel unseen and off the cultural radar. "I feel invisible, like when you're in the bars or walking down the street or at some charity events or even at the health club . . . Gay guys are all about other gay guys . . . So, I guess there is a little bit of an invisibility thing. You could be purple and not be noticed if you were a woman." This extreme example inspired her partner to chime in: "You could be naked standing there, and you'd be fine." In a separate conversation, another woman added, "It's just guys everywhere. And guys aren't paying attention to me." Although "women are welcome too," in the words of a fourth lesbian, "they are gayborhoods," after all. They are "not the lesbianhood, or whatever," which this woman and others imagine as a different type of urban space.

In a 2010 interview with the *New York Observer*, Sharon Zukin offered a provocative image of lesbians as "canaries in the urban coal mine." Intrigued, the journalist reflected on the relationship between gender and the city: "[L]esbians are handy urban pioneers, dragging organic groceries and prenatal yoga to the 'frontier' neighborhoods they make hospitable for the rest of us. In three to five years."[8] Journalists, scholars, and residents share the same wisdom about what we can describe as a process of incubation, formation, change, and resurrection. Lesbians come first, and they create a Girlstown for themselves. This is a period of incubation since, for reasons that we will explore shortly, there is not always widespread awareness that the area is a gay district. Lesbians and some gay men, however, generally know that an area exists specifically for women. Thus, subcultural knowledge and awareness circulates during this period of incubation. Consider the recollections of one gay man, "In the '90s, Andersonville was known as 'Lesbiantown.' The lesbians were living there and fixing up some properties. We were down here [in Boystown], they're up there. We each had our neighborhoods."

Gay men arrive next, pushed out from where they were before by rising rents and a straight presence that exceeds what is for many of them a comfortable balance of inclusion and integration. They follow the trailblazing lesbians. As gay men arrive in larger numbers, and because they have more financial resources than lesbians, they build more visible commercial institutions. Soon after, the identity of the area gradually shifts from Girlstown to Boystown 2 (or Mandersonville). During this transition, the composition of the old gayborhood (Boystown, in this case) becomes straighter, and some of its queer businesses close. Meanwhile, the residential texture of the new area becomes gayer (although increasingly dominated by men) and new commercial establishments open. Many lesbians feel priced out at this point, leave, and then migrate to an adjacent neighborhood to the north. Being canaries in the urban coal mine, they initiate another period of incubation in the new place where they settle. Straights arrive last, after the gay men, and the cycle repeats.

Jason Cox saw this process happen in Andersonville: "The lesbians came here, the gay men followed behind, fixed everything up, the lesbians got priced out and moved to other places. Are there still lesbians in the neighborhood? Absolutely. But are there enough where you would call it Girlstown? Not really." One woman who had lived in the neighborhood for a decade agreed: "It was Girlstown when I first moved here. That's the perception I had of it. I think since then, especially over the last four years or so, gay men have come into the neighborhood." I repeatedly heard some version of what she said: first come the lesbians, then the gay men, and finally the straights who, in larger numbers, eventually erode the queer vibe. "When I first moved here, this place was Girlstown," she continued, "but slowly, the gay men are moving in. And now, it seems like a lot of straight couples with children are moving in too." In the course of our conversation, she offered an economic "theory" (her word) for gayborhood change: "My friends and I have this theory. Lesbians move into cheap, run-down, kind of ghettoish neighborhoods, which Andersonville was years ago. They fix it up a little bit. And then once it's fixed up, the gay men move in and really spruce it up. And then the straight couples are like, 'Oh, this is nice. Let's move here.'" This familiar refrain frequently ends with a level of heterosexual presence that leaves many gays and lesbians feeling restless and that motivates them to build a new gayborhood somewhere else.

The story can have a different ending. Maureen Martino who, recall, directs the Lakeview Chamber of Commerce, thinks that lesbians should mimic gay men: "Look at Andersonville. It used to be very well known for lesbian communities. It used to be 'Girlstown.' Now you've got more boys going up there than girls. And what's happening to the girls? They're losing their position in Andersonville. What they need to do is open more lesbian bars or businesses." The presence of such institutions matters, as we know, but perhaps more important is the question of property ownership. If lesbian business owners controlled their own real estate, like gay men do in Boystown, then the gender identity of Andersonville would be more firmly anchored into the ground.[9] Maybe this is why "the city has not pronounced Andersonville as Girlstown," Alex Papadopoulos mused. There is no equivalent in Andersonville to the phallic rainbow pylons that adorn the streets of Boystown. To draw attention to this gendered disparity, *Time Out Chicago* ran a comedic April Fool's story entitled, "Andersonville to Evulve: New Markers Will Pay Lip Service to Girlstown." The story poked much fun, but in doing so, it offered tremendous insights into gender and urban planning:

> Andersonville resident and out activist Pat Bushman recalls her first big encounter with Boystown's phallic street statues more than ten years ago. "I was pushing my cat Xena in her stroller up North Halsted when I bumped into one of those ugly rainbow-colored penis things," says Bushman of the pylons the city constructed in '98 to officially designate North Halsted as gay-identified 'hood Boystown. "Suddenly, I had an idea."
>
> After a nearly decade-long initiative, Bushman, cofounder of Concerned Lesbians Investing in Tomorrow, has convinced Chicago to officially designate Far North Side nabe Andersonville a lesbian enclave. The city will erect a series of decorative markers to be placed on Clark Street between Foster and Bryn Mawr Avenues by this fall.
>
> "There are more than 25,000 dykes living on the North Side and, quite frankly, I'd like to see the city try and live without the $1,879 we spend annually on bars and nightlife," Bushman tells us over a pint of Guinness at Andersonville bar T's. Japanese automaker Subaru has agreed to pay for the Georgia O'Keeffe–inspired markers, which will be "handcrafted from recycled materials we hauled back from last summer's Michigan Womyn's Music Festival," Bushman says.

But some residents oppose C.L.I.T. "This is really disheartening," says one anonymous gay man who settled on Balmoral Avenue with his partner last year. "For the better part of the last two decades, gay men have worked hard to scrub Andersonville of its hardware stores, softball fields and vegan coffee shops. The fate of its brunch scene now hangs in the balance."[10]

Many residents spoke with me about the idea of installing "vaginal, vulva-looking structures in Andersonville," as one gay man put it. Even though it was a joke, Joe Hollendoner felt "really pleased, not because I think we need to reclaim another gay neighborhood, but because queer women should have some visibility. Gay men just kind of push women out of spaces."

Economic inequality between men and women is a major reason why male-dominated gayborhoods look and feel different than areas that have a distinct lesbian presence. "Lesbians usually cannot afford what gay men can," which compels them "to go farther north to buy something they can afford," one woman explained. Said another, "A lot of it is economics and affordability. The economic situation for women is very, very different. Gay men generally are much more affluent than gay women. Overall, women are not earning what men are earning." A third woman also agreed, "The economic issue cannot be overlooked, because that might be as much of a driver as anything." Research confirms these suspicions. In their 2012 study, entitled "Beyond Stereotypes: Poverty in the LGBT Community," Brad Sears and Lee Badgett found:

> There are approximately 9 million LGBT people in the United States, and almost half of these are lesbian and bisexual women. In addition to facing sexual orientation discrimination, these women also face sex discrimination in education and the workplace and the persistent wage gap in the US. Twenty-four percent of lesbians and bisexual women are poor, compared with only 19% of heterosexual women. (It's not that gay and bisexual men aren't poor, but their poverty rates are roughly equal [13%] to those of heterosexual men.)[11]

The pattern of multiple gayborhoods, one for lesbians and another principally defined by gay men, exists in many cities. A well-traveled woman described lesbian "sub-gayborhoods" that she had seen across the United States: "Gay neighborhoods tend to be male-dominated in general. But in almost every city I've been to, there's always been a little sub-gayborhood where most of the women live that's not really acknowledged or designated." But other lesbians certainly know about it. She surveyed the country, "There's an equivalent community space where women tend to be, like Andersonville for here, the J.P. in Boston, South Park in San Diego, in Philly it's West Philly or Northern Liberties. Even in Houston, the guys are in Montrose, but the women are in the Heights." We see it in Brooklyn too, where lesbians from the other boroughs of New York and the surrounding suburbs tend to cluster in Park Slope. Once enough of them arrived, women rebranded the area as "Dyke Slope."[12] Places like Andersonville and Park Slope, where lesbians cluster, are similar but not identical to the more visible gayborhoods that are dominated by men. "It's always close, it's similar, and there's some cross-pollination," the metropolitan woman explained, "but for residential space, women almost always tend to live in less expensive regions that are tucked away."

When gayborhoods first formed in the coming out era, they were defined mostly by gay men. Distinct lesbian settlements emerged in the 1970s and 1980s, and they were influenced by feminist politics, rather than the sexual marketplaces that more often typified the places where gay men congregated. As a result, lesbian neighborhoods then and to this day consist of clusters of homes located near countercultural institutions, like artsy theaters, alternative bookstores, coffee shops, bike shops, and cooperative grocery stores. This gives them a quasi-underground character, it makes them seem more hidden, and thus it makes them harder to find for those who are not in the know. But lesbian neighborhoods are "always close" and "similar" to the commercially visible gayborhoods, even if women prefer to build their spaces around informal networks of friends or semiformal and transitory institutions like co-ops.

I often heard references to these differences between men and women in their socializing habits. "We're different genders. We connect in different ways," one lesbian remarked. When I asked her to explain, she elaborated, "The social [bar] scene for men is the way that they connect with each other. Women prefer to connect in a different environment and in different ways. We settle down earlier in life too, than men. The age band for the gay men in that scene is probably much wider than the lesbian age band. We phase out of it in the mid- to late-thirties and start nesting at home." Another woman agreed: "Lesbians like to hunker down and stay in, where you'll see men out cruising. We like to stay on our patios, drink our beer, and have our barbecues. That's why you don't see us walking around." A third added, "Men have the money to go into those bars because that's the type of activities they want to be entertained [by]. Women have house parties or gatherings, or we would rather go out to dinner—but in small social settings. Not to say that women don't go out to bars, but generally speaking, it takes a lot of effort to draw women out to bars."

When I asked people if they still referred to Andersonville as Girlstown, most of them said no with a sigh. "We stopped around 2004-ish," one woman told me, "when we started thinking that it was more of a gay neighborhood." What is the difference between Girlstown and a gayborhood? "A gay neighborhood would encompass lesbians, but we didn't talk about it just being a lesbian place," which is what the moniker Girlstown implies—greater concentration. A lesbian presence in Andersonville dwindled as more gay men moved into the area. By the summer of 2010 when I did my interviews, more people called it "Mandersonville" or "Boystown 2" than Girlstown.

Several women resented being priced out and displaced by gay men. "We do blame the gay men a lot," one woman confessed. Andersonville's commercial composition changed dramatically after gay men arrived in larger numbers. There is now an abundance of home decor stores, which inspired *Time Out* magazine to characterize the area as "the unofficial design mecca" of Chicago.[13] "These stores didn't exist before," one woman told me. "It doesn't feel nearly as neighborhoodly and homey, which I associated with women's relationships." Another resident was usually unaware of being a woman or a lesbian in the neighborhood. "If I'm annoyed," she qualified, "then I'm conscious of being a gay woman." What annoys her? "Every time I see a new [home decor] shop open up, I get annoyed because they are almost always opened by gay men." For her, these stores signal that Girlstown is losing its lesbian flavor. The presence of gay men, much more so than even straight people, makes her lesbian identity salient. "There wasn't as much resistance and resentment to straights moving in as there was to the Mandersonville movement," another woman explained. I found this counterintuitive since gays and lesbians are both sexual minorities, while straights are part of the dominant group. How did she account for this? "The straight couples are guests in our community. The gay men are coming in to pillage. Imperialism is coming up from Boystown."

Not everyone had such a damning response, even while most lamented the changes in gender composition: "I didn't feel hostility toward gay men," one woman told me, "but there was definitely a little hostility that we no longer had our own place anymore." Said another, "They can swallow us whole, but we can't swallow them whole. That's where the resentment comes from: they already have Boystown. If they take Girlstown, where are we going to go?" These arguments—home decor stores as symbols of urban change, "they already have Boystown," "they can swallow us whole," "we no longer had our own place anymore"—are all similar to those that both gay men and lesbians make against straight newcomers into Boystown. As we walk through Andersonville, we realize that there is a similar discontent between lesbians and gay men, a cultural infighting if you will,[14] in addition to conflicts between gays and straights.

As more gay men move to Andersonville, some lesbians are again migrating north, this time to Rogers Park. "The lesbians are moving north now to Rogers Park since the gay boys are taking over the neighborhood," one woman told me. But why are lesbians moving north? Why not west or south? Like Boystown, Andersonville remains an important symbol, which is why the adjacent Rogers Park neighborhood is a preferred destination for many women. Rogers Park has a "proximal relationship" to Andersonville, to conjure a phrase we heard once before. It has cheaper real estate, but it is still close enough and connected to the energy of the old lesbian neighborhood.

For more than a decade, Andersonville was home to the annual Chicago Dyke March, a noncommercial and explicitly political alternative to the annual gay pride parade that moves through the streets of Boystown. The Dyke March cemented the identity of Andersonville as a lesbian space. Beginning in 2008, however, it left Andersonville. Organizers now stage it in different neighborhoods across the city. One woman explained why they did this: "In Chicago the march has taken place in Boystown, and for over ten years in the Andersonville neighborhood. But after the march of 2007, organizers and community members began to ask what would happen if the march took place in different neighborhoods, and how would this change the march into a movement. So in 2008 and 2009, Dyke March took place in Pilsen, a predominantly Mexican neighborhood in Chicago, with between 1,000 to 2,000 participants." Organizers now move the march to a new neighborhood every two years. In doing this, "we also do solidarity work with other organizations, [offer] education on LGBTQ issues, and organize and collaborate in fund-raisers and parties, which is how we have evolved from an event-planning committee to a more holistic collective."[15]

Relocating to a new neighborhood every two years creates a visual reminder that Chicago has multiple mini-enclaves of queer people. But it also has the potential to undermine the identity of Andersonville, the most symbolically potent lesbian neighborhood. Organizer Clarissa Gonzalez agrees that this could happen, but she adopts a more comprehensive understanding of the relationship between a neighborhood and its identity:

Is it [the lesbian identity of Andersonville] just because there's a march that's happening once a year? Or is it because there are lots of businesses geared toward this community? Is it because there are spaces that are created for the community? If taking out the march and having it go around the rest of Chicago diluted its lesbianism—I don't know if it's really diluting it. If we took out one bar and the march stayed there, then would it still be a lesbian space? If this can't hold down [if the neighborhood cannot maintain a lesbian identity without the Dyke March], then was it ever really a lesbian space? Or was it a place where the march was happening? If an identity can that easily and quickly lose itself with one thing taken away, then the identity did not have a solid foundation.

Neighborhood identity is greater than just one business or one event, of course, and this is why moving the Dyke March every two years will create more spaces for queer women across the city, rather than risk taking away the one, and only one, they have.

THE PAST, PRESENT, AND FUTURE

When gays and lesbians move out of an existing gayborhood, where do they go next? A historic-geographic mapping of Chicago shows a sequentially northward movement. Gays and lesbians were first visible in Towertown, and from there they moved up along the lakefront to Old Town, New Town, and Boystown. Even in today's era of alleged dispersion, there is a collective northward migration to Andersonville. That gay and lesbian relocation is collectively patterned in this way shows that social networks and a search for community are factors that continue to inform where they choose to live. In addition, that straight presence in Boystown motivates gays and lesbians to move out troubles idealistic arguments about inclusion and integration. Thus, post-gay claims that sexual orientation is receding into the background and that gays and lesbians prefer sexually mixed company live side by side with seemingly contradictory impulses of distinction, exclusion, and separatism.

Although we spent time only in Chicago, the trend of gayborhood revival is not unique to it. We saw the same thing in New York, San Francisco, and Washington, DC. This is not to suggest that people in all these cities simply recreate new gayborhoods in the image of older ones. Reinvention does not mean replication. Gays and lesbians, just like the rest of us, are creatively adjusting to the times.

In our wayfaring, we also challenged the assumption that there can be only one gayborhood in a city. We must change the frame of our conversation away from a notion of *the* gayborhood to gayborhoods and other queer geographies in the plural. Although Boystown still anchors queer commercial activity in Chicago, there are many "smaller colonies," "little pockets," and "mini-enclaves" that same-sex families with children, older gays, people of color, and lesbians are pioneering. These are not all formal gayborhoods, and some of them never will be, but they are places that have a perceptible sexual charge. We met families and older gays in earlier chapters when we developed the metaphor of a trigger as an explanation for why gayborhoods are changing. Rather than asking them to tell us yet again why they were leaving the gayborhood, however, this time we inquired into where they were going next—and we discovered abundant evidence for cultural archipelagos along the way.

Another reason why archipelagos form is because queer people of color are creating unique spaces for themselves, such as the African American hangouts on the south and west sides of Chicago, along with the emergence of distinct scenes for Latino and Asian queer communities. We saw similar developments in New York with Hell's Cocina and the Chocolate Chelsea. All of these urban spaces are separate from the more visible, commercial, and mainstream gayborhood, and they reiterate a need for safe spaces for gays and lesbians of color. Some of them may not participate in white social networks, as Charles Nero suspected, but it is unclear whether the result is a paradox or a surprising proliferation of new queer spaces. He is right that "the multicultural guiding ideals about homosexuality as a subculture" conflict with "the homogeneity of the so-called gay ghetto." We all live in a society where racism is alive and well, after all. But in an act of exquisite agency, queer people of color are forming new gayborhoods of their own, rather than disappearing off the cultural map.[16]

Not only are gayborhoods overwhelmingly white, but they are also decidedly male. Sociologists for a long time assumed that only gay men have territorial aspirations. Manuel Castells set the terms of debate back in 1983:

> *Lesbians, unlike gay men, tend not to concentrate in a given territory,* but establish social and interpersonal networks . . . *[L]esbians do not acquire a geographical basis* . . . [T]here is a major difference between men and women in their relationship to space. Men have sought to dominate, and one expression of this domination has been spatial . . . *Women have*

rarely had these territorial aspirations: their world attaches more importance to relationships and their networks are ones of solidarity and
affection . . . So when gay men try to liberate themselves from cultural
and sexual oppression, they need a physical space from which to strike
out. Lesbians on the other hand tend to create their own rich, inner
world and a political relationship with higher, societal levels. Thus,
they are "placeless" . . . *[W]e can hardly speak of lesbian territory* [emphasis
added].

These days, sociologists and everyday people reject the assertion
that lesbians are placeless. In the Park Slope neighborhood of
Brooklyn, for example, a local resident said, "Being a dyke and living in the Slope is like being a gay man and living in the Village."
Or consider the tiny town of Northampton, Massachusetts, with its
population of thirty thousand. Many consider it the most famous
"lesbian mecca" in the United States, as we know. Writing for *Newsweek*, Barbara Kantrowitz certainly defined it in this way: "Lesbians
have a mecca, too. It's Northampton, Mass. a.k.a. Lesbianville,
USA . . . Northampton has been a lesbian haven since the late 1970s.
'If you're looking for lesbians, they're everywhere,' said Diane Morgan," who coordinates an annual summer festival. The town had a
lesbian mayor, Mary Clare Higgins, who held a near-record tenure
of political office (six terms of two years each, 1999–2011). Clearly,
lesbian geographies exist, they are urban and rural, and they contribute to cultural archipelagos across the country (table 6.1).[17]

This table reports 2010 US Census data, and it shows that lesbians
are spatially concentrated.[18] Although women share some areas
with men (in three cases: Provincetown, Rehoboth Beach, and the
Castro), they often live in less urbanized places than gay men—and
all of their zip codes are much less concentrated overall than those
of gay men. Economic factors account for this. Like all women relative to all men, lesbians have less disposable income, and the table
confirms that female households are located in lower-income areas.
This might limit lesbian territoriality, which is probably why Castells and others have overlooked lesbian enclaves for so long, but
it does not negate it. Lesbians, without a doubt, contribute to the
diversity of queer geographies.[19]

TABLE 6.1 Highest Zip Code Concentrations of Same-Sex Male and Female Couples

	Male couples				Female couples			
Zip code	Location	% of all households	Median price per sq. foot		Zip code	Location	% of all households	Median price per sq. foot
94114	Castro, San Francisco, CA	14.2	671		02657	Provincetown, Cape Cod, MA	5.1	532
92264	Palm Springs, CA	12.0	146		01062	Northampton, MA	3.3	187
02657	Provincetown, Cape Cod, MA	11.5	532		01060	Northampton, MA	2.6	189
92262	Palm Springs, CA	11.3	136		02130	Jamaica Plain, Boston, MA	2.4	304
33305	Wilton Manors, Fort Lauderdale, FL	10.6	206		19971	Rehoboth Beach, DE	2.4	187
90069	West Hollywood, Los Angeles, CA	8.9	481		95446	Guerneville, north of San Francisco, CA	2.2	197
94131	Noe Valley / Glen Park / Diamond Heights, San Francisco, CA	7.4	564		02667	Wellfleet, Cape Cod, MA	2.2	340
75219	Oak Lawn, Dallas, TX	7.1	160		94619	Redwood Heights / Skyline, Oakland, CA	2.1	230
19971	Rehoboth Beach, DE	7.0	187		30002	Avondale Estates, suburban Atlanta, GA	1.9	97
48069	Pleasant Ridge, suburban Detroit, MI	6.8	107		94114	Castro, San Francisco, CA	1.9	671

Source: 2010 U.S. Census, analyzed by Jed Kolko, Trulia Trends, "Welcome to the Gayborhood," Huffington Post, June 15, 2012.

Gayborhoods are de-gaying and growing at the same time. This is a curious contradiction to be sure. They meet the many needs of women and men, people of color and whites, trans- and cisgender individuals, families and singles, older and younger people, those who hail from small towns, city dwellers, suburbanites, and rural folk. Gayborhoods are invested with symbolic importance, and they nurture material anchors that sway the decisions of the community as a whole at the same time as they speak to smaller segments of it. We have taken an incredible journey to arrive at these realizations, although we have answered as many questions as we have asked new ones along the way. The time has come, therefore, to think about what this all means for the future and fate of gay neighborhoods—and for urban life more generally.

Conclusions

What, in the end, should we make of cries like "there goes the gay-borhood"? When we listened to hundreds of people from across the United States share their impressions about gay districts, we heard an extraordinary range of responses, not only about why these urban areas are changing, but also how they will endure and live to see another tomorrow. Residents addressed what cultural iconography is or is not visible to them on the sidewalks and in the storefronts, the numerous options they perceive for where they can comfortably live both within the city and beyond it, how they and their friends decide which one to select, the major junctures in life that trigger them to move, where they go next, how they interact with their gay and straight neighbors, and the social consequences of the Internet in this vibrant mix. Our travels have opened our eyes to the enduring yet evolving relationship between sexuality and the city, the causes and consequences of urban change, the diverse and dynamic cultures of a place, the experiences of a marginalized community on the doorstep of equality, and the protean meanings and material expressions of the gayborhood in America.

WHY GAYBORHOODS ARE CHANGING

By focusing on shifting cultural understandings of sexuality, which we saw in our periodization of the closet, coming out, and post-gay eras, we cast new light on familiar questions of residential choice (how do we decide where to live?) and urban forms (why do neighborhoods develop and change?). Pockets of places where sexual minorities socialize date back to the closet era in the form of "scattered gay places." Since there were no neighborhoods that were yet identifiably queer in composition or character, these small clusters generally formed in bohemian sections of the city where people had a high tolerance for nonconformity and unconventional lifestyles.

Gayborhoods, as such, are modern urban artifacts of the coming out era. They first formed after World War II, and they flourished some decades later after the Stonewall riots. This abbreviated history reminds us of a simple fact: gay neighborhoods have not always been around. And they have never been exclusively queer, even after they arrived on the urban scene. Perpetual change is a reality of city life, but gay districts are not sliding down a slope toward their demise. This is neither the time nor the place for us to sing a requiem for the impending death of great American gayborhoods. What we have discovered sharply contrasts with the conclusion that gay neighborhoods are "largely a thing of the past," as Don Reuter asserts in his book, where he offers a "nostalgic look" at them.[1]

That said, demographers did show us that rates of sexual segregation for male and female same-sex households in the United States have decreased over the last decade. The quantitative index of dissimilarity that they use, however, did not tell much about the motivations of people who actually live in a gayborhood, those who hope to move to one someday, those who have left them behind, or those who reject them outright. A bird's-eye statistical view is a fine place to start—we used it, after all, when we began our own journey—but it leaves us with little more than a numerical description of a much more nuanced process.

Gayborhoods are de-gaying and "deconcentrating," as those demographers say. A buzz about what this means and their future fate has gained momentum in the pages of newspapers across the country, in opinion polls, academic and policy circles, and in casual coffee shop banters. We asked people to talk about the polymorphic meanings of these demographic shifts and, by doing so, we learned how residential flux in the gayborhoods that they call home is related to broader changes in queer life and in our societal discussions about sexuality. We quickly realized that the interesting question to ask was not *whether* gayborhoods are changing—this much we assumed—but rather, and more germane, *why* and *how* are they changing? And what are the consequences of those changes for individuals, communities, and urban landscapes?

The post-gay era featured prominently in our conversations and musings. Homosexuality is becoming more accepted every day, and sexual minorities are blending in with heterosexuals across the United States—in big, medium-sized, and small cities, the suburbs, and in rural areas alike. Echoing Nate Silver, who we met in the opening pages, gays and lesbians today are much more likely to say that they are "ethnically straight." Such an assimilationist and mainstreaming mindset is the primary feature of a post-gay era and, in the first half of our travels, we sought to explain how it affects city life. We discovered that the significance of the specific streets that define a gayborhood is dissolving in the minds of many post-gays. They retain a sense of safety and freedom that those streets once promised when the world was more hostile toward them, but now they stretch those feelings far beyond the gayborhood to most other parts of the city as well. We called this an expansion mechanism. The phrase "San Francisco is our Castro," seeing the gayborhood in Chicago as spanning the entire North Side, or calling Northampton "Lesbianville, USA" were among the most prominent examples that we heard from residents.

People also shrugged their shoulders when we asked them about sexual orientation. Who cares if you are gay, they said? And who cares if you are straight? We called this nonchalance an impulse toward cultural sameness. This post-gay sensibility is the opposite of the "gay imaginary" that emerged during the great gay migration, which produced a perception that gays and lesbians comprised a people who were culturally distinct from heterosexuals.[2] When a realtor from Fort Lauderdale told us, "No one gives a good goddamn if you are gay or straight," we realized that sexual orientation is receding in primacy for how many of us define ourselves and for how we relate with one another. Post-gays see themselves as culturally comparable to their heterosexual neighbors—who tend to think the same way. Some of this mutual affinity is a function of overlapping social networks. Friendships today are more sexually heterogeneous, voluntary, and driven by common tastes and activities rather than an oppressed minority group identity predicated on a sense of shared struggle among only nonheterosexuals. "There is more of a mix now, like people just don't care," one Chicagoan told us. And remember as well what Dyke March organizer Clarissa Gonzalez said: "You don't need to be queer for me to feel like you're family." As our networks change, the assumption attenuates that minorities have more in common with one another than they do with the majority. And without this assumption, it is just as easy for gays and lesbians to leave the gayborhood as it is for straights to move into them.

In the coming out era, sexual segregation, along with the independence that gay people achieved by claiming their own territory, promoted a perception that they belonged to a quasi-ethnic community, and it advanced gay rights (recall the Tavern Guild, for instance). Integration in a post-gay era, therefore, may signal the ideals of equality realized, at least in terms of who lives where and how we interact with our neighbors in the course of our everyday lives. But equality comes with a cultural cost. Gayborhoods are artifacts of urban planning, but in the coming out era, they also embodied distinct queer cultures and communities. Today, however, they are straightening and becoming mainstream. Recall the lesbian couple from New Jersey who smoothly said, "Here, we're just part of a neighborhood. We weren't the gay girls next door; we were just neighbors. We were able to blend in, which is what you want to do, rather than have the scarlet letter on our heads." Or the men from Houston: "We're not 'those people in Montrose.' We're the people next door." And even the punchy sentiments of Quentin Crisp: "When I asked somebody, 'Why do you want to cut yourself off from nine-tenths of the human race?' he said, 'I have nothing in common with them.' But he has everything in common with them except his funny way of spending the evening."

We need to rethink the meaning of sexual diversity. In the coming out era, people used the word "diversity" in a pretty standard way: as a measure of demographic differences, either between people (gays are distinct and thus diverse from straights) or within a group of people (the diversity among gay men, lesbians, bisexuals, and transgender individuals). Politically, the word implied an inclusive, integrated community, as in the notion of "unity through diversity," which inspired activists as they assembled early pride parades in their gayborhoods. As they organized the very first event on June 28, 1970, in New York, the Christopher Street Liberation Day Umbrella Committee released the following message to participants: "Welcome to the very first anniversary celebration of the Gay Liberation movement. We are united today to affirm our pride, our life-style, and our commitment to each other. Despite political and social differences we are united on this common ground: for the first time in history, we are together as *The* Homosexual Community." Activists defined their internal diversity as a source of strength, and they merged it with the language of "community," "celebration," "pride," and "unity" in this first commemoration of the Stonewall riots in the gayborhood where the police raid occurred.[3]

Post-gays still use the word "diversity" to describe the demographic makeup of their community, but they also use it in some new ways. The idea now signifies different ways of life at the individual level—but without a presumption that those differences cohere into a community that shares a unique worldview. As Crisp said, gay people have "everything in common with nine-tenths of the human race." This new definition of diversity grows from a sexual politics that is associated with neoliberalism. An economic policy that is procorporate, anti–big government, and free market–based, neoliberalism promotes a particular brand of sexual politics, what American studies scholar Lisa Duggan describes as a "privatized, depoliticized, gay culture anchored in domesticity and consumption." Post-gays who subscribe to a neoliberal ethic fight for the right to sexual privacy. For them, the meaning of diversity has moved away from references to demographic differences and a group of people who is united through those differences (we gays comprise a people, much like an ethnic group, with distinctively shared interests) to an individualism and private pluralism (my sexuality is a private matter related to how I spend my evenings). No longer self-evidently the characteristic of a community that its members celebrate, diversity is now the property of a person who is domesticated and privatized, often weakly or superficially connected to a community, and whose sexual identity has receded in its centrality. Recall the quibble that a New Yorker had with Richard Goldstein: "All gay Americans want is for others to acknowledge that sexual orientation doesn't make a dammed difference about anything." If we attach the meaning of diversity to a proud public community, rather than a private person, then according to the man who wrote this letter, we are "doing incredible harm in encouraging the notion that gay people are fundamentally different and exist outside the mainstream." Out gays and lesbians do not pretend that they are heterosexual, of course, but like Crisp and this angry New Yorker, they are reluctant to attribute any special significance to that difference. This is why the nighttime activity of gay people is "funny": sex is the final frontier of distressing difference.

POST-GAY WOES

The post-gay era creates a puzzle for sexual minorities as they struggle with how to preserve their culture. If by "culture" we mean to say a particular way of life of a group of people, and if that way of life in a post-gay era expresses itself through arguments that we are just like you (or cultural sameness, as we called it), and we can live anywhere in the city (or expansion), then how is it possible for gay people to preserve distinct sexual cultures and place-based communities? Daniel Mendelsohn was right to wonder, in the title of his cover story for *New York Magazine*, "When Did Gays Get So Straight?" Amid the social and legislative advances of the last few decades, sexual minorities have moved from the "exoticized gay margin to the normalized straight center." Their substance and style today are "increasingly hard to differentiate from those of the straight mainstream." For Mendelsohn, this shift represents the "heterosexualization of gay culture." In recent years, gay and lesbian lives have suffered from "a classic assimilationist ailment (c.f., Jews): You can't take away what was most difficult about being gay without losing what made gay culture interesting in the first place . . . [Y]ou realize that, at least culturally speaking, oppression may have been the best thing that could have happened to gay culture. Without it, we're nothing."[4] Stripped of what once made them interesting, gays and lesbians suffer a huge cultural loss, despite the happiest of endings that the post-gay era promises.

These kinds of questions about the meaning of gayborhood change (does it signal the loss of a community or the dawn of equality?) and its relationship to a way of life (are gayborhoods necessary to preserve sexual cultures?) are among a number of puzzles that captivated us as we traveled across the country. Why did we find that a strong spiritual connection with the gayborhood remains intact for some gays and lesbians, even after they move out from it, while others, like Urvashi Vaid, shun them as "a more spacious closet"? Consider another caution that social theorist Michael Warner makes about the circular underbelly of assimilationist arguments: "Sex and sexuality are disavowed as 'irrelevant' in an attempt to fight stigma. But the disavowal itself expresses the same stigma!" Ultimately, it is "hard to claim that homosexuality is irrelevant as long as you feel the need to make the claim." The scarlet letter remark from the New Jersey lesbian couple we met illustrates this contradiction. Warner also exposes the trouble with the quest for being perceived as normal: "To be fully normal is, strictly speaking, impossible. Everyone deviates from the norm in some way. Even if one belongs to the statistical majority in age group, race, height, weight, frequency of orgasm, gender of sexual partners, and annual income, then simply by virtue of this unlikely combination of normalcies one's profile would already depart from the normal." This leads him to wonder, "Is it normal to want to be normal?"[5]

These are all genuine questions, and they do not have simple answers. Maybe they are not meant to be definitively answered. To ask them, as we have on several occasions, creates space for a much-needed debate about sexuality and urban life in America. Assimilation advocates like Michelangelo Signorile argue that mainstreaming expands options for how to be gay. It allows an entire city to become the functional equivalent of the gayborhood, as we saw. Others, like Bruce Bawer, propose that assimilation prevents urban ghettoization and social ills like poverty, crime, and the scarlet letter of stigma that accompany it. Finally, Andrew Sullivan asserts that assimilation allows homosexuality to enter the public sphere. We know, for example, that straight people are more likely to know openly gay and lesbian people today, and that more straight people live in gayborhoods. This affects their attitudes about homosexuality. In a March 2013 survey of 1,051 adults nationwide, the Pew Research Center, in an effort to learn about "growing support for gay marriage," identified individuals who in the last ten years have rethought their support for it. The survey asked, "What made you change your mind about same-sex marriage?" Roughly a third of the respondents said that their views changed because they now personally know someone who is gay, be it a friend, family member, or a neighbor. Knowing someone who is gay, therefore, or living next door to that person, makes you more accepting of them, and it changes your opinion about issues related to gay equality. This process also contributes to the changing demographic composition of gay neighborhoods. The more gays and lesbians that a straight person meets, the more tolerant that person will become of them, and the more comfortable he or she will feel about socializing in a gayborhood—and maybe living in one someday.[6]

On the flip side, however, are devotees of distinction and separation like Daniel Harris and Daniel Mendelsohn, who counter that assimilation is socially homogenizing, and that it erases a unique queer sensibility that has been a long-standing source of cultural innovation in America. Recall our discussion about the Harlem Renaissance, for instance, where we learned the lesson that concentrated urban settings are crucibles where minority cultures and consciousness flourish. Urvashi Vaid dismisses the claim that gays have assimilated as a mere illusion. She argues that what we have instead is a state of "virtual equality." Why else would more than a quarter of Americans still prefer to not have gays and lesbians as their neighbors, as we saw earlier? Finally, Michael Warner cautions that celebrating assimilation too quickly downplays "a stone wall of hardcore homophobia and heterosexual domination."[7]

This debate is not just academic; it also rings true in the lives of many sexual minorities across the country. In a different June 2013 nationally representative survey of 1,197 LGBT American adults, the Pew Research Center finds "different points of view about how fully they should seek to become integrated into the broader culture." Nearly half their respondents (49%) say that "the best way to achieve equality is to become part of mainstream culture and institutions such as marriage." An equal share, however, say that "LGBT adults should be able to achieve equality while still maintaining their own distinct culture and way of life." This division also expresses itself in attitudes about gayborhoods. More than half of the respondents (56%) say that "it is important to maintain places like LGBT neighborhoods and bars," while 41 percent "feel these venues will become less important over time."[8]

To reconcile these opposing views, we need to acknowledge that the effects of the post-gay era, including an impulse to integrate and a disinterest in the gayborhood, are uneven. According to sociologist Steve Seidman, assimilation and sexual privacy resonate most with those gays and lesbians whose behavior "conforms to traditional gender norms, who link sex to intimacy, love, monogamy, and preferably marriage, and who restrict sex to private acts that exhibit romantic or caring capacity." Such people are "enthralled by respectability," Jane Ward argues, obsessed with being perceived as normal, as Warner said earlier, and they are the ones who are likely to say that gayborhoods are passé. We met many such champions of assimilation, but we also spoke with queer youth, people of color, small-town gays, and transgender individuals who say otherwise, and who remain deeply invested in gay neighborhoods.[9]

As post-gays obsess over being perceived as normal and respectable, and as they abandon the gayborhood, more straights move in and stumble through challenges of their own. Once they arrive, for example, some prefer to say that they live in a "diverse neighborhood" rather than a "gay neighborhood," as we heard several times. The difference is subtle but not trivial. Characterizing a neighborhood as "diverse" detaches it from any particular community, and it invites heterosexuals into it. We are no longer primed to think about sexual orientation at all. In fact, the straights who say this do not consider these urban areas as exclusively *of* gay people: the home base for a community of sexual minorities. Instead, they perceive the gayborhood as a place *for* all individuals, regardless of whether you are gay or straight. Diversity, rather than gay, is a more palatable term for many heterosexuals who live in a gayborhood. It helps them "to overcome their discomfort with being 'out of place' in gay space," in the insightful words of British geographer Gavin Brown.[10]

Furthermore, opinion polls that show heterosexual acceptance of gays and lesbians imply a progressive politics that they do not always deserve. Consider the unsettling observations that sociologist Theodore Greene made at a drag race in Washington, DC, during the fall of 2010:

On the last Tuesday of every October, hundreds of straight and gay people crowd the sidewalks of 17th Street in DC in order to cheer on approximately fifty drag queens racing in stiletto heels from P Street NW to R Street NW. As the drag queens paraded along the street, taking photos with the spectators, and hamming it up to the audience, a young gay white couple began lightly kissing each other on the lips. A 30-something white man with a young girl hoisted on his shoulders pats one of the gay men on the shoulder and asked him if the young men would refrain from kissing in front of his daughter. One of the gay men responded by asking . . . why he feared his daughter watching two men showing affection "in their neighborhood." A white woman standing next to the man [objects] that their kissing was not appropriate on the street. The second gay man retorted that it was a "gay festival," and that if they had a problem with it, they should not be here. As the arguing escalated, another straight couple jumps into the argument, saying that the father meant no real harm, and reminds the gay couple how lucky they should be that this event has the support of straight people. The gay couple repeated that they *belonged* here, and they should go elsewhere if they didn't like what they saw. Frustrated, the straight couples pushed their way through the crowd away from the gay couple.[11]

The discomfort that some straights feel with being out of place in a gay space is in plain view in this example of straights who protest a basic act of intimacy between same-sex couples—during a gay festival in a gayborhood, at that—and who "remind" gays of the good fortune of their "support." What does this mean? I suspect that some straights who live in gayborhoods are not as politically progressive as they might think.

Consider next the many conflicts that surround bachelorette parties in gayborhood bars. The Abbey, a popular venue in West Hollywood, recently implemented a "bachelorette ban." In a 2012 press release, the owners explained that their new policy is in response to "an offensive heterosexual tradition [that] flaunts marriage inequality in the face of gays and lesbians" (this was before the 2013 Supreme Court decision that reinstated same-sex marriage in California):

"Every Friday and Saturday night, we're flooded with requests from straight girls in penis hats who want to ogle our go-gos, dance with the gays and celebrate their pending nuptials. They are completely unaware that the people around them are legally prohibited from getting married," said David Cooley, Founder of The Abbey. "Over the past 22 years, The Abbey has been a place that accepts everyone, gay, straight, lesbian, transgender, bisexual and everything in between. We love our straight girlfriends and they are welcome here, just not for bachelorette parties."[12]

Maybe these women think they are being open-minded when they decide to celebrate at a gayborhood bar, even though gays and lesbians at the time could not legally marry. One female resident agreed that this was hypocritical: "If you're a straight woman who supports LGBT rights and gay marriage, you should understand this ban. If you don't understand why this ban is in place and think it's unfair that you can't celebrate your upcoming marriage in a gay bar, then maybe you should rethink how much you support LGBT rights and what it really means to support gay marriage."[13]

Business owners in Washington, DC, went a step further. When partygoers enter the gay bar Town Danceboutique, "They are asked to sign a petition in support of gay marriage. Owner Ed Bailey sends the petition to the customer's representative in Congress." This move takes the performance out of the assumption of progressiveness and thus authenticates it. Bailey says, "The girls want to come and see the dancers. I don't think it's on their mind at all, 'We can get married and, oh, you can't.' I don't think the girls are malicious in their intent." Chicago residents agree that when straights perform progressiveness, they do so out of ignorance, not intentional malice. A bar in Boystown called Cocktail banned bachelorette parties in 2009. "We appreciate that these women are not homophobic and want to party with us," a gay man remarked. "But with all that's going on in the media about us not being able to marry, are these women willing to march with us or raise money with us or work to change somebody's attitude to help us get equal rights?"[14]

Just as the presence of conflict between gays and straights over matters that are directly related to sexuality can indicate the performance of progressiveness, so too can its absence. Recall those straight gayborhood residents in Chicago who felt indifferent about their gay neighbors and said that they do not think about them or notice them very much at all. Would these straights do anything to preserve a gayborhood or its history? When we pressed them to comment on the *gay* part of the gayborhood, some defensively retorted that integration is the desired outcome that gay people have been seeking all along. This dismissal absolved them of political engagement, since they are apparently doing their part by not making a big deal about the fact that they live in a gayborhood. Their inaction, in other words, freed them from any real responsibility. Vague acceptance of a group or indifference to it is not enough, and coexistence does not always translate to active support or learning what members of a minority group need in order to survive. It would be interesting to survey a large number of randomly sampled gayborhood residents, ask them about various forms of political engagement, and then compare the results by sexual orientation. How many times last year or last month did you write to your congressperson in support of gay and lesbian rights? How many times did you march in a local demonstration whose purpose was to draw attention to gay and lesbian rights? How many times did you volunteer at a gay or lesbian organization? How often did you donate money to a gay or lesbian charity? How often did you post something in support of gay rights on your Facebook status or in a tweet?

A blissful but nonmalicious ignorance about sexual inequality, along with political absolution and inaction, are the main modes of what I call a *performative progressiveness*. Sexual integration is not necessarily a sign of progress, since some straights who live in a gayborhood are not in political solidarity with gays and lesbians. These straights, along with those neoliberal post-gays who seek privacy and move out from the gayborhood, undermine these otherwise emancipatory urban areas across the country.

ANOTHER TOMORROW

The term post-gay is part of an American cultural obsession with the prefix post-. In a 2003 *Los Angeles Times* story entitled, "In 'Post' Culture, the Prefix Is In," Mary McNamara comments, "Enter the brave new post-everything world in which we mark our rejection of past cultural movements, and our refusal to commit to new ones, with one little word: 'post.' In the past few years, Americans have been told that society is becoming post-black, post-ethnic, post-ironic, post-feminist, and post-political." This worldview is rooted in what communication studies scholar Mary Douglas Vavrus describes as "a generally decent, if misguided, belief that our society has reached a moment in which we are living out our lives on a level playing field." Public conversations about whether Americans are post-gay (or post-black and post-racial) presume that conflicts have eased,[15] not that we have eliminated them altogether. Progress exists alongside continuing problems. Neal Broverman, in the title of an opinion essay that he published in the *Advocate* in July 2013, captures this important insight: "If Racism Is Alive and Well, Homophobia Has Lots of Good Years Left." He is right. As an example, the June 2013 Pew Survey we looked at earlier finds that an overwhelming share of LGBT Americans (92%) say that society has become more accepting of them over the past decade, and they expect this trend to continue. However, relatively few (19%) of these same individuals say that "there is a lot of social acceptance for the LGBT population today." A majority (59%) says there is "some," and 21 percent say there is "little or no acceptance today."[16]

Post-gay does not mean post-discrimination. This will ensure that gayborhoods live on to see another tomorrow. "There are always going to be bigots and homophobes in the world, and they're always going to have really loud voices," a gay man reminded us in this book. "And people who are in minority groups are always going to perceive that lots of people are discriminating against them, even if they're not." This, recall him saying, "is going to cause them to want to go to places where they feel safe." It does not matter "whether or not they're needed," said another man, because "the perception will be that they are needed." Thus, anyone who argues that we do not *need* gayborhoods anymore is missing the point. Acceptance has limits. If prejudice and discrimination are "alive and well" in a world of legislative equality, as Broverman correctly recognizes about race, then imagine what life must be like for sexual minorities when employers, landlords, schools, hospitals, adoption agencies, and even the federal government can legally discriminate against them.[17] This is why we heard one somber story after another from queer youth of color, transgender individuals, those who hail from small towns, and many other people, like Carolyn and Brian, who still see the gayborhood as a safe harbor.

Residents, business owners, political figures, and city officials are also working tirelessly to ensure that the cultural and institutional character of existing gayborhoods will survive into the future, despite the demographic flux. We met people who are investing in anchors, like Sidetrack and the Center on Halsted in Boystown or Women and Children First in Andersonville, while gay and lesbian business owners are encouraging one another to maintain economic control over their real estate. They are also crafting a dense commercial and leisure zone, like the lively nightlife strip on Halsted Street. Finally, activists, politicians, public figures, and city officials are working together to install monuments of historical commemoration and collective memory, such as the art deco rainbow pylons that line Halsted Street and the outdoor Legacy Walk. These are quite powerful, as they transform a gayborhood into a symbolically charged heritage space where sexual minorities can connect with their history and thus feel a sense of perpetuity despite the relentless passage of time.

We discovered these two and several other trends in the second half of our trip. All of them caution against misreading gayborhood change as synonymous with their decline. It is true that some gays and lesbians are leaving the gayborhood and dispersing across the city, but where they go next is not random. Dispersion is an urban reality that is unexpectedly patterned. Birds of a feather insist on flocking together, regardless of whether society becomes more postgay, whether more straights tolerate or even accept homosexuality, whether gays and lesbians assimilate into the mainstream, whether they have more straight friends, and regardless of whether sexual orientation recedes into the background of social life.

This propensity for minority group members to stick together is called homophily, and we saw two ways in which it is compatible with residential dispersion. First, sometimes gay people want to be around other gay people in general. When their homes become too expensive or too straight, they migrate collectively and revive the gayborhood somewhere else. In Chicago, there has been a sequentially northward movement for more than a century now. Gays and lesbians were first visible in Towertown, and from there they moved adjacently to Old Town, New Town, and then to Boystown. Today, it is tempting to feel a sense of loss when we realize that gay people are leaving Boystown. But this is historically short-sighted. If we concluded that gayborhoods in Chicago were outmoded, then we would miss an ongoing, systematic gay migration north to Andersonville.

In the coming out era, gayborhoods were islands of meaning in a city that was flooded with heterosexual hostilities. When the "biggie bang," as Scott called it, happened in the post-gay era, the mindset of gays and lesbians expanded from these isolated islands to the entire city, which they now see as filled with meaningful living and socializing options. This does not signal the end of American gayborhoods; on the contrary, they are growing. Gays and lesbians can take the tone of the primary gayborhood, which they have set, and creatively reattach it to many of the places where they are moving. The migration patterns of specific groups of people like same-sex families, aging gays, people of color, and lesbians have become more visible in recent years, and they also account for some of this urban variety. This is also why Andersonville is not the "next" gayborhood, a word that implies that it will singularly replace Boystown. Instead, Andersonville is a "new" gayborhood—or "another" gayborhood, more likely. Therefore, in a moment of theoretical irony, the tenets of the post-gay era support a generative notion of multiplicity, which we captured in our provocative image of cultural archipelagos. Archipelagos are not exclusive to big cities like Chicago, New York, or San Francisco. We also visited settlements in small cities, medium-sized cities, the suburbs, and in rural areas. None of these areas houses what we conventionally consider a gay mecca, but each is a place where today we see large increases in gay and lesbian newcomers.

Established gayborhoods, emerging concentrations, and all the other "little planets of gays" are quite diverse fiscally. Consider the findings of a June 2012 national real estate analysis: "While pricey areas like San Francisco's Castro district and Southern California's West Hollywood are still prime gayborhoods, there are some more affordable ones that are home to many same-sex couples." Several of these "leading gayborhoods," such as the Detroit suburb of Pleasant Ridge and Avondale Estates near Atlanta, have "much lower housing prices." This recent analysis debunks the widely circulating notion that gayborhoods change, and potentially disappear, because gays are priced out of them. The reality is that there are "gayborhoods for many budgets."[18] These areas may not have that je ne sais quoi, center-of-the-queer-universe feeling that the Castro once had, but this does not mean that they are culturally insignificant.

It is precisely because sexual minorities still want to be near one another, even while they are also blending into the multicultural mosaic, that our national landscape today is defined by queer geographies—in the plural—of new and next gayborhoods and maybe even gay Potemkin villages; mini-enclaves and mini-gay areas; gay-friendly, straight-friendly, and diverse areas; commercial centers and residential clusters; scattered gathering places; smaller colonies; and little pockets and planets of gays in cities of different sizes, the suburbs, and in rural areas alike. Acceptance *and* same-sex sexuality are palpable on the streets of all these places. We live in a world, therefore, not of shriveling sexual and spatial expressions but instead of extraordinary growth and new possibilities. The queer spirit has become more plastic and portable in a post-gay era, and this helps gayborhoods to evolve in exciting ways as many different gender and sexual minorities reinvent their relationship with them, and thus the city itself, in profound ways.

ACKNOWLEDGMENTS

The image of the solitary scholar is so misleading. Yes, solitude characterizes some of our creative craft, but the production of new knowledge is also undeniably social. It is my pleasure, therefore, to thank the many people without whom I could never have embarked on, let alone completed, the remarkable journey that resulted in the book you now hold in your hands.

I dedicate this book to the Princeton Society of Fellows. I had the immeasurably good fortune to join this interdisciplinary community of scholars. I held the LGBT-Cotsen postdoctoral fellowship from 2008–11. Cosponsored by charter trustee Lloyd E. Cotsen and the Fund for Reunion/Princeton Bisexual, Transgendered, Gay and Lesbian Alumni Association, the award provides three years of support for young scholars who study sexuality. The Joseph Henry House was my intellectual home, and an ideal place to build this project from the ground up. I thank Leonard Barkan, Mary Harper (with fondness), Susan Stewart, and Carol Rigolot for their visionary leadership, and Susan Coburn, Cass Garner, and Penny Stone for administrative support. Thanks as well to my cohort members—Lucia Allais, Eduardo Canedo, Yaacob Dweck, and Ricardo Montez—and indeed all the fellows for their camaraderie. I am also grateful for the warm welcome in the sociology department at Princeton, where I had the privilege of working with Paul DiMaggio and Doug Massey. Their hearts are as open as their minds are brilliant.

From the East Coast of the United States, I traveled nearly three thousand miles to the West Coast of Canada, where I accepted my first assistant professorship in the sociology department at the University of British Columbia. What I began in Princeton I finished in the Olympic city of Vancouver. I am not Canadian (a Chicago native, actually), and I had no prior friendship or familial networks in the area. As you can imagine, then, the enthusiasm that

I received upon my arrival in July 2011 helped to ease my transition and nerves. The department and the university provided abundant resources for me on the home stretch of this book. A special thanks to Neil Guppy, the former department head; Darrin Lehman, the former dean of the Faculty of Arts; and Gage Averill, the current dean, for their confidence and investment in my career. They played a pivotal role in granting me a one-year leave so that I could complete my fellowship at Princeton. Thanks as well to the Peter Wall Institute for Advanced Studies, especially Janis Sarra, the dazzlingly talented director. During my second year at UBC, I won a competitive Early Career Scholars fellowship for my work. This program selects a small group of untenured assistant and recently tenured associate professors from all academic disciplines across the university. The 2012–13 cohort, of which I was a member, included scholars from anthropology, architecture, English, genetics, linguistics, ophthalmology, philosophy, physical therapy, psychology, sociology, and zoology. The structure and mission of the Princeton Society of Fellows resembles that of the UBC Institute for Advanced Studies. This felicitous alignment created continuity across my postdoctoral and assistant professor experiences.

The six years it took me to research and write this book have been graced by exquisitely gifted people. For their intellectual companionship, I thank Chris Bail (conceptualizing the media as a data source), Delia Baldassarri (statistical savvy), Ellen Berrey (scholarship on diversity), Matt Brim (fabulously queer perspectives on questions of separatism and integration), Joe Broderick (Princeton IRB), Aaron Brost (queer market research), Kathleen Cioffi (assistance with maps and charts), Alexander Davis (inter-rater reliability tests), John D'Emilio (how historical events affect same-sex location patterns), Steve Engel (provocative conversations about performative progressiveness), John Evans (NVivo guidance), Dave Frech (professional photographs), Josh Gamson (queer parenting research), Gary Gates (2009 ACS data on same-sex households), Theo Greene (navigating the literature on gay neighborhoods), William Guthe (GIS training), Christina Hanhardt (how historical events affect same-sex location patterns), Kathy Hull (queer parenting research), Marcus Hunter (general insights into urban sociology), Mary Luebbe (Humanities and Social Sciences reference librarian at UBC for help with the US Census), Ryan Mulligan (managing copyrights), Jon Norman (general insights into urban sociology), Martin O'Connell (at the US Census Bureau for help with counting same-sex households), Wenona Rymond-Richmond (crime rates in gay neighborhoods), Matt Salganick (statistical savvy), Tsering Wengyal Shawa (GIS instruction), Cathy Slovensky (expert copy editing), Amy Spring (index of dissimilarity), Tim Stewart-Winter (how historical events affect same-sex residential patterns), Verta Taylor (queer parenting research), and Transcription Professionals. Paula Kamen owns the last-mentioned company, which I have used since my graduate student days, and Chris Heidenrich completed all my interview transcriptions speedily and even shared her musings about them. Last but certainly not least, I would like to acknowledge the 125 Chicagoans who I interviewed. This book would have been impossible had they not agreed to share their time and personal stories with me. Thank you so much. I hope that I have faithfully rendered your experiences. I am especially grateful to Billy Gerardi for opening his beautiful home to me during the summer of 2010 when I conducted my fieldwork.

For their good spirits and reliably inspiring conversations, I express my gratitude to friends and colleagues alike: Rumee Ahmed, Debbie Bazarsky, Brent Camilleri, Ayesha Chaudhry, Scott Conway, Jon David, Michaela DeSoucey, Eric Enderlin, Neil Fancourt, David Frank, Ron Garcia, Jeremy Gottschalk, Debbie Gould, Kiley Hamlin, Ryan Kerian, Jeff Kosbie, Bob Leschke, Riley McMitchell, David Mejias, Vincent Metallo, Nick Meyer, Caroline Mildner, Shaylih Muehlmann, Emily Quinn, Jeremie Benoit Rosley, Mikel Ross, Wendy Roth, Trent Shaw, Paul Steinke, Nicole Van Cleve, Janet Vertesi, Mike Wong, Stu Zirin, and the sociology department at UCSD (especially Amy Binder, John Evans, and John Skrentny, three magnificent scholars for whom I feel great affection).

I was the beneficiary of much material support along the way. Mary Harper and Susan Stewart at the Princeton Society of Fellows vetted grant applications. I thank them for their patience and guidance. This research would not have been possible without the financial support of Princeton University's Committee on

Research in the Humanities and Social Sciences. David Grazian invited me to pen an essay on gayborhoods for *Contexts*. I am grateful for this early opportunity to think through my ideas. A warm thanks to the late Jim Clark, who arranged my first meeting with Princeton University Press. The Institute for Advanced Studies at UBC gave me a course buyout, and I was able to use this gift of time to finish the book. A heartfelt thanks to all the individuals who gave me permission to reproduce their photographs and art. Finally, I thank Dave Frech, Mike Hines, and Jessica Randklev for their brainstorming efforts on creative possibilities for the cover of this book.

Some stars in my life have shined so brightly that I must acknowledge their light one by one. A profound thanks to my colleague Neil Gross. He read a draft of this entire manuscript before it was published—and some chapters several times. This book is far better because he read it first. An equally profound thanks to my developmental editor, David Lobenstine. He, too, read the entire manuscript, line by line, and guided me on how to tinker boldly and beautifully to reframe and rethink, alter the tone, and other shifts too numerous to name. His mind is a thing of beauty. I also am extremely fortunate for the hands-on involvement of Eric Schwartz, the sociology and cognitive sciences editor at Princeton University Press. Eric is a masterful editor. He mentored me on subtle matters of craft, and he generously welcomed my thoughts on the production of this book. I am honored that the Princeton Studies in Cultural Sociology series editors Paul DiMaggio, Michele Lamont, Bob Wuthnow, and Viviana Zelizer took an interest in this project and included it in their illustrious list. Two anonymous reviewers provided page after page of constructively critical comments. Reviewing a book manuscript is a noble yet selfless task. They brought my research to a level of sophistication that I could not have possibly reached otherwise. Thank you. Any remaining errors, oversights, or stylistic stumbles are entirely mine, I'm afraid.

These are long lists, I know, but each person has had an indelible impact on me, my mind, my heart, and, of course, the pages of this book. I am fortunate to feel the admiration that I do. That they stretch from Princeton to Chicago to Vancouver—and so many places in between—testifies to the grace that surrounds my life.

My last breaths of gratitude I save for Gary Baker: for your limitless love and unending enthusiasm from start to finish on this project. What an adventure! I am so happy to open and close these pages with you.

THE LANGUAGE OF SEXUALITY

Sexual minorities regularly debate how to characterize their collective selves. This conversation has often expressed itself as a string of letters. The "gay" community and the "gay" rights movement of the 1970s, for example, became the "gay and lesbian" community and the "gay and lesbian" rights movement in the 1980s. Later that decade came "bisexuals," and then "transgender" people were rhetorically represented in the 1990s. And so the letters expanded from G to GL to GLB to GLBT. Self-identified "queers" also arrived on the scene in the 1990s. The group sometimes expressed itself as "GLBTQ," and at other times the word "queer" became a shorthand for an ever-expanding list. The appeal of queer increased as other groups demanded inclusion: those who were questioning their sexuality, intersexed peoples, two-spirited individuals, and even straight allies. To represent each one resulted in an unwieldy acronym: GLBTQQITA.

It is never easy to characterize all nonheterosexual and noncisgender persons, given their tremendous diversity. I follow a three-part strategy in this book. First, I mostly speak of "gays and lesbians" specifically and narrowly, and I periodically reference "sexual minorities," "gay people," and "gays" when making general statements about the group, especially when those statements are connected with a quote. This is an artifact of my data. My interviewees overwhelmingly identified as gay or lesbian, and so it is an accurate way to describe them. In addition, the journalists who I quote in this book also mostly spoke with lesbians and gay men. Therefore, this is less an arbitrary decision than it is an empirical reflection.

Second, when I know that a person self-identifies as bisexual, transgender, open, fluid, queer, or something else (either because I interviewed someone who identifies in one or more of these ways or because the journalist makes it clear), then I use that respective term. In other words, I acknowledge bisexual, transgender, and other voices when they speak for themselves and on their own terms. It is useful to separate these groups since research suggests that the residential decisions of bisexuals and transgender people are different from those of lesbians and gay men (and even lesbians, in turn, make decisions that are distinct from gay men). Because I have considerably less evidence on where bisexuals and transgender people choose to live, I feel that it would be irresponsible of me to make unsubstantiated claims about them.

Finally, I use a different approach when I make analytic remarks. I interchangeably use "gay people," "gays," "gays and lesbians," "the gay community," and "gay culture" when I want to emphasize the collective yet singular nature of the group. However, I use "queers," "queer people," "queer communities," and "queer culture" when I want to emphasize the collective nature of the group yet be mindful of its internal diversity or to make a point that emphasizes differences from heterosexuals. I realize that the word "queer" can denote a particular political view, but I do not use it in this way. Instead, I use it to invoke a cultural queering, if you will, or those myriad ways in which the divisions between "straight" cultures and "gay" cultures are sometimes blurring and at other times standing in stark contrast from one another.

Conversations about urban areas have not been as rhetorically complex. "Gayborhood" never expanded to "gay and lesbian neighborhood," "gay, lesbian, bisexual neighborhood," and so on. I use gay neighborhood, gayborhood, gay district, and gay village interchangeably to denote a physical area of the city. This decision stems from specific principles of cultural analysis that direct me to use the actual words of my respondents, rather than superimposing my own analyst-selected categories onto them. Some scholars of race and ethnicity may object to my use of "enclave" as a synonym for neighborhood since they conceptualize it as a geographically bound, horizontally and vertically integrated economy. I generally do not use it as a result, unless it is part of a quote. I speak of "queer spaces" deliberately when I want to emphasize the presence of a greater diversity of nonheterosexuals, think about areas other than urban neighborhoods, or when I want to advance arguments that are counterhegemonic and non-heteronormative. I only use "gay ghetto" when it is part of a direct quote, given its particular and charged meanings in urban scholarship. Finally, I sometimes distinguish "lesbian spaces" and "lesbian neighborhoods" from "gay male-dominated gayborhoods" when I want us to think carefully about gender differences, and I use "same-sex male" and "same-sex female households" when I discuss census results.

I use the term "sexuality" throughout the book. Some readers might wonder if this is an oversimplification since contemporary notions of gay men, lesbians, bisexuals, transgender people, and queer people also refer to a sociocultural identity or status, not just a sexual one. Sexuality is a word that people use all the time, of course, but our ubiquity of usage does not signal unanimity over what it means. Most people still regard sexuality as a personal and private matter, an intimate topic that concerns our individual desires, libidos, experiences, moralities, subjectivities, bodily pleasures, and general eroticisms. Yet, I maintain that sexuality is also remarkably social, political, and cultural, which is why I think it is important for us to use this particular word.

Clearly, there is no simple or singular solution for how to engage with the extraordinary diversity of human sexualities. Precision, context, evidence, and representational integrity are the principles that guide me in my discussions throughout this book.

APPENDIX:
WHAT ARE GAYBORHOODS?
HOW DO WE STUDY THEM?

WHAT ARE GAYBORHOODS?

Neighborhoods, Ann Forsyth argues, are a "basic building block of urban areas." Residents who live in the same area generally feel a "psychological unity" with one another, Suzanne Keller adds. But what is a *gay* neighborhood, specifically? There are many ways to think about these particular types of urban areas. A gayborhood can be a "ghetto" for disadvantaged sexual minorities; the site of real or "imagined communities" of like-minded queer people; a "quasi-ethnic" settlement that promotes identity development; a "safe space" to which queer moral refugees retreat for shelter from heterosexual hostility; a "site of resistance" from which activists can overcome antigay violence; an "urban land market" that promotes economic vitality and revitalization; and an "entertainment district" of consumption and tourism.[1]

Scholars published some of the earliest studies on gayborhoods in the 1970s. Martin Levine, for example, defined them as urban areas with an institutional concentration (a cluster of commercial establishments), a distinct culture area (a perceptible presence of nonheterosexuals on the streets and their images on billboards, posters, or in store windows), social isolation (discrimination compels queer people to restrict their social lives with one another), and residential concentration. Stephen Murray added that gayborhoods are based in specific spaces—he calls this "territory" and "geographical distinctness"—and major "gay meccas" like New York and San Francisco are institutionally complete with basic social services, like churches, travel agencies, hair salons, pharmacies, and those that are profitable, such as bars and bathhouses.[2]

Over the next two decades, researchers examined clues for institutional concentration in particular by relying on community periodicals, tourism guides, and business listings. Levine used this "ecological method," as he calls it, to create maps of "gay gathering places."[3] Although he could make maps of institutional clusters, Levine and others could not do the same for residences in 1979, since the US Census did not track same-sex households, which it now does, or individual sexual orientation, which it still does not.

Manuel Castells and Karen Murphy offered an innovative solution three years later. They used five types of data to establish the spatial boundaries of the gay community, each of which produced a distinct map: (a) they interviewed key informants to create a map of residential concentration (solving Levine's problem); (b) they looked at 1977 Voters' Registrar data files to find "multiple male households in each urban unit" (a second solution to the same problem); (c) they examined the spatial distribution of voting patterns for openly gay candidate Harvey Milk in a San Francisco citywide election from 1975 (a new measure that others had not considered); (d) believing that "gay bars tend to overlap with gay residential areas," they searched for bar listings in *Bob Damron's Address Book*; and (e) they mapped gay businesses by reviewing the Golden Gate Business Association Directory. All five sources showed "a similar spatial pattern of gay residence."[4]

The census first asked about same-sex households in 1990, but that data proved unusable for the many reasons we have already considered in this book. It was not until 2000 that the Census Bureau collected the first set of unaltered and thus unbiased data, which scholars could use to identify same-sex location patterns. While they still did not ask about individual sexual orientation, sexual behavior, or sexual attraction—"three common ways used to identify gay men and lesbians in surveys"—they did inquire into how people in a household were related to one another. There were two options: related persons (which would include husband/wife, son/daughter, and brother/sister pairs) and unrelated persons. Gary Gates, in a paper he coauthored with Jason Ost, explains how researchers made inferences about lesbians and gay men from these categories: "Since 1990, the Census Bureau has included an 'unmarried partner' category to describe an unrelated household member's relationship to the householder. If the householder designates another adult of the same sex as his or her unmarried partner, the household counts as a same-sex unmarried-partner household."[5]

In addition to the census, we can also use municipal markings to find (and measure) gayborhoods. In a nationally unprecedented move in 1997, Chicago installed tax-funded rainbow pylons along Halsted Street to celebrate the area's queer character. Two years later, "the Newcastle City Council became the first City Council in the UK to announce it was actively seeking to develop a 'gay village,' which it did by designating one of its neighborhoods as the 'Pink Triangle.'" In April 2007, Philadelphia became the second American city to mark one of its neighborhoods as gay by officially renaming a portion of the Washington Square West district in Center City as "the Gayborhood." The city added thirty-six rainbow flags underneath street signs that bordered the area, which extends from Eleventh to Broad Street and from Pine to Locust. A *Philadelphia Daily News* headline declared, "New Signs Make It Official: We Have a 'Gayborhood.'" Finally, in July 2013, the city of Vancouver, in British Columbia, installed four permanent rainbow-colored crosswalks at the intersection of Davie and Bute Streets in the heart of the Davie Village gayborhood. This was the first fixed installation in Canada.[6]

In summary, there are four ways that we can conceptualize gay neighborhoods:

1. *Geography*: gayborhoods are identifiable in space and place, typically by one or two specific streets that locals can point out on a map.
2. *Culture*: nonheterosexuals "set the tone," to borrow a pithy yet powerful phrase from George Chauncey. There is a perceptible presence of them on the streets, and images of their lives appear on billboards, community newspapers, posters, store signs, and bus stops. The neighborhood is also the site of events like the annual gay pride parade.[7]
3. *Residences*: while everyone who lives in a gayborhood does not self-identify as LGBTQ, many people certainly do (a statistically sizable proportion, in fact).

4. *Organizations*: there is a cluster of commercial establishments, especially gay bars, bathhouses/sex clubs, bookstores, progressive churches, political and nonprofit organizations, and community centers that cater to the LGBT demographic. They appeal to those who live in the neighborhood, of course, but also to those who live elsewhere yet visit and/or socialize in it.

HOW DO WE STUDY GAYBORHOODS? NATIONAL TRENDS

To understand why and how gayborhoods across the country are changing, I first looked at 2000 and 2010 US Census collections. The census provides demographic data about the location of same-sex partner households in the United States at one point in time and their migration over time (when we compare the 2000 and 2010 counts). I also looked at several opinion polls that track how societal attitudes toward homosexuality have changed. Finally, I collected 617 newspaper articles from seventeen different sources. This public conversation includes twenty-seven urban, suburban, and rural locations, and it spans forty years of coverage, from 1970 to 2010 (I chose 1970 as my start date in light of theoretical arguments that gayborhoods flourished after the Stonewall riots of 1969). I used the following sources: the *Advocate, Boston Globe, Boston Herald, Chicago Sun-Times, Chicago Tribune, Houston Chronicle, Los Angeles Times, New York Times, Philadelphia Daily News, Philadelphia Inquirer, San Diego Union-Tribune, San Francisco Chronicle, Seattle Post-Intelligencer, USA Today, Village Voice, Washington Post,* and *Washington Times.*

I selected these newspapers using what sociologists call maximum variation sampling. According to Michael Quinn Patton, this approach gathers "information-rich cases . . . from which one can learn a great deal about issues of central importance," instead of "gathering little information from a large, statistically significant sample." The strategy approximates probability sampling by extending the statistical principle of regression to the mean. In other words, my sample includes attitudes that may be extreme yet also those that are representative of how most people think. Table A.1 lists the locations that the newspaper articles feature.[8]

TABLE A.1 US Gayborhoods

City	Frequency	Percent
San Francisco, CA	103	16.7
Chicago, IL	73	11.8
Philadelphia, PA	65	10.5
New York City, NY		
All boroughs	63	10.2
Unspecified	52	8.4
Multiple Cities	43	7.0
San Diego, CA	43	7.0
International Cities	37	6.0
Washington, DC	26	4.2
Seattle, WA	20	3.2
Boston, MA	18	2.9
Resort Towns		
Asbury Park, NJ; Fire Island, NY; Key West, FL;		
Northampton, MA; Provincetown, MA	18	2.9
Houston, TX	12	1.9
Suburbs	11	1.8
Dallas, TX	9	1.5
Los Angeles / West Hollywood	8	1.3
Florida		
Orlando, South Beach, and Sarasota	4	0.7
Pittsburgh, PA	4	0.6
Detroit, MI	3	0.5
Baltimore, MD	2	0.3
Atlanta, GA	1	0.2
Columbus, OH	1	0.2
Saint Louis, MO	1	0.2
Total	617	100

I gathered articles using Lexis-Nexis Academic, a full-text database of newspapers. I searched for seven keywords in singular and plural forms: Boystown (a phrase particular to Chicago), gay enclave(s), gay ghetto(s), gay neighborhood(s), gay village(s), gayborhood(s), and homosexual neighborhood(s). These are the phrases that academics, municipal governments (e.g., city websites), marketing and advertising agencies, journalists, and activists all tend to use. Ubiquity of usage, however, does not mean that these are the only ways of communicating about queer spaces. Some readers may object that lesbians are not represented in these key-words and that, as a result, I have systematically neglected them in this book. As a robustness check, I searched for the phrase "lesbian neighborhood(s)" within the same parameters, and I retrieved only five results. Two of these were already in my sample, and two others were not about gender and urban areas at all (the phrase was part of a longer string: "Columbia Heights Gay and Lesbian Neighbor-hood Association"). This means that I missed only one newspaper article in my original data collection, which reported on the Park Slope neighborhood of Brooklyn. Fortunately, several articles within my sample discussed this well-known lesbian neighborhood. Thus, while it is true that the story for women is sometimes differ-ent than it is for gay men, my sampling strategy does not prevent me from engaging in this important conversation.[9]

I did not do a similar search within the LGBT media because writers who work within this genre use the same keywords much more casually. A press may describe local events within the gay-borhood or at a bar in the gayborhood. Therefore, including the LGBT media would artificially inflate the sample size of articles that addressed the topic while reducing the number of articles that addressed the questions that motivated me in this book. As another robustness check, however, I searched for the same keywords in the "LGBT Life" database (a functional equivalent of Lexis-Nexus). This produced 2,928 articles. There was no way for me to system-atically sample from within this population, which then introduced the possibility of selection bias into my data set. I included the *Village Voice* because it was part of the Lexis-Nexus database, and I included the *Advocate* because it returned a more manageable fifty-five articles, all of which I include in my analysis. The gay press more often emphasizes the symbolic aspects of gayborhoods, whereas the mainstream press focuses on economic dimensions. My findings may underemphasize the former. This is one among a number of reasons why I also interviewed actual gayborhood residents, as I discuss below.[10]

I coded each article deductively by looking for several indicators of assimilation and the post-gay era. Thomas Cook calls this approach "multiple operationalism" or "critical multiplism."[11] I used it to find references to intergroup interactions, group distinctions, integration, the centrality of sexuality in self-identity and social life, network structures (homophily or heterogeneity), references to antigay stigma and discrimination, and anything to do with residential choice (for gays and straights) and urban forms. I also looked at the year each article was published, its title, source, placement (front page or elsewhere), story type (news, letters, opinions), word count, centrality (gayborhoods as central to the discussion or not), and the location covered. My total sample included 1,446 pages of single-spaced text. Articles averaged 1,153 words and ranged from 31 to 8,656 words. Sixty-six articles (10.7%) appeared on the front page; there were 567 (91.9%) news stories and 50 (8.1%) letters and opinion-editorial pieces; and discussions of gayborhoods were central in 145 (23.7%) stories (471 stories, while still discussing gay neighborhoods, were generally about other issues). Table A.2 details the distribution of articles over time.

Of my 617 articles, 396 (64.2%) addressed gay residential choice. In other words, the journalist included interview transcripts from self-identified gay or lesbian individuals who explained why they did

TABLE A.2 Gayborhood Coverage over Time

Years	Frequency	Addressed gay residential choice	%	Addressed straight residential choice	%
1970–74	1	0	0	0	0
1975–79	7	7	100	1	14.3
1980–84	7	5	71.4	2	28.6
1985–89	26	15	57.7	0	0
1990–94	95	64	67.4	2	28.6
1995–99	136	88	64.7	16	11.8
2000–04	177	111	62.7	12	6.8
2005–09	168	106	63.1	31	18.5
Totals	617	396	64.2	64	10.4

TABLE A.3 Gayborhood Gays

Code	Why do gays live in gayborhoods?	Kappa
Community building	They house gay communities.	.395, p<.001
Diversity	They are multicultural areas.	1.00, p<.001
Gentrification	They have investment potential.	.214, p<.043
Mating markets	They promise sex and love.	.417, p<.001
Niche markets	They nuture gay businesses.	1.00, p<.001
Safe spaces	They protect against homophobia.	.270, p<.001
Social movements	They catalyze political mobilization.	1.00, p<.001
Voting bloc	They express gay electoral strength.	1.00, p<.001

or did not live in a gayborhood. These responses cohered into eight major themes, each of which has a yes-or-no reply. Articles could contain more than one main idea, of course, although they did not always. Table A.3 shows these themes.[12]

Sixty-four articles (10.4%) addressed straight residential choice. In this case, the journalist interviewed self-identified heterosexuals who explained why they lived in a gayborhood, specifically. Their responses clustered into five major motivations, with similar yes-or-no replies, some of which resemble the reasons that gays and lesbians expressed. Table A.4 shows these themes.

The media waxed and waned in its coverage of gayborhoods over time, although figure A.1 shows an overall crescendo in coverage. The distance between the first line and the second two suggests that gayborhoods are newsworthy for reasons other than residential choice. Reporters used them as a context to discuss police harassment, review restaurant openings, publicize hate crimes, profile political candidates and newly elected officials, chronicle social and medical developments related to HIV and AIDS, impart lessons about gay and lesbian history, address antigay discrimination, debate new developments in urban planning, draw comparisons with women's and black civil rights, and extend international comparisons with gay and lesbian life in other countries.

TABLE A.4 Gayborhood Straights

Code	Why do straights live in gayborhoods?	Kappa
Chicness	They are chic and attractive.	.805, p < .001
Family friendliness	They are a good place to raise a family.	.660, p < .001
Gentrification	They have investment potential.	.484, p < .001
Diversity	They are multicultural areas.	.316, p <. 001
Safety	They have low crime rates.	1.00, p < .001

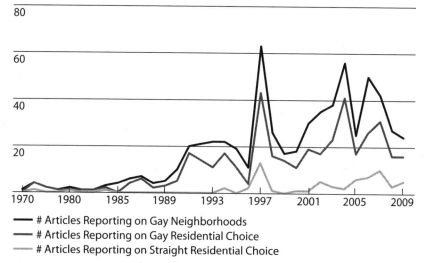

——— # Articles Reporting on Gay Neighborhoods
——— # Articles Reporting on Gay Residential Choice
⋯⋯⋯ # Articles Reporting on Straight Residential Choice

FIGURE A.1 Gayborhood coverage and conversational crests, 1970–2009.

There were three conversational crests across these forty years. Two major events occurred during the initial peak (1996–98). The first, as I have already mentioned, was Chicago's move to officially recognizing a section of its Lakeview neighborhood as Boystown. The year 1997 also marked a most-wanted manhunt for Andrew Cunanan, a then twenty-seven-year-old gay man from San Diego who committed a two-week, cross-country killing spree of at least five people, including fashion designer Gianni Versace. The three-month search concluded eight days after Versace's murder on July 23, 1997, when Cunanan shot himself aboard a Miami houseboat.

During the second cycle (2003–5), the Greater Philadelphia Tourism Marketing Company launched a multimillion-dollar television and magazine ad campaign to lure lesbian and gay tourists to their city. The "Get your history straight and your nightlife gay" catchy marketing moment made Philadelphia "the first destination in the world to produce a gay-themed television commercial [and magazine ads soon after] . . . Never before has a US city, resort, or international destination used [media] advertising to invite gay travelers to visit." Also in this spell—as of July 20, 2005—Canada legalized same-sex marriage with the enactment of its Civil Marriage Act. Local court decisions began in 2003 when Ontario (on June 10) and British Columbia (on July 8) legally recognized same-sex marriages in their respective provinces. By December 2004, six of ten provinces and one of three territories allowed gays and lesbians to legally marry. Legislators in the House of Commons requested the Canadian Supreme Court to weigh in on the issue, and on December 8, 2004, it released an affirmative announcement that jolted American headlines: "For Gays, Toronto Is the Marrying Kind" (*Washington Post*) and "Top Court in Canada OKs Gay Marriage" (*San Francisco Chronicle*) are two examples.[13]

On April 18, 2007, during the third spike (2006–8), Philadelphia became the second American city to officially demarcate one of its neighborhoods as gay. A *Philadelphia Daily News* headline declared, "New Signs Make It Official: We Have a 'Gayborhood.'" This final period also witnessed aggravated anxieties over straight in-migration, as the following headlines attest: "S.F.'s Castro District Faces an Identity Crisis: As Straights Move In, Some Fear Loss of the Area's Character" (*San Francisco Chronicle*), "In San Francisco's Castro District, a Cry of 'There Goes the Neighborhood'" (*Washington Post*), "Gay Enclaves Face Prospect of Being Passé: Gay Enclaves, Once Unique, Lose Urgency" (*New York Times*), "Last Call: Why the Gay Bars of Boston Are Disappearing" (*Boston Globe*), and "Won't You Be My Gaybor? Gay Neighborhoods Worry about Losing Their Distinct Identity" (*Chicago Tribune*).[14]

HOW DO WE STUDY GAYBORHOODS? LOCAL MEANINGS

I used a 2 × 2, neighborhood-by-sexual-orientation design to inter-view 125 Chicagoans from Boystown and Andersonville. I spoke with a snowball sample of twenty-five self-identified gay and lesbian residents of Boystown, twenty-five self-identified straight residents of Boystown, twenty-five gay and lesbian residents of Andersonville, and twenty-five straight residents of Andersonville. I also met with twenty-five business owners, government officials, representatives of nonprofit community organizations, realtors, developers, and various public officials from both neighborhoods (table A.5). This group included the following: retail merchants; two professors who worked at local universities; Joe Hollendoner, the founding director of the Broadway Youth Center, a nonprofit organization in Boys-town that works with queer, transgender, and other at-risk youth; Ed Devereux, the owner of the gay and lesbian bookstore in Boys-town (Unabridged) and Linda Bubon, the co-owner of the feminist bookstore in Andersonville (Women and Children First); two Dyke March organizers who have assembled the event in Andersonville; a straight female realtor and a gay male realtor; Maureen Martino, the executive director of the Lakeview East Chamber of Commerce; Jason Cox, the associate director of the Andersonville Chamber of Commerce; Christina Pinson, the executive director of the Gay and Lesbian Chamber of Commerce; four Boystown bar owners (Jim

TABLE A.5 Chicago Interviews

	Gays and Lesbians	Straights	Total interviews by neighborhood
Boystown	25 interviews	25 interviews	N = 50 residents
Andersonville	25 interviews	25 interviews	N = 50 residents
Business owners and public figures	22 interviews	3 interviews	N = 25 (from both neighborhoods)
Total interviews by sexual orientation	N = 72	N = 53	N = 125

Gates, who owns Little Jim's, the first gay bar to open in Boystown; Stu Zirin and John Dalton, who co-own Minibar and the D.S. Tequila Company, the newest bars to open in Boystown; and Art Johnson, who owns Sidetrack, the largest bar in the neighborhood); Bernard Cherkasov, the CEO of Equality Illinois, the state's largest political lobbying group; Modesto Tico Valle, the CEO of the Center on Halsted, Chicago's LGBT community center; straight and gay volunteer board members of the Nettelhorst School, a public elementary school in Boystown; Marge Summit, a Chicago Gay and Lesbian Hall of Fame member and lesbian activist who owned an early bar in the neighborhood (His 'n Hers); and Tom Tunney, who was the alderman for the Forty-Fourth Ward, which includes Boystown.

It is impossible to randomly sample gays and lesbians because there is no way to identify the population. However, we can use some statistical principles to approximate probability sampling in these types of "hidden populations." Such "respondent-driven techniques," as scholars call them, use a variation of chain-referral, or a snowball mechanism that is sensitive to community structure, geographic clusters, and social networks. Recall that I use interviews to understand the meanings that people assign to the places that they call home, not to calculate central tendencies. This is why I can rely on the intuition of a hidden populations approach. The idea is to study networks within a population, each of which is heterogeneous in its contacts (or friendship circles) yet geographically clustered. The chain of friends in each network "should be large enough so that the recruitment continues even if some subjects choose not to recruit." Multiple selection waves "allow the sampling process to explore parts of the network that may have had a zero probability of being included as a seed." Each of these is called a "long chain," and they avail the "small world problem" that the "average path length between any two people is often quite short."[15] I lived in Chicago for nearly ten years prior to doing my fieldwork. Yet I only knew 1/25 Boystown straights, 6/25 Boystown lesbians and gay men, 2/25 Andersonville straights, and 7/25 Andersonville lesbians and gay men.

I met people from diverse backgrounds (table A.6). Their occupations ranged from students and waiters to attorneys, physicians, professors, and everything in between, including the unemployed. I interviewed copy editors and grant writers, massage therapists, interior designers, hairstylists, social workers, flight attendants, models, stay-at-home moms and dads, part-time bartenders and professional mixologists, graphic and web designers, dog walkers, and cat sitters.

The Boystown gay and lesbian sample is slightly skewed toward older individuals who are more established in the neighborhood, those who own, gay men, whites, and those who are partnered. The Boystown straight sample is comparatively younger and less established in the neighborhood, yet with more owners and more women. This group is also mostly white and more partnered. Roughly equal numbers of gays and lesbians and straights are part of a household with children. The Andersonville gay and lesbian sample is younger than Boystown, less established, roughly balanced in terms of home ownership or renting, and it has a slightly smaller range on both accounts. But it too is skewed toward gay men, whites, and those who are partnered. The Andersonville straight sample is slightly older than Boystown, equally established in the neighborhood, slightly more female, heavily white, balanced in terms of owners and renters, and mostly partnered.

My interviews averaged fifty-one minutes, and they ranged from twenty-five to eighty minutes. Most were one-on-one, but I sometimes interviewed couples together. I transcribed each interview, and this produced 1,573 pages of single-spaced text. I used the NVivo data analysis software to analyze this data line by line. I focused on indicators of the post-gay era (deductive codes that referenced assimilation and the recession of sexual identity) along with counterfactual challenges to it (inductive codes for the continuing significance of gay neighborhoods and sexual identity, including references to safe spaces, collective memory, and urban conflicts). I assembled my codes into "meaning structures" by thinking about that analytic space where post-gay themes overlapped with references to specific urban sexual cultures.[16] What can indicate the

TABLE A.6 Interview Profiles

	LGBs		Straights	
Boystown	Average Age: 41		Average Age: 34	
	Age Range: 21–61		Age Range: 24–59	
	Average Residence: 10.4 years		Average Residence: 5.8 years	
	Residence Range: 0.25–31 years		Residence Range: 1–13 years	
	17 gay men	(68%)	9 men	(36%)
	5 lesbians	(20%)	16 women	(64%)
	3 bisexual women	(12%)		
	20 whites	(80%)	21 whites	(84%)
	1 Asian	(4%)		
	1 Hispanic/Latino	(4%)	1 Hispanic/Latino	(4%)
	3 multiracial	(12%)	3 multiracial	(12%)
	9 renters	(36%)	10 renters	(40%)
	16 owners	(64%)	15 owners	(60%)
	7 singles	(28%)	6 singles	(24%)
	18 partnered	(72%)	19 partnered	(76%)
	4 with kids	(16%)	6 with kids	(24%)
Andersonville	Average Age: 35		Average Age: 38	
	Age Range: 28–51		Age Range: 30–54	
	Average Residence: 4.8 years		Average Residence: 5.9 years	
	Residence Range: 0.25–17 years		Residence Range: 0.25–20 years	
	16 gay men	(64%)	11 men	(44%)
	9 lesbians	(36%)	14 women	(56%)
	19 whites	(76%)	22 whites	(88%)
	2 African-Americans	(8%)		
	1 Asian	(4%)		
	1 Hispanic/Latino	(4%)		
	2 multiracial	(8%)	3 multiracial	(12%)
	11 renters	(44%)	12 renters	(48%)
	14 renters	(56%)	13 owners	(52%)
	5 singles	(20%)	7 singles	(28%)
	20 partnered	(80%)	18 partnered	(72%)
	3 with kids	(12%)	10 with kids	(40%)
Public Figures and Business Owners	Average Age: 46		Average Age: 41	
	Age Range: 26–75		Age Range: 39–45	
	Average Residence: 12.5 years		Average Residence: 11.7 years	
	Residence Range: 2–30 years		Residence Range: 10–15 years	
	16 gay men	(64%)	3 straight women	(12%)
	1 bisexual woman	(4%)		
	5 lesbians	(20%)		
	19 whites	(76%)	3 whites	(12%)
	3 Hispanics/Latinos	(12%)		
	2 renters	(8%)	0 renters	(0%)
	20 owners	(80%)	3 owners	(12%)
	9 singles	(36%)	1 single	(4%)
	13 partnered	(52%)	2 partnered	(8%)
	5 with kids	(20%)	2 with kids	(8%)

presence of an urban sexual way of life in a milieu characterized by the *absence* of cultural distinctions between groups of residents? Satisfying answers had to achieve dual goals of social world sensitivity (an idea must be meaningful for those who live and socialize in Chicago gayborhoods) and analysis (an idea must help me answer the questions that motivate this book).

My triangulated approach to data collection and analysis is in the service of better understanding why gayborhoods first formed, why they are changing today, how they can survive to see another tomorrow, what the corporeal and brick-and-mortar border wars that surround gayborhoods can teach us about the relationship between sexuality and the city, what it means to be post-gay, how our sexuality operates as a unique driver for an otherwise common process of urban change, how our sexuality affects the character and composition of urban spaces, how it informs the decisions we make about where to live and whether to move, and what all of this means for the future of urban life in America.

NOTES

INTRODUCTION

1. Patricia Leigh Brown, "Gay Enclaves Face Prospect of Being Passé," *New York Times*, October 30, 2007, A1.

2. Title on the cover: "There Goes the Gayborhood?" Title of the story inside the paper: "Culture Clash: Boystown Shifting as More Families Move In," by Kyra Kyles, *Chicago Tribune (RedEye)*, December 10, 2007, 6.

3. Sabrina Tavernise, "New Numbers, and New Geography, for Gay Couples," *New York Times*, August 25, 2011. For an academic study of declining segregation, see Spring (2013).

4. Are there cross-national differences in how sexuality and the city are related? See Knopp (1998) for a comparative study of Minneapolis, Edinburgh, London, and Sydney. Other international studies include Cape Town, South Africa (Tucker 2009); a twenty-city comparison within Germany (Drever 2004); Hong Kong, China (Kong 2012); London, England (Houlbrook 2005); a comparison of London and Birmingham, UK (Collins 2004); Newcastle, UK (Casey 2004); Paris, France (Sibalis 2004); Sydney, Australia (Faro and Wotherspoon 2000; Markwell 2002); Toronto, Canada (Murray 1979); and Vancouver, Canada (Lo and Healy 2000).

5. For more on the defining and differentiating features of gay neighborhoods, see Castells (1983), Castells and Murphy (1982), Chauncey (1994), Collins (2004), Doan and Higgins (2011), Levine (1979), Mills et al. (2001), and Murray (1979 and 1992).

6. For more on the functions of these enclaves, see Evans and Boyte (1986), Florida (2002), Gates and Ost (2004a:2–6), Mansbridge and Morris (2001), Murray (1996), and Usher and Morrison (2010:283).

7. "Are Gay Neighborhoods Worth Saving?," GLBT Historical Society, November 10, 2006, www.glbthistory.org/news/1110_gayneighbors.html.

8. "There Goes the Gaybourhood: A New, Straight Crowd Is Discovering Church and Wellesley," by Micah Toub, *Globe and Mail*, March 24, 2007, M1; "Church and Wellesley under Review, Community Planning Study Underway," *The 519 Blog*, April 26, 2013, http://www.the519.org/blog/tag/village-study/.

9. Vaid's quote, "Under Glass," by Bruce Bawer, *New York Times*, October 29, 1995, section 7, 24; Sophia's quote, "Cheek by Jowl," by John Freeman Gill,

New York Times, July 10, 2005, section 14, 1; Frank's quote, "Move Over West Hollywood, Silver Lake Is the True Gay Mecca," by Tyler Trykowski, *LA Weekly*, April 19, 2013.

10. See Frisch (2002) for a characterization of this oversight as a "heterosexist project."

11. To learn more about Florida's arguments, see Florida (2002 and 2005) and Florida and Gates (2001).

12. Scholars debate whether same-sex households have higher or lower incomes compared to married heterosexual couples (Badgett 1995, 1997, and 2001; Black et al. 2003). Some assume that same-sex households have greater net disposable income since they are less likely to have children and therefore less likely to incur those associated expenses (Black et al. 2002).

13. The fact that scholars use economic arguments to explain analytically distinct outcomes, such as neighborhood formation and change, is one reason why Sharon Zukin (1987) criticizes the concept of gentrification for being disorganized. For more on the importance of politics and culture in our understanding of cities, see Borer (2006). For a sociological argument that neighborhood change occurs in "forms beyond gentrification," see Owens (2012). Most scholars downplay the explanatory role of culture in urban change because they see it as epiphenomenal, as a mere aggregation of individual residential decisions, or they see it as outright irrelevant (Lauria and Knopp 1985:163). Herbert Gans, for example, asserts that "culture *per se* is not a useful explanatory tool" given its "antipathy toward structural issues such as hierarchy, inequality, and power" (2007:159–60). Other scholars have shown the many ways in which urban cultures matter (e.g., Abrahamson 2005; Borer 2006; Zukin 1989, 1995, 2010). Those who advocate for incorporating culture into urban analysis reply, "Exploring the ways people actively, rather than passively, construct meaning, and how those processes are often both sources of conflict and compromise, is to take an *affirmative* view of culture" (Borer 2007:159). A study of gayborhoods must integrate cultural perspectives with economic and political approaches in order to assess how shifting power dynamics affect sexuality and the city. Forest argues that "symbolic struggles over the meaning of places often coincide with economic and political struggles" (1995:134), even though most studies have "focused on political, rather than symbolic-cultural issues." It is useful to think about gayborhoods as "center[s] of meaning" (Mitchell 2000:177), since it is "impossible to imagine one [queer culture and identity] without the other [geographic space]" (Sibalis 2004:1750). Spatial concentrations produce "political strength and cultural freedom" (Castells and Murphy 1982:238). For more on creative class workers, see Florida (2002 and 2005). For the spatial response quote, see Lauria and Knopp (1985:152).

14. Armstrong (2002:53).

15. Seidman (2002). For the coining of "post-gay," see Collard (1998) and Ghaziani (2011). Silver's quote is from Andy Towle, "Nate Silver: Sexually Gay but Ethnically Straight," Towleroad, December 18, 2012.

16. Bergquist and McDonald (2006:vii).

17. For the birth of the homosexual as a "species," see Foucault (1978:43). David Halperin challenges Foucault by asking, "Is there a history of sexuality?" Halperin answers, "Sex has no history. It is a natural fact, grounded in the functioning of the body, and, as such, it lies outside of history and culture." Sexuality, however, is different: "Sexuality is not a somatic fact; it is a cultural effect. Sexuality, then, does have a history" (Halperin 1993:416). For more on sexuality and capitalism, see D'Emilio (1993). His "product of history" quote is from page 468, and the "imperative to procreate" quote is from page 470. For the relationship between capitalism and gender, see Knopp (1992:663–64). For the functions of sex in the Victorian era, see Katz (2007), and refer to Katz (1990:11) for the "heterolust" quote. For an example of how gays and lesbians created a rich collective life despite societal characterizations of them as pathological, see Timmons (1990).

18. For topography, bourgeois, tone, and Paul and Joe quotes, see Chauncey (1994:23, 227–28). See page 244 for arguments about Harlem. The Forsyth quote is from Forsyth (2001:343). For more on urban "men's lives and gay identities" in the twentieth century, see Loughery (1998).

19. For evidence about literacy rates, see Faderman (1999:56). For the Buffalo lesbian community, see Kennedy and Davis (1993). The "cultures of resistance" quote is from page 2, and the recollections are from page 45. Don Mitchell uses the imagery of a "fragmented spatiality" to describe closet era lesbian spaces (2000:192), which has clear similarities with Forsyth's notion of "scattered gay places." The "well of loneliness" is an allusion to a 1928 fiction novel by British author Radclyffe Hall ([1928] 2005). For a discussion of cross-dressing women in 1920s Chicago and San Francisco, see San Francisco Lesbian and Gay History Project (1989:192).

20. See Chauncey (1994:2–6) for a discussion of the closet as a "spatial metaphor" and three popular myths that perpetuate the fallacy that gay and lesbian life during the closet era was devoid of institutional or cultural character. The "normative city" quote is from page 23. Sodom and Gomorrah, *Call Her Savage*, and Degenerates quotes are from page 234. For the "straight state," see Canaday (2009).

21. For nationwide coming out, see D'Emilio and Freedman (1997:289); Wittman's quotes, Wittman (1970:67–68); San Francisco population and census data, D'Emilio (1989:459–60). Gay bars inspired sexual minorities to build "a society within a society" (Castells 1983:157), and they "channel[ed] urban gay life into a particular path of growth—away from stable private networks [of the closet era] and toward public commercial establishments" (Berube 1990:126).

22. For the 1951 ruling, see Castells (1983:141); the quote is from 157. See Sibalis (2004) for a similar perspective. The war transformed gays into a "quasi-ethnic minority" (D'Emilio 1983; Stein 1997; Wright 1999:173).

23. For "symbol" quote, see Adam (1995:81). For "the making of the Stonewall myth," see Armstrong and Crage (2006).

24. A recurring theme in queer theory and politics is what Scott Herring calls a "compulsion to urbanism" that "codifies the metropolitan as the terminus of queer world making." He challenges an urban/rural binary that demands "migration [away] from wicked little towns" to the city, which becomes "the sole locus for queer community, refuge, and security" (Herring 2010:10). For more on "queer diffusion," see Cooke and Rapiano (2007) and Knopp and Brown (2003:288). For queer communities in the countryside, see Bell and Valentine (1995); Browne (2008); Forsyth (1997); Gray (2009); Kirkey and Forsyth (2001); McCarthy (2000); Phillips, Watt, and Shuttleton (2000); and Smith and Holt (2005). In the suburbs, see Brekhus (2003), Hodge (1995), Langford (2000), Lynch (1992), and Tongson (2011).

25. Many scholars focus on the Castro and its legendary status as a "gay mecca" (Boyd 2005; D'Emilio 1989; Duggins 2002; Mitchell 2000:189; Stryker 2002; Stryker and Van Buskirk 1996; Wittman 1970). While much of this research provides a community history, some of it is also more generalizable (Adler and Brenner 1992; Black et al. 2002; Castells 1983; Castells and Murphy 1982; Collins 2004; Murray 1992; Weston 1995).

26. For more on historical accidents, see Collins (2004:1792, 1800). This "historical argument," as I call it, is the first of five formal explanations for why gayborhoods form and change. The argument also applies to international cases. For example, the decriminalization of homosexuality in 1967 prompted gayborhoods to form in the English cities of London, Brighton, Manchester, and Newcastle. For additional cases, see Aldrich (2004), Berube (1990), Chauncey (1994), D'Emilio (1983 and 1993), D'Emilio and Freedman (1997), Duggins (2002), Heap (2003 and 2009), Newton (1993), Stryker (2002), Stryker and Van Buskirk (1996), and Weston (1995). For more on the "great gay migration," see Newton (1993:44) and Weston (1995:255). The "gay imaginary" quote is from Weston (1995:257).

27. For an overview of "economic arguments," the second of five classes of explanation for gayborhood formation and change, see Knopp (1990:347), Florida (2002), Collins (2004:1790), and Cooke and Rapiano (2007:296). The research that I report in this section comes from Black et al. (2002). The quote is from pages 64–65.

28. For research on correlations with amenities and housing stock, see Anacker and Morrow-Jones (2005:390, 406) and Black et al. (2002:55). For more on freed-up resources, see Black et al. (2002:54).

29. Spring (2013:691).

30. Ruth Glass (1964) first coined the term "gentrification." Sharon Zukin offers an often-cited definition as "the conversion of socially marginal and working-class areas of the central city to middle-class residential use" by "private-market investment capital in downtown districts" (1987:129). For research on the precipitating factors of gentrification, see Brown-Saracino (2007), Spain (1993), and Zukin (1987). Justin Ocean, "Change of Pace," *Advocate*, November 2009, issue 1032, 44; Lamm's quote, "Focus on Hillcrest," by Lori Weisberg and Roger M. Showley, *San Diego Union-Tribune*, July 27, 1997, A1; Morten's quote, "Chicago Hails District as Symbol of Gay Life," by Dirk Johnson, *New York Times*, August 27, 1997, A14. Realtor reports suggest that gayborhoods are politico-economic expressions of elite interests (e.g., an alliance of businesses, government officials, realtors, and home owners) that comprise what John Logan and Harvey Molotch call a "growth machine," a coalition that profits through particular land use patterns (Logan and Molotch 1987; Molotch 1976). For more on the white flight of the 1960s, see Wilson (1987). For more on "islands of decay in seas of renewal," along with the reverse notion of "islands of renewal in seas of decay," see Berry (1985) and Wyly and Hammel (1999). For more on "taming the urban wilderness," see N. Smith (1986) and Spain (1993:158). For more on the role that gays and lesbians play in gentrification, see Brown-Saracino (2007), Gale (1980), Knopp (1990), and Zukin (1987).

31. Chauncey (1994:229). For additional research that defines gays and lesbians as economic actors, see Black et al. (2002), Collins (2004), Florida (2002), and Kasinitz (1988). To learn more about the relationship between economic arguments and factors like politics and culture, see Borer (2006).

32. For more on the political functions of gayborhoods, see Murray (1979 and 1992), Sibalis (2004), and Usher and Morrison (2010). This type of argument is also called "the emancipatory city thesis" (Collins 2004:1799; Lees 2000:392). For overviews, see Castells (1983), Murray (1996), and Hayslett and Kane (2011). For Castell's quote and for more on gays and lesbians as "moral refugees," see Castells (1983:161) and Wittman (1970:67–68). For gayborhoods as beacons of tolerance, see Weston (1995:262). For gayborhoods as liberated zones, see Castells (1983:139, 168). For gayborhoods as promised lands, see Humphreys (1979:140). All of these, along with framings of gayborhoods as safe spaces, comprise a "political argument" for gayborhood formation and change, the third of five classes of explanation.

33. Pamela Allen first used the term "free space" in 1970 to explain how to build an autonomous women's movement (1970:6). This is also the source for the "personal is political" quote. For more on hand-holding and kissing in gayborhoods, see Sibalis (2004:1748). For a widely cited discussion of free spaces, see Evans

and Boyte (1986:17). Scholars use many different terms to describe these settings, including abeyance structures (Verta Taylor), cultural laboratories (Carol Mueller), cultures of solidarity (Rick Fantasia), free social spaces (Robert Fisher and Joseph Kling), free spaces (Sara Evans and Harry Boyte), halfway houses (Aldon Morris), havens (Eric Hirsch), independent spaces (Ruth Needleman), protected spaces (Mary Ann Tétreault), safe spaces (William Gamson), sequestered social sites (James Scott), social movement communities (Steven Buechler), social spaces (Craig Calhoun), spatial preserves, and liberated zones (Rick Fantasia and Eric Hirsch). References include Buechler (1990), Calhoun (1983), Evans and Boyte (1986), Fantasia (1988), Fantasia and Hirsch (1995), Fisher and Kling (1990), Gamson (1996), Hirsch (1990), Morris (1984), Mueller (1994), Needleman (1994), Scott (1990), Taylor (1989), and Tétreault (1993). Early gay social thinkers were also a part of this conversation (Wittman 1970:67–68). For contemporary examples, see Castells (1983:139, 168), Castells and Murphy (1982:237), Forest (1995:137), Hanhardt (2008:63), Myslik (1996:168), Sibalis (2004:1748), and Weston (1995:262, 268). For a critique of this research, see Polletta (1999). John Gallagher's quote is from "Location, Location, Location," *Advocate*, June 24, 1997, issue 736, page unnoted. For the *New York Times* quote, see David Shaftel, "Under the Rainbow," *New York Times*, March 25, 2007, section 14, 1.

34. Denny Lee's quote is from "Street Fight," *New York Times*, March 31, 2002, section 14, 1. For a sociological treatment of this "sexuality argument," the fourth class of explanation for gayborhood formation and change, see Laumann et al. (1994) and Laumann et al. (2004:40, 357). For an interdisciplinary consideration of public sex in queer spaces, see Leap (1999). For additional research with a sexuality focus, see Collins (2006), Doan and Higgins (2011:15), Humphreys (1975), Laumann et al. (2004), and Sides (2009). For men, this manifested in a "pleasure-seeking logic" (Armstrong 2002:42, 43, 185) that linked politics with public space, while lesbians organized their social world around eroticized butch-femme roles (Kennedy and Davis 1993:151–52).

35. John Morgan Wilson, "WeHo, Warts and All," *Advocate*, December 21, 2004, issue 929, page unnoted. For more on the role that gay people played in the municipal incorporation of West Hollywood, see Forest (1995); Michael Lavers, "The Queer Issue: The New Gayborhoods of Fort Greene, Sunset Park, and Jackson Heights," *Village Voice*, June 24, 2009, page unnoted.

36. Hindle (1994:11). The DC study is from Myslik (1996:166). The resident who is quoted is from New York. Although he was not a part of the study, he nonetheless breathed life into the numbers from the DC study. See Michelle Garcia, "Race, Class, and Sex Breed Contempt in Greenwich Village," *Washington Post*, September 18, 2006.

37. Murray (1992:109). For more on the institutional elaboration of a quasi-ethnic community, see Epstein (1987) and Murray (1979:165).

38. Quattrochi's quote, "Neighborhood Report: West Village," by Randy Kennedy, *New York Times*, June 19, 1994, 6; Nolan's quote, "A Milestone in the Fight for Gay Rights: A Quiet Suburban Life," by Jane Gross, *New York Times*, June 30, 1991, 16; Elizabeth Kastor, "Fill-in-the-Blanks: For Gay Men, Self-Invention Can Be a Key to Self-Discovery," *Washington Post*, July 31, 1997, B01.

39. Dan Levy, "A 'Soft-Focus' Look at the Castro," *San Francisco Chronicle*, March 15, 1997, E1; Paula Span, "Greenwich Time: On the Stonewall Anniversary, a Gay Tour of Village History," *Washington Post*, June 22, 1994, D1.

40. Joseph Coates, "Bringing Clarity to an Elusive Reality," *Chicago Tribune*, May 2, 1991, 3. See Durkheim (1912) on communal affirmation. In this way, a gayborhood is much like a "homeland" (Weston 1995:265). It promises a path to membership in the gay and lesbian community (Murray 1992:107). For more examples of this "community argument," the fifth and final class of explanation for gayborhood formation and change, see Castells and Murphy (1982:256), Escoffier (1975), and Herrell (1993). Stephen Murray debates Robert Bellah and his colleagues who, in their book *Habits of the Heart*, seek "to preserve the sacred term 'community' from application to what they term 'lifestyle enclaves.'" Murray thinks this category is "based on the 'narcissism of similarity' in patterns of leisure and consumption." He applies each of Bellah et al.'s three criteria for a "real community" (institutional completeness, commitments among geographically concentrated people that they carry beyond their private lives into public endeavors, and a collective memory that preserves their past) to gay people and concludes that they "fit all the criteria suggested by sociologists to define 'community' as well as or better than urban ethnic communities do" (Bellah et al. 1985; Murray 1992:108, 114).

41. James Collard, "New Way of Being," *New York Times*, June 21, 1998, SM13; and "Leaving the Gay Ghetto," *Newsweek*, August 17, 1998, 53. In his *Newsweek* piece, Collard credits Burston with coining the term post-gay. For more on the "de-gaying" of gayborhoods, see Ruting (2008:260). The term "post-queer" has also recently entered the English lexicon, although it means something quite different. Anchored in queer theory (e.g., Seidman 1996), some scholars use it to argue that the theoretical framework neglects the "institutional organization of sexuality" and the "complex developmental processes attendant to sexual identification" (Green 2002:523). Others use it to critique queer theory's binary conception of the world as either queer or heteronormative (C. Cohen 2001; Ruffolo 2009).

42. The 2010 Census statistic is from Gates and Cooke (2011); Hanhardt's quote is from Hanhardt (2008:65).

43. For more on the resurgence of gentrification and the role that gays and lesbians play in it, see Doan and Higgins (2011). See page 7 of their article for remarks on "super-gentrifiers" and page 16 for threats to the "cultural icons of queer neighborhoods." For Florida on Colbert, see Colbert (2007 [July 16]). LGBT population statistics can be found online at the Williams Institute. For more on the "pillaging of gay culture," see Doan (2007:15).

44. See Rushbrook (2002:183) on the geography of cool. For more on the Gay Index, see Florida (2002) and Gates and Ost (2004b). For more on the predictive capacity of the Gay Index, see Hanhardt (2008:63). For more on global cities, see Sassen (2001). See Rushbrook (2002:183) for more on secondary cities. See page 188 for her "places of culture and consumption" and "marker of cosmopolitanism" quotes. See page 193 for her discussion about the shift from regulation to marketing. For more on "Disneyfying" cities, see Zukin (1995 and 1998). She calls this "Disneyitis." For sociological research on "entertainment districts," see Lloyd (2006) and Lloyd and Clark (2001). For arguments about "cosmopolitan buffets" in cities, see E. Anderson (2011) and Rushbrook (2002:188). For Collins's quote, see Collins (2004:1793, 1798).

45. For quotes, see Ruting (2008:266) and Rushbrook (2002:196). See Owens (2012:346) for an argument about urban change that happens in "forms beyond gentrification."

46. For more on straight allies, see Ghaziani (2011) and Meyers (2008). For more on intergroup interactions as an operation for assimilation, see Waters (1990 and 2000) and Waters and Ueda (2007). "Assimilation" defines the post-gay era. It is a social factor. "Integration," on the other hand, is its outcome. It is a relational effect of assimilation. Furthermore, I also use assimilation instead of integration (cf., Brown-Saracino 2011) because the latter implies a wide incorporation of the minority group that is invalid in the post-gay era. Mostly white, middle-class, cisgendered men and women are self-presenting like straights. I address these issues in the conclusion.

47. Lydia Saad, "Americans' Acceptance of Gay Relations Crosses 50% Threshold," Gallup Politics. See also "Gay and Lesbian Rights," poll at www.gallup.com /poll/1651/gay-lesbian-rights.aspx; "Behind Gay Marriage Momentum, Regional Gaps Persist," Pew Research Center, November 9, 2012; "It's Not Just City Folks: Gays and Lesbians Experience Striking Gains in Acceptance in All Regions and Subgroups of America," *Sociologists for Women in Society*, December 11, 2012; Jon Cohen, "Gay Marriage Support Hits New High in Post-ABC Poll," *Washington Post* online, March 18, 2013.

48. See "Windsor v. United States," *SCOTUSblog*, http://www.scotusblog.com.

49. Seidman (2002:2, 6, 86, and 88). For more on assimilation, see Fischer (1999:217).

50. Paul Aguirre-Livingston, "Dawn of a New Gay," *The Grid*, June 9, 2011. For a counterargument on the importance of sexual orientation among the younger generations, see Russell, Clarke, and Clary (2009).

51. G. Brown (2006:136, 140).

52. D'Emilio and pilgrimage quotes, Myslik (1996:167–68).

53. Robert David Sullivan, "Last Call: Why the Gay Bars of Boston Are Disappearing," *Boston Globe*, December 2, 2007, E1. For more on how gay business closings can "sever" ties between residents and the neighborhood, see Usher and Morrison (2010:277) and Steven Kurutz, "Savoring a Last Cup at a Place All Their Own," *New York Times*, August 26, 2005, section B, column 1, 3. For more on the symbolic role of place, see Vaisey (2007).

54. R. D. Sullivan, "Last Call: Why the Gay Bars of Boston Are Disappearing." For the "virtual pleasure" and "real-world fun" quotes, see Usher and Morrison (2010:279). For the international study, see Rosser, West, and Weinmeyer (2008:588). Sandy's quote, "In San Francisco's Castro District, a Cry of 'There Goes the Gayborhood,'" by Lisa Leff, *Washington Post*, March 18, 2007, D01; William's quote, "Hub's Gays Revel in Societal Changes," by Marie Szaniszlo, *Boston Herald*, June 11, 2006, 6.

55. For more on gayborhoods as safe spaces for straight women, see Collins (2004:1794). The heterosexual male gaze quote is from Casey (2004:454); Charles M. Blow, "Gay? Whatever, Dude," *New York Times* online, June 4, 2010; Dan Levy, "There Goes the Neighborhood," *San Francisco Chronicle*, May 26, 1996, Z1.

CHAPTER 1. BEYOND THE GAYBORHOOD

1. John Caldwell, "Where We Live," *Advocate*, March 27, 2007, issue 982, page unnoted. Results: "The Advocate Poll," *Advocate*, April 24, 2007, issue 984, page unnoted. For Gates's research on Census 2000, see Gates and Ost (2004a and 2004b). He indicates on page 19 that "same-sex unmarried partners were present in 99.3 percent of all counties in the United States." For his analysis of 2010, see Gates and Cooke (2011). He does not offer an explanation for why the number decreased to 93 percent.

2. For more on assimilation, defined as the intermixing of two groups, see Waters (1990, 2000) and Waters and Ueda (2007). For "separation of socially defined groups," see Massey, Rothwell, and Domina (2009:74). To learn more about the meaning of an "even" residential distribution, see Massey and Denton (1993:20). For earlier work on segregation and assimilation, see Massey (1981) and Massey and Denton (1988). For later writings, see Charles (2003). Recent research also includes socioeconomic status, language, and intermarriage as dimensions of assimilation (Waters and Jiménez 2005). For more on the dissimilarity index,

see Reardon and O'Sullivan (2004) and Rugh and Massey (2010). For research related to ethnocentrism, prejudice, and stereotyping, see Allport (1954) and Charles (2003:186, 189).

3. The data in the table reports mean segregation scores in 2000 and 2010, weighted by the number of male-male or female-female partner households in a place, for the one hundred most populous places in 2010. "Different-Sex households" include "husband-wife households" and "male-female unmarried partners." A paired t-test shows $p < 0.001$ for both male and female same-sex households. Segregation scores for race and class are from the same one hundred places in 2010. The source, including the quote in the text, is from Spring (2013:699).

4. For differences between statistical and perceptual integration, see Rich (2009:829).

5. Josh Benson, "Welcome to the Rainbow State," *New York Times*, September 5, 2004, 14NJ; for Domestic Partnership Act, see http://www.state.nj.us/treasury /pensions/dp-page.shtml. In 2006, New Jersey passed a "Civil Union Law" to recognize same-sex relationships. Lisa Leff's quote is from "In San Francisco's Castro District, a Cry of 'There Goes the Gayborhood.'"

6. James McCown, "Proud Owners," *Boston Globe*, May 23, 2004, J1; Vaid on leaving the ghetto, "Gay Rights: Wrong Strategy?" by Adam Goodheart, *Washington Post*, November 21, 1995, E2; Vaid on the spacious closet, "Under Glass," by Bruce Bawer, *New York Times*, October 29, 1995, section 7, 24. See Vaid (1995) for her thoughts on "virtual equality."

7. Smith's quote, "An 'Anti' Electorate Tries to Regain Control," by Debbie Howlett, *USA Today*, October 26, 1993, A5; R. D. Sullivan, "Last Call: Why the Gay Bars of Boston Are Disappearing."

8. Philip Bennett, "Southie Revising a Bad Rap: Gays Increase Their Presence but Raise No Alarms," *Boston Globe*, September 28, 1991, 25.

9. Wyatt Buchanan, "S.F.'s Castro District Faces an Identity Crisis," *San Francisco Chronicle*, February 25, 2007, A1.

10. Leah Garchik, "Daily Notebook," *San Francisco Chronicle*, June 8, 1998, D8. For an argument about why San Francisco might represent the nation, see Armstrong (2002).

11. Castro bar owner quote, Dan Levy, "There Goes the Neighborhood"; unauthored story from Philadelphia, "Briefly . . . Nation/World," *Philadelphia Daily News*, March 13, 2007, 11; Romesburg quote, "In San Francisco's Castro District, a Cry of 'There Goes the Gayborhood,'" by Lisa Leff.

12. Judith Gaines, "Some Lesbians Feel Left Out of Their 'Home Town,'" *Boston Globe*, May 15, 1999, B1.

13. Diane Daniel, "Where Diversity and Arts Shine," *Boston Globe*, February 15, 2006, D8.

14. Jen Christensen and John Caldwell, "Welcome to the Gayborhood," *Advocate*, June 20, 2006, page unnoted. For more suburban gay flight, see Brekhus (2003).

15. Stewart's quote, "Our Towns," by Matthew Purdy, *New York Times*, November 10, 1999, B1; Wayne's quote, "In and Out of Roanoke: In the Aftermath of a Mass Shooting, One Town's Gay Population Tries to Find Its Place on Main Street," by Liza Mundy, *Washington Post*, February 18, 2001, W10.

16. See note 15 in the introduction.

17. For white ethnic identity, see Waters (1990). For its situational nature, see Nagel (1994 and 1997).

18. For a theory of migration that includes push and pull factors, see Lee (1966). Quotes in this section, Marc Fisher, "With Their Circle Seemingly Broken, Gays Face Change," *Washington Post*, May 2, 2002, B1.

19. Carol Christian, "Gays Celebrate How Far They've Come," *Houston Chronicle*, June 17, 2001, A37. For the "trouble with normal" and the politics of "shame," see Warner (1999a) and Halperin and Traub (2010), respectively. For stigma and the management of spoiled identity, see Goffman (1963).

20. Karen De Witt, "Gay Presence Leads Revival of Declining Neighborhoods," *New York Times*, September 6, 1994, A14.

21. A. Sullivan (1996). Tim Nolan's quote is from Jane Gross's article, "A Milestone in the Fight for Gay Rights: A Quiet Suburban Life," *New York Times*, June 30, 1991, section 4, 16.

22. Crisp's quote, "Quentin Crisp as Resident Wit," by Edward Guthman, *San Francisco Chronicle*, June 13, 1997, C6; Bill's quote, "Retirement Community for Gays Under Development in Florida," by Craig Wilson, *USA Today*, November 23, 1994; Lucas's quote, "Talks with Gay Playwrights Offered in Course at Purchase," by Alvin Klein, *New York Times*, December 5, 1999, section 14WC, 8; Baim's quote, "Gaytown Enters Gray Area of Community Naming," by Mary Schmich, *Chicago Tribune*, August 17, 1997, 1.

23. Goldstein's quote, the letters to the editor that it provoked, and his response to them are all from "Unguided Tour: Queer Notions," *Village Voice*, July 14, 1998, J'Accuse section, 6.

24. The quote in this section is from Sibalis (2004:1739). Levine (1979) is the most systematic in his appraisal of whether the term "ghetto" applies to gayborhoods (the term "lavender ghetto" is from page 182). Drawing on Wirth (1928), he identifies the four defining features that I reviewed in this section, and he applies each to gay concentrations in Boston, New York, Chicago, San Francisco, and Los Angeles. His results are mixed. Some communities meet all the requirements for a ghetto, whereas others meet only some. "These communities represent different stages in ghetto development," he concludes (Levine 1979:201). Loïc Wacquant

(2011:7) offers another perspective on the ghetto. He argues that it is not a natural area, in the ecological sense, but a "socio-organizational device" that has four elements: stigma, constraint, spatial confinement, and institutional parallelism. The urban formation that results "is a distinct space, containing an ethnically homogenous population, which finds itself forced to develop within it a set of interlinked institutions that duplicate the organizational framework of the broader society from which that group is banished and supplies the scaffolding for the construction of its specific 'style of life' and social strategies" (Wacquant 2000:383). See the same source for "institutional encasement." For "anti-ghettos," see Wacquant (2008:115).

25. Sedgwick (1990:22). For more on Kinsey, see Condon (2004). In the movie *Kinsey*, Alfred Kinsey (played by Liam Neeson) delivers the quote in reference to his research on gall wasps about twelve minutes into the film. For celebrating and suppressing differences, see Bernstein (1997).

26. Jane Gross, "A Milestone in the Fight for Gay Rights: A Quiet Suburban Life," *New York Times*, June 30, 1991, section 4, 16; Leal's quote, "There Goes the Neighborhood," by Dan Levy; Cohn's quote, "Area Gay Couples Settled, Middle-Aged, Study Finds," by D'Vera Cohn, *Washington Post*, June 13, 2003, B1.

27. Andrew Sullivan, "The End of Gay Culture and the Future of Gay Life," *Chicago Sun-Times*, November 27, 2005, B1. For more on "the new gay teenager," see Savin-Williams (2005).

28. John Caldwell, "Where We Live," *Advocate*, March 27, 2007, issue 982, page unnoted; Kyra Kyles, "Culture Clash: Boystown Shifting as More Families Move In," 6.

29. Benoit Denizet-Lewis, "Young Gay Rites," *New York Times*, April 27, 2008, section MM, 28.

30. P. L. Brown, "Gay Enclaves Face Prospect of Being Passé."

31. Lonnae O'Neal Parker, "Just Another Way to Be Suburban," *Washington Post*, June 29, 2009, B1. For classic social research on master identities and their "insensitivity to context," see Bearman and Stovel (2000:75). For the way in which "master statuses" take precedence over other identities, see Hughes (1945).

32. Ian Lovett, "Changing Nature of West Hollywood, Long a Gay Haven, Becomes an Election Issue," *New York Times*, March 6, 2011. For Sullivan's arguments, see A. Sullivan (2004:146).

33. Donovan Slack, "Culture Clash in Bay Village," *Boston Globe*, January 27, 2003, B1; Chris's quote, "Hub's Gays Revel in Societal Changes," by Marie Szaniszlo, *Boston Herald*, June 11, 2006, 6.

34. Adam H. Graham, "Where the Gays Are," *Advocate*, April 8, 2008, issue 1005, page unnoted.

35. "A Survey of LGBT Americans: Attitudes, Experiences and Values in Changing Times," Pew Research Center, June 13, 2013. See http://www.pew research.org/packages/lgbt-in-changing-times. The quotes are from page 14.

36. R. D. Sullivan, "Last Call: Why the Gay Bars of Boston Are Disappearing"; P. L. Brown, "Gay Enclaves Face Prospect of Being Passé."

37. From the Grindr website, http://grindr.com/learn-more. For a critique about how Grindr and other gay mobile dating apps can be "intimidating, negative, and noninclusive," see Carl Sandler, "Gay-on-Gay Bullying: The New Mean Girls," *Huffington Post*, May 25, 2012; Thomas Rogers, "The Pines' Summer of Discontent," *New York Magazine*, July 21, 2012.

38. Keith Darc, "Adapting to the Times: Gay Newspapers Face Competition, but Publishers Remain Optimistic," *San Diego Union Tribune*, April 5, 2007, C1.

39. Larry Fish, "A Landmark Gay Bookstore Is Closing," *Philadelphia Inquirer*, January 15, 2003, C1.

40. "Gay Retirees: The Next Big Untapped Target Market?" CARP, http://www.carp.ca; on safe housing, see Janet Thomson, Manmeet Ahluwalia, and Sunnie Huang, "Gay Seniors Struggling to Find 'Safe' Retirement Housing," CBC News, April 15, 2013.

41. Erinn Cawthon, "N.Y. High School Names Same-Sex Couple as 'Cutest' in Yearbook," CNN online, June 5, 2013.

CHAPTER 2. THE HAPPIEST ENDING

1. For examples of early studies in the Chicago School, see Kornblum (1974), Park (1915 and 1925), Suttles (1968), Wirth (1928), and Zorbaugh (1929). Contemporary studies focus on race and class (Pattillo-McCoy 2000; Pattillo 2007; Wilson 1987 and 1996; Wilson and Taub 2006), art and music (Grazian 2003; Lloyd 2006), and sometimes sexuality (Laumann et al. 2004). Sexual laboratory quote, Heap (2003:458); 2010 US Census statistics from http://2010.census .gov/2010census/popmap/.

2. For more on the notion of a global city, see Abu-Lughod (1999) and Sassen (2001:3–4). For more on secondary cities and their branding strategies, see Rushbrook (2002:188). For the "cosmopolitan canopy," see E. Anderson (2011).

3. See Clark for an argument that "no city represents the nation or the world" (2011:236). See Lloyd for an argument that Chicago is "perhaps the most studied city in the world" (2006:14). John D'Emilio argues, "The GLBT history of Chicago is vastly underwritten in comparison to New York, San Francisco or L.A. . . . We don't know the story of queer Chicago yet." See Jason Heidemann, "A Gay Old Time," *Time Out Chicago*, April 14, 2010.

4. For more on the sexual character of Boystown and Andersonville, see Bergquist and McDonald (2006:vii).

5. "Boystown, Chicago," BGC website, http://bgclive.com/board/viewtopic .php?pid=173545019.

6. See Lane (2003) for a characterization of Andersonville as a Swedish American Landmark Neighborhood. For more on Andersonville's lesbian and gay history, see Brown-Saracino (2009:37–39).

7. See Joseph Erbentraut, "Making Us Count: Chicago Queer Couples in the Census," *Windy City Times*, April 20, 2011, www.windycitymediagroup.com /gay/lesbian/news/ARTICLE.php?AID=31459 for more statistics. The numbers change if you broaden Andersonville boundaries to include Edgewater and parts of Uptown. See Joe Zekas, "Is Andersonville Chicago's 'Premier Residential LGBT Neighborhood?'" YoChicago website, August 4, 2011.

8. See Erbentraut, "Making Us Count," *Windy City Times*, April 20, 2011.

9. Interpretive frameworks quote, Zerubavel (1997:23–24); "islands of meaning" quote, Zerubavel (1991:21). For a review of research on culture and cognition, see DiMaggio (1997).

10. For research on the city as a growth machine, see Logan and Molotch (1987) and Molotch (1976).

11. For Obama's speech, see "Obama Urges Morehouse Graduates to 'Keep Setting an Example,'" by Mark Landler, *New York Times* online, May 19, 2013. For the Cook County Human Rights Ordinance (No. 93-0-13), see http://www.qrd .org. It was approved on March 16, 1993, and it became effective on May 21, 1993.

12. Wirth (1938:11).

13. The prediction that contact will reduce prejudice is called the "contact hypothesis" (Allport 1954). Allport did not consider whether this applied to gay-straight interactions. Other scholars, however, have demonstrated that his hypothesis holds true for sexuality (Herek 1986; Herek and Capitanio 1996; Herek and Glunt 1993). For research on the media as a type contact, see Capsuto (2000), Gross (2001), Russo (1987), and Walters (2001). The idea that being gay today is "no big deal" has generated critical research on the hazards of being "mainstream" and "normal" (Chasin 2000; Vaid 1995; Warner 1999a).

14. For the terms that women use to define their sexuality, see Diamond (2003 and 2008) and Fahs (2009).

15. One way to resolve this contradiction is to distinguish cultural and institutional sources of oppression. The former make "loosening categories a smart strategy," while the latter "make tightening categories a smart strategy." Gayatri Spivak calls this "operational essentialism." See Gamson (1995:400, 403) for a review.

16. For more on subcultures and ethnic groups, see Abrahamson (2005). For sociological writings on space and place, see Dreier, Mollenkopf, and Swanstrom

(2004); Gans (2002); and Gieryn (2000). For studies on the meaning of "community," see Hunter (1974), Putnam (2000 and 2007), Tonnies (1957), and Vaisey (2007).

17. Lauster and Easterbrook (2011).

18. For more on the relationship between organizational names and collective identity, see Ghaziani (2011).

19. Jenel Nels, "Stanley Cup Heads to Pride Parade," NBC online, June 22, 2010, http://www.nbcchicago.com; Roman Modrowski, "Cubs Have Float in Chicago Pride Parade," June 24, 2010, ESPN Chicago, http://sports.espn.go.com.

20. For the Harlem Renaissance, see Watson (1995) and Wintz (1988).

21. Other examples of classic urban research that emphasizes race and class include Gans (1962), Kornblum (1974), and Suttles (1968). For contemporary studies, see E. Anderson (1985 and 1992), Duneier (1999), Massey and Denton (1993), Pattillo-McCoy (2000), Pattillo (2007), and W. J. Wilson (1987 and 1996). For the epistemology of sexuality and its distinctiveness, see Sedgwick (1990); the quote is from page 75. For a view that introduces race into Sedgwick's arguments, see Ross (2005). For "us versus them" and "us and them," see Ghaziani (2011).

22. For the Facebook group of Heterosexual Awareness Month, see https://www.facebook.com/heterolAwareness; for the group's general website, see http://heterosexualawarenessmonth.com/. For news coverage, see Cavan Sieczkowski, "Heterosexual Awareness Month Kicks Off, Facebook Page Offers Ways to Celebrate," *Huffington Post* online, July 10, 2013.

CHAPTER 3. TRIGGERS

1. Jacobs (1961:47). The Chicago School of Urban Sociology also emphasized diversity (Fischer 1975; Park and Burgess 1925; Simmel 1903). See Berrey (2005) for a review of how the diversity concept informs contemporary city life, along with Bell and Hartman (2007:895) and Glazer (1997) for an assessment of diversity in everyday discourse. For a recent example of a study of neighborhood diversity that emphasizes race and class yet ignores sexuality, see Crowder, Pais, and South (2012). For "new immigrant enclaves" in New York, see Kirk Semple, "Take the A Train to Little Guyana," *New York Times* online, June 8, 2013. For a review of research on homophily, see McPherson, Smith-Lovin, and Cook (2001).

2. According to Fischer, "One indicator of assimilation is spatial distribution within urban areas" (1999:217).

3. For research on developmental changes in conformity among adolescence, see Berndt (1979) and Brown, Eicher, and Petrie (1986). For research on adults, see Charles and Carstensen (2010) and Pasupathi (1999).

4. For NGLTF research results, see Cianciotto and Cahill (2003). Psychologist Ritch Savin-Williams (2005:1) is a major proponent of "the new gay teenager," and he develops the idea in his book of the same title. There is debate on whether teenagers are really post-gay. Russell, Clarke, and Clary (2009) find that the majority of nonheterosexual youth (71%) endorse "historically typical sexual identity labels." Only a small portion identify as "questioning" (13%) or "queer" (5%). Nine percent of their sample elected "alternative labels that describe ambivalence or resistance to sexual identity labels, or fluidity in sexual identities." They conclude, "Lesbian, gay, and bisexual identities remain relevant for contemporary adolescents." In a different study, Stuart Biegel argues, "Despite significant advances for gay and transgender persons in the United States, the public school environment remains daunting, even frightening, as evidenced by numerous high-profile incidents of discrimination, bullying, violence, and suicide" (2010). When scholars challenge the label "fluidity," they often reference Lisa Diamond's (2008) research on women's sexuality.

5. Vary (2006); for additional research on identity changes in young people, see Ghaziani (2011), Houvouras and Carter (2008), McAdam (1988), and Seidman (2002:11).

6. It Gets Better Project, http://www.itgetsbetter.org/pages/about-it-gets-better-project.

7. For census statistics, see http://www.census.gov/prod/2011pubs/acsbr10-03.pdf. For the Williams Institute, see "As Overall Percentage of Same-Sex Couples Raising Children Declines, Those Adopting Almost Doubles—Significant Diversity among Lesbian and Gay Families," Williams Institute online, January 25, 2012. There are important racial differences: "Childrearing is substantially higher among racial/ethnic minorities, and African-Americans, in particular, are 2.4 times more likely than their White counterparts to be raising children." For the "gayby boom," see John Blake, "'Gayby Boom': Children of Gay Couples Speak Out," CNN online, June 28, 2009, and Susan Donaldson James, "'Gayby Boom' Fueled by Same-Sex Parents," ABC News online, August 3, 2009.

8. Edelberg and Kurland (2009:xxi, 122, 157).

9. "It Gets Better, Starting in Elementary School," How to Walk to School, http://howtowalktoschool.com/. See also "Nettelhorst's Pride Fabric Fence," Facebook, https://www.facebook.com/note.php?note_id=86630698310.

10. Rex W. Huppke, "Chicago School to March in Pride Parade," *Chicago Tribune* online, April 11, 2011.

11. The myth of the gay man as child molester and recruiter for homosexuality is perhaps the most destructive weapon that antigay activists use to stoke public fears about homosexuality (e.g., Anita Bryant's 1977 campaign to overturn a Dade County, Florida, ordinance that barred discrimination against lesbians and gay

men). According to the American Psychiatric Association, however, "homosexual men are not more likely to sexually abuse children than heterosexual men are." There is no evidence for the myth that gay men molest children at higher rates than heterosexual men. See Evelyn Schlatter and Robert Steinback, "10 Anti-Gay Myths Debunked," Southern Poverty Law Center (SPLC), http://www.splcenter.org/.

12. See Laumann et al. (2004); the footnoted discussion is on page 96n4. For MSM study, see Bolding et al. (2007). This was based in the UK. A different 2002 study surveyed 609 MSM in Atlanta and found that 75 percent reported using the Internet to access gay-oriented websites, and 34 percent reported having met a sexual partner online (Benotsch, Kalichman, and Cage 2002).

13. Hilbert and Lopez (2011).

14. For research on how the Internet adds to other forms of communication and community, see Wellman and Haythornthwaite (2002) and Wellman et al. (2003). For a study that explicitly asks whether virtual communities are "true communities," see Driskell and Lyon (2002).

15. For the many functions of gayborhoods, see Gates and Ost (2004a:2–6), Myslik (1996), and Usher and Morrison (2010).

16. For Jim Owles's statement, see Armstrong (2002:104–5).

17. Rubin (1993).

18. Fischer (1999:213–14). He acknowledges that "nonethnic subcultures differ in many ways from ethnic ones" (216), and he lists "gay communities" as among these nonethnic subcultures. That said, he does not document how the diversity of the gay community affects the decisions that individuals make about where in the city to live, nor does he speak with members of the gay community for their thoughts about assimilation.

CHAPTER 4. CULTURAL ARCHIPELAGOS

1. For quotes, see Smith and Gates (2001:1) and Gates and Ost (2004a:20); for 2010 Census analysis of households, see O'Connell and Feliz (2011).

2. For Census 2000 quote, see Gates and Ost (2004b:20); for Census 2010 quote, see O'Connell and Feliz (2011:7).

3. Quotes are from Gates and Ost (2004b:20).

4. McPherson, Smith-Lovin, and Cook (2001:415).

5. For more on lesbian and gay location patterns in the Gilded Age, see Papadopoulos (2005); on important meeting places, and to learn more about Rush Street and lesbians, see Heap (2008:8–11); for Kinsey, see Kinsey, Pomeroy, and Martin (1948).

6. Papadopoulos (2005:236); Stephanie Banchero, "Rift Threatens Unity of North Halsted Plan to Recognize Gay Pride," *Chicago Tribune*, September 24, 1997, 1.

7. Kyra Kyles, "Culture Clash: Boystown Shifting as More Families Move In," 6.

8. Michael Lavers, "The Queer Issue: The New Gayborhoods of Fort Greene, Sunset Park, and Jackson Heights," page unnoted.

9. Brinster's quote, "A Landmark Gay Bookstore Is Closing," by Larry Fish, *Philadelphia Inquirer*, January 15, 2003, C1; Michelle Garcia, "Race, Class and Sex Breed Contempt in Greenwich Village," *Washington Post*, September 18, 2006, A3.

10. Brinster's quote, "A Landmark Gay Bookstore Is Closing," by Larry Fish; Gary Lee, "Sojourn through Gay America: From Provincetown to San Francisco, Taking the Pulse of the Country for Gay and Lesbian Travelers," *Washington Post*, July 23, 1995, E1; Denny Lee, "Street Fight," *New York Times*, March 31, 2002, section 14, 1.

11. For more on Potemkin, see "Did 'Potemkin Villages' Really Exist?," Straight Dope website, and "Grigory Aleksandrovich Potemkin," *Encyclopaedia Brittanica* online.

12. Lynn Yaeger, "Chasing Rainbows," *Village Voice*, June 29, 2004, 15; Motoko Rich, "TURF: Edged Out by the Stroller Set," *New York Times*, May 27, 2004, F1.

13. Shaftel, "Under the Rainbow."

14. Ibid.

15. Chauncey (1994:228). For examples of research on the stages of gentrification, see Brown-Saracino (2009), Gale (1980), Kasinitz (1988), Knopp (1997), Laska and Spain (1980), Levy and Cybriwsky (1980), London (1980), and Zukin (1987).

16. Marc Fisher, "With Their Circle Seemingly Broken, Gays Face Change," *Washington Post*, May 2, 2002, B1.

17. On South Boston, see Philip Bennett, "Southie Revising a Bad Rep: Gays Increase Their Presence but Raise No Alarms," *Boston Globe*, September 28, 1991, 25; on Oakland, see Jim Herron Zamora, "Oakland: Gays in the Mainstream," *San Francisco Chronicle*, June 25, 2004, B1.

18. For more on the relationship between gay households and economic development, see Florida (2002).

19. P. L. Brown, "Gay Enclaves Face Prospect of Being Passé."

20. Jen Christensen and John Caldwell, "Welcome to the Gayborhood," *Advocate*, June 20, 2006, page unnoted. For Brekhus's research on suburban gays, see Brekhus (2003).

21. Jane Gross, "A Quiet Town of Potlucks, Church Socials, and Two Dads: Gays Find a Warm Welcome in a New Jersey Suburb," *New York Times*, December 4, 2000, B1.

22. Ruth Schubert, "Same-Sex Couples Stand Up for Count: Semi-Rural Vashon Island a Surprising Top Choice for Gays and Lesbians," *Seattle Post-Intelligencer*, July 12, 2001, B1.

23. Thomas Ginsberg, "Census Finds Gays, Lesbians in Diverse and Distinct Areas," *Philadelphia Inquirer*, August 16, 2001, A01.

24. The statistics in this section are from Gary Gates, "LGBT Parenting in the United States," Williams Institute, February 2013, 5, http://williamsinstitute .law.ucla.edu/wp-content/uploads/LGBT-Parenting.pdf. For a comparison with Census 2000, see Gates (2003). For research on gay and lesbian families, see Bernstein and Reimann (2001), Gates et al. (2007), Ryan and Berkowitz (2009), and Stacey (2003).

25. Gates (2013), "LGBT Parenting in the United States."

26. "Metro Areas with Highest Percentages of Same-Sex Couples Raising Children Are in States with Constitutional Bans on Marriage," Williams Institute online, May 20, 2013.

27. Claire Wilson, "Gay Retirement Communities Are Growing in Popularity," *New York Times*, November 20, 2005, "National Perspectives" section. For demographics of GLBT seniors, see Cornelius Frolik, "Gay Seniors Fear Bias," Williams Institute online, January 17, 2012.

28. Ibid. For more on being "beyond the closet," see Seidman (2002).

29. Many of these observations have scholarly support: for de-gaying, or deconcentration, see Reynolds (2009), Ruting (2008), and Spring (2012 and 2013); for safe harbors, see Doan (2007) and Hanhardt (2008); for survival, or integration and retention, see Browne and Bakshi (2011) and Collins (2004); for revival as adjacent reconcentration, see Hayslett and Kane (2011); for revival as fringe reconcentration, see Doan and Higgins (2011); for multiplication, or subgroup reconcentration, see Ettorre (1978), Gates and Cooke (2011), and Valentine (2000); for medium- and small-sized cities, see D'Emilio (1993), Florida (2002), and Gates and Ost (2004a); and for suburbs and rural areas, see Brekhus (2003), Gray (2009), and Herring (2010).

30. Research on gayborhoods and queer spaces often focuses on big cities like Chicago, LA, New York, San Francisco, and West Hollywood. Fewer studies look at small and medium-sized cities. See D'Emilio (1993), Florida (2002), and Gates and Ost (2004a) for general overviews. Notable exceptions include Columbus, Ohio (Hayslett and Kane 2011); Minneapolis, Minnesota (Murphy, Pierce, and Knopp 2010); New Orleans, Louisiana (Knopp 1997); and a comparative study of Duluth, Minnesota, and Seattle, Washington (Knopp and Brown 2003). Some research that is based in small cities, such as Buffalo, New York (Kennedy and Davis 1993); Ithaca, New York (Brown-Saracino 2011); Northampton, Massachusetts (Forsyth 1997; Kirkey and Forsyth 2001; Smith and Holt 2005); and Vancouver, British Columbia (Bouthillette 1997; Lo and Healy 2000), is actually about gender differences—and thus subgroup reconcentration—rather than the emergence of gayborhoods in nontraditional, small, and medium-sized cities. In the interest of not conflating two distinct analytic possibilities, I do not classify the latter as an example of the former, and I maintain a separate discussion

of suburbanism and ruralism (Brekhus 2003; Browne 2008; Gray 2009; Herring 2010; Kennedy 2010; Lynch 1992; Newton 1993; Tongson 2011).

CHAPTER 5. RESONANCE

1. For the actual study, see Schafer and Shaw (2009). The figure in the text is adapted from Lisa Wade, "Who Do Americans Prefer Not to Have as Neighbors?," *Sociological Images* blog, Society Pages website, May 14, 2010.

2. Castells and Murphy (1982:257).

3. Thomas and Thomas (1928:572).

4. Smelser (1963:8).

5. Jeff Michel owns the copyright for the artwork. In an e-mail correspondence with him, Jeff told me the following: "One last thing I do want to stress is that we haven't made this shirt since 2006 and that was at the request of Major League Baseball. We produced parody shirts from 2005 until earlier this year [in 2013], but have stopped because the cost of fighting with MLB way outweighed any profits made."

6. David Sokol, "Not Your Average LGBT Center," *Advocate*, April 24, 2007, 15; Mike Thomas, "An Equal Opportunity Hang Out," *Chicago Sun-Times*, March 29, 2007, 35. For more on how the post-gay era affects organizational names, see Ghaziani (2011).

7. Doan (2007:62).

8. Adapted from Doan (2007:66). She snowball sampled 149 people at two professional conferences, one in Atlanta in the fall of 2000 and the other in Philadelphia during the spring of 2001. Her sample includes individuals from twenty-nine states and four overseas countries. The average age was forty-six.

9. Weston (1995).

10. For the idea of cities as a "beacon of tolerance," see ibid., 282.

11. A host of other derogatory and urban-centric terms are also available at our disposal, including bumpkin, hillbilly, redneck, Hicksville, boondocks, backwater, the middle of nowhere, the sticks, the backwoods, the hinterlands, and the outskirts (Herring 2010:1).

12. Cisgender contrasts with transgender. In the former, there is a match between the gender you are assigned at birth, your body, and your personality. For more on the meaning of cisgender, see Schilt and Westbrook (2009).

13. Coates, "Bringing Clarity to an Elusive Reality," 3.

14. For more on anchor institutions, see "Overview," Penn IUR, http://penn iur.upenn.edu/research/anchor-institutions.

15. Murray (1979:168); for more on quasi-ethnic identity, see Murray (1979 and 1996:4). This is part of a wider debate over whether gay identity is essential or socially constructed (Epstein 1987 and 1999).

16. For more on the history of gay migration patterns in Chicago, see Papado-poulos (2005).

17. For cosmopolitanism quote, see Rushbrook (2002:183). For a transnational feminist critique and a discussion of its lesbian-inflected nature, see Puar (2002). For a mainstream, urban sociological consideration of how tourism creates a symbolic economy, see Zukin (1995). See E. Anderson (2011) for general remarks on cosmopolitanism. The discussion in this section is consistent with market research. The "travel and leisure industry vendors and municipalities eager for tourist dollars recognized the size and affluence of the gay market segment and were able to match their amenities and sites to the segment's needs" (Branchik 2006:230).

18. Bergquist and McDonald (2006:16).

19. To learn more about the business alliance, see www.northalsted.com.

20. See Bennett (2010); the quotes are from chapter 1.

21. See Bergquist and McDonald (2006:17).

22. Jessica Kwong, "SF Gay History Museum Finds Home, Identity," *San Francisco Chronicle*, January 12, 2011, C-1.

23. See the Legacy Project, http://legacyprojectchicago.org/.

24. For Frank Kameny Way, see Lou Chibbaro Jr., "'Kameny Way' Ceremony Highlights Capital Pride Events," *Washington Blade*, June 8, 2010; see also Greene (2011). For Harvey Milk Street, see Mike Spradley, "San Diego Dedicates Harvey Milk Street," *Huffington Post*, May 26, 2012. For June as Pride Month, see White House press release, "Lesbian, Gay, Bisexual, and Transgender Pride Month, 2009," June 1, 2009, Office of the Press Secretary. For Stonewall Inn as a historic landmark, see David W. Dunlap, "Stonewall, Gay Bar that Made History, Is Made a Landmark," *New York Times*, June 26, 1999, 1. For Christopher Park, see the website of the City of New York Parks and Recreation.

25. For Dufty quote, see Scott James, "Change with a Straight Face Barrels into the Castro," *New York Times*, May 7, 2011. For academic research on collective memory, see Armstrong and Crage (2006), Griffin and Bollen (2009), Irwin-Zarecka (1994), Olick and Robbins (1998:106), and Wagner-Pacifici (1996).

CHAPTER 6. REINVENTION

1. Hayslett and Kane (2011:145); they argue that "geographic clustering may also be a protective mechanism" for gays and lesbians (ibid.) and that "geographic concentration and neighborhood barriers suggest that gay men may either face explicit barriers to specific neighborhoods or that the generalized hostility in the U.S. culture encourages clustering as a protective mechanism" (151).

2. McPherson, Smith-Lovin, and Cook (2001); the quotes are from the abstract and pages 429–30.

3. My knowledge of migrations within a city is mostly anecdotal, with the exception of San Francisco (Duggins 2002; Hunter 2010; Valocchi 1999). For a working paper on DC, see Greene (2011).

4. For more on post-gay collective identity, along with an "us and them" framework, see Ghaziani (2011).

5. Zukin (1987, 1995, and 2010).

6. Nero (2005:231).

7. Michael Lavers, "The Queer Issue: The New Gayborhoods of Fort Greene, Sunset Park, and Jackson Heights."

8. Guelda Voien, "Lesbians as 'Canaries in the Urban Coal Mine,'" *New York Observer* online, April 23, 2010.

9. For scholarship on lesbian neighborhoods, see Adler and Brenner (1992: 29–31), Bouthillette (1997:219), Brown-Saracino (2011), Ettorre (1978), Forsyth (2001:346), Rothenberg (1995), and Valentine (2000:3). The idea that these areas are "quasi-underground" comes from page 31 of Adler and Brenner's research.

10. Authorship unnoted, "Andersonville to Evulve," *Time Out Chicago*, March 31, 2010.

11. For the 2012 study, see Brad Sears and Lee Badgett, "Beyond Stereotypes: Poverty in the LGBT Community," Williams Institute online, June 2012. Other research has returned mixed results. For example, Badgett shows that lesbians and gay men earn *less* than their straight counterparts, even after we control for education, age, race, and other factors (2001). Current work shows that while gay men continue to earn *less* than straight men, lesbians now earn *more* than straight women. See Joe Clark, Gay Money project website, http://joeclark.org /gaymoney/facts/. Some research suggests that gay male couples' incomes and lesbian couples' incomes are similar to *each other*, although this has not been widely validated (see the same website under the heading "Other facts").

12. Michael Lavers, "The Queer Issue: The New Gayborhoods of Fort Greene, Sunset Park, and Jackson Heights."

13. Kevin Aeh and Jessica Herman, "Andersonville's Top 10 Best Home-Decor Shops," *Time Out Chicago*, September 30, 2009.

14. Infighting is not always a bad thing; it can be generative for minority group members. Research shows that the expression of a difference of opinion, or the offering of a discrepant view, can clarify what it means to belong to a group, and it can concretize shared strategic visions (Ghaziani 2008).

15. For more information on this strategy, see the Chicago Dyke March Collective's (CDMC) webpage, http://chicagodykemarch.wordpress.com/.

16. Nero (2005:228).

17. Castells (1983:140). For an argument that Castells offers a "simplistic assumption" about lesbians, see Binnie and Valentine (1999:176), and for the

assertion that such an assumption is an outright "lie," see Mitchell (2000:193). For Park slope lesbians, see Rothenberg (1995:179). On Northampton, Massachusetts, see Barbara Kantrowitz, "A Town Like No Other," *Newsweek*, June 20, 1993. "Lesbianville, USA" has been racially critiqued in the same way as its gay male counterparts. Kantrowitz observes, "Northampton isn't a utopia for all lesbians, either. It's mostly a white community, with few minorities. 'I'm going to Berkeley or New York,' says one black Amherst college student who wears her hair in dreadlocks and is studying to be a percussionist in an Afrofunk band." For more on lesbian geographies, see Valentine (2000). For more on lesbian spaces, see Doan and Higgins (2011:8). For more on urban lesbian concentrations, see Elwood (2000), Ettorre (1978), Kennedy and Davis (1993), Lo and Healy (2000), and Podmore (2006). For more on rural lesbian concentrations, see Brown-Saracino (2011), Browne (2008), Forsyth (1997), and McCarthy (2000).

18. Jed Kolko (*Trulia Trends* chief economist), "Welcome to the Gayborhood," *Huffington Post* online, June 15, 2012; for the blog post by Suzy Kimm, see "America's Gayest ZIP Codes, in Two Tables," *Washington Post* online, June 16, 2012.

19. There are at least five reasons why lesbians and gay men tend to make different decisions about where to live: (1) men and women have different needs to control space (Castells 1983); (2) women have less socioeconomic power than men (Adler and Brenner 1992; Badgett 1997:68–69; Badgett 2001; Black et al. 2002:69; Knopp 1990:349 and 1997:59); (3) men are more influenced by sexual marketplaces and commercial institution building, whereas women are more motivated by feminism, countercultures, and informal institutions (Bouthillette 1997; Brown-Saracino 2011; Ettorre 1978; Knopp 1997:58; Laumann et al. 2004); (4) female same-sex partner households are more likely to have children, and thus they have different needs for housing, especially the type and quality of housing stock (Black et al. 2000; Bouthillette 1997); and (5) lesbians are more likely to live in "less populous regions" (Cooke and Rapiano 2007:295), often rural environments (Kazyak 2011 and 2012; Wolfe 1979), while gay men are more likely to select urban areas. Cooke and Rapiano (2007:288, 296) refer to all these gender differences as the "Gay and Lesbian Exceptionalism Hypothesis."

CONCLUSIONS

1. Reuter (2008:108).

2. Weston (1995:257).

3. Armstrong (2002:106–10), emphasis added.

4. For the definition of culture as a "way of life," see Williams (1976:90). Daniel Mendelsohn, "We're Here! We're Queer! Let's Get Coffee!," *New York Magazine*, September 30, 1996, 31.

5. Warner (1999:46, 48, 54–55). For arguments about "gay shame," or the idea that homosexuality has become too respectable for its own good, see Halperin and Traub (2009).

6. How to be gay (Signorile 1997); urban ghettoization (Bawer 1993); and public-private split (A. Sullivan 1996). For the Pew Research Poll, see "Growing Support for Gay Marriage: Changed Minds and Changing Demographics," Pew Research Center, March 20, 2013. A quarter of respondents say that their personal views have changed as they have thought about the issue or simply because they have grown older. Eighteen percent say that the world is different now than it was before.

7. Cultural innovation (Harris 1997); virtual equality (Vaid 1995); and hardcore homophobia (Warner 1999). Warner's quote is from Seidman (2002:5). See the same source (pages 2–6) for the debate between assimilation and diversity.

8. Pew Survey, "A Survey of LGBT Americans: Attitudes, Experiences and Values in Changing Times," Pew Research Center, June 13, 2013, http://www .pewresearch.org/. The quotes are from pages 12–13. Gay men are most likely of any LGBT subgroup to say that gayborhoods and gay bars are still important (68%).

9. See Seidman (2002:189) for additional post-gay problems. The "enthralled by respectability" quote is from Ward (2008). These problems remind us that the "charmed circle" and its "outer limits" are alive and well today (Rubin 1993; Warner 1999:23). For the desire to be perceived as normal, see Warner (1999 and 1999:25, 66–68). Lisa Duggan calls this a politics of "homonormativity" (2002 and 2003). It encourages gay people to strive for tolerance, which is a "grudging form" of assimilation in which the boundaries of sex, gender, and sexuality remain unchallenged (Jakobsen and Pellegrini 2003).

10. G. Brown (2006:133).

11. Greene (2011:6).

12. Hadley Tomicki, "The Abbey Bans Bachelorette Parties until Marriage Equality Is Reached," Grub Street, http://losangeles.grubstreet.com/2012/05 /the-abbey-bans-bachelorette-parties.html.

13. See the comment of "Andi in Wonderland" in "Iconic Gay Bar, The Abbey, Bans Bachelorette Parties Until Marriage Legal for Gays," *LGBTQ Nation* online, May 26, 2012.

14. On DC, see Associated Press, "Boystown Gay Bar Bans Bachelorette Parties," *Huffington Post*, first posted July 16, 2009, updated May 25, 2011; on Chicago, see Dawn Turner Trice, "Gay Rights Battle Puts Strain on Parties," *Chicago Tribune*, March 23, 2009.

15. For too long now, scholars have struggled to promote sexuality as a legitimate mode of intellectual inquiry, and they have often justified its study by comparing it to race. This can be quite fruitful, of course, but urban research already

overemphasizes race (and class), and it neglects sexuality. There is, however, an "epistemological distinctiveness of gay identity and gay situation in our culture" (Sedgwick 1990:75). The contrasting ways in which we acquire knowledge about race and sexuality, along with the historical trajectories through which their respective discourses and silences flow, warrant the study of sexuality on its own terms. For more on postracialism, postblackness, and colorblindness, see Kaplan (2011) and Touré (2011).

16. Mary McNamara, "In 'Post' Culture, the Prefix Is In," *Los Angeles Times*, August 31, 2003. Vavrus's quote is from Vavrus (2010:222); Neal Broverman, "If Racism Is Alive and Well, Homophobia Has Lots of Good Years Left," *Advocate*, July 18, 2013; Pew Survey, "A Survey of LGBT Americans," Pew Research Center online, June 13, 2013, http://www.pewresearch.org/. The quotes are from pages 1 and 6.

17. For a listing of gay rights in the United States, state by state, see *The Guardian* online, http://www.theguardian.co.uk/world/interactive/2012/may/08/gay -rights-united-states/. A June 2013 national study by the US Department of Housing and Urban Development, entitled "An Estimate of Housing Discrimination Against Same-Sex Couples," confirmed that same-sex couples are discriminated against in the rental housing market, even when business is conducted online; see http://www.huduser.org/portal/publications/fairhsg/discrim_samesex.html. See also Lauster and Easterbrook (2011).

18. Quotes are from Trudy Ring, "Study: Gayborhoods for Many Budgets," *Advocate* online, June 16, 2012. For the study itself, see Jeff Kolko, "Welcome to the Gayborhood," *Trulia Trends*, June 15, 2012, http://trends.truliablog.com/.

APPENDIX

1. For "basic building block," see Forsyth (2001:343); on psychological unity, see Keller (1968:87); on gayborhoods as ghettos, see Wirth (1928) and Wittman (1970); on real communities, see Murray (1992); on imagined communities, see B. Anderson (1983); on quasi-ethnic settlements, see Abrahamson (2005), Epstein (1987), and Murray (1979); on safe spaces, see Allen (1970), Castells (1983), and Evans and Boyte (1986); on sites of resistance, see Myslik (1996); on urban land markets, see Black et al. (2002), Florida (2002), Knopp (1997), and Molotch (1976); and on entertainment districts, see Lloyd and Clark (2001) and Rushbrook (2002).

2. For examples of early studies, see Ettorre (1978), Harry (1974), Levine (1979), Murray (1979:167–69), Wittman (1970), and Wolfe (1979).

3. Levine (1979:185–86).

4. Castells and Murphy (1982:238–40).

5. Gates and Ost (2004a:20).

6. On Newcastle, see Casey (2004:450); on Philadelphia, see Damon C. Williams, "New Signs Make It Clear: We Have a 'Gayborhood,'" *Philadelphia Daily News*, April 19, 2007; on Vancouver, see Mike Hager, "Davie Street Village Gets First Permanent Rainbow Crosswalk in Canada," *Vancouver Sun*, July 30, 2013.

7. Chauncey (1994:228).

8. For more on maximum variation sampling, see List (2004) and Patton (1987: 52). For more on regression to the mean, see Shadish, Cook, and Campbell (2002).

9. See Ghaziani and Ventresca (2005) and Williams (1976) for more information on a keywords methodology.

10. For more on the differences between gay and straight presses, see Forest (1995:141).

11. Cook (1985).

12. For media discussions of residential choice, specifically, I used retroductive coding, which alternates between deductive and inductive inferences (Ragin 1994) to balance concerns of reliability and validity (Stemler 2001). Principles of cultural analysis directed me to ground my inductive codes in the actual language of the newspaper articles, rather than those that are "superimposed by the analyst" (Griswold 1987:1096). By opening up the possibility of multiple codes per article, I correct a common criticism of content analysis as ignoring multiple meanings (Gottdiener 1995:19–22; Steinberg 1999:740). I hired a graduate research assistant to compute a Cohen's Kappa statistic for each theme. The Kappa statistic assesses inter-rater reliability in the content analysis of categorical, often dichotomous variables. It is a more robust measure than the calculation of percent agreement, because Kappa incorporates chance (J. Cohen 1960; Neuendorf 2002:141). It is considered "the standard measure of research quality" for content analysis (Kolbe and Burnett 1991:248). Kappa values range from 0 to 1.0. High values redress the common criticism of subjectivity and suggest instead that the coding categories are objective (Lombard, Snyder-Duch, and Campenella Bracken 2005). An independent rater coded a 10 percent random sample of articles.

13. John Fischer, "Ground-breaking TV Ad Set to Promote 'Gay-Friendly' Philly," About.com online; Gary Lee, "For Gays, Toronto Is the Marrying Kind," *Washington Post*, March 14, 2004, 1; Rona Marech, "Top Court in Canada OKs Gay Marriage," *San Francisco Chronicle*, December 10, 2004, A1.

14. Damon C. Williams, "New Signs Make It Official," *Philadelphia Daily News*, April 19, 2007, 22; Wyatt Buchanan, "S.F.'s Castro District Faces an Identity Crisis," *San Francisco Chronicle*, February 25, 2007, A1; Lisa Leff, "In San Francisco's Castro District, a Cry of 'There Goes the Gayborhood,'"; P. L. Brown, "Gay Enclaves Face Prospect of Being Passé"; R. D. Sullivan, "Last Call: Why the Gay Bars of Boston Are Disappearing"; Associated Press, "Won't You Be My Gaybor?

Gay Neighborhoods Worry about Losing Their Distinct Identity," *Chicago Tribune*, March 13, 2007, 3.

15. For more on hidden populations, see Salganik and Heckathorn (2004). Respondent-driven techniques are sensitive to community structure (Goel and Salganik 2009), geographic clusters (Sudman, Sirken, and Cowan 1988:991), and social network ties (Bernard et al. 2010). For more on network chains, see Salganik and Heckathorn (2004:201–2; 204–8).

16. Cicourel (1964:50).

WORKS CITED

Abrahamson, Mark. 2005. *Urban Enclaves: Identity and Place in the World*. New York: Worth Publishers.

Abu-Lughod, Janet L. 1999. *New York, Chicago, Los Angeles: America's Global Cities*. Minneapolis: University of Minnesota Press.

Adam, Barry D. 1995. *The Rise of the Gay and Lesbian Movement*. New York: Twayne.

Adler, Sy, and Johanna Brenner. 1992. "Gender and Space: Lesbians and Gay Men in the City." *International Journal of Urban and Regional Research* 16:24–34.

Aldrich, Robert. 2004. "Homosexuality and the City: An Historical Overview." *Urban Studies* 41:1719–37.

Allen, Pamela. 1970. *Free Space: A Perspective on the Small Group in Women's Liberation*. New York: Times Change Press.

Allport, Gordon Willard. 1954. *The Nature of Prejudice*. Reading, MA: Addison-Wesley.

Anacker, Katrin B., and Hazel A. Morrow-Jones. 2005. "Neighborhood Factors Associated with Same-Sex Households in U.S. Cities." *Urban Geography* 26:385–409.

Anderson, Benedict. 1983. *Imagined Communities*. New York: Verso.

Anderson, Elijah. 1985. "Race and Neighborhood Transition." Pp. 99–127 in *The New Urban Reality*, edited by P. E. Peterson. Washington, DC: Brookings Institution.

———. 1992. *Streetwise: Race, Class, and Change in an Urban Community*. Chicago: University of Chicago Press.

———. 2011. *The Cosmopolitan Canopy: Race and Civility in Everyday Life*. New York: Norton.

Armstrong, Elizabeth A. 2002. *Forging Gay Identities: Organizing Sexuality in San Francisco, 1950–1994*. Chicago: University of Chicago Press.

Armstrong, Elizabeth A., and Suzanna M. Crage. 2006. "Movements and Memory: The Making of the Stonewall Myth." *American Sociological Review* 71:724–51.

Badgett, M. V. Lee. 1995. "The Wage Effects of Sexual Orientation Discrimination." *Industrial and Labor Relations Review* 48:726–39.

———. 1997. "Beyond Biased Samples: Challenging the Myths on the Economic Status of Lesbians and Gay Men." Pp. 65–71 in *Homo Economics: Capitalism,*

Community, and Lesbian and Gay Life, edited by A. Gluckman and B. Reed. New York: Routledge.

———. 2001. *Money, Myths, and Change: The Economic Lives of Lesbians and Gay Men*. Chicago: University of Chicago Press.

Bawer, Bruce. 1993. *A Place at the Table: The Gay Individual in American Society*. New York: Simon and Schuster.

Bearman, Peter S., and Katherine Stovel. 2000. "Becoming a Nazi: A Model for Narrative Networks." *Poetics* 27:69–90.

Bell, David, and Gill Valentine. 1995. "Queer Country: Rural Lesbian and Gay Lives." *Journal of Rural Studies* 11:113–22.

Bell, Joyce M., and Douglas Hartman. 2007. "Diversity in Everyday Discourse: The Cultural Ambiguities and Consequences of 'Happy Talk.'" *American Sociological Review* 72:895–914.

Bellah, Robert N., Richard Madsen, William M. Sullivan, Ann Swidler, and Steven T. Tipton. 1985. *Habits of the Heart*. Berkeley: University of California Press.

Bennett, Larry. 2010. *The Third City: Chicago and American Urbanism*. Chicago: University of Chicago Press.

Benotsch, Eric G., Seth Kalichman, and Maggi Cage. 2002. "Men Who Have Met Sex Partners via the Internet: Prevalence, Predictors, and Implications for HIV Prevention." *Archives of Sexual Behavior* 31:177–83.

Bergquist, Kathie, and Robert McDonald. 2006. *A Field Guide to Gay and Lesbian Chicago*. Chicago: Lake Claremont Press.

Bernard, H. Russell, Tim Hallett, Alexandrina Lovita, Eugene C. Johnsen, Rob Lyerla, Christopher McCarty, Mary Mahy, Matthew J. Salganik, Tetiana Saliuk, Otilia Scutelniciuc, Gene A. Shelley, Petchsri Sirinirund, Sharon Weir, and Donna F. Stroup. 2010. "Counting Hard-to-Count Populations: The Network Scale-Up Method for Public Researchers." *Sexually Transmitted Infections* 86:iii1–iii5.

Berndt, Thomas J. 1979. "Developmental Changes in Conformity to Peers and Parents." *Developmental Psychology* 15:608–16.

Bernstein, Mary. 1997. "Celebration and Suppression: The Strategic Uses of Identity by the Lesbian and Gay Movement." *American Journal of Sociology* 103:531–65.

Bernstein, Mary, and Renate Reimann. 2001. *Queer Families, Queer Politics*. New York: Columbia University Press.

Berrey, Ellen. 2005. "Divided over Diversity: Political Discourse in a Chicago Neighborhood." *City and Community* 4:143–70.

Berry, Brian J. L. 1985. "Islands of Renewal in Seas of Decay." Pp. 69–96 in *The New Urban Reality*, edited by P. E. Peterson. Washington, DC: Brookings Institution.

Berube, Allan. 1990. *Coming Out Under Fire: The History of Gay Men and Women in World War Two*. New York: Plume.

Biegel, Stuart. 2010. *The Right to Be Out: Sexual Orientation and Gender Identity in America's Public Schools*. Minneapolis: University of Minnesota Press.

Binnie, Jon, and Gill Valentine. 1999. "Geographies of Sexuality: A Review of Progress." *Progress in Human Geography* 23:175–87.

Black, Dan A., Hoda R. Makar, Seth G. Sanders, and Lowell J. Taylor. 2003. "The Earning Effects of Sexual Orientation." *Industrial and Labor Relations Review* 56:449–69.

Black, Dan, Gary Gates, Seth Sanders, and Lowell Taylor. 2000. "Demographics of the Gay and Lesbian Population in the United States: Evidence from Available Systematic Data Sources." *Demography* 37:139–54.

———. 2002. "Why Do Gay Men Live in San Francisco?" *Journal of Urban Economics* 51:54–76.

Bolding, Graham, Mark Davis, Graham Hart, Lorraine Sherr, and Jonathan Elford. 2007. "Where Young MSM Meet Their First Sexual Partner: The Role of the Internet." *AIDS and Behavior* 11:522–26.

Borer, Michael Ian. 2006. "The Location of Culture: The Urban Culturalist Perspective." *City and Community* 5:173–97.

———. 2007. "Culture Matters: A Reply to Gans." *City and Community* 6:157–59.

Bouthillette, Anne-Marie. 1997. "Queer and Gendered Housing: A Tale of Two Neighborhoods in Vancouver." Pp. 213–32 in *Queers in Space: Communities, Public Places, Sites of Resistance*, edited by G. B. Ingram, A.-M. Bouthillette, and Y. Retter. Seattle: Bay Press.

Boyd, Nan Alamilla. 2005. *Wide-Open Town: A History of Queer San Francisco to 1965*. Berkeley: University of California Press.

Branchik, Blaine J. 2006. "Out in the Market: The History of the Gay Market Segment in the United States." In *Handbook of Niche Marketing*, edited by T. Dalgic. New York: Haworth Press.

Brekhus, Wayne. 2003. *Peacocks, Chameleons, Centaurs: Gay Suburbia and the Grammar of Social Identity*. Chicago: University of Chicago Press.

Brown, B. Bradford, Sue Ann Eicher, and Sandra Petrie. 1986. "The Importance of Peer Group ('Crowd') Affiliation in Adolescence." *Journal of Adolescence* 9:73–96.

Brown, Gavin. 2006. "Cosmopolitan Camouflage: (Post-)gay Space in Spitalfields, East London." Pp. 130–45 in *Cosmopolitan Urbanism*, edited by J. Binnie, J. Holloway, S. Millington, and C. Young. New York: Routledge.

Brown, Patricia Leigh. 2011. "Gay Enclaves Face Prospect of Being Passé." *New York Times*, October 30, 2007, A1.

Brown-Saracino, Japonica. 2007. "Virtuous Marginality: Social Preservationists and the Selection of the Old-Timer." *Theory and Society* 36:437–68.

———. 2009. *A Neighborhood that Never Changes: Gentrification, Social Preservation, and the Search for Authenticity*. Chicago: University of Chicago Press.

———. 2011. "From the Lesbian Ghetto to Ambient Community: The Perceived Costs and Benefits of Integration for Community." *Social Problems* 58:361–88.

Browne, Kath, and Leela Bakshi. 2011. "We Are Here to Party? Lesbian, Gay, Bisexual, and Trans Leisurescapes Beyond Commercial Gay Scenes." *Leisure Studies* 30:179–96.

Browne, Katherine. 2008. "Imagining Cities, Living the Other: Between the Gay Urban Idyll and Rural Lesbian Lives." *Open Geography Journal* 27:25–32.

Buechler, Steven M. 1990. *Women's Movements in the United States*. New Brunswick: Rutgers University Press.

Calhoun, Craig. 1983. "The Radicalism of Tradition: Community Strength or Venerable Disguise and Borrowed Language?" *American Journal of Sociology* 88: 886–914.

Canaday, Margot. 2009. *The Straight State: Sexuality and Citizenship in Twentieth-Century America*. Princeton, NJ: Princeton University Press.

Capsuto, Steven. 2000. *Alternate Channels: The Uncensored Story of Gay and Lesbian Images on Radio and Television*. New York: Ballantine Books.

Casey, Mark. 2004. "De-Dyking Queer Spaces: Heterosexual Female Visibility in Gay and Lesbian Spaces." *Sexualities* 7:446–61.

Castells, Manuel. 1983. *The City and the Grassroots: A Cross-Cultural Theory of Urban Social Movements*. Berkeley: University of California Press.

Castells, Manuel, and Karen Murphy. 1982. "Cultural Identity and Urban Structure: The Spatial Organization of San Francisco's Gay Community." Pp. 237–59 in *Urban Policy Under Capitalism*, edited by N. I. Fainstein and S. F. Fainstein. London: Sage.

Charles, Camille Zubrinsky. 2003. "The Dynamics of Racial Residential Segregation." *Annual Review of Sociology* 29:167–207.

Charles, Susan T., and Laura L. Carstensen. 2010. "Social and Emotional Aging." *Annual Review of Psychology* 61:383–409.

Chasin, Alexandra. 2000. *Selling Out: The Gay and Lesbian Movement Goes to Market*. New York: Palgrave.

Chauncey, George. 1994. *Gay New York: Gender, Urban Culture, and the Making of the Gay Male World, 1890–1940*. New York: Basic Books.

Cianciotto, Jason, and Sean Cahill. 2003. "Education Policy: Issues Affecting Lesbian, Gay, Bisexual and Transgender Youth." National Gay and Lesbian Task Force, Washington, DC.

Cicourel, Aaron V. 1964. *Method and Measurement in Sociology*. New York: Free Press.

Clark, Terry Nichols. 2011. "The New Chicago School: Notes Towards a Theory." Pp. 220–41 in *The City Revisited: Urban Theory from Chicago, Los Angeles, and New York*, edited by D. R. Judd and D. Simpson. Minneapolis: University of Minnesota Press.

Coates, Joseph. 1991. "Bringing Clarity to an Elusive Reality." *Chicago Tribune*, May 21.

Cohen, Cathy J. 2001. "Punks, Bulldaggers, and Welfare Queens: The Radical Potential of Queer Politics?" In *Sexual Identities, Queer Politics*, edited by M. Blasius. Princeton, NJ: Princeton University Press.

Cohen, Jacob. 1960. "A Coefficient of Agreement for Nominal Scales." *Educational and Psychological Measurement* 20:37–46.

Colbert, Stephen. 2007 (July 16). *The Colbert Report*.

Collard, James. 1998. "Leaving the Gay Ghetto." *Out Magazine*, August 17, 53.

Collins, Alan. 2004. "Sexual Dissidence, Enterprise and Assimilation: Bedfellows in Urban Regeneration." *Urban Studies* 41:1789–1806.

———. 2006. "Cities of Pleasure: Sex and the Urban Socialscape." New York: Routledge.

Condon, Bill. 2004. *Kinsey*. Los Angeles: Twentieth Century Fox Film Corporation.

Cook, Thomas D. 1985. "Postpositivist Critical Multiplism." Pp. 21–62 in *Social Science and Social Policy*, edited by R. L. Shotland and M. M. Mark. London: Sage.

Cooke, Thomas J., and Melanie Rapiano. 2007. "The Migration of Partnered Gays and Lesbians between 1995 and 2000." *Professional Geographer* 59:285–97.

Crowder, Kyle, Jeremy Pais, and Scott J. South. 2012. "Neighborhood Diversity, Metropolitan Constraints, and Household Migration." *American Sociological Review* 77:325–53.

D'Emilio, John. 1983. *Sexual Politics, Sexual Communities: The Making of a Homosexual Minority in the United States, 1940–1970*. Chicago: University of Chicago Press.

———. 1989. "Gay Politics and Community in San Francisco since World War II." Pp. 456–73 in *Hidden from History: Reclaiming the Gay and Lesbian Past*, edited by M. Duberman, M. Vicinus, and G. Chauncey. New York: New American Library Books.

———. 1993. "Capitalism and Gay Identity." Pp. 467–76 in *The Lesbian and Gay Studies Reader*, edited by H. Abelove, M. A. Barale, and D. M. Halperin. New York: Routledge.

D'Emilio, John, and Estelle B. Freedman. 1997. *Intimate Matters: A History of Sexuality in America*. Chicago: University of Chicago Press.

Diamond, Lisa. 2003. "Was It a Phase? Young Women's Relinquishment of Lesbian/Bisexual Identities Over a 5-Year Period." *Journal of Personality and Social Psychology* 84:352–64.

———. 2008. *Sexual Fluidity: Understanding Women's Love and Desire.* Cambridge, MA: Harvard University Press.

DiMaggio, Paul. 1997. "Culture and Cognition." *Annual Review of Sociology* 23:263–87.

Doan, Petra L. 2007. "Queers in the American City: Transgendered Perceptions of Urban Space." *Gender, Place, and Culture* 14:57–74.

Doan, Petra L., and Harrison Higgins. 2011. "The Demise of Queer Space? Resurgent Gentrification and the Assimilation of LGBT Neighborhoods." *Journal of Planning Education and Research* 31:6–25.

Dreier, Peter, John Mollenkopf, and Todd Swanstrom. 2004. *Place Matters: Metropolitics for the Twenty-First Century.* Lawrence: University Press of Kansas.

Drever, Anita I. 2004. "Separate Spaces, Separate Outcomes? Neighborhood Impacts on Minorities in Germany." *Urban Studies* 41:1423–39.

Driskell, Robyn Bateman, and Larry Lyon. 2002. "Are Virtual Communities True Communities? Examining the Environments and Elements of Community." *City and Community* 1:373–90.

Duggan, Lisa. 2002. "The New Homonormativity: The Sexual Politics of Neoliberalism." Pp. 175–94 in *Materializing Democracy: Toward a Revitalized Cultural Politics*, edited by R. Castronovo and D. D. Nelson. Durham, NC: Duke University Press.

———. 2003. *The Twilight of Equality? Neoliberalism, Cultural Politics, and the Attack on Democracy.* Boston: Beacon.

Duggins, Jim. 2002. "Out in the Castro: Creating a Gay Subculture, 1947–1969." Pp. 17–28 in *Out in the Castro: Desire, Promise, Activism*, edited by W. Leyland. San Francisco: Leyland Publications.

Duneier, Mitchell. 1999. *Sidewalk.* New York: Farrar, Straus and Giroux.

Durkheim, Emile. 1912. *The Elementary Forms of Religious Life.* New York: Free Press.

Edelberg, Jacqueline, and Susan Kurland. 2009. *How to Walk to School: Blueprint for a Neighborhood Renaissance.* New York: Rowman and Littlefield.

Elwood, Sarah A. 2000. "Lesbian Living Spaces: Multiple Meanings of Home." *Journal of Lesbian Studies* 4:11–27.

Epstein, Steven. 1987. "Gay Politics, Ethnic Identity: The Limits of Social Constructionism." *Socialist Review* 15:9–54.

———. 1999. "Gay and Lesbian Movements in the United States: Dilemmas of Identity, Diversity, and Political Strategy." Pp. 30–90 in *The Global Emergence of Gay and Lesbian Politics*, edited by B. D. Adam, J. W. Duyvendak, and A. Krouwel. Philadelphia: Temple University Press.

Escoffier, Jeffrey. 1975. "Stigmas, Work Environment and Economic Discrimination against Homosexuals." *Homosexual Counseling Journal* 2:8–17.

Ettorre, E. M. 1978. "Women, Urban Social Movements and the Lesbian Ghetto." *International Journal of Urban and Regional Research* 2:499–520.

Evans, Sara M., and Harry C. Boyte. 1986. *Free Spaces: The Sources of Democratic Change in America.* Chicago: University of Chicago Press.

Faderman, Lillian. 1999. "A Worm in the Bud: The Early Sexologists and Love Between Women." Pp. 56–67 in *The Columbia Reader on Lesbians and Gay Men in Media, Society, and Politics,* edited by L. Gross and J. D. Woods. New York: Columbia University Press.

Fahs, Breanne. 2009. "Compulsory Bisexuality? The Challenges of Modern Sexual Fluidity." *Journal of Bisexuality* 9:431–49.

Fantasia, Rick. 1988. *Cultures of Solidarity: Consciousness, Action, and Contemporary American Workers.* Berkeley: University of California Press.

Fantasia, Rick, and Eric L. Hirsch. 1995. "Culture in Rebellion: The Appropriation and Transformation of the Veil in the Algerian Revolution." Pp. 144–59 in *Social Movements and Culture,* edited by H. Johnston and B. Klandermans. Minneapolis: University of Minnesota Press.

Faro, Clive, and Garry Wotherspoon. 2000. *Street Seen: A History of Oxford Street.* Carlton: Melbourne University Press.

Fischer, Claude S. 1975. "Toward a Subcultural Theory of Urbanism." *American Journal of Sociology* 80:1319–41.

———. 1999. "Uncommon Values, Diversity, and Conflict in City Life." Pp. 213–28 in *Diversity and Its Discontents: Cultural Conflict and Common Ground in Contemporary American Society,* edited by N. J. Smelser and J. C. Alexander. Princeton, NJ: Princeton University Press.

Fisher, Robert, and Joseph Kling. 1990. "Leading the People: Two Approaches to the Role of Ideology in Community Organizing." Pp. 71–90 in *Dilemmas of Activism: Class, Community, and the Politics of Local Mobilization,* edited by J. Kling and P. S. Posner. Philadelphia: Temple University Press.

Florida, Richard. 2002. *The Rise of the Creative Class.* New York: Basic Books.

———. 2005. *Cities and the Creative Class.* New York: Routledge.

Florida, Richard, and Gary Gates. 2001. "Technology and Tolerance: The Importance of Diversity to High-Technology Growth." Washington, DC: Brookings Institution.

Forest, Benjamin. 1995. "West Hollywood as Symbol: The Significance of Place in the Construction of a Gay Identity." *Environment and Planning D: Society and Space* 13:133–57.

Forsyth, Ann. 1997. "'Out' in the Valley." *International Journal of Urban and Regional Research* 21:36–60.

———. 2001. "Sexuality and Space: Nonconformist Populations and Planning Practice." *Journal of Planning Literature* 15:339–58.

Foucault, Michel. 1978. *The History of Sexuality*. Vol. 1. New York: Vintage Books.

Frisch, Michael. 2002. "Planning as a Heterosexist Project." *Journal of Planning Education and Research* 21:254–66.

Gale, Dennis E. 1980. "Neighborhood Resettlement: Washington, D.C." Pp. 95–115 in *Back to the City: Issues in Neighborhood Renovation*, edited by S. B. Laska and D. Spain. New York: Pergamon Press.

Gamson, Joshua. 1995. "Must Identity Movements Self-Destruct? A Queer Dilemma." *Social Problems* 42:390–407.

Gamson, William A. 1996. "Safe Spaces and Social Movements." *Perspectives on Social Problems* 8:27–38.

Gans, Herbert J. 1962. *The Urban Villagers: Group and Class in the Life of Italian Americans*. New York: Free Press.

———. 2002. "The Sociology of Space: A Use-Centered View." *City and Community* 1:329–48.

———. 2007. "But Culturalism Cannot Explain Power: A Reply to Borer." *City and Community* 6:159–60.

Gates, Gary J. 2003. "Gay and Lesbian Families in the Census: Couples with Children." Washington, DC: Urban Institute Press.

———. (February) 2013. "LGBT Parenting in the United States." Williams Institute, http://williamsinstitute.law.ucla.edu/.

Gates, Gary J., M. V. Lee Badgett, Jennifer Ehrle Macomber, and Kate Chambers. 2007. "Adoption and Foster Care by Gay and Lesbian Parents in the United States." Washington, DC: Urban Institute Press.

Gates, Gary J., and Abigail M. Cooke. 2011. "United States Census Snapshot: 2010." Los Angeles: Williams Institute.

Gates, Gary J., and Jason Ost. 2004a. *The Gay and Lesbian Atlas*. Washington, DC: Urban Institute Press.

———. 2004b. "Getting Us Where We Live." *Gay and Lesbian Review* 11:19–21.

Ghaziani, Amin. 2008. *The Dividends of Dissent: How Conflict and Culture Work in Lesbian and Gay Marches on Washington*. Chicago: University of Chicago Press.

———. 2011. "Post-Gay Collective Identity Construction." *Social Problems* 58:99–125.

Ghaziani, Amin, and Marc J. Ventresca. 2005. "Keywords and Cultural Change: Frame Analysis of Business Model Public Talk, 1975–2000." *Sociological Forum* 20:523–59.

Gieryn, Thomas F. 2000. "A Space for Place in Sociology." *Annual Review of Sociology* 26:463–96.

Glass, Ruth. 1964. *London: Aspects of Change*. London: Centre for Urban Studies and MacGibbon and Kee.

Glazer, Nathan. 1997. *We Are All Multiculturalists Now*. Cambridge, MA: Harvard University Press.

Goel, Sharad, and Matthew J. Salganik. 2009. "Respondent-Driven Sampling as Markov Chain Monte Carlo." *Statistics in Medicine* 28:2202–29.

Goffman, Erving. 1963. *Stigma: Notes on the Management of Spoiled Identity*. New York: Simon and Schuster.

Gottdiener, Mark. 1995. *Postmodern Semiotics: Material Culture and the Forms of Postmodern Life*. Oxford, UK: Blackwell.

Gray, Mary L. 2009. *Out in the Country: Youth, Media, and Queer Visibility in Rural America*. New York: New York University Press.

Grazian, David. 2003. *Blue Chicago: The Search for Authenticity in Urban Blues Clubs*. Chicago: University of Chicago Press.

Green, Adam Isaiah. 2002. "Gay but Not Queer: Toward a Post-Queer Study of Sexuality." *Theory and Society* 31:521–45.

Greene, Theodore. 2011. "Sexual Orientation, Sexual Identity, and the Politics of Place." In Northwestern University Sexuality Project Working Paper, Evanston, Illinois.

Griffin, Larry J., and Kenneth A. Bollen. 2009. "What Do These Memories Do? Civil Rights Remembrance and Racial Attitudes." *American Sociological Review* 74:594–614.

Griswold, Wendy. 1987. "The Fabrication of Meaning: Literary Interpretation in the United States, Great Britain, and the West Indies." *American Journal of Sociology* 92:1077–1117.

Gross, Larry. 2001. *Up From Invisibility: Lesbians, Gay Men, and the Media in America*. New York: Columbia University Press.

Hall, Radclyffe. [1928] 2005. *The Well of Loneliness*. London, UK: Wadsworth.

Halperin, David M. 1993. "Is There a History of Sexuality?" Pp. 416–31 in *The Lesbian and Gay Studies Reader*, edited by H. Abelove, M. A. Barale, and D. M. Halperin. New York: Routledge.

Halperin, David M., and Valerie Traub. 2010. *Gay Shame*. Chicago: University of Chicago Press.

Hanhardt, Christina B. 2008. "Butterflies, Whistles, and Fists: Gay Safe Street Patrols and the New Gay Ghetto, 1976–1981." *Radical History Review* Winter: 60–85.

Harris, Daniel. 1997. *The Rise and Fall of Gay Culture*. New York: Hyperion.

Harry, Joseph. 1974. "Urbanization and the Gay Life." *Journal of Sex Research* 10:238–47.

Hayslett, Karen, and Melinda D. Kane. 2011. "'Out' in Columbus: A Geospatial Analysis of the Neighborhood-Level Distribution of Gay and Lesbian Households." *City and Community* 10:131–56.

Heap, Chad. 2003. "The City as a Sexual Laboratory: The Queer Heritage of the Chicago School." *Qualitative Sociology* 26:457–87.

———. 2008. "Gays and Lesbians in Chicago: An Overview." In *Out and Proud in Chicago: An Overview of the City's Gay Community*, edited by T. Baim. Chicago: Surrey Books.

———. 2009. *Slumming: Sexual and Racial Encounters in American Nightlife, 1885–1940*. Chicago: University of Chicago Press.

Herek, Gregory M. 1986. "The Instrumentality of Attitudes: Toward a Neofunctional Theory." *Journal of Social Issues* 42:99–114.

Herek, Gregory M., and John P. Capitanio. 1996. "'Some of My Best Friends': Intergroup Contact, Concealable Stigma, and Heterosexuals' Attitudes Toward Gay Men and Lesbians." *Personality and Social Psychology Bulletin* 22:412–24.

Herek, Gregory M., and Eric K. Glunt. 1993. "Interpersonal Contact and Heterosexuals' Attitudes Toward Gay Men: Results from a National Survey." *Journal of Sex Research* 30:239–44.

Herrell, Richard. 1993. "The Symbolic Strategies of Chicago's Gay and Lesbian Pride Day Parade." Pp. 225–52 in *Gay Culture in America*, edited by G. Herdt. Boston: Beacon Press.

Herring, Scott. 2010. *Another Country: Queer Anti-Urbanism*. New York: New York University Press.

Hilbert, Martin, and Priscila Lopez. 2011. "The World's Technological Capacity to Store, Communicate, and Compute Information." *Science* 332:60–65.

Hindle, Paul. 1994. "Gay Communities and Gay Space in the City." Pp. 7–25 in *The Margins of the City: Gay Men's Urban Lives*, edited by S. Whittle. Hants, UK: Arena.

Hirsch, Eric L. 1990. *Urban Revolt: Ethnic Politics in the Nineteenth-Century Labor Movement*. Berkeley: University of California Press.

Hodge, Stephen. 1995. "'No Fags Out There': Gay Men, Identity and Suburbia." *Journal of Interdisciplinary Gender Studies* 1:41–48.

Houlbrook, Matt. 2005. *Queer London: Perils and Pleasures in the Sexual Metropolis, 1918–1957*. Chicago: University of Chicago Press.

Houvouras, Shannon, and J. Scott Carter. 2008. "The F Word: College Students' Definitions of a Feminist." *Sociological Forum* 23:234–56.

Hughes, Everett Cherrington. 1945. "Dilemmas and Contradictions of Status." *American Journal of Sociology* 50:353–59.

Humphreys, Laud. 1975. *Tearoom Trade: Impersonal Sex in Public Places*. New York: Aldine de Gruyter.

———. 1979. "Exodus and Identity: The Emerging Gay Culture." Pp. 134–47 in *Gay Men: The Sociology of Male Homosexuality*, edited by M. P. Levine. New York: Harper and Row.

Hunter, Albert. 1974. *Symbolic Communities: The Persistence and Change of Chicago's Local Communities*. Chicago: University of Chicago Press.

Hunter, Marcus. 2010. "All the Gays Are White and All the Blacks Are Straight: Black Gay Men, Identity, and Community." *Sexuality Research and Social Policy* 7:81–92.

Irwin-Zarecka, Iwona. 1994. *Frames of Remembrance: The Dynamics of Collective Memory*. New Brunswick, NJ: Transaction.

Jacobs, Jane. 1961. *The Death and Life of Great American Cities*. New York: Vintage Books.

Jakobsen, Janet R., and Ann Pellegrini. 2003. *Love the Sin: Sexual Regulation and the Limits of Religious Tolerance*. New York: New York University Press.

Kaplan, H. Roy. 2011. *The Myth of Post-Racial America*. New York: Rowman and Littlefield.

Kasinitz, Philip. 1988. "The Gentrification of 'Boerum Hill': Neighborhood Change and Conflicts over Definitions." *Qualitative Sociology* 11:163–82.

Katz, Jonathan Ned. 1990. "The Invention of Heterosexuality." *Socialist Review* 20:7–33.

———. 2007. *The Invention of Heterosexuality*. Chicago: University of Chicago Press.

Kazyak, Emily. 2011. "Disrupting Cultural Selves: Constructing Gay and Lesbian Identities in Rural Locations." *Qualitative Sociology* 34:561–81.

———. 2012. "Midwest or Lesbian? Gender, Rurality, and Sexuality." *Gender & Society* 26:825–48.

Keller, Suzanne. 1968. *The Urban Neighborhood: A Sociological Perspective*. New York: Random House.

Kennedy, Elizabeth Lapovsky, and Madeline D. Davis. 1993. *Boots of Leather, Slippers of Gold: The History of a Lesbian Community*. New York: Routledge.

Kennedy, Michael. 2010. "Rural Men, Sexual Identity, and Community." *Journal of Homosexuality* 57:1051–91.

Kinsey, Alfred C., Wardell B. Pomeroy, and Clyde E. Martin. 1948. *Sexual Behavior in the Human Male*. Bloomington: Indiana University Press.

Kirkey, Kenneth, and Ann Forsyth. 2001. "Men in the Valley: Gay Male Life on the Suburban-Rural Fringe." *Journal of Rural Studies* 17:421–41.

Knopp, Lawrence. 1990. "Some Theoretical Implications of Gay Involvement in an Urban Land Market." *Political Geography Quarterly* 9:337–52.

———. 1992. "Sexuality and the Spatial Dynamics of Capitalism." *Environment and Planning D: Society and Space* 10:651–69.

———. 1997. "Gentrification and Gay Neighborhood Formation in New Orleans: A Case Study." Pp. 45–64 in *Homo Economics: Capitalism, Community, and Lesbian and Gay Life*, edited by A. Gluckman and B. Reed. New York: Routledge.

———. 1998. "Sexuality and Urban Space: Gay Male Identity Politics in the United States, the United Kingdom, and Australia." Pp. 149–76 in *Cities of Difference*, edited by R. Fincher and J. M. Jacobs. New York: Guilford Press.

Knopp, Lawrence, and Michael Brown. 2003. "Queer Diffusions." *Environment and Planning D: Society and Space* 21:409–24.

Kolbe, Richard H., and Melissa S. Burnett. 1991. "Content-Analysis Research: An Examination of Applications with Directives for Improving Research Reliability and Objectivity." *Journal of Consumer Research* 18:243–50.

Kong, Travis S. K. 2012. "A Fading Tongzhi Heterotopia: Hong Kong Older Gay Men's Use of Spaces." *Sexualities* 15:896–916.

Kornblum, William. 1974. *Blue Collar Community*. Chicago: University of Chicago Press.

Kyles, Kyra. 2007. "Culture Clash: Boystown Shifting as More Families Move In." *Chicago Tribune (RedEye)*, December 10.

Lane, Kerstin B. 2003. *Andersonville: A Swedish-American Landmark Neighborhood*. Chicago: Swedish American Museum Center.

Langford, Barry. 2000. "Margins of the City: Towards a Dialectic of Suburban Desire." Pp. 63–78 in *De-Centering Sexualities: Politics and Representations Beyond the Metropolis*, edited by R. Phillips, D. Watt, and D. Shuttleton. New York: Routledge.

Laska, Shirley Bradway, and Daphne Spain. 1980. *Back to the City: Issues in Neighborhood Renovation*. New York: Pergamon Press.

Laumann, Edward O., John H. Gagnon, Robert T. Michael, and Stuart Michaels. 1994. *The Social Organization of Sexuality*. Chicago: University of Chicago Press.

Laumann, Edward O., Stephen Ellingson, Jenna Mahay, Anthony Paik, and Yoosik Youm. 2004. *The Sexual Organization of the City*. Chicago: University of Chicago Press.

Lauria, Mickey, and Lawrence Knopp. 1985. "Toward an Analysis of the Role of Gay Communities in the Urban Renaissance." *Urban Geography* 6:152–69.

Lauster, Nathanael, and Adam Easterbrook. 2011. "No Room for New Families? A Field Experiment Measuring Rental Discrimination against Same-Sex Couples and Single Parents." *Social Problems* 58:389–409.

Lavers, Michael. 2009. "The Queer Issue: The New Gayborhoods of Fort Greene, Sunset Park, and Jackson Heights." *Village Voice*, June 24.

Leap, William L. 1999. *Public Sex/Gay Space*. New York: Columbia University Press.

Lee, Everett S. 1966. "A Theory of Migration." *Demography* 3:47–57.

Leff, Lisa. 2007. "In San Francisco's Castro District, a Cry of 'There Goes the Gayborhood.'" *Washington Post*, March 18, 2007, D01.

Lees, Loretta. 2000. "A Reappraisal of Gentrification: Towards a 'Geography of Gentrification.'" *Progress in Human Geography* 24:389–408.

Levine, Martin P. 1979. "Gay Ghetto." Pp. 182–204 in *Gay Men: The Sociology of Male Homosexuality*, edited by M. P. Levine. New York: Harper and Row.

Levy, Dan. 1996. "There Goes the Neighborhood." *San Francisco Chronicle*, May 26, Z1.

Levy, Paul R., and Roman A. Cybriwsky. 1980. "The Hidden Dimensions of Culture and Class: Philadelphia." Pp. 138–55 in *Back to the City: Issues in Neighborhood Renovation*, edited by S. B. Laska and D. Spain. New York: Pergamon Press.

List, Dennis. 2004. "Maximum Variation Sampling for Surveys and Consensus Groups." Adelaide, Australia: Audience Dialogue.

Lloyd, Richard. 2006. *Neo-Bohemia: Art and Commerce in the Postindustrial City.* New York: Routledge.

Lloyd, Richard, and Terry Nichols Clark. 2001. "The City as an Entertainment Machine." *Critical Perspectives on Urban Redevelopment* 6:357–78.

Lo, Jenny, and Theresa Healy. 2000. "Flagrantly Flaunting It? Contesting Perceptions of Locational Identity Among Urban Vancouver Lesbians." Pp. 29–44 in *From Nowhere to Everywhere: Lesbian Geographies*, edited by G. Valentine. New York: Harrington Park Press.

Logan, John R., and Harvey L. Molotch. 1987. *Urban Fortunes: The Political Economy of Place.* Berkeley: University of California Press.

Lombard, Matthew, Jennifer Snyder-Duch, and Cheryl Campenella Bracken. 2005. "Practical Resources for Assessing and Reporting Intercoder Reliability in Content Analysis Research Projects." Vol. 2006. Pdf available at http://ils.indiana.edu/faculty/hrosenba/www/Research/methods/lombard_reliability.pdf.

London, Bruce. 1980. "Gentrification as Urban Reinvasion: Some Preliminary Definitional and Theoretical Considerations." Pp. 77–92 in *Back to the City: Issues in Neighborhood Renovation*, edited by S. B. Laska and D. Spain. New York: Pergamon Press.

Loughery, John. 1998. *The Other Side of Silence.* New York: Owl Books.

Lynch, Frederick R. 1992. "Nonghetto Gays: An Ethnography of Suburban Homosexuals." Pp. 165–201 in *Gay Culture in America: Essays from the Field*, edited by G. Herdt. Boston: Beacon Press.

Mansbridge, Jane, and Aldon Morris. 2001. *Oppositional Consciousness: The Subjective Roots of Social Protest.* Chicago: University of Chicago Press.

Markwell, Kevin. 2002. "Mardi Gras Tourism and the Construction of Sydney as an International Gay and Lesbian City." *GLQ: A Journal of Lesbian and Gay Studies* 8:81–99.

Massey, Douglas S. 1981. "Dimensions of the New Immigration to the United States and the Prospects for Assimilation." *Annual Review of Sociology* 7:57–85.

Massey, Douglas S., and Nancy A. Denton. 1988. "The Dimensions of Residential Segregation." *Social Forces* 67:281–315.

———. 1993. *American Apartheid: Segregation and the Making of the Underclass.* Cambridge, MA: Harvard University Press.

Massey, Douglas S., Jonathan Rothwell, and Thurston Domina. 2009. "The Changing Bases of Segregation in the United States." *Annals of the American Academy of Political and Social Science* 626:74–90.

McAdam, Doug. 1988. *Freedom Summer.* New York: Oxford University Press.

McCarthy, Linda. 2000. "Poppies in a Wheat Field: Exploring the Lives of Rural Lesbians." *Journal of Homosexuality* 39:75–94.

McPherson, J. Miller, Lynn Smith-Lovin, and James M. Cook. 2001. "Birds of a Feather: Homophily in Social Networks." *Annual Review of Sociology* 27:415–44.

Mendelsohn, Daniel. 1996. "When Did Gays Get So Straight? How Queer Culture Lost Its Edge." *New York*, September 30, 24–31.

Meyers, Daniel J. 2008. "Ally Identity: The Politically Gay." Pp. 167–87 in *Identity Work in Social Movements*, edited by J. Reger, D. J. Myers, and R. L. Einwohner. Minneapolis: University of Minnesota Press.

Mills, Thomas C., Ron Stall, Lance Pollack, Jay P. Paul, Diane Binson, Jesse Canchola, and Joseph A. Catania. 2001. "Health-Related Characteristics of Men Who Have Sex with Men: A Comparison of Those Living in 'Gay Ghettos' with Those Living Elsewhere." *American Journal of Public Health* 91:980–83.

Mitchell, Don. 2000. *Cultural Geography.* Malden, MA: Blackwell.

Molotch, Harvey L. 1976. "The City as a Growth Machine: Toward a Political Economy of Place." *American Journal of Sociology* 82:309–32.

Morris, Aldon. 1984. *The Origins of the Civil Rights Movement: Black Communities Organizing for Change.* New York: Free Press.

Mueller, Carol. 1994. "Conflict Networks and the Origins of Women's Liberation." Pp. 234–63 in *New Social Movements: From Ideology to Identity*, edited by E. Larana, H. Johnston, and J. R. Gusfield. Philadelphia: Temple University Press.

Murphy, Kevin P., Jennifer L. Pierce, and Larry Knopp. 2010. *Queer Twin Cities.* Minneapolis: University of Minnesota Press.

Murray, Stephen O. 1979. "Institutional Elaboration of a Quasi-Ethnic Community." *International Review of Modern Sociology* 9:165–78.

———. 1992. "Components of Gay Community in San Francisco." Pp. 107–46 in *Gay Culture in America*, edited by G. Herdt. Boston: Beacon Press.

———. 1996. *American Gay.* Chicago: University of Chicago Press.

Myslik, Wayne. 1996. "Renegotiating the Social/Sexual Identities of Places: Gay Communities as Safe Havens or Sites of Resistance?" Pp. 156–69 in *Bodyspace: Destabilizing Geographies of Gender and Sexuality*, edited by N. Duncan. New York: Routledge.

Nagel, Joane. 1994. "Constructing Ethnicity: Creating and Recreating Ethnic Identity and Culture." *Social Problems* 41:152–76.

———. 1997. *American Indian Ethnic Renewal*. New York: Oxford University Press.

Needleman, Ruth. 1994. "Space and Opportunities." *Labor Research Review* 20:5–20.

Nero, Charles. 2005. "Why Are the Gay Ghettos White?" Pp. 228–45 in *Black Queer Studies*, edited by E. P. Johnson and M. G. Henderson. Durham, NC: Duke University Press.

Neuendorf, Kimberly A. 2002. *The Content Analysis Guidebook*. Thousand Oaks, CA: Sage.

Newton, Esther. 1993. *Cherry Grove, Fire Island: Sixty Years in America's First Gay and Lesbian Town*. Boston: Beacon Press.

O'Connell, Martin, and Sarah Feliz. 2011. "Same-Sex Couple Household Statistics from the 2010 Census." Washington, DC: US Census Bureau.

Olick, Jeffrey K., and Joyce Robbins. 1998. "Social Memory Studies: From 'Collective Memory' to the Historical Sociology of Mnemonic Practices." *Annual Review of Sociology* 24:105–40.

Owens, Ann. 2012. "Neighborhoods on the Rise: A Typology of Neighborhoods Experiencing Socioeconomic Ascent." *City and Community* 11:345–69.

Papadopoulos, Alex. 2005. "From 'Towertown' to 'Boystown' and 'Girlstown': Chicago's Gay and Lesbian Geographies." In *Chicago's Geographies: Metropolis for the 21st Century*, edited by R. P. Green, M. J. Bouman, and D. Grammenos. Washington, DC: Association of American Geographers.

Park, Robert E. 1915. "The City: Suggestions for the Investigation of Human Behavior in the City Environment." *American Journal of Sociology* 20:577–612.

———. 1925. "The City." Pp. 1–46 in *The City: Suggestions for Investigation of Human Behavior in the Urban Environment*, edited by R. E. Park and E. W. Burgess. Chicago: University of Chicago Press.

Park, Robert E., and Ernest W. Burgess. 1925. *The City: Suggestions for Investigation of Human Behavior in the Urban Environment*. Chicago: University of Chicago Press.

Pasupathi, Monisha. 1999. "Age Differences in Response to Conformity Pressure for Emotional and Nonemotional Material." *Psychology and Aging* 14:170–74.

Pattillo, Mary. 2007. *Black on the Block: The Politics of Race and Class in the City*. Chicago: University of Chicago Press.

Pattillo-McCoy, Mary. 2000. *Black Picket Fences: Privilege and Peril Among the Black Middle Class*. Chicago: University of Chicago Press.

Patton, Michael Quinn. 1987. *How to Use Qualitative Methods in Evaluation*. Newbury Park, CA: Sage.

Phillips, Richard, Diane Watt, and David Shuttleton. 2000. *De-Centering Sexualities: Politics and Representations Beyond the Metropolis*. New York: Routledge.

Podmore, Julie A. 2006. "Gone 'Underground'? Lesbian Visibility and the Consolidation of Queer Space in Montreal." *Social and Cultural Geography* 7:595–625.

Polletta, Francesca. 1999. "'Free Spaces' in Collective Action." *Theory and Society* 28:1–38.

Puar, Jasbir. 2002. "A Transnational Feminist Critique of Queer Tourism." *Antipode* 34:935–46.

Putnam, Robert D. 2000. *Bowling Alone: The Collapse and Revival of American Community*. New York: Simon and Schuster.

———. 2007. "E Pluribus Unum: Diversity and Community in the Twenty-first Century." *Scandinavian Political Studies* 30:137–74.

Ragin, Charles C. 1994. *Constructing Social Research*. Thousand Oaks, CA: Pine Forge Press.

Reardon, Sean F., and David O'Sullivan. 2004. "Measures of Spatial Segregation." *Sociological Methodology* 34:121–62.

Reuter, Don. 2008. *Greetings from the Gayborhood: A Nostalgic Look at Gay Neighborhoods*. New York: Abrams.

Reynolds, Robert. 2009. "Endangered Territory, Endangered Identity: Oxford Street and the Dissipation of Gay Life." *Journal of Australian Studies* 33:79–92.

Rich, Meghan Ashlin. 2009. "'It Depends on How You Define Integrated': Neighborhood Boundaries and Racial Integration in a Baltimore Neighborhood." *Sociological Forum* 24:828–53.

Ross, Marlon B. 2005. "Beyond the Closet as Raceless Paradigm." Pp. 161–89 in *Black Queer Studies: A Critical Anthology*, edited by E. P. Johnson and M. G. Henderson. Durham, NC: Duke University Press.

Rosser, B. R. Simon, William West, and Richard Weinmeyer. 2008. "Are Gay Communities Dying or Just in Transition? Results from an International Consultation Examining Possible Structural Change in Gay Communities." *AIDS Care* 20:588–95.

Rothenberg, Tamar. 1995. "'And She Told Two Friends': Lesbians Creating Urban Social Space." Pp. 165–81 in *Mapping Desire: Geographies of Sexualities*, edited by D. Bell and G. Valentine. London: Routledge.

Rubin, Gayle S. 1993. "Thinking Sex: Notes for a Radical Theory of the Politics of Sexuality." Pp. 3–44 in *The Lesbian and Gay Studies Reader*, edited by H. Abelove, A. Barale, and D. M. Halperin. New York: Routledge.

Ruffolo, David. 2009. *Post-Queer Politics*. London: Ashgate.

Rugh, Jacob S., and Douglas S. Massey. 2010. "Racial Segregation and the American Foreclosure Crisis." *American Sociological Review* 75:629–51.

Rushbrook, Dereka. 2002. "Cities, Queer Space, and the Cosmopolitan Tourist." *GLQ: A Journal of Lesbian and Gay Studies* 8:183–206.

Russell, Stephen T., Thomas J. Clarke, and Justin Clary. 2009. "Are Teens 'Post-Gay'? Contemporary Adolescents' Sexual Identity Labels." *Journal of Youth and Adolescence* 38:884–90.

Russo, Vito. 1987. *The Celluloid Closet: Homosexuality in the Movies.* New York: Perennial.

Ruting, Brad. 2008. "Economic Transformations of Gay Urban Spaces: Revisiting Collins' Evolutionary Gay District Model." *Australian Geographer* 39:259–69.

Ryan, Maura, and Dana Berkowitz. 2009. "Constructing Gay and Lesbian Parent Families 'Beyond the Closet.' " *Qualitative Sociology* 32:153–72.

Salganik, Matthew J., and Douglas D. Heckathorn. 2004. "Sampling and Estimation in Hidden Populations Using Respondent-Driven Sampling." *Sociological Methodology* 34:193–239.

San Francisco Lesbian and Gay History Project. 1989. "'She Even Chewed Tobacco': A Pictorial Narrative of Passing Women in America." Pp. 183–94 in *Hidden from History,* edited by M. B. Duberman, M. Vicinus, and G. Chauncey. New York: New American Library.

Sassen, Saskia. 2001. *The Global City.* Princeton, NJ: Princeton University Press.

Savin-Williams, Ritch C. 2005. *The New Gay Teenager.* Cambridge, MA: Harvard University Press.

Schafer, Chelsea E., and Greg M. Shaw. 2009. "Tolerance in the United States." *Public Opinion Quarterly* 73:404–31.

Schilt, Kristen, and Laurel Westbrook. 2009. "Doing Gender, Doing Heteronormativity: 'Gender Normals,' Transgender People, and the Social Maintenance of Heterosexuality." *Gender & Society* 23:440–64.

Scott, James C. 1990. *Domination and the Arts of Resistance: Hidden Transcripts.* New Haven: Yale University Press.

Sedgwick, Eve Kosofsky. 1990. *Epistemology of the Closet.* Berkeley: University of California Press.

Seidman, Steven. 1996. *Queer Theory/Sociology.* Cambridge, MA: Blackwell.

———. 2002. *Beyond the Closet: The Transformation of Gay and Lesbian Life.* New York: Routledge.

Shadish, William R., Thomas D. Cook, and Donald T. Campbell. 2002. *Experimental and Quasi-Experimental Designs for Generalized Causal Inference.* New York: Houghton Mifflin.

Shaftel, David. 2007. "Under the Rainbow." *New York Times,* March 25, section 14, 1.

Sibalis, Michael. 2004. "Urban Space and Homosexuality: The Example of the Marais, Paris' 'Gay Ghetto.'" *Urban Studies* 41:1739–58.

Sides, Josh. 2009. *Erotic City: Sexual Revolutions and the Making of Modern San Francisco.* New York: Oxford University Press.

Signorile, Michelangelo. 1997. *Life Outside.* New York: HarperCollins.

Simmel, Georg. 1903. "The Metropolis and Mental Life." Pp. 324–39 in *Georg Simmel: On Individuality and Social Forms,* edited by D. N. Levine. Chicago: University of Chicago Press.

Smelser, Neil J. 1963. *Theory of Collective Behavior*. New York: Free Press.

Smith, Darren P., and Louise Holt. 2005. "Lesbian Migrants in the Gentrified Valley and Other Geographies of Rural Gentrification." *Journal of Rural Studies* 21:313–22.

Smith, David M., and Gary J. Gates. 2001. "Gay and Lesbian Families in the United States: Same-Sex Unmarried Partner Households." Washington, DC: Human Rights Campaign.

Smith, Neil. 1986. "Gentrification, the Frontier, and the Restructuring of Urban Space." In *Gentrification of the City*, edited by N. Smith and P. Williams. Winchester, MA: Allen and Unwin.

Spain, Daphne. 1993. "Been-Heres versus Come-Heres: Negotiating Conflicting Community Identities." *Journal of the American Planning Association* 59:156–71.

Spring, Amy L. 2012. "Deconcentration of Urban Gay Enclaves: Evidence from the 2000 and 2010 U.S. Censuses." In *Annual Meetings of the American Sociological Association*. Denver, CO.

———. 2013. "Declining Segregation of Same-Sex Partners: Evidence from Census 2000 and 2010." *Population Research and Policy Review*, 32:687–716.

Stacey, Judith. 2003. "Gay and Lesbian Families: Queer Like Us." In *All Our Families: New Policies for a New Century*, edited by M. A. Mason, A. Skolnick, and S. D. Sugarman. New York: Oxford University Press.

Stein, Peter L. 1997. *The Castro*. KQED.

Steinberg, Marc W. 1999. "The Talk and Back Talk of Collective Action: A Dialogic Analysis of Repertoires of Discourse among Nineteenth-Century English Cotton Spinners." *American Journal of Sociology* 105:736–80.

Stemler, Steve. 2001. "An Overview of Content Analysis." *Practical Assessment, Research, and Evaluation* 7, http://PAREonline.net/getvn.asp?v=7&n=17.

Stryker, Susan. 2002. "How the Castro Became San Francisco's Gay Neighborhood." Pp. 29–34 in *Out in the Castro: Desire, Promise, Activism*, edited by W. Leyland. San Francisco: Leyland Publications.

Stryker, Susan, and Jim Van Buskirk. 1996. *Gay by the Bay: A History of Queer Culture in the San Francisco Bay Area*. San Francisco: Chronicle Books.

Sudman, Seymour, Monroe G. Sirken, and Charles D. Cowan. 1988. "Sampling Rare and Elusive Populations." *Science* 240:991–96.

Sullivan, Andrew. 1996. *Virtually Normal: An Argument about Homosexuality*. New York: Vintage.

———. 2004. *Same-Sex Marriage: Pro and Con, A Reader*. New York: Vintage Books.

Sullivan, Robert David. 2007. "Last Call: Why the Gay Bars of Boston Are Disappearing." *Boston Globe*, December 2, E1.

Suttles, Gerald D. 1968. *The Social Order of the Slum*. Chicago: University of Chicago Press.

Taylor, Verta. 1989. "Social Movement Continuity: The Women's Movement in Abeyance." *American Sociological Review* 54:761–75.

Tétreault, Mary Ann. 1993. "Civil Society in Kuwait: Protected Spaces and Women's Rights." *Middle East Journal* 47:275–91.

Thomas, William Isaac, and Dorothy Swaine Thomas. 1928. *The Child in America: Behavior Problems and Programs*. New York: Knopf.

Timmons, Stuart. 1990. *The Trouble with Harry Hay: Founder of the Modern Gay Movement*. Boston: Alyson Publications.

Tongson, Karen. 2011. *Relocations: Queer Suburban Imaginaries*. New York: New York University Press.

Tonnies, Ferdinand. 1957. *Community and Society*. Translated by C. P. Loomis. New York: Harper.

Touré. 2011. *Who's Afraid of Post-Blackness*. New York: Free Press.

Tucker, Andrew. 2009. *Queer Visibilities: Space, Identity and Interaction in Cape Town*. Malden, MA: Wiley-Blackwell.

Usher, Nikki, and Eleanor Morrison. 2010. "The Demise of the Gay Enclave, Communication Infrastructure Theory, and the Transformation of Gay Public Space." Pp. 271–87 in *LGBT Identity and Online New Media*, edited by C. Pullen and M. Cooper. New York: Routledge.

Vaid, Urvashi. 1995. *Virtual Equality: The Mainstreaming of Gay and Lesbian Liberation*. New York: Anchor Books.

Vaisey, Stephen. 2007. "Structure, Culture, and Community: The Search for Belonging in 50 Urban Communes." *American Sociological Review* 72:851–73.

Valentine, Gill. 2000. *From Nowhere to Everywhere: Lesbian Geographies*. Binghamton, NY: Harrington Press.

Valocchi, Steve. 1999. "The Class-Inflected Nature of Gay Identity." *Social Problems* 46:207–24.

Vary, Adam B. 2006. "Is Gay Over?" *Advocate*, June 20:100.

Vavrus, Mary Douglas. 2010. "Unhitching from the 'Post' (of Postfeminism)." *Journal of Communication Inquiry* 34:222–27.

Wacquant, Loïc. 2000. "The New 'Peculiar Institution': On the Prison as Surrogate Ghetto." *Theoretical Criminology* 4:377–89.

———. 2008. "Ghettos and Anti-Ghettos: An Anatomy of the New Urban Poverty." *Thesis Eleven* 94:113–18.

———. 2011. "A Janus-Faced Institution of Ethnoracial Closure: A Sociological Specification of the Ghetto." Pp. 1–31 in *The Ghetto: Contemporary Global Issues and Controversies*, edited by R. Hutchinson and B. Haynes. Boulder, CO: Westview.

Wagner-Pacifici, Robin. 1996. "Memories in the Making: The Shapes of Things that Went." *Qualitative Sociology* 19:301–22.

Walters, Suzanna Danuta. 2001. *All the Rage: The Story of Gay Visibility in America*. Chicago: University of Chicago Press.

Ward, Jane. 2008. *Respectably Queer: Diversity Culture in LGBT Activist Organizations*. Nashville, TN: Vanderbilt University Press.

Warner, Michael. 1999. *The Trouble with Normal: Sex, Politics, and the Ethics of Queer Life*. New York: Free Press.

Waters, Mary C. 1990. *Ethnic Options: Choosing Identities in America*. Berkeley: University of California Press.

———. 2000. "Immigration, Intermarriage, and the Challenges of Measuring Racial/Ethnic Identity." *American Journal of Public Health* 90:1735–37.

Waters, Mary C., and Tomás R. Jiménez. 2005. "Assessing Immigrant Assimilation: New Empirical and Theoretical Challenges." *Annual Review of Sociology* 31:105–25.

Waters, Mary C., and Reed Ueda. 2007. *The New Americans: A Guide to Immigration since 1965*. Cambridge, MA: Harvard University Press.

Watson, Steven. 1995. *The Harlem Renaissance: Hub of African-American Culture, 1920–1930* New York: Pantheon.

Wellman, Barry, and Caroline Haythornthwaite. 2002. *The Internet in Everyday Life*. Malden, MA: Blackwell.

Wellman, Barry, Anabel Quan-Haase, Jeffrey Boase, Wenhong Chen, Keith Hampton, Isabel Díaz, and Kakuko Miyata. 2003. "The Social Affordances of the Internet for Networked Individualism." *Journal of Computer-Mediated Communication* online. Vol. 8, issue 3.

Weston, Kath. 1995. "Get Thee to a Big City: Sexual Imaginary and the Great Gay Migration." *GLQ: A Journal of Lesbian and Gay Studies* 2:253–77.

Williams, Raymond. 1976. *Keywords: A Vocabulary of Culture and Society*. New York: Oxford University Press.

Wilson, William Julius. 1987. *The Truly Disadvantaged: The Inner City, the Underclass, and Public Policy*. Chicago: University of Chicago Press.

———. 1996. *When Work Disappears: The World of the New Urban Poor*. New York: Knopf.

Wilson, William Julius, and Richard P. Taub. 2006. *There Goes the Neighborhood: Racial, Ethnic, and Class Tensions in Four Chicago Neighborhoods and Their Meaning for America*. New York: Vintage.

Wintz, Cary D. 1988. *Black Culture and the Harlem Renaissance*. Houston: Rice University Press.

Wirth, Louis. 1928. *The Ghetto*. Chicago: University of Chicago Press.

———. 1938. "Urbanism as a Way of Life." *American Journal of Sociology* 44:1–24.

Wittman, Carl. 1970. *A Gay Manifesto*. New York: Red Butterfly Publication.

Wolfe, Deborah. 1979. *The Lesbian Community*. Berkeley: University of California Press.

Wright, Les. 1999. "San Francisco." Pp. 164–89 in *Queer Sites: Gay Urban Histories since 1600*, edited by D. Higgs. New York: Routledge.

Wyly, Elvin, and Daniel J. Hammel. 1999. "Islands of Decay in Seas of Renewal: Housing Policy and the Resurgence of Gentrification." *Housing Policy Debate* 10:711–71.

Zerubavel, Eviatar. 1991. *The Fine Line: Making Distinctions in Everyday Life*. New York: Free Press.

———. 1997. *Social Mindscapes: An Invitation to Cognitive Sociology*. Cambridge, MA: Harvard University Press.

Zorbaugh, Harvey Warren. 1929. *The Gold Coast and the Slum: A Sociological Study of Chicago's Near North Side*. Chicago: University of Chicago Press.

Zukin, Sharon. 1987. "Gentrification: Culture and Capital in the Urban Core." *Annual Review of Sociology* 13:129–47.

———. 1989. *Loft Living: Culture and Capital in Urban Change*. New Brunswick, NJ: Rutgers University Press.

———. 1995. *The Cultures of Cities*. Oxford, UK: Blackwell.

———. 1998. "Urban Lifestyles: Diversity and Standardisation in Spaces of Consumption." *Urban Studies* 35:825–39.

———. 2010. *Naked City: The Death and Life of Authentic Urban Places*. New York: Oxford University Press.

INDEX

Page numbers followed by *f* indicate a figure; those with *t* indicate a table.

Abrahamson, Mark, 82
Adam, Barry, 16
adjacent resettlement, 153, 213
Adler, Sy, 308n9
affirmative view of culture, 288n13
age factors, 240, 258–59, 302n4; maturation and, 103–8, 224–26, 236; media reports of, 51–55, 61–62; new gay youth and, 52–55, 62, 108–16, 302n4; retirement planning and, 62, 157–59. *See also* parenting and family life
Aguirre-Livingston, Paul, 28–29
Albuquerque, New Mexico, 137t, 140t, 153
Allen, Pamela, 291n33
Allport, Gordon Willard, 300n13
American Community Survey, 52, 68
anchor institutions, 32, 145, 150–53, 161t, 189–98, 206, 257
Andersonville (Chicago), 65–69, 143, 239; boundaries of, 66–68; Chamber of Commerce of, 71, 192, 282; collective relocation to, 210–19, 257–58; Dyke March of, 238–39, 281; families with children in, 220–22; gay commercial activity in, 236–37; Girlstown moniker for, 11–12, 185, 210, 230, 232–34, 236; Green Genes store of, 118, 225; lesbian migration from, 237; lesbian population of, 230–39, 258; mature gays in, 224–26; same-sex partner households in, 68–69, 300n7; Swedish identity of, 203, 204f; Women and Children First bookstore in, 68, 79, 192–93, 230, 257, 281. *See also* interviews in Chicago
Angelo, Gregory, 149
antigay bias, 167–76, 206, 256–57. *See also* safe harbors
anti-ghettos, 50
archipelagos. *See* geographic trends
Asbury Park, New Jersey, 140t, 275t

assimilation, 9–10, 24–31; contradictory reasoning on, 80–82, 249–55, 300n15, 310n9; cultural sameness and, 41–50, 52–54, 75–97, 99–101, 245–49, 294n46; definition of, 28, 294n46; dimensions of, 295–96nn2–3; expanded residential imagination and, 69–75, 77, 98–99, 112–13; media examination of, 36–50, 60–63; minority group infighting about, 49; public opinion on, 26–27, 35, 250–52, 310n6, 310n8; vs. separationist views, 86–95, 100, 110–12, 169–74, 251–52
Atlanta, Georgia, 17, 137t, 139t, 242t, 259, 303n12
Austin, Texas, 17, 136, 137t, 139t
Avondale Estates (Atlanta suburb), 139t, 242t, 259

bachelorette parties, 4–5, 253–54
Badgett, Lee, 234, 308n11
Bailey, Ed, 254
Baim, Tracy, 47–48
Baltimore, Maryland, 139t, 158t, 275t
Banchero, Stephanie, 142
Banks, Ernie, 95
Bawer, Bruce, 250
Bellah, Robert, 293n40
benign indifference (among straights), 84–86, 99–100
Bennett, Larry, 198
Bennett, Phillip, 40
Benson, Josh, 37–38
Berwyn, Illinois, 223
Biegel, Stuart, 302n4
big cities, 64–65, 136, 139–40f, 141, 153, 305n30
Big Cup coffee shop (New York City), 29–30, 146
biggie bang theory, 219–20, 258

The Birdcage, 127
Birmingham, Alabama, 17
bisexual (as term), 267–68
bisexual individuals, 11, 25, 108
Black, Dan, 17
the Black church, 218
blacks. *See* race
Blow, Charles, 30–31
Bob Damron's Address Book, 272
Bond, Monique, 121
Boston, Massachusetts, 29–30, 39–40, 137t, 139t, 158, 242t
Boystown (Chicago), 1, 10, 65–69, 202–5, 239; aging out of, 224–26; anchor institutions of, 145, 189–98, 257; boundaries of, 65–66, 67f; Center on Halsted of, 5, 66, 145, 169, 176–82, 192, 257, 282; changing demographics of, 66; collective migration from, 161t, 210–19, 239, 257–58; commercial center of, 1, 47, 65, 176, 193–98; emergence of, 142–43, 211, 258; gay pride parades of, 93–95, 120–21, 142, 238; Legacy Project and Legacy Walk of, 145, 207–8, 255; lesbian residents of, 230–31; maps of, 66f, 67f, 84f; official designation of, 65, 279; property ownership in, 190–91; proximity to Wrigleyville of, 83–84, 171–74, 306n5; rainbow-colored pylons of, 1, 65, 91, 193, 198–208, 233, 257, 273; safety discourses on, 166–88; same-sex partner households in, 68–69; straight residents of, 4–5, 69, 74–75, 89–92, 212–13; tourism in, 197; whiteness of, 227. *See also* interviews in Chicago; Lakeview
Brekhus, Wayne, 43, 154
Brenner, Johanna, 308n9
Brinster, Kim, 143–44, 145
Broadway Youth Center (Chicago), 177–79, 181–82, 281
Brokeback Mountain, 127
Broverman, Neal, 256
Brown, Gavin, 29, 252
Brown, Patricia Leigh, 1, 54–55, 153
Bubon, Linda, 79–80, 110, 192, 281
Bucio, Edith, 71, 227, 228
Buffalo, New York, 14, 17
bullying, 177–79
Burr, Robin, 176
Burston, Paul, 23–31

Caldwell, John, 53, 153–54, 295n1
Call Her Savage, 14–15
Cambridge, Massachusetts, 29, 139t
Canaday, Margot, 14
Carroll, Kevin, 62
Casey, Mark, 30
Castells, Manuel, 167, 240–41, 272, 291n32, 308n17
Castro district (San Francisco), 1, 4, 22, 219, 290n26; commercial center of, 152; cost of living in, 258–59; expansion of, 72; gay departure from, 41, 61; GLBT History Museum of, 207; as immigrant neighborhood, 40–41; rates of same-sex partner households in, 241, 242t
causal reasoning (neighborhood integration), 80, 82
census data. See demographic trends; U.S. Census
Center on Halsted (Chicago), 5, 66, 145, 169, 176–82, 192, 257, 282
Charlotte, North Carolina, 17
Chauncey, George, 13, 14, 19, 150, 273
Chelsea (New York City), 5, 143–50, 219; Big Cup coffee shop in, 29–30, 146; HIV/AIDS in, 145–46; same-sex partner households in, 149; straight residents of, 146–47
Cherkasov, Bernard, 71, 76–77, 201, 282
Chestnut Hill (Boston area), 155–56, 163
Chicago, 64–69; Dyke March of, 238–39, 281; ethnic and cultural enclaves of, 198; gayborhoods in, 65–69; gay pride parades of, 93–95, 120–21, 142, 238; as global city, 64–65; homophobia in, 171–74; Legacy Project of, 145, 207–8, 255; maps of, 66f, 67f, 83, 84f; population of, 64; queer narratives of, 65; same-sex partner households in, 68–69, 300n7; same-sex partners with children in, 220–24; as secondary city, 24, 64–65; shifting of gayborhoods in, 141–45, 163–64, 211–19, 239, 257–58. *See also* Boystown (Chicago); interviews in Chicago
Chicago Blackhawks, 94–95
Chicago Cubs, 94–95
Chicago School of Urban Sociology, 64, 75–76
childhood/teenage years. *See* new gay teens and youth

child molestation myth, 123, 302n11
children. *See* parenting and family life
Christensen, Jen, 153–54
Christian, Carol, 45
Christopher Street. *See* Greenwich Village
Christopher Street Liberation Day Umbrella Committee, 247–48
Church-Wellesley Village (Toronto), 2, 4
Cincinnati, Ohio, 39, 42
Circuit, 127
circular reasoning (neighborhood integration), 80–82, 99
cisgender (as term), 306n12
Cleveland, Ohio, 17
closet era, 8, 12–15, 244–45, 289nn17–20; in Chicago, 97, 142; contemporary traces of, 228
cluster effect (as term), 196, 211
Coates, Joseph, 23, 189, 293n40
Cohn, D'Vera, 51–52
Colbert, Stephen, 25
The Colbert Report, 25
Collard, James, 24, 28, 293n41
collective memory of gay neighborhoods, 144–45, 164, 201–2, 205–9, 257, 283
collective relocation, 161t, 210–19, 239, 257–58, 307n1
Collins, Alan, 16, 26
Columbia, South Carolina, 16
Columbus, Ohio, 137t, 139t, 158t, 275t
coming out era, 8–9, 15–23; bohemian spaces in, 42; gay ghettos of, 49; institutional encasement in, 50; motto of, 28; Roman analogy of, 29; safe harbors of, 109–10; sexual segregation in, 247
commemorative activities, 161t, 198–209, 247, 257. *See also* historic preservation
commercial concentration, 2, 152–53, 164, 193–98, 271, 274
community, 21–22, 82; of the gayborhood, 21–23, 59–60, 82, 126–27, 293n40; via social networking, 57–60, 62–63, 123–27, 303n12
community argument for gayborhood formation, 293n40
contact hypothesis, 76, 300n13
Cook, James, 139–40f, 141, 214
Cook, Thomas D., 277
Cook County. *See* Chicago
Cook County Human Rights Ordinance, 74
Cooke, Thomas J., 308n19

Cooley, David, 254
Cox, Jason, 71, 192, 282
Crisp, Quentin, 47, 247, 248–49
critical multiplism, 277
Cruising, 127
Cubs baseball (Chicago), 83, 84f, 171–74, 306n5
cultural absorption. *See* assimilation
cultural archipelagos. *See* geographic trends
cultural gayness, 44, 53
cultural preservation (neighborhood integration), 81–82, 93, 99
cultural sameness, 99–100; Chicago interviews on, 75–97; contact hypothesis and, 76, 300n13; contradictory reasoning of, 80–82, 249–55, 300n15, 310n9; media reports of, 44–50, 61; queer perspectives on, 75–82, 99, 246–47, 300n13; straight concerns of reverse discrimination and, 84, 95–97, 100; straight desires for sexual integration and, 83, 86–95, 100; straight expressions of indifference and, 83–87, 99–100, 246–47, 254–55
Cunanan, Andrew, 279–80

Dadey, Dick, 46
D'Alessandro, Joe, 40, 44
Daley, Richard, 198
Dallas, Texas, 2, 137t, 139t, 242t, 275t
Dalton, John, 78, 196, 282
Daniel, Diane, 42
Darc, Keith, 59–60
data: from Chicago interviews, 11–12, 64–101, 281–83, 284t, 313n15; from media accounts, 10, 35–63, 274–81, 312n12. *See also* demographic trends; geographic trends; U.S. Census
Davie Village (Vancouver), 2, 58, 273
Davis, Madeline, 14
Decatur, Georgia, 137t, 140f, 141, 163
deconcentration (as term), 2, 60, 160, 245
Defense of Marriage Act (DOMA), 27
D'Emilio, John, 13, 15, 29, 289n17
demographic trends, 11, 133–41, 274, 275t; of children of same-sex partners, 17–18, 55, 116, 302n7; of financial resources of lesbians and gays, 231–32, 234, 236–37, 241, 258–59, 308n11; Gay Index of, 25–26, 135–41; of geographic

demographic trends (*continued*)
distribution of same-sex couples,
36–50, 135–41, 156f, 157, 159–65, 241,
242t, 308n17, 308n19; maps of, 135f; of
post-World-War-II urban households,
15; of poverty rates among lesbians,
234; of rates of segregated spaces,
36–37, 245, 295–96nn2–3; of same-sex
partner households, 1–2, 11, 24–25,
55, 134–35, 151, 153, 242t, 295n1; of
same-sex partner households in Cook
County, 68–69; of same-sex partner
households in NYC, 149; of same-sex
partner households with children,
156–57, 158t; of social intolerance,
167–69; of social-networking hook-ups,
123–24, 303n12; of straight residents
of gayborhoods, 2, 24–25. *See also* geographic trends
Denizet-Lewis, Benoit, 54
Denver, Colorado, 137t, 139t
Des Moines, Iowa, 16
Detroit, Michigan, 17, 158t, 242t, 259, 275t
developmental factors. *See* age factors
Devereux, Ed, 190, 191, 195, 281
diaspora metaphors, 59–60
discrimination. *See* antigay bias
dissimilarity index, 36–37, 60, 245,
295–96nn2–3
dissimilarity meaning measure, 37, 60
diversity: detachment from particular
community in, 252–54; of gay people,
127–29, 247–49, 303n18; neoliberalism
and, 248, 255
Doan, Petra, 182–83, 306n8
Domestic Partnership Act of 2003 (New
Jersey), 38
Downtown Chicago, 142
Driving While Black (DWB), 171
Dufty, Bevan, 208
Duggan, Lisa, 248
Dupont Circle (Washington, D.C.), 2, 21,
44, 151, 219
Duran, John, 56
Durkheim, Emile, 23, 293n40
Dyke March (Chicago), 77, 227, 238–39, 281
Dyke Slope. *See* Park Slope

East Bay area (California), 152, 191, 219
economic factors, 7–8, 17–18, 26, 288n12;
Chicago interview accounts of, 71; in

creation of new gayborhoods, 142–45,
148–50, 258–59, 290n27; of gay commercial centers, 152–53, 193–98, 231–34;
in lesbian migration, 231–32, 234,
236–37, 241, 308n11; media accounts of,
45; of urban renewal and gentrification,
18–19, 24–25, 143–45, 288n13, 291n30
Edelberg, Jacqueline, 119–20
Edgewater (Chicago), 68, 212, 300n7
education. *See* schools
El Paso, Texas, 153
Empire State Pride Agenda, 46
The Epistemology of the Closet (Sedgwick), 50
Erbentraut, Joseph, 68–69
Essex County (New Jersey), 154, 163. *See
also* New Jersey
ethnically straight identity, 9, 44, 46, 166,
246
ethnic enclaves, 25–26, 81–82, 197–98
expansion mechanism, 246. *See also* residential imagination

family life. *See* parenting and family life
Feliz, Sarah, 135
female same-sex partner households. *See*
same-sex partner households
financial resources. *See* economic factors
Fire Island (New York), 16, 275t
Fischer, Claude, 128, 303n18
Fisher, Marc, 151
Florida, Richard, 7, 25
fluidity, 80, 267–68
Forsyth, Ann, 13, 271, 289n19
Fort Greene (New York City), 230
Fort Lauderdale, Florida, 17, 43, 46,
137–39t, 242t, 246
Fort Myers, Florida, 158
Fort Worth, Texas, 153
Foucault, Michel, 12–13, 289n17
Frank Kameny Way (Washington, D.C.),
208
Freedman, Estelle, 15
free spaces, 19–20, 291n33. *See also* safe
harbors
future of gayborhoods. *See* persistence
of gayborhoods; reinventing the
gayborhood

Gallagher, John, 19–20
Gans, Herbert, 288n13
Garcia, Michelle, 144

Gargano, Ed, 66

Gates, Gary: on gay choices of where to live, 17, 43, 153; U.S. Census analysis by, 35, 134–36, 137–40f, 149, 156f, 157, 272–73

Gates, Jim, 211, 282

gay (as term), 267–68

gay bars: aging out of, 104–6; as anchor institutions, 117, 272, 282; bachelorette parties in, 4–5, 253–54; of the closet era, 8, 13–15; of the coming out era, 15–16, 211; community-building role of, 217, 289n21; the Internet's impact on, 57–59; of the post-gay era, 29–30, 44, 50, 57–60; post-gay iconography in, 78–79, 89–90, 91f; public opinion on, 252, 310n8

gayborhoods: anchor institutions of, 32, 145, 150–53, 161t, 164, 189–98, 206, 257; benefits and amenities of, 2–3, 17–18, 290n24; border zones of, 174–75; characteristics and definition of, 2, 8, 268–69, 271–74; commercial centers of, 1, 47, 65, 152–53, 164, 176, 193–98, 231–34, 274; community functions of, 21–23, 59–60, 82, 126–27, 293n40; cultural and institutional relevance of, 32, 162, 188–89, 197; de-gaying of, 24, 128, 160, 161t, 243, 245; emergence of, 15–20, 211, 244–45, 290nn26–27; examples of, 2, 16; "ghetto" depictions of, 23, 39–40, 42, 46–50, 73, 247, 297n24; history of, 8–10, 12–31; identification and mapping of, 272–81; impact of HIV/AIDS on, 145–46; as islands of meaning, 69–70, 72, 76, 88, 98, 258; lesbian presence in, 192–93, 230–31; as male spaces, 183, 233, 235, 240–41; new formation of, 8, 141–59, 161t, 162–63; novelty and sex shops of, 105; political role of, 2–3, 16, 74, 90–93, 291n32; preservation activities in, 81–82, 145, 150–51, 160–62, 198–209, 255, 257; promotion and tourism in, 3, 25–26, 44, 64, 197, 280, 294n44, 307n17; property ownership in, 145, 150–51, 164, 190–91, 233–34; queer iconography of, 1, 65, 78–79, 89–91, 118, 193, 198–208, 233, 257, 273; as safe spaces, 19–20, 30–31, 72–73, 109–10, 161t, 162, 166–88, 206, 214; scholarly

understandings of, 6–8; sexuality and love functions of, 20–21, 59–60, 98–99, 103–4, 291n35; shifting archipelagos of, 141–59; stereotyped depictions of, 127, 302n11; straight residents of, 4–5, 7, 24–25, 31–32, 69, 146–48, 160, 161t, 169–74, 232; whiteness of, 226–27, 240. *See also* persistence of gayborhoods; reinventing the gayborhood; shrinking of gayborhoods

gayby boom. *See* parenting and family life

Gay.com, 58

gay culture: coolness factors in, 25–26, 64, 81–82, 294n44; cultural gayness in, 44, 53; diversity and dynamism of, 127–29, 247–49, 303n18; ethnically straight identity in, 9, 44, 46, 166, 246

gay ghettos. *See* gayborhoods; ghettos

gay identity, 44; declining identity politics and, 110, 112–14, 161t; decreased primacy of sexual orientation and, 5–6, 7, 28–29, 52–54, 73, 78, 79–80, 88–89, 154–55, 166, 246; epistemological distinctiveness of, 97, 310n15; essentialist vs. constructionist debates on, 300n15, 306n15; vs. ethnically straight identity, 9, 44, 46, 166, 246; self-identification and coming out as, 108–10, 113–15, 302n4; stereotypes of, 127, 302n11. *See also* post-gay era

gay imaginary, 16, 246

Gay Index, 25–26, 135–41; cities in, 136–37, 139–40f, 141; towns and neighborhoods in, 138f

"Gay Liberation" (Segal), 208

Gay Liberation Movement, 247–48. *See also* gay rights

gay marriage, 27, 39, 134; Canadian legalization of, 280; child-rearing and, 156; legal bans on, 157, 253–54; public support for, 250–51, 310n6

gay pride parades, 93–95, 120–21, 142, 238

gay rights, 81, 90–93; contradictions of achieved equality in, 80–82, 249–55, 300n15; post-racial comparisons with, 92–93; privacy concerns in, 252; for same-sex partner adoptions, 56; straight performative progressiveness on, 252–55. *See also* gay marriage; legal environment

gay-straight alliances (GSA), 177–78

gender, 230–41. *See also* lesbians

gentrification, 7, 24–25, 288n13; of gayborhoods, 18–19, 24–25, 291n30; second wave of super-gentrifiers in, 25–26, 65, 144–45, 294n43

geographic clustering (as term), 211

geographic trends, 135–65, 240, 242t, 275t; in cities/metropolitan areas, 153, 164–65, 309n19; in concentrations of female-partner households, 241, 242t, 308n17, 308n19; of cultural archipelago formation, 135–41, 159–65, 305nn29–30; economic and class factors in, 142–45, 148–50, 241; gay-friendliness vs. gay-identity in, 148–51, 164; of homophily, 141, 214–19, 257–58; multiple-migrating gayborhood model in, 41, 141–59, 161t, 162–63, 258–59; on rates of segregated spaces, 36–37, 245, 295–96nn2–3; of safety concerns, 157, 161t, 162; of senior housing, 157–59; of straight in-migration, 146–48, 151–52, 160, 161t; in suburbs and rural areas, 153–57, 161t, 163–64, 305n30, 309n19. *See also* reinventing the gayborhood

geography of cool, 25

Georgetown (Washington, D.C.), 219

ghettos: four features of, 49–50; as segregated spaces, 23, 39–40, 42, 46–50, 73, 247, 271, 297n24

Ginsberg, Thomas, 155–56

Girlstown (Chicago), 11–12, 185, 210, 230, 232–34, 236. *See also* Andersonville

Glass, Ruth, 291n30

GLBT Historical Society of Northern California, 3, 41, 207

GLBT History Museum (the Castro), 207

global cities, 64–65

Gold Coast (Chicago), 141–42, 191

Goldstein, Richard, 48, 248–49

Gonzalez, Clarissa, 77, 227–30, 238–39, 246–47

Gorton, Don, 151

great gay migration, 16–18, 98, 246

Greene, Theodore, 252–53

Green Genes, 118, 225

Greensboro, North Carolina, 17

Greenwich Village (New York City), 2, 20, 22–23, 143–44, 164–65, 219; Christopher Street Liberation Day Umbrella Committee of, 247–48; commercial center of, 152; expansion of, 71–72;

HIV/AIDS in, 145–46; Oscar Wilde Bookshop of, 60, 63, 143; same-sex partner households in, 149; Stonewall riots in, 16, 19, 143, 146, 208, 248; straight in-migration to, 147

Grindr app, 58–60, 63, 124

Gross, Jane, 51, 154–55

Gross, Rachel, 120

growth machine, 71, 291n30

Guerneville (San Francisco suburb), 138t, 139t, 141, 242t

Gulfport, Florida, 42

Habits of the Heart (Bellah et al.), 293n40

Haight Ashbury (San Francisco), 136, 138t

Hall, Radclyffe, 289n19

Halperin, David, 289n17

Hammel, Daniel, 18

Harris, Daniel, 251

Harvey Milk Street (San Diego), 208

Hatch, Richard, 52–53

Hayslett, Karen, 307n1

Heap, Chad, 64, 142

Heilman, John, 55

Hell's Kitchen (New York City), 2, 143, 146–50, 219

Herring, Scott, 290n24

Heterosexual Awareness Month, 100

heterosexualization of gay culture, 249–55, 310n9

Higgins, Mary Clare, 241

Hillcrest (San Diego), 2, 208

Hindle, Paul, 21

historical argument for gayborhood formation, 290n26

historic preservation, 81–82, 145, 150–51, 160–62, 198–209; Boystown's Legacy Walk and, 145, 207–8, 257; Castro's GLBT History Museum and, 207; straight residents' commitment to, 255

history of gayborhoods, 8–9, 12–31; in the closet era, 8, 12–15, 244–45, 289nn17–20; in the coming out era, 8–9, 15–23; in the post-gay era, 8–10, 23–31, 100–101, 174, 245–59, 293n41

HIV/AIDS, 117, 127, 145–46, 172, 178, 187

Hollendoner, Joe, 177–79, 181–82, 233, 281

home values, 17, 25, 288n12

homophily, 102–3, 128, 141, 257–58, 277; among same-sex parents with children, 220–24; of collective relocation, 214–19

Houston, Texas, 2, 45, 137–38t, 158t, 235, 275t

How to Walk to School (Kurland and Edelberg), 119–20
Human Rights Campaign (HRC), 121–22
Humphrey, Laud, 19
Hydrate bar, 90–91

identity politics, 110, 112–14, 161t. *See also* gay identity
imagination. *See* residential imagination
index of dissimilarity, 36–37, 60, 245, 295–96nn2–3
institutional anchors. *See* anchor institutions
institutional encasement, 50
institutional systems of inequality, 87–88, 96, 100, 300n15
integrated spaces, 83, 86–95, 100, 110–12, 169–74, 251–52. *See also* assimilation
the Internet, 30, 101; community and, 30, 57–60, 62–63, 123–27, 214; safety considerations and, 126; social networking on, 62–63, 303n12
interviews in Chicago, 11–12, 64–101, 276; on assimilation and expanded residential imagination, 69–75, 77, 98–99, 112–13; coding and analysis of, 283–84; on economic factors, 71; with officials and community leaders, 70–71, 76–80, 282; on power and politics, 74, 81; queer perspectives in, 75–82, 99–101, 300n13; on safe spaces, 72–73, 166–88; sampling methodology for, 281–83, 284t, 313n15; straight perspectives in, 82–97, 99–101
intolerance, 167–76, 206, 256–57. *See also* safe harbors
islands of meaning, 69–70, 72, 76, 88, 98, 258
Isperduli, Tina, 225
It Gets Better Project, 62, 114–15

Jackson Heights (New York City), 229–30
Jacobs, Jane, 102
Jamaica Plain (Boston), 223, 235, 242t
Johnson, Art, 70–71, 190, 217, 282

Kameny, Franklin, 9, 208
Kane, Melinda D., 307n1
Kansas City, Missouri, 137t, 140f
Kantrowitz, Barbara, 241, 308n17
Kastor, Elizabeth, 22
Katz, Jonathan Ned, 13

Keller, Suzanne, 271
Kennedy, Elizabeth Lapovsky, 14
Kennedy Anthony, 27
Key West, Florida, 138t, 275t
Kidder, Tracy, 42
King, Rodney, 87
Kinsey, Alfred, 50, 123, 142
Knopp, Lawrence, 8
Kohler, Bob, 20
Kurland, Susan, 119–20
Kurutz, Steven, 29–30
Kwong, Jessica, 207
Kyles, Kyra, 1, 53

Lakeview (Chicago), 68, 83, 142–43; Chamber of Commerce of, 193, 232–33, 291; Nettelhorst School of, 119–22, 282; Wrigley Field in, 83, 84f, 171–74, 306n5. *See also* Boystown
Lambertville, New Jersey, 10, 140t
Lamm, Michael, 18
language of sexuality, 267–69
large cities, 136, 139–40f, 141, 153, 305n30
Latina/o enclaves, 228–30, 240
Laumann, Edward, 123
Lauria, Mickey, 8
Lavers, Michael, 21, 143–44, 229–30
Leal, Susan, 51
Lee, Denny, 20, 145–46
Lee, Gary, 145
Leff, Lisa, 38
Legacy Project, 145, 207–8, 257. *See also* Boystown
legal environment: Chicago perspectives on, 74, 81, 170–71; for gay marriage, 157, 253–54, 280; at local level, 37–39, 74; for same-sex partner adoptions, 56. *See also* gay rights
Lesbian, Gay, Bisexual, and Transgender Pride Month, 208
lesbians, 192–93, 230–41, 276; in Boystown, 230–31; feminist and countercultural institutions of, 235–36; financial resources of, 231–32, 234, 236–37, 241, 308n11; geographic concentrations of, 241, 242t, 258, 308n17, 308n19; invisibility of, 231, 233–34, 308n9; maturation and settling down among, 236; sub-gayborhoods of, 235; urban pioneering by, 231–32, 237; use as term of, 267. *See also* Andersonville; Girlstown
lesbian spaces (as term), 269

Lesbianville. *See* Northampton
Levine, Martin P., 271–72, 297n24
Levy, Dan, 22, 31
lifecycle effects, 224. *See also* age factors
Lincoln Park (Chicago), 142
Lingle, Larry, 60
Livesay, Harry, 45
Logan, John, 291n30
Longtime Companion, 127
Los Angeles, California, 17, 87, 137t, 140t, 242t, 275t. *See also* West Hollywood
Louisville, Kentucky, 17, 153
Lucas, Craig, 47

magical beliefs, 169
mainstreaming, 48, 128, 220, 246, 250. *See also* assimilation
male same-sex partner households. *See* same-sex partner households
mall effect, 194–96
Mandersonville (Chicago), 11, 225, 232, 236–37. *See also* Andersonville
Manhole bar, 90–91
Manhunt.net, 124
marriage, 56. *See also* gay marriage
Martino, Maureen, 193, 232–33, 281–82
Match.com, 124
maturation. *See* age factors
maximum variation sampling, 274
McCown, James, 38–39
McNamara, Mary, 255–56
McPherson, J. Miller, 141, 214
mecca, 22–23, 189, 241
media examinations of where gays live, 10, 35–63, 274–81; on age factors, 51–55, 61–62; on assimilation, 36–50, 60–63; on cultural sameness, 45–50, 61; on economic factors, 45; gay ghetto themes in, 23, 39–40, 42, 46–50; on the Internet, 57–60, 62–63; on local legal environments, 37–39; on parenting and families, 55–57, 61–62; sampling and coding of, 274–81, 312n12; on small towns and suburbs, 42–47, 52, 55, 153–57
medium-sized cities, 136, 139–40f, 141, 161t, 163–64, 305n30
Mendelsohn, Daniel, 249, 251
Meunier, John, 40
Meyers, Daniel, 26
Miami, Florida, 15, 25, 127, 137t. *See also* South Beach

Miami Shores, Florida, 138f, 139f
Michel, Jeff, 306n5
Milk, Harvey, 207, 208, 272
mini-enclaves. *See* multiplication of mini-enclaves
Minneapolis–St. Paul, Minnesota, 137t, 139–40t
Mitchell, Don, 289n19
Modern Family, 127
Molotch, Harvey, 291n30
Montrose (Houston), 2, 45, 138t, 235, 247
moral refugees, 19, 40–41, 70, 72–73, 98, 109–10, 271
Morgan, Diane, 241
Morten, Mary, 18
Muenstermann, Heather, 225
multiple operationalism, 277
multiplication of mini-enclaves, 41, 161t, 210, 219–40, 258–59; age factors in, 224–26; cultural infighting and, 237, 308n14; gendered nature of, 230–39; racial factors in, 226–30, 308n17; specificity of groups in, 210, 220
Murphy, Karen, 167, 272
Murray, Stephen, 21–22, 190, 271, 293n40
Myslik, Wayne, 29

National Gay and Lesbian Task Force (NGLTF), 39
neighborhoods, 271
neoliberal politics, 248–49
Nero, Charles, 226, 230
Nettelhorst School (Chicago), 119–22, 282
Neubecker, David, 120–22
new gayborhoods. *See* geographic trends; reinventing the gayborhood
new gay paradigm, 5, 9
new gay teens and youth, 52–55, 62, 108–16, 302n4; bullying of, 177–79; expanded residential imagination of, 112–13; It Gets Better Project for, 62, 114–15; new gayborhoods of, 149–50; racial considerations for, 178–82, 206, 257; restrictions on interviews with, 115, 176–77; safe spaces and programs for, 176–82, 192, 281; on segregated spaces, 110–12; self-identification and coming out of, 108–10, 113–15, 302n4; straight friends of, 112, 113
New Jersey, 10, 37–38, 140t, 154–55, 163
The New Normal, 127

New Orleans, Louisiana, 15, 140t
New Town (Chicago), 142, 161t, 211, 239, 258
New York City, 5, 20, 22–23; Gay Index of, 137f; HIV/AIDS in, 145–46; legal environment of, 38; racial and ethnic mini-enclaves in, 229–30; rates of same-sex partner households in, 138–39f; shifting gayborhoods of, 143–51, 164–65. *See also* Greenwich Village
Nolan, Tim, 22, 46–47
Northampton, Massachusetts, 42, 61, 138–39t, 241, 242t, 308n17
North Druid Hills, Georgia, 137t, 140f, 141

Oakland, California, 17, 137–39t, 152–53, 191, 242t
Oakland Park, Florida, 136, 138t, 139t
Oak Lawn (Dallas), 2, 242t
Oak Park (Chicago), 222–24
Obama, Barack, 74, 92, 208
Ocean, Justin, 18
O'Connell, Martin, 135
O'Connell, Sue, 59
O'Neal Parker, Lonnae, 55
open (as term), 267–68
operational essentialism, 300n15
Orlando, Florida, 137t, 139t, 275t
Oscar Wilde Bookshop, 60, 63, 143
Ost, Jason, 134–36, 137–38f, 272–73
out-migration. *See* geographic trends
Owles, Jim, 127

Palm Springs, California, 138t, 139t, 242t
Papadopoulos, Alex, 142, 192, 205, 233
parenting and family life, 17–18, 61–62, 116–23, 240; adoption laws and, 56; Chicago-area interviews on, 116–23; demographic trends on, 156; in female-partner households, 308n19; geographic distribution of, 153–56, 157, 158t, 222–24, 258; homophily in choice of location in, 220–24; media reports on, 55–57; racial and ethnic variations in, 302n7; school considerations in, 57, 62, 117, 118–22, 154, 221. *See also* parenting
Park Slope (Brooklyn, New York City), 143, 235, 241, 276
Patton, Michael Quinn, 274
pedophilia myth, 123, 302n11

performative progressiveness, 252–55
persistence of gayborhoods, 133–34, 150–53, 164, 257; anchor institutions and, 32, 145, 150–53, 161t, 164, 189–98, 206, 257; future outlook for, 239–43; preservation activities and, 81–82, 145, 150–51, 160–62, 164, 198–209, 255, 257; promotion and tourism in, 3, 25–26, 44, 64, 197, 280, 294n44, 307n17; property ownership and, 145, 150–51, 164, 190–91, 233–34; psychological spaces for sexual expression and, 189, 197, 206; safety considerations and, 166–88, 206; U.S. Census data on, 133–41
Pfeiffer, Richard, 121
Philadelphia, Pennsylvania, 15, 25, 137t, 273, 275t, 280. *See also* Washington Square West
Phoenix, Arizona, 137t, 140t
pink ghettos, 152–53, 164
Pink Triangle (Newcastle, U.K.), 273
Pinson, Christina, 282
Plano, Texas, 57
Plattsburgh, New York, 43
Pleasant Ridge (Detroit suburb), 139t, 242t, 259
Pokela, Julie, 42
political argument for gayborhood formation, 291n31
politically gay heterosexuals, 26
Portland, Oregon, 40, 137f, 139f
post- (as prefix) designations, 255–57, 310n15
post-feminist era, 256
post-gay era, 8–10, 23–31, 100–101, 245–59, 293n41; cultural sameness beliefs of, 44–50, 75–97, 99–101, 246–47, 249; decline of identity politics in, 110, 112–14, 161t; decreased primacy of sexual orientation in, 5–6, 7, 28–29, 52–54, 73, 78, 79–80, 88–89, 154–55, 166, 246; expanded residential imagination of, 69–75, 77, 98–99, 112–13, 151–59; gay ghettos of, 50, 247; heterosexualization of gay culture in, 80–82, 249–55, 300n15, 310n9; homophily in, 102–3, 215–19, 257–58; iconography of, 78–79, 89–90, 91f, 118, 257; the Internet in, 30, 57–60, 62–63, 101, 123–27, 303n12; maturation and settling down in, 103–8;

post-gay era (*continued*)
neoliberal politics of, 248–49, 255; new
gay teenagers of, 52–55, 62, 108–16,
302n4; resistance to reductive understandings of gayness in, 44, 248–51; TV
and film portrayals in, 52–53. *See also*
assimilation; persistence of gayborhoods; reinventing the gayborhood
post-queer (as term), 293n41
post-racial era, 92, 256
Potemkin villages, 146
preservation activities. *See* historic
preservation
Pritchard, Bill, 53–54
property ownership, 145, 150–51, 164,
190–91, 233–34
Provincetown, Massachusetts, 138t, 139t,
141, 241, 242t, 272t
public opinion, 26–27, 274; on assimilation, 251; on gay marriage, 250–51,
310n6; on heterosexual acceptance of
gays, 252–55, 256; on integrated neighborhoods, 35, 251–52, 310n8
Putnam, New York, 62

quasi-ethnic identity, 306n15
Quattrochi, Regina, 22
queer (as term), 267–68
Queer as Folk, 127
queer communities (as term), 268
Queer Eye for the Straight Guy, 127
queer geographies, 159–65. *See also* geographic trends
queer people of color. *See* race
queer spaces (as term), 268–69
queer youth. *See* new gay teens and youth

race, 240, 310n15; in multiplication of
mini-enclaves, 226–30, 258–59, 308n17;
in safety considerations for queer
youths of color, 178–82, 206, 257
rainbow-colored pylons, 198–202, 207,
273
Rapiano, Melanie, 308n19
Rehoboth Beach, Delaware, 139t, 241,
242t
reinventing the gayborhood, 8, 141–59,
161t, 162–63, 210–43, 257–59; collective relocation and revival in, 161t,
210–19, 239, 257–58, 307n1; future
outlook for, 239–43; multiplication

into mini-enclaves in, 41, 210, 219–40,
258–59; principle of homophily in,
215–19, 220–24, 257–58
residential concentration, 152–53, 164,
193–94, 213, 271, 273
residential imagination, 69–75, 77, 98–99,
112–13, 151–59
retirement housing, 62, 157–59
Reuter, Don, 245
reverse discrimination of straights, 84,
95–97, 100
revival. *See* collective relocation
Rich, Meghan Ashlin, 37
Rich, Motoko, 146–47
Roanoke, Virginia, 43–44
Rogers Park (Chicago), 68, 223, 227–28, 237
Romesburg, Don, 4, 41
rural areas. *See* suburban and rural areas
Rushbrook, Dereka, 25
Ruting, Brad, 26

safe harbors, 19–20, 72–73, 161t, 162,
166–88, 206, 214, 291n33; in the coming out era, 109–10; legal landscapes
of, 157, 170–71; for people from smaller
communities, 183–88, 306n11; social
intolerance and, 167–76, 256–57; for
transgender individuals, 182–86, 206,
257, 306n8, 306n12; for women, 30–31;
for young gays and queers of color, 169,
176–82, 206, 257
Salt Lake City, Utah, 139t, 158t, 163
same-sex marriage. *See* gay marriage
same-sex partner households: census identification of, 134–35, 272–73; children
and parenting in, 17–18, 55–57, 116–23,
153–57, 158t, 220–24; location of, 35,
116, 241, 242t, 295n1, 308n17, 308n19;
segregation of, 36–37; terminology for,
269; widespread increase in, 153. *See
also* demographic trends; geographic
trends
Sanders, Seth, 17
San Diego, California, 15, 17, 137t, 139t,
208, 235
San Francisco, California, 15–18, 41–42, 61,
72, 113, 246; Gay Index of, 137t; GLBT
History Museum of, 207–8; Harvey
Milk's election in, 272; rates of same-
sex partner households in, 138t, 139t,
141, 152, 242f. *See also* Castro district

San Francisco Gay Men's Community Initiative, 58
Santa Fe, New Mexico, 139t, 158
Sarasota, Florida, 47, 275t
Savage, Dan, 62, 114–15
Savin-Williams, Ritch, 52, 109, 302n4
scattered gay places, 12–15, 228, 244
schools, 57, 62; bullying in, 177–79; gay-straight alliances (GSA) in, 177–78; parent considerations of, 57, 62, 117, 118–22, 154, 221
Schubert, Ruth, 155
Sears, Brad, 234
Seattle, Washington, 2, 17, 137t, 139t, 275t
secondary cities, 64–65, 153
Sedgwick, Eve, 50, 97, 310n15
Segal, George, 208
segregated spaces, 46, 247; "gay ghetto" language of, 23, 39–40, 42, 46–50, 73, 271, 297n24; as islands of meaning, 69–70, 72, 76, 88, 98, 258; rates of, 36–37, 60, 245, 295–96nn2–3; sexual integration vs., 86–95, 100, 110–12, 169–74, 251–52
Seidman, Steve, 9, 28, 176, 252
separate spaces. See segregated spaces
sexuality: decreased primacy of orientation in, 5–6, 7, 28–29, 52–54, 73, 78, 79–80, 88–89, 154–55, 166, 246; diversity among gays of, 127–29, 247–49, 303n18; invention of, 289n17; as mode of intellectual inquiry, 256, 310n15; for new gay teenagers, 108–10; as term, 269. See also assimilation; straight residents of gayborhoods
sexuality argument for gayborhood formation, 292n34
sexual minorities (as term), 267
The Sexual Organization of the City (Laumann et al.), 123
Shaftel, David, 148–49
Shand, Jeff, 143
Sherrill, Kenneth, 143
shrinking of gayborhoods, 1–12, 244–49; economic factors in, 7–8, 45, 288n12; gentrification in, 7, 288n13, 291n30; historical accidents and, 16, 290n26; increased tolerance and, 5–6, 7, 9, 73. See also post-gay era
Sibalis, Michael, 49, 297n24
Sidetrack bar, 190, 196–97, 217, 257, 282

Signorile, Michelangelo, 250
Silver, Nate, 9, 44, 46, 245–46
Slack, Donovan, 56
small cities, 136, 139–40f, 141, 153, 163–64
small towns, 42–45, 163–64. See also suburban and rural areas
Smelser, Neil, 169
Smith, David, 39, 134
Smith, Neil, 18
Smith-Lovin, Lynn, 141, 214
social intolerance, 167–76, 206, 256–57. See also safe harbors
social networking, 30, 57–60, 62–63, 123–27, 303n12
Sokol, David, 176
Sopel, Brent, 94–95
South Beach (Miami), 2, 127, 275t
South Boston, 39–40, 151–52
South End (Boston), 2, 39–40, 57, 138t, 151–52
Southern cities, 17
South Orange, New Jersey, 154, 163. See also New Jersey
South Park (San Diego), 235
South Side (Chicago), 141–42, 227–28
Span, Paula, 22
spatial contagion (as term), 211
Spivak, Gayatri, 300n15
Spring, Amy, 36–37
Stein, Peter, 40–41
Stemm, Greg, 42
stereotypes of gay people, 127, 302n11
Stewart, Daniel, 43
St. Louis, Missouri, 17, 139t, 275t
Stonewall Inn riots, 16, 19, 143, 146, 208, 248
straight allies movement, 26
straight nights, 30
straight residents of gayborhoods, 2, 24–25, 31–32, 146; in Chicago's Boystown, 4–5, 69, 74–75, 89–92; on concerns of reverse discrimination, 84, 95–97; on cultural sameness, 46, 82–97, 99–101, 246–47; expressions of indifference by, 83–87, 99–100, 246–47, 254–55; in-migration and diversification by, 146–48, 151–52, 160, 161t, 232, 252–54; interviews with, 82–97; performative progressiveness of, 252–55; on safety, 30–31; on sexual integration, 83, 86–95, 100, 110–11; as super-gentrifiers, 25, 144–45, 294n43;

straight residents of gayborhoods (*continued*)
threshold levels and tipping points of,
146–48, 169–74, 212–14
strollers (baby carriages), 4, 146–47
sub-gayborhoods, 235
suburban and rural areas, 42–47, 52, 55,
153–57, 161t, 163–64, 305n30; lesbian
concentrations in, 241, 242t, 308n19;
parenting and family life in, 153–57,
158t, 222–24; safety considerations in,
157, 185, 306n11
Sullivan, Andrew, 46, 52–53, 56, 250
Sullivan, Robert David, 29, 39, 57–58
Summit, Marge, 282
super-gentrifiers, 25, 144–45, 294n43

Tavern Guild, 15–16
Taylor, Lowell, 17
teens. *See* new gay teens and youth
Tenderloin (San Francisco), 219
terminology, 267–69
Thomas, Mike, 176
Thomas Theorem, 167
Tico Valle, Modesto, 71, 78, 179, 182,
191–92, 282
tolerance, 5–6, 7, 166–67; cultural sameness and, 75–97, 99–101, 246–47, 249;
formation of gayborhoods and, 17–20;
post-gay era assimilation and, 9–10,
24–31, 52–54, 73, 294n46. *See also* safe
harbors; social intolerance
Top 10 Neighborhoods, 137f
Top 10 Towns, 137f
Top 25 Cities, 137f, 139–40f
Toronto, Ontario, 2, 4, 28, 160, 280
Toub, Micah, 4
tourism, 3, 25–26, 44, 64, 197, 280,
294n44, 307n17
Towertown (Chicago), 141–42
transgender (as term), 267–68
transgender individuals, 182–86
Tunney, Tom, 70, 76, 79, 176, 282
Twin Peaks (San Francisco), 136, 138t

Unabridged bookstore, 145, 190, 196–97,
281
United States v. Windsor, 27
Uptown (Chicago), 68, 300n7
urban life, 31–32; block-by-block organization of, 174–75; demographic trends in,
135–41; diversity in, 127–29, 247–49,

252–54, 303n18; homophily in, 102–3,
128, 141, 214–19, 257–58; mechanisms
of change in, 41, 61, 162–63; promotion
of queer spaces of, 3, 25, 44, 197. *See also*
suburban and rural areas
urban renewal, 18–19, 24–25, 291n30. *See
also* gentrification
U.S. Census, 133–41, 274; on concentrations of female-partner households,
241, 242t; on same-sex households
raising children, 156–57; on same-sex
partner households, 134–35, 272–73;
underestimation of nonheterosexual
population in, 11, 134, 136; on
unmarried-partner households, 136. *See
also* demographic trends
us/them thinking, 54, 97, 223

Vaid, Urvashi, 5, 39, 250
Vancouver, British Columbia, 10, 25, 58,
273
Vary, Adam, 109
Vashon Island (Seattle), 140t, 155, 163
Vavrus, Mary Douglas, 256
Venator, Michael, 45
Venice, Italy, 49
Versace, Gianni, 279–80
Virginia Beach, Virginia, 153, 158t

Wacquant, Loïc, 50, 297n24
Wan, Danny, 152
Ward, Jane, 252
Warner, Michael, 250–52
Washington, D.C., 17, 252–54; Frank
Kameny Way of, 208; Gay Index
of, 137t; rate of same-sex partner
households in, 139t; shifting gay com-
munities in, 162, 219; suburban gay
homeowners of, 52. *See also* Dupont
Circle
Washington Square West (Philadelphia), 2,
38, 273, 280–81
Weber, Tim, 225
"We're here, we're queer" chant, 28
West Hollywood (Los Angeles), 20–21,
54, 138t, 139t, 242t; The Abbey bar of,
253–54; aging population of, 55–56;
cost of living in, 258–59. *See also* Los
Angeles
Weston, Kath, 16
When Boys Fly, 127

Williamsburg (Brooklyn, New York City), 147
Williams Institute, 116, 157, 308n11
Wilson, Claire, 157–59
Wilson, John Morgan, 20–21
Wilton Manors (Fort Lauderdale), 138t, 139t, 242t
Wirth, Louis, 75–76, 97
Wittman, Carl, 15
women. *See* lesbians; straight residents of gayborhoods
Women and Children First bookstore, 68, 79, 192–93, 230, 257, 281

Worcester, Massachusetts, 16
World War II, 8–9, 13–15, 142, 197, 245
Wrigley Field (Chicago), 83, 84f, 171–74, 306n5
Wyly, Elvin, 18

youth. *See* new gay teens and youth

Zamora, Jim Herron, 152
Zerubavel, Eviatar, 69
Zirin, Stu, 70, 78, 195–96, 201, 282
Zukin, Sharon, 224, 231, 288n13, 291n30
Zwicky, Arnold, 109

PRINCETON STUDIES IN CULTURAL SOCIOLOGY

Origins of Democratic Culture: Printing, Petitions, and the Public Sphere in Early-Modern England by David Zaret

Bearing Witness: Readers, Writers, and the Novel in Nigeria by Wendy Griswold

Gifted Tongues: High School Debate and Adolescent Culture by Gary Alan Fine

Offside: Soccer and American Exceptionalism by Andrei S. Markovits and Steven L. Hellerman

Reinventing Justice: The American Drug Court Movement by James L. Nolan, Jr.

Kingdom of Children: Culture and Controversy in the Homeschooling Movement by Mitchell L. Stevens

Blessed Events: Religion and Home Birth in America by Pamela E. Klassen

Negotiating Identities: States and Immigrants in France and Germany by Riva Kastoryano, translated by Barbara Harshav

Contentious Curricula: Afrocentrism and Creationism in American Public Schools by Amy J. Binder

Community: Pursuing the Dream, Living the Reality by Suzanne Keller

The Minds of Marginalized Black Men: Making Sense of Mobility, Opportunity, and Future Life Chances by Alford A. Young, Jr.

Framing Europe: Attitudes to European Integration in Germany, Spain, and the United Kingdom by Juan Dez Medrano

Interaction Ritual Chains by Randall Collins

On Justification: Economies of Worth by Luc Boltanski and Laurent Thévenot, translated by Catherine Porter

Talking Prices: Symbolic Meanings of Prices on the Market for Contemporary Art by Olav Velthuis

Elusive Togetherness: Church Groups Trying to Bridge America's Divisions by Paul Lichterman

Religion and Family in a Changing Society by Penny Edgell

Hollywood Highbrow: From Entertainment to Art by Shyon Baumann

Partisan Publics: Communication and Contention across Brazilian Youth Activist Networks by Ann Mische

Disrupting Science: Social Movements, American Scientists, and the Politics of the Military, 1945–1975 by Kelly Moore

Weaving Self-Evidence: A Sociology of Logic by Claude Rosental, translated by Catherine Porter

The Taylorized Beauty of the Mechanical: Scientific Management and the Rise of Modernist Architecture by Mauro F. Guillén

Impossible Engineering: Technology and Territoriality on the Canal du Midi by Chandra Mukerji

Economists and Societies: Discipline and Profession in the United States, Britain, and France, 1890s to 1990s by Marion Fourcade

Reds, Whites, and Blues: Social Movements, Folk Music, and Race in the United States by William G. Roy

Privilege: The Making of an Adolescent Elite at St. Paul's School by Shamus Rahman Khan

Making Volunteers: Civic Life after Welfare's End by Nina Eliasoph

Becoming Right: How Campuses Shape Young Conservatives by Amy J. Binder and Kate Wood

The Moral Background: An Inquiry into the History of Business Ethics by Gabriel Abend

There Goes the Gayborhood? by Amin Ghaziani